D1607361

Architecture on Ice

McGill-Queen's/Beaverbrook Canadian Foundation Studies in Art History

MARTHA LANGFORD and SANDRA PAIKOWSKY, series editors

Recognizing the need for a better understanding of Canada's artistic culture both at home and abroad, the Beaverbrook Canadian Foundation, through its generous support, makes possible the publication of innovative books that advance our understanding of Canadian art and Canada's visual and material culture. This series supports and stimulates such scholarship through the publication of original and rigorous peer-reviewed books that make significant contributions to the subject. We welcome submissions from Canadian and international scholars for book-length projects on historical and contemporary Canadian art and visual and material culture, including Native and Inuit art, architecture, photography, craft, design, and museum studies. Studies by Canadian scholars on non-Canadian themes will also be considered.

Architectu

McGill-Queen's University Press   Montreal & Kingston • London • Chicago

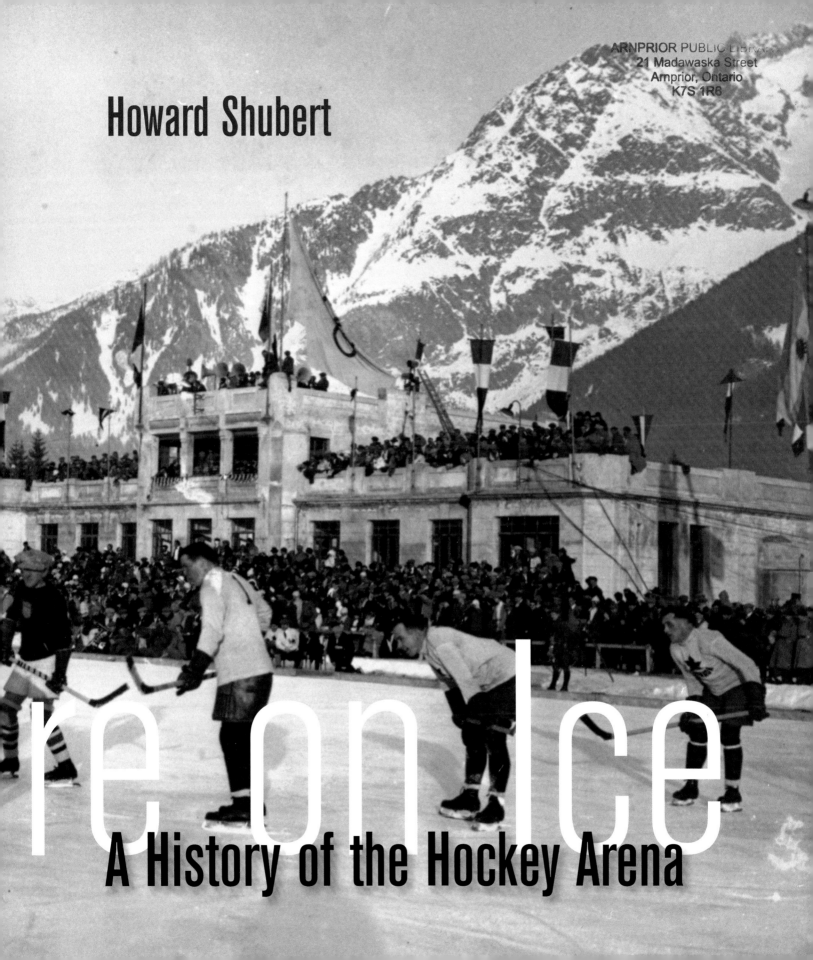

Howard Shubert

re on Ice

A History of the Hockey Arena

© McGill-Queen's University Press 2016

ISBN 978-0-7735-4813-8

Legal deposit third quarter 2016
Bibliothèque nationale du Québec

Printed in Canada on acid-free paper

This book has been published with the help of a grant from the Canadian Federation for the Humanities and Social Sciences, through the Awards to Scholarly Publications Program, using funds provided by the Social Sciences and Humanities Research Council of Canada.

Funding has also been provided by the Visual Arts Section of the Canada Council for the Arts (Assistance for the Promotion of Architecture Program).

McGill-Queen's University Press acknowledges the support of the Canada Council for the Arts for our publishing program. We also acknowledge the financial support of the Government of Canada through the Canada Book Fund for our publishing activities.

Library and Archives Canada Cataloguing in Publication

Shubert, Howard, 1954–, author
Architecture on ice : a history of the hockey arena / Howard Shubert.

(McGill-Queen's/Beaverbrook Canadian Foundation studies in art history)
Includes bibliographical references and index.
ISBN 978-0-7735-4813-8

1. Hockey arenas. 2. Hockey arenas – Design and construction. 3. Hockey arenas – Social aspects. 4. Hockey arenas – History. 5. Public architecture. I. Title. II. Series: McGill-Queen's/Beaverbrook Canadian Foundation studies in art history

NA6860.S58 2016   725'.84   C2016-903200-0

Contents

Acknowledgments

The idea for this book originated at a family lunch down the street from the Montreal Forum. The restaurant was decorated with hockey sticks and photographs of Canadiens hockey players. My brother Irwin, then a PhD candidate at Simon Fraser University, proposed that we combine his experience in urban geography and insights gained from creating and teaching a course on hockey and communications with my own expertise in architectural history to write a book about hockey arenas. One of the great delights of working on a book that has provided only pleasure was the two years that Irwin and I collaborated in its planning and early research. Life intervened. Irwin gracefully stepped back and I continued the work solo but Irwin's original vision, his insistence that hockey arenas were worth investigating, has animated my work ever since.

A seed grant from the Institut de recherche en histoire de l'art (IRHA) enabled me to hire Beryl Corber, the first of several supremely capable research assistants. After a presenta-tion of my research to IRHA colleagues, Kurt Forster commented that what I seemed to be saying was that the hockey arena never existed. Thanks to Kurt for intuiting this key idea and revealing it to me before I had recognized it myself.

A three-year grant from the Social Sciences and Humanities Research Council of Canada (SSHRC) kick-started the research and allowed me to travel extensively. At McGill University David Covo and Alberto Pérez-Gómez at the School of Architecture provided an institu-tional base from which to administer the grant, and Will Straw, director of the McGill Institute for the Study of Canada, offered advice and library access at a key moment. Clare Backhouse, Nathalie Senecal, and Sharon Vattay proved enthusiastic research assistants, uncovering gold in archives and newspaper microfilms. In Kansas City, Stuart Smith and Carrie Wobbe supplied documen-tation and images and arranged interviews with architects Blake Ellis, Steve Hotujac, and Gordon Wood at Ellerbe Beckett and with

Chris Carver and Rick Martin at HOK Sports, all of whom patiently talked about their work and answered my questions.

A sabbatical from my job at the Canadian Centre for Architecture (CCA) advanced my work significantly and I am grateful to Nicholas Olsberg for first proposing and then supporting my request for a six-month leave. During my time off, Cammie McAtee, my colleague in the Prints and Drawings Department, carried my workload in addition to her own. Cammie's friendship, intelligent guidance, and support have been a source of comfort and delight to me over the years. It was during a CCA lunch break at Le Faubourg Ste-Catherine that Cammie, Réjean Legault, and I cheered the Canadiens as they paraded to the Molson Centre.

Colleagues, friends, relatives, and even acquaintances have responded with remarkable enthusiasm to this book project over the years, sending me clippings and links to articles. I want to thank my CCA colleagues who offered support and encouragement and kept me sane, in particular: Lorraine Brown, Paul Chenier, Louise Désy, Nadia Di Fiore, Renata Guttman, Kathryn Kollar, Alain Laforest, Colin McWhirter, Marc Pitre, Karen Potje, Judy Silverman, and Alexis Sornin. My discussion of Toronto's Air Canada Centre derives largely from the daily drama unfolding in Toronto newspapers. My father, Alex Shubert, diligently clipped and mailed these articles to me. I regret that he did not live to see the results of his contribution.

Discussion with colleagues, friends, and family have clarified my thinking at many points along the way. My friend and former teacher Nick Adams was a steadfast source of encouragement and the model of a fearless, generous, and committed scholar. Réjean Legault, Cammie McAtee, and Geoffrey Simmins read and commented on publication and grant proposals. Over the course of my work on this book, my daughter Amanda Shubert grew from a precocious teenager into a scholar able to advise me on issues of postmodernism. Ed Dimendberg, a CCA scholar-in-residence during my year directing that program, became a mentor, generously reviewing texts and offering advice on publication strategies. Ed supplied this book's title and perhaps its very existence, for he counselled me, when at a low point I considered shifting to another topic, not to "give up on my first love." Other family and friends who offered support and love include Lil Mingail, Ben Shubert, Pauline Shubert, and Steve Vineberg.

Over the years I presented aspects of my research at conferences organized by the Gorsebrook Research Institute ("Putting It on Ice"), the North American Society for Sport History (NASSH), the Society of Architectural Historians (SAH), and the Society for the Study of Architecture in Canada (SSAC). I am grateful for the response and encouragement received at these conferences and for the support and input from the following individuals: Russell Field, J.W. (Bill) Fitsell, Roger Godin, Jack Grinold, Stephen Hardy, Robert Hill, Gary Hughes, Dick Irvin, Dana Johnson, Bruce Kidd, Brian Libby, Daniel Mason, Dietrich Neumann, Larry Richards, J. Andrew Ross, Rhodri Windsor-Liscombe, and David Whitson.

Among the many librarians and archivists who answered my queries and tracked down images, I want to mention: Craig Campbell, Hockey Hall of Fame; Karen Cover, World Figure Skating Museum and Hall of Fame; Linda Fraser, Canadian Architectural Archives; and Janet Parks, Avery Architectural and Fine Arts Library. Thanks to the librarians and staff of the Pointe Claire Public Library, in the congenial atmosphere of which large parts of this book were written. Róisín Heneghan of heneghan peng architects graciously supplied information and images of her firm's project, Bigfoot. Chrissy Parent of the Florida Panthers went beyond the call of duty, commissioning a made-to-order photograph of the BB&T Center. A casual conversation with my next-door neighbour revealed not only that she was related to Thomas Duggan but that she possessed never-before-seen correspondence documenting her grandfather's role in introducing NHL hockey to the United States. Thanks to Pat Duggan for allowing me to access this material, to quote from, and to reproduce some of it.

From my first conversation with Jonathan Crago, my editor at McGill-Queen's University Press (MQUP), I felt that I was in confident and competent hands. Jonathan was immediately enthusiastic about the project and never wavered. I greatly appreciated his support, especially in sensitively guiding me through the sometimes tortuous process of grant applications and reader reports. Thanks to the entire MQUP team, to managing editor Ryan Van Huijstee, to the light-handed touch of my copy editor, Curtis Fahey, and to the talented designer of the book's cover, David Drummond.

I am especially grateful to the two anonymous readers who contributed constructive feedback and specific suggestions that enabled me to rethink some basic ideas, to eliminate sketchy ones, to reinforce my overarching argument, and especially to bolster the book's introduction, contextualizing and clarifying my interdisciplinary approach. Thanks to Brigitte Desrochers and the Canada Council for the Arts for a grant that guaranteed a richly illustrated book.

Finally, no amount of thanks could adequately acknowledge the importance of my wife's love and support. In spite of being taught high school English by former NHL coach Roger Neilson (he had her punctuate – he shoots he scores), Rachelle still regards televised hockey as a spontaneous soporific, all the more reason to marvel at her willingness to hear me discourse on all aspects of hockey and architectural history. The journey has been sweeter with her by my side.

Architecture on Ice

Introduction

North America's Most Important Overlooked Cultural Buildings

Architecture on Ice examines the architecture, history, and economics of skating rinks and hockey arenas. It looks at the places and spaces, primarily in cities, where people skate and play hockey and where audiences watch them, revealing them as crucibles of meaning. Architecture enlarged the possibilities of both sports – first by protecting participants in northern climates against the elements, then by extending the season and eventually by eliminating weather, calendar, and geography altogether. People now skate and play hockey year-round, from Detroit to Dallas and from Dublin to Dubai. This book charts the development of buildings for skating and hockey, from simple wooden sheds erected for nineteenth-century amateur practitioners to today's fully wired, multi-purpose entertainment complexes where professional athletes perform before mass audiences, both live and virtual.

These physical structures and spaces, both contained and geographic, exist at the intersection of multiple story lines, overlapping histories of architecture, sport, economics, and socio-cultural life. One of my goals in writing this book has been to disentangle these narratives, to focus a light on the particular history and significance of skating and hockey venues so that they might be revealed and better understood.

Two histories are particularly intertwined in the pages that follow. This book engages in a dialogue between hockey history and architectural history. This is hardly surprising in a study of building typology. Advances in medicine and medical practice inevitably affected the design, function, and use of hospital buildings while the growth of the automobile industry, expansion of roadways, and the extension of cities have seen a corresponding response in the number, design, and location of gas stations. Professional hockey's financial success, expansion, and continued growth across North America was achieved in lock-step with developments in the solidity, scale, and sophistication of its architecture. The designers of the earliest hockey arenas took into account the sport's rules and requirements, while the buildings, once they existed, transformed how the game was played and watched.

The first three parts of this book document the symbiotic relationship between skating, hockey, and the buildings constructed for these sports through the 1960s. Today, however, hockey no longer determines the design of buildings in which this sport is played. It is not that hockey and its architecture have parted ways but rather that the relationship has evolved. In the fourth and final part of the book, I examine how hockey was reconceived as spectacle, becoming fully incorporated as a product of the entertainment/media firmament. Hockey is now played, and consumed, within buildings more appropriate to this revised conception. My argument is that today's commercial entertainment centres, the current venues in which the National Hockey League (NHL) plays its matches, no longer depend on hockey to define their designs.

This book investigates the interaction of architecture and ice. While it deals with buildings for skating and, to a lesser extent, curling, the ice sports for which enclosed buildings were first constructed, the book's primary focus is hockey and, more specifically, the professional hockey arena. In designing buildings for skating and hockey, architects and builders introduced novel solutions to accommodate the unique requirements of ice sports. But architecture soon altered the sports it sheltered. Architecture determined where, when, and how people skated and played hockey. Covered rinks and arenas were essential to the popularization of these sports across North America in the nineteenth century and to the commercial success of professional hockey in the twentieth century. Architecture changed the way these sports were performed and experienced and recodified the relationship between player and spectator. As society changed and clients demanded new buildings, commercial sports facilities changed the way spectators interacted with and consumed ice sports. In these respects, buildings for skating and hockey diverge from the typical script for the development of a building type, where architectural form is defined by functional demands.

Yet, for many people, it is not large-capacity commercial sports facilities that come to mind when they conjure an ice rink but the smaller, community facilities where so many of us first encountered indoor ice, whether as hockey playing youths or as adults, cradled coffee cups in hand, watching our children's early morning figure-skating or hockey practices. Such buildings are not only ubiquitous; they serve a vital cultural role for their communities. The website Arenamaps.com lists nearly three thousand indoor and outdoor rinks in Canada, over one thousand in Ontario alone.[1]

However, my goal in writing what is primarily a typological study was to reveal and explain the development of ice rinks from naturally occurring surfaces to massive entertainment complexes. Curling rinks, figure-skating, and community rinks appear at various points throughout this book. But the road map that emerged – from ice rink to hockey arena and beyond – sped through, or bypassed altogether, these related buildings because they contributed only fleetingly to this history. Curling and figure skating were significant to the development of this building type early, but not later. Community arenas, with their modest budgets and public agendas, introduced no innovations to the type; they followed the example of commercial facilities in larger cities, from form and function to the centrality of multi-functionality to their programs. Community arenas dot the local streets of this road map, not its highways. Similarly, speed skating and its highly specialized and less commonly occurring buildings make no appearance here.

I was initially cool to the idea of studying hockey arenas when the subject was first proposed to me. As an architectural historian I found the buildings uninspiring. Part shed, part commercial establishment, the hockey arena introduced neither formal nor stylistic innovation to architectural discourse or development. Though technically and functionally complex, few buildings for skating and hockey would make it onto anyone's architectural "highlight reel." This reflects their origins as relatively simple, unpretentious structures, often little more than barns – a term still used to describe them.[2] A small number of hockey buildings do deserve greater recognition as works of architecture and they are discussed here in detail as individual monuments, in a manner consistent with architectural history. But as I looked more closely at these buildings, delving into the history of their development and considering them through a wider interpretive lens, it became clear that the sources of their importance lay beyond aesthetics and architectural debate. Pursuing this story has taken me into many delightfully unexpected corners, from the nineteenth-century fashion for "elevator" skirts to electronic pucks and an outdoor hockey match played at Caesars Palace in Las Vegas.

Buildings for skating and hockey occupy a territory similar to what architectural historian Paula Lupkin has called the "middle ground" in reference to YMCA buildings.[3] As with YMCA buildings, architects, but not famous ones, design most hockey facilities. Neither high nor low culture, they can be best described as middlebrow buildings, standardized and undistinguished but for their scale. They cede the higher ground to monuments by greater architects even as they claim the status of urban landmarks. For Lupkin, YMCA buildings blend into the background of their urban settings. Perhaps this is because their individual users visit them so habitually that the buildings can hold little mystery for them. Hockey facilities, by contrast, provide the focus for less frequent but more intense communal experiences that evoke strong emotional responses, responses that spectators come to associate with the buildings themselves, regardless of their architectural merits.

Style and architectural innovation are the typical means architectural historians use to categorize and assess buildings, yet neither is especially helpful in discussing facilities for skating and hockey. To be sure, the design of nineteenth- and early-twentieth-century skating rinks reflected prevailing architectural tastes, from Italianate to Beaux-Arts, just as their later twentieth-century counterparts are clothed in Modern materials and idiom. But analyzing how well or (mostly) poorly these buildings are designed or assessing their novelty would miss the point of their importance. In fact, this is precisely why these buildings have been overlooked by architectural historians. Instead, I want to uncover and analyze the forces that brought these buildings into being – who, how, why, when – and which led them to change over time. In taking this approach, I am following the lead of scholars such as Annmarie Adams and Richard Longstreth in their analyses of building typology. In her study of hospital architecture, Adams employed a "hybrid, experimental approach to an architectural typology" in arguing that "interpreting the social history of the built environment means considering style as a tool used by hospital architects, rather than a category of analysis."[4] Longstreth avoided "a study of architectural typology in the usual sense" or "a strict architectural, urban, or business history in the traditional sense of those terms" because the retail complexes he examined in his 1997 book, *City Center to Regional Mall: Architecture, the Automobile, and Retailing in Los Angeles 1920–1950*, were defined less by physical attributes than by ownership, management, tenancy, and merchandising. He believed his subject called for a more integrated approach.[5]

Building typology may be considered a subcategory of architectural history. Typological studies inevitably involve a dialogue between the history of architecture and the discipline or function to which a building type is devoted, whether banking, art, medicine, or ice sports, to name but a few. Any such work owes a debt to Nikolaus Pevsner's *History of Building Types*.[6]

For Pevsner, writing in the mid-1970s, style was the domain of architectural history while function was the concern of social history, and he was primarily interested in the former, in discovering the stylistic origins of building types and in tracing their subsequent histories. Pevsner conceived the architect's role as an intellectual one, that of responding to the functional components of a building type by determining its appropriate architectural expression. It was understood by him that the architect need intervene in a novel way only when a building presented a unique set of functional requirements.

Today, architects and architectural history have exceeded the boundaries set by Pevsner in 1976 and those now writing about the built environment concern themselves with an expanded range of issues, incorporating many aspects of social, economic, and cultural history. In writing about architecture on ice, I am less interested in the formal and stylistic choices made by architects than I am in the ways their buildings work. I have found it more useful to foreground the role of clients, spectators, and the larger society that participated in the production and use of these buildings, especially as these actors and their needs changed over time.

Most studies of building typology conform to a "form follows function" script, according to which architects develop and refine a particular building type in response to functional requirements demanded by clients – for example, a large banking hall, teller's cages, and an imposing façade to encourage client confidence, for banks. But the story of how buildings for skating and hockey evolved diverges from this script in significant ways. The first buildings to accommodate ice sports operated seasonally and to survive economically they had to accommodate additional functions. Multi-functionality remained the norm for these buildings, to such an extent that this book posits that the "hockey arena," a building designed solely for that use, may never have existed. This is quite different from architectural historian Carol Meeks's assertion that the railway train shed was born in 1830 and died in 1904, owing both its rise and its demise to the engineers who initially discovered ever more daring ways to span space, until they uncovered more efficient if less exciting means to achieve that building's goal of sheltering passengers and dispersing smoke.[7]

Skating rinks and hockey arenas differ from the usual building-type script in another important way. In designing the earliest buildings for skating and hockey, architects transposed to a bounded space the requirements of these sports as they were formerly engaged in out-of-doors. But once enclosed, the sports themselves were transformed. The various ways in which this occurred and the reasons why appear and reappear throughout this study, with particular emphasis in the final chapter. Indeed, explaining how, why, and when this happened is one of the major contributions that architectural history brings to this subject.

Typology, style, and cutting-edge architectural developments proved inadequate filters through which to analyze the history and meaning of these buildings for another reason. The locus of this book stretches beyond the confines of the buildings that enclose ice rinks to encompass an expanded sports landscape – the places and spaces of the sport and its enthusiasts, both physical and virtual. Similarly, the book looks beyond the achievements of individual architects to consider the clients, users, and supporting communities who contributed to and were affected by these buildings over the course of their existence. The book therefore presents a dialogue not only between architecture and sport but within architecture. I employ a hybrid methodology – part architectural history, part cultural-landscape studies, part vernacular architecture analysis – and an interdisciplinary approach incorporating history, politics, and economics as well as urbanism and aspects of scholarship on media, the entertainment industry, and contemporary culture.

Those who study vernacular architecture are usually looking at common, often humble, architect-less buildings and landscapes in order to discover insights into the culture that produced them. And they are interested in the life of these buildings, how users modify them over time.[8] Such an approach has proved extremely useful in studying the earliest, wooden structures for skating that were raised throughout eastern Canada and the northeast United States into the twentieth century. These buildings came into being as a consequence of social and economic forces. They helped shape the experience of the sports they housed and were frequently modified by users as needs and circumstances changed.

0.1
Winter Olympics hockey match, Chamonix, France, 1924. Fans gather at rink's edge with no intervening boards.

As suitable subjects for in-depth study, skating rinks and hockey arenas have suffered a fate similar to that of summer camps, insane asylums, and YMCA buildings, which have been examined recently by, in turn, architectural historians Abigail Van Slyck, Carla Yanni, and Paula Lupkin. Like their subjects, buildings for skating and hockey seem to fall into a methodological no-man's-land between architectural history and vernacular architecture studies.[9] For example, Yanni explains that asylums were too large, expensive, formal, and professional to interest historians of vernacular architecture yet their architects were not famous enough to appeal to architectural historians.[10]

This book concentrates on buildings for skating and hockey in North America. Hockey first appeared in Canada and by the early twentieth century both ice sports were popular enough in Canada and the northern United States to sustain numerous amateur and professional hockey leagues and the construction of hundreds of arenas. Europe lagged far behind in the construction of covered rinks. As late as 1936, when the Winter Olympics were held at Garmisch-Partenkirchen, Germany, hockey matches were still being played on outdoor rinks, as had been the case for the Olympics held in 1924 and 1928.[11]

While hockey was first played outdoors, and then in buildings originally constructed for skating, once professional hockey achieved success, by the early 1920s, hockey buildings predominated. After this date, skaters, if they skated indoors, did so in hockey arenas. Specialized structures to accommodate curlers and speed skaters continue to be erected throughout the world (the latter in very small numbers). But commercial ice events, whether featuring hockey, figure skaters, or costumed characters (Disney on Ice), soon occurred exclusively within buildings conceived first and foremost for hockey.

Community arenas across North America far outnumber their larger, commercial counterparts. I refer to them only briefly, yet they deserve a study of their own, one that would inevitably touch upon architecture, vernacular architecture studies, and local and social history. My concern here has been with understanding the history and development of buildings for skating and professional hockey. Community arenas do not contribute anything new to this storyline.

Architecture is not a requirement for playing sports. Grassy fields and frozen ponds abound. Sport existed, and continues to exist, in the absence of buildings in which games may be played. According to a Prairie baseball enthusiast, circa 1910: "Every town would have a pasture with a chicken wire backstop, and when you was gonna have a game you'd chase the town cows off it and scrape up the cow plops and that was about it."[12] Substitute snow on outdoor ice surfaces for cow plops on pastures and you have the comparable experience of early skaters and hockeyists.

At their most elemental, skating and hockey rinks consist of nothing more than a patch of natural or artificial ice. Ice surfaces have been laid within existing structures (barns, drill sheds, warehouses) and in buildings specifically designed for the purpose. What does a hockey arena look like? What are its defining characteristics? The basic recipe does not change, regardless of geographical location, construction materials, overall dimensions, or intended audience (community participants or professional athletes and their fans). A vast, sheltering roof and retaining walls encompass a massive interior volume, around the perimeter of which runs an oval grandstand, punctuated by four-foot-high boards where it meets and encloses a sheet of ice. Other amenities for the accommodation of fans and players – change rooms, restaurants, washrooms, score clocks – may be provided. Like the arenas of ancient Rome, to which they ultimately refer, all such buildings dispose spectators around an event in such a way that they become an audience. Visible each to several, audience members are both spectators and actors; they become enfolded into the larger spectacle on offer.

If this was all that hockey arenas were, and did (brought spectators in proximity to hockey matches), then there would be little ambiguity in discussing them. But the recipe I have outlined above can be, and was, put to many other uses. Whether purpose-built or adapted, architecture on ice always serves multiple functions. A key issue that runs throughout this book concerns architects' difficulties in defining skating rinks and hockey arenas as a distinct and recognizable architectural form precisely because of their slippery program, a problem made all the more difficult as they morphed from rink to arena to coliseum to centre. (When is a hockey arena a hockey arena? Is it still a hockey arena if there is no ice and people are playing basketball?) Yet, in spite of this ambiguity, which neutralized architects' ability to design skating rinks and hockey arenas expressive of their functions, architecture affected both sport and spectator in fundamental ways.

Once buildings for sport exist, they create what sports historian Brian Nelson has called, in reference to baseball stadiums, "a box to contain a drama."[13] This book explores the changing experience of that drama within buildings for skating and hockey and how the conjunction of sports, spectatorship, and architecture has evolved over the past one hundred and fifty years. What do these buildings mean for the communities that build them?

Hockey facilities are some of our largest enclosed gathering spaces, capable of seating as many as 21,000. They have served as quasi-public places of assembly for shared rituals – mass assemblies of social, political, entertainment, and sporting events. It might even be argued that the common rules of sport, acknowledged by all who choose to enter these places of exercise and entertainment, more successfully unite North Americans of diverse language, politics, age, race, or national heritage than any other cultural activity. In their historic and continuing role as venues for a multiplicity of events – from political rallies to Stanley Cup matches, from trade shows to rock concerts – skating rinks and hockey arenas have played a central role in the lives of a broad cross-section of the North American populace. The transmission of these events, via electronic and print media, has further extended their reach to people who might never enter these buildings, thereby expanding the hockey facility's spatial realm of influence far beyond the physical confines of the building.

Arenas have even been accorded the status of secular shrines in the hearts and minds of some. When Montreal Canadiens hockey great Howie Morenz died in 1937, his funeral service was held at the Montreal Forum before ten thousand faithful fans. And when that same venerable building closed in 1996, after seventy-two years of continuous operation, the event was attended with all the pomp, ceremony, and symbolism typically associated with the de-consecration of a major religious building, vivid acknowledgment of the mythic status this building had achieved.

The emotional frenzy attending the closing of the Montreal Forum was in large part a public-relations-induced event, orchestrated to favourably dispose the public toward the new Molson

0.2
Fans in stands, Sharks at Canucks, 2013. This is how we spectate today.

(now Bell) Centre, with its roughly three thousand extra seats to fill. But Montreal's experience was not isolated. In Boston, Chicago, Detroit, and Toronto, great trouble was taken to smooth public perception of the transition to new buildings and of the inevitable destruction of their hockey teams' former homes. Such efforts recognize the widespread emotional hold that sports buildings exert on our collective psyches, and the economic stakes at play. How many other civic buildings arouse such broad-based enthusiasm?

But not only major league sports facilities in metropolitan centres can achieve exalted status. A British settler in Canada, describing the centrality of the skating rink to winter life, observed in 1878 that "the rink is the great winter amusement [where] the bands play and young people meet to skate, to dance on skates and to amuse themselves."[14] In a review of skating and hockey buildings at the Calgary Exhibition Grounds, the author noted that, by about 1921, "the Arena was not only a hockey center. As time passed, the Arena became Calgary's 'everything center.'"[15] One hundred years after the first covered rinks, nothing much had changed. In their 1989 book *Home Game*, Ken Dryden and Roy MacGregor revealed how the humble, ubiquitous Quonset-hut-type arenas that dot the Canadian landscape serve as de facto cultural centres, the glue that binds many small communities together. They recount the compelling story of Radisson, Saskatchewan, a prairie town of 434 people faced with the challenge of replacing their structurally unsound rink. The authors interviewed locals who referred to their rink as "the grand central gathering place for the young and old … the backbone of the community … the gathering place for the winter months." And they speculated on the impact of its loss: "We know of other towns that have lost their rinks. The towns die overnight."[16]

Between 1990 and 2010 twenty-eight new NHL arenas were constructed across North America at a total cost of over $5 billion. This remarkable construction boom effected a nearly complete sea change in the places where professional hockey is played. These massive sport/entertainment complexes are not just different from their predecessors. They mark a fundamental break with the past. Although they are often promoted as important public and cultural facilities – like town halls, museums, and airports – and as debates have raged over their public funding, discussion of these buildings rarely focuses on their architecture. Relatively little is known about the history of this building type.

Hockey has been a topic of immense popularity and intense cultural identification for Canadians and the sport has also been fervently followed in specific northern locales in the United States. The sport has given rise to a vast literature in both fiction and non-fiction genres, to poetry, to movies, and to music and to art.[17] The most common publications to treat hockey facilities are popular building histories. They follow a standard, biographical script; after an opening chapter looking at previous buildings (ancestors), they proceed to detail memorable events, either chronologically or by type (circus, entertainment, hockey, basketball).[18]

Scholars of architecture have paid relatively little attention to sports facilities, including skating rinks and hockey arenas. In 2005 sports journalist and author Simon Kuper observed that "stadiums are becoming keynote urban buildings, as cathedrals were in the Middle Ages and opera houses more recently."[19] Yet, with the exception of a few recent studies by an architectural and a sports historian that point to the depth and range of investigation that is possible, the hockey arena is absent from architectural history, even while related building types such as movie theatres and shopping malls have been studied.[20] My own previously published work has dealt with a single building (Montreal Forum), explored the theme of spectatorship, and offered thumbnail histories of the hockey arena, the skeletal outlines of the present study.[21]

Researchers in other disciplines have actively and profitably investigated aspects of hockey's architecture, referring to sports facilities in studies of urbanism, sports history, culture, and anthropology. Sports historians focus on specific geographical regions, chronological moments, and the economics of early hockey.[22] Sociologists and urban historians have studied contemporary hockey facilities, characterizing them as highly commercialized and mediatized works. Their interest has been on how media, technology, and the entertainment industry have contributed to the "spectacularization" of public space.[23]

Though undoubtedly valuable, most of these earlier studies inevitably decontextualize buildings for sport, either considering individual buildings as mere containers or isolating them as material evidence without considering their architectural history. Media, technology, and entertainment have been factors in the conception and design of hockey architecture since Maple Leaf Gardens opened in 1931, with its gondola for Foster Hewitt's radio broadcasts and an advanced sound system. And the development from outdoor to indoor rink and then to arena is also the story of commercial interests transforming the relationship between performers and spectators. The 1964 and 1965 Beatles tours of North America ushered in a new era of rock concerts, henceforth invariably held in arenas. The impact of this phenomenon on the conception and design of subsequent arenas is still with us. Its implications for architecture will be investigated here for the first time.

Today's multi-purpose sport facilities evolved from simple curling and skating rinks, first erected in Canada beginning in the 1850s. How and why did these buildings evolve? What were the influences and pressures that affected their design and development? How did we get here from there? In tracing the history of this building typology, changes in name – from rink to arena to coliseum to centre – provide clues, alerting us to corresponding changes to these buildings'

0.3
"Grand Skating Carnival at Halifax," 1882. This is how we participated over one hundred years ago.

form, function, and use. But a funny thing happened on the way to the forum. As the professional hockey arena emerged, developed, and evolved, it also disappeared. In 1999 Brian Brisbin, architect of Toronto's Air Canada Centre, stated, "Simply put, the 'arena' is dead."[24] As this book unfolds, we will see why this is true and how it happened.

What do rinks, arenas, forums, and "gardens" look like and what goes on inside them? Where are they located? What does it feel like to participate in activities or attend events within them? How have these features and experiences shifted over time? For instance, what happens when buildings for participation become places of spectatorship and commerce? When and why did these changes occur? To answer these questions, the narrative travels from Montreal to Los Angeles, from Vancouver to Nashville. And we will also journey in time, from nineteenth-century costume-clad revellers dancing to polka music on ice skates to twenty-first-century fans in shorts and T-shirts doing the "wave" and hamming it up for the Jumbotron screen.

The book is organized chronologically, with its four parts devoted to six distinct phases that I have identified in the development and history of buildings for skating and hockey: (1) indoor skating rinks (1852–1904); (2) first spectator arenas (1898–1912); (3) first NHL arenas (1920–31); (4) NHL expansion-era arenas (1960–83); (5) corporate entertainment centres (1990–2010); (6) Sports-anchored developments (SADS) (2012–) (see Table 1). While the divisions correspond to changes in building form, the interest has been in highlighting how these changes reflect broader issues: of architecture, sports, and history, to be sure, but also economics, commerce, urbanism, technology, music, politics, media, gender relations, and the entertainment industry.

Part One traces the origins of buildings for skating, curling, and hockey from simple barns, primarily in Canada, to the first dedicated hockey rinks equipped with artificial ice in both Canada and the United States. The ownership, design, and siting of these buildings is discussed, with an emphasis on the architectural origins of this building type, on the activities the buildings made possible, and on how enclosed, covered rinks affected the game of hockey. The years 1852 to 1912 parallel hockey's establishment and growing popularity. The development of professional hockey leagues is examined in the context of other competing sports. The close link between the economics of early hockey and its buildings is revealed.

Part Two looks at the first permanent spectator arenas that arose in Canada and the United States between 1920 and 1931, focusing on their design characteristics, siting, and economics. It was during this so-called Golden Age of Sport that urban audiences came into possession of the required disposable income and leisure time to attend sporting and other mass-entertainment events. Formed in 1917, the NHL emerged as the premiere professional league in North America and a mini building boom saw the construction of new buildings for eight of the league's ten teams, several of which would continue in operation for over fifty years. Two Canadian buildings – the Montreal Forum (1926) and Maple Leaf Gardens (1931) in Toronto – are analyzed in depth in order to better understand how and why they achieved near mythical status as shrines for their supporters.

Architecture was the pivotal means by which the NHL expanded into the United States. The history of Madison Square Garden is unfolded, revealing subtle yet significant differences between its origins and mode of operation from that of most other hockey venues. The commercial foundations of this entertainment palace provided an alternate model for the staging of hockey. This is the model that will prevail later in the century, directly informing the conception of today's sport-entertainment complexes.

Part Three examines the period of professional hockey expansion that began in the late 1960s. Economics, urban politics, television, and new construction methods all affected the siting and design of arenas. Post-war North America witnessed a demographic shift. As populations gravitated to new suburbs, many sports teams followed suit, constructing new facilities there. For teams that remained in the urban core, new arena projects were often linked to plans for urban revitalization.

Architects' novel deployment of glass, steel, and concrete, inspired by the accomplishments of engineer-architects such as Buckminster Fuller and Pier Luigi Nervi, produced arenas of formal simplicity, clarity, and beauty. Before the 1960s, arenas shared few common features that might have helped characterize them as a distinct building type. Buildings like the Los Angeles Forum (1967) and the Oakland-Alameda County Coliseum (1966) were among the first recognizable arenas. It seemed possible to imagine that they could serve as models that would define this building type for the future, as had occurred earlier in the century for classic American ballparks. But an alternate model for the staging of sport and entertainment, typified by New York's Madison Square Garden (1968) and by Houston's Astrodome (1964), triumphed in this age of entertainment and mass celebrity (the Beatles, Muhammad Ali). These two buildings emerged as spectacular sites in which sports, entertainment, architecture, and the omnipresence of television became firmly entwined.

In Part Four, the book's final section, the outcome of these developments on the design of hockey facilities and on hockey spectatorship becomes apparent within a new crop of sport-entertainment complexes that arose at the end of the twentieth century. Corporate owners demanded facilities that would enable them to capitalize on new and existing revenue streams: private boxes, naming rights, in-arena advertising, merchandising, and restaurants. This new breed of facility was intended for a new species of spectator – mobile, affluent, less knowledgeable, and less devoted.

These buildings directly answer the characterization of this era by social and cultural critics as one dominated by capitalism, consumption, media, and new technologies of communication and computerization. Whether referred to as "Consumer Society," "Media Society," or "Society of Spectacle," these critics agree that the present age is one dominated by an ever-present mass media that has itself become reality. Spectator experience within these facilities is characterized by fragmentation and recombination through pastiche. This corresponds to the philosopher Jean Baudrillard's description of the "hyperreal," in which the "real" is absorbed by televisual screens. The cybernetic images they broadcast become reality.

As sports facilities returned to the urban core during this period, issues of urbanism and public financing came to the fore. Across North America, cities built new sports facilities as lures to attract professional sports franchises, often vying with each other when doing so. If you build it they will come, but if you don't they might go. At the end of the twentieth century, corporate owners discovered a new way to expand the scope and economic return of sport-entertainment complexes. SADs are large-scale retail, residential, commercial, and real estate projects developed around a sports-entertainment facility. L.A. Live, built up around the Staples Center (beginning in 2007), and Brooklyn's Atlantic Yards, anchored by the Barclays Center (2012), are two examples. Though the sports facility arguably "anchors" these developments, the hockey arena, as a distinct identifiable building, has disappeared.

One of the ironies of this study is that the hockey arena may never have existed as a unique and fully defined building type. From their origins in the nineteenth century, purpose-built buildings for skating and hockey were multi-functional. To survive economically they were transformable, in the beginning from season to season, today from day to day. Furthermore, hockey has often been played in buildings constructed for entirely different purposes, from boat-building barns to opera houses. In architectural terms, building types are defined and distinguished by their functional requirements. The architectural brief for today's sport-entertainment complexes requires an adaptable, multi-functional space capable of seating large audiences for diverse events, while outside they are expected to exhibit some of the characteristics of civic buildings – plazas, towers, and apparent accessibility – in order to justify the huge public expenditures they increasingly entail. This uninspiring, all-purpose recipe accurately predicts the generic quality of the resulting architecture. Today, little distinguishes arenas for basketball from those for hockey beyond a change of playing surface and the rearrangement of some seats. It may be more accurate to describe this book as a study of the spaces and places in which hockey has been played; the hockey arena, as such, may be a phantom.

Finally, even if "hockey arena" may not be the correct term to describe these ambiguous buildings, I will show that they have nonetheless played a central role in their communities' cultural life for nearly two centuries. Whether known as rinks, arenas, forums, gardens, or centres, these buildings helped shape the sports and entertainment events they hosted. And as part of an expanded "sportscape," they contributed to and influenced urban, social, and political life. Skating rinks and hockey arenas may be North America's most important overlooked cultural buildings.

1.1
Quebec City Skating Rink, 1852. The first purpose-built skating rink in the world.

Part One

In the Beginning:
Indoor Rinks for Skating, Curling, and Hockey,
1852–1912

1.2
Victoria Skating Rink, Montreal, 1862. Men and women,
adults and children: exercise, conversation, and flirting,
all in one grand all-encompassing space.

1

Outdoor Games – Indoor Games

"The rink is the great winter amusement [where] the bands play and young
people meet to skate, to dance on skates and to amuse themselves."
– J.J. Rowan, *The Emigrant and Sportsman in Canada*

"I should be truly glad to see the police interfere whenever hockey is commenced."
– Henry Roxborough, *The Stanley Cup Story*

Introduction

Before there was architecture on ice there was only ice. In this chapter I begin by examining the
spaces and places of skating and winter sport that existed before architects were invited to intervene. Where, why, how, and for whom did people skate? This history and the wide range of social
practices that defined skating culture up to and including the nineteenth century influenced
the form, function, and use of the buildings that followed. Throughout the nineteenth century,
skating was primarily a participatory activity. Architecture initially provided shelter and comfort,
first for skaters and then for hockey players. But as the century came to a close, these same
conditions encouraged the presence of ever greater numbers of spectators, which exposed the
limitations of existing buildings to meet such demand.

Nineteenth-Century Urban Skating Rinks

People have skated out-of-doors since at least the twelfth century, first as a means of transportation and then for exercise and pleasure.[1] When we talk about skating out-of-doors we are
generally describing a social experience, with people engaged in a number of related but different
physical activities, both individual and communal. All skaters glide over an ice surface on skates
but each person may have different motivations and goals and, were they not on skates, we might
call what they are doing by other names. At the rink we see: individuals exercising and practising
their figures; couples skating hand-in-hand or dancing; groups of young people playing games,
racing, and chasing one another; parents helping children to skate; non-skaters being pushed
in chairs or sleds; people falling on the ice and being helped to their feet; people putting on or
adjusting their skates; people standing and socializing. At any moment a person engaged in one

1.3
Belle Isle Skating Pavilion, Detroit, 1900. In summer it served the needs of boating enthusiasts.

activity may shift to another.[2] The London correspondent for *The Times* compared idle skaters at Montreal's Victoria Skating Rink in 1862 to "swallows on a cliff" and described how they "dashed off and swept away as if on the wing over the surface."[3] The fixed space of the skating rink within which these simultaneous and fluidly changing activities take place functions as a cross between public park, gymnasium, and dance hall. It is these functional characteristics that will define the program of all nineteenth-century skating rinks, whether open-air or enclosed: social intercourse, physical activity, and mingling of the sexes.

Nineteenth-century outdoor skating rinks in urban settings, though they featured natural or naturally occurring ice surfaces, were in other respects man-made, controlled, and spatially defined. At New York's Central Park as at other similar locations, the ice needed tending. Falling snow and that which built up after hours of skating had to be cleared. Its disposal by shovel, usually along the perimeter of the ice surface, created snow banks that further defined the skating area and also served non-skaters as a safe vantage point from which to view the action. Dangerous spots such as protrusions or thin ice had to be marked for the safety of skaters. The Philadelphia Skating Rink at Fairmount Park was noted for its life-saving equipment, which included long ladders, poles with hooks, axes, and ropes, all used to rescue unfortunates who had fallen through the ice.[4] Amenities such as warming huts (sometimes elaborate pavilions such as that at Belle Isle, Detroit), refreshment booths, benches, and skate-rental kiosks that were provided for the convenience of skaters, and that were often located at "entrance" points like those close to tramway and bus stops, further delimited space and controlled experience. Most skating ponds posted rules, many of which were aimed at dampening the rambunctiousness of young men in order to encourage the presence of young women who, it was felt, might otherwise be deterred from participating. Private skating rinks even featured fences to keep out non-paying customers (see Image 1.25 below).

When the first covered ice rinks were constructed in the mid-nineteenth century, they transposed to indoor settings some six centuries of skating practice on freely accessible frozen ponds, streams, and lakes. Even as the earliest of these buildings accommodated this long tradition they reshaped skating experience in ways both small and large. The inevitable compromises and transformations that resulted from the conjoining of ice, architecture, and participation will be replayed to varying degrees in the history of every other sport that has experienced this shift.

Between 1860 and 1890 ice skating enjoyed a phenomenal burst of popularity in North America. This popularity gave rise to specialized fashions, an increase in ice-skate patents, and the construction of the first indoor rinks.[5] It was the skating culture in existence at this moment, the second half of the nineteenth century, that defined the characteristics of indoor skating rinks. What were the parameters of skating experience at this date? Who were the participants and how did they interact? And what was the nature of the spaces in which this activity took place?

A "skating pond" had been indicated on Frederick Olmsted and Calvert Vaux's original plans for Central Park in New York.[6] It opened in the winter of 1858–59 and by 1866 the daily average attendance at the Central Park skating rink had reached twenty thousand, with evening skating taking place under gas lamps.[7] This skating rink extended its presence throughout the city. To alert skaters to the availability of good ice for skating, a ball was hoisted on the Arsenal building, at 64th Street and Fifth Avenue in Central Park, while the city's streetcars also signalled this condition with small flags.[8] A similar arrangement existed in Brooklyn where the streetcars were equipped with a red ball, which when raised indicated good skating conditions at Prospect Park.[9] Further evidence of skating's growing popularity at this date can be found in industry, art, and literature. Registrations of ice skate patents increased from 17 during the 1850s to 149 for the 1860s.[10]

Love on the Ice

Ice skating became a favoured subject of popular novels, newspapers, poems, songs, and lithographs. While of questionable literary merit, the following passage from a romantic novel entitled *The Admiral's Niece, A Tale of Nova Scotia*, published in London in 1858, allows insights into the contemporary customs and mores of ice skating in North America.

"What a glorious day it is, not a cloud. I hope your skates are in good order, girls? The ice is perfect; I scarcely ever saw it so smooth."

They were soon all prepared for the ice.

Kate and Ada, enveloped in their furs, their dresses gracefully looped up (showing a bright scarlet petticoat trimmed with black velvet, made rather short so as not to impede their movements in skating) looked bewitching. St. John gazed at Ada's tiny feet in admiration, and on reaching the ice begged to be allowed to fasten on her skates, an honor she smilingly accorded him.

"Dangerous work that, St. John," said Lord D —, coming up to them; "those are the prettiest little trotters in the world, more than enough to steal any man's heart from him. They stole mine the first time I ever saw them; did they not Ada."

"Come my Lord, don't be saucy; you are at my mercy on the ice, you know, so I advise you to take care," and with a merry laugh she glided gracefully and swiftly away.[11]

This passage describes nearly all of the conventions touching upon the social experience of skating during the late nineteenth century. We see, for instance, that skating was a popular physical and social activity for both men and women, one that allowed for more relaxed relations between people; that the sport enabled men and women to flirt, and to touch, in ways that would not have been permitted under normal circumstances; that specialized fashions in women's clothing already existed; and that men and women participated as equals – it was even accepted that women could surpass men in ability although cartoons, popular songs, and novels frequently included scenes in which women are rescued by men after having fallen through the ice.

Other winter sports, such as curling, were reserved for socializing among a restricted elite of men. Women might attend as spectators but it was not until 1894 that the first ladies' curling club was formed, in Montreal. The delay was apparently owing to the "copious quantities of whiskey said to be consumed at bonspiels."[12] Similar circumstances prevailed within the world of snowshoeing, where women were deemed too delicate to accompany men on their frequent "tramps" and could expect no more than to marry a snowshoe man.[13] By contrast, outdoor and indoor skating rinks were quickly perceived as spaces for both sexes. Writing in 1860, Charles Wolley encouraged women to join the men at Central Park and fantasized about "what a charming thing it will be to see five hundred cherry-cheeked healthy beauties – goddesses in crinoline and mortals in plumptitudinous loveliness – gliding, whirling, and now and then sitting down, without exactly intending it, on the slippery ice."[14] According to Edwin Bullinger, women were not slow to respond. He reports that, at the Washington Skating Club in Brooklyn, "the great feature of the pond was the vast number of ladies, who … flocked to the pond in multitudes; in fact it sometimes appeared as if the pond was for their exclusive use."[15] Women's changing attitude toward skating was remarked upon by the American author of an illustrated guidebook published in 1867:

Ten years ago a lady on skates was not only a rare and novel sight in this vicinity, but any fair one … who in such a way would have dared to brave the opinion of "her set" and to have outraged their sense of feminine propriety by appearing in public on skates, would have been driven forth from the sacred circles of the then fashionable

coteries of the city in disgrace. Now the very reverse is the case, for the selfsame fair one is now tabooed as "slow" and not "up to the times" if she can not do the "outside circle" or the "grape-vine twist" on skates in the best style of the art.[16]

Skating rinks quickly became scenes for heterosexual recreation, "providing intoxicating opportunity for men and women to meet – and touch."[17] A reporter for the *New York Times* remarked on the unrestricted freedom with which men and women interacted on Parisian rinks in 1891, noting how "the girls skate with one gentleman all the afternoon, beyond the sight of mama, who would be nearly frantic were the same thing to occur in a ballroom."[18] A similar situation existed for the sport of croquet, which also gained popularity at this date. According to Patricia Campbell Warner, "the croquet lawn became famous as a meeting ground for young eligibles, as a socially acceptable place to carry on flirtations."[19] A late-nineteenth-century poem revels in the opportunities for flirtatiousness and the potential for physical contact with the female sex that skating offered but that would have been otherwise prohibited:

1.4
Currier and Ives, *Central Park, Winter, the Skating Pond*, 1862. Pavilions, kiosks, and other man-made structures and interventions defined and delimited naturally occurring outdoor rinks.

There are tiny waists you may put your arm round
     (Don't attempt it on land – that's all!),
And white warm hands you may clasp till charm-bound,
     (Just in case they should chance to fall);
There are tresses trailing and bright eyes glowing,
     Lips that laugh when you lend a hand,
And dainty ankles they can't help showing
     (Quite by accident – understand!),
     Sing Tan-tarra-ti,
     A-skating we hie,
The jolliest sport in the world, say I![20]

William Howard Russell, *The Times* war correspondent who arrived in Montreal after having reported on the American Civil War from March 1861 to April 1862, visited Montreal's Victoria Skating Rink not long after it opened in 1862 and remarked that it was "crowded with women, young and old, skating or preparing to skate, for husbands."[21]

The Social Context: Skating Rinks as Sites of Democracy

From its beginnings in North America, ice skating was understood and practised as a democratic sport. In cold weather ice was plentiful and free of access. Ice skates were relatively cheap to buy and they could also be rented from outdoor kiosks. The democratic underpinnings of ice skating were enshrined in the handbook published by the Brooklyn Skating Rink Association for the 1868–69 season, which states: "Skating, in a moral and social point, is particularly suited to our republican ideas as a people. The millionaire and mechanic, the lady of fashion and those of humbler rank, all meet together to enjoy this fascinating and beautiful exercise. All can skate alone or associate with those most agreeable to themselves, and none are held responsible for the action or standing of others."[22]

    The fact that it is difficult to maintain one's dignity on ice skates, even for experts, is a further characteristic of the sport that serves to unite skaters in a kindly and non-judgmental fellowship. A skating manual of the period warned readers, "No parlor etiquette can be maintained on the ice-pond. Whoso goes there must bid goodbye to stateliness and formality and become one of the democracy of skaters. All are equal on the common level of the iron runners."[23] Yet another contemporary manual, Henry Chadwick's *Handbook of Winter Sports*, first published in New York in 1867, expands on and refines these ideas by comparing American skating ponds with other sites of social interaction. His observations identify the skating rink as a place of joyous and unfettered pleasure, where participants were freed from the normal rules and social obligations of society:

    At the skating-pond we meet friends and acquaintances, not as we meet them in the
    street, where a passing bow or a minute's converse is all the intercourse we can have
    with them; nor as at the evening party, where the positions of host and guests places
    them upon a formal footing; nor as at the church or lecture-room, where one's

attention is especially devoted to other matters. But we meet them on a footing of equality … where we can converse for a few minutes or an hour; where we can listen and be heard, see and be seen; laugh and frolic without fear of offense; where we can assist those in trouble, meet with and dispense courtesy.[24]

In this regard, nineteenth-century skating rinks correspond to sociologist Ray Oldenburg's definition of "third places," which he characterizes as public places on neutral ground where people can gather and interact. His prime examples are the sidewalk cafés of Paris, London pubs, the piazzas of Florence, and the coffeehouses of Vienna, places that offer an "escape or time out from life's duties and drudgeries."[25] Such places, he argues, enable chance meetings and spontaneous acts. What goes on inside "is largely unplanned, unscheduled, unorganized, and unstructured," while their mood is a playful one in which "joy and acceptance reign over anxiety and alienation."[26] Distinct from both home and work (first and second places), these spaces are, for Oldenburg, central to local democracy and community vitality. They promote social equality by levelling the status of guests, because the "third place" is "by its nature, an inclusive place. It is accessible to the general public and does not set any formal criteria of membership and exclusion."[27]

The First Indoor Rinks

Covered rinks allowed patrons to escape winter's cold temperatures, harsh winds, and blowing snow and eliminated the immediate danger of falling through thin ice on ponds or streams. Newspaper accounts of skating fatalities were a constant through the nineteenth century and contemporary painted and published images of outdoor skating scenes invariably included at least one figure falling through the ice.[28] Indoor rinks fitted with gas lights permitted skaters and curlers to practise their sport beyond the limits of daylight-shortened winter days and also made possible evening competition and social events.[29] The first indoor ice rinks, for curling, were erected in the eastern provinces of Canada as early as 1837. Many were probably no more than sheets of ice laid down within existing wooden barns or sheds that had been retrofitted

1.5
Caledonian Curling and Skating Club rink, Toronto. Opened 1875 and used for both curling and skating until it was replaced by the Mutual Street Arena in 1912 (see Image 4.5).

for the purpose, a practice that continued even later in the century for both curling and skating rinks.[30] This practice was often a means of putting to use structures that otherwise would have been idle during the winter months. For example, on 20 December 1884, the Dey Brothers, a prominent family of Ottawa boat builders, opened the first of three commercial skating rinks in one of the family's boat works, located to the east of the Rideau Canal.[31]

Curling, like most nineteenth-century sports, was initially an upper-class pursuit and the first purpose-built curling rinks, appearing in Canada by about 1870, were located in urban centres, to allow their members easy access. The buildings comprised two parts, a long shed to house the rinks and a clubhouse for subscribed members. The two- or three-storey clubhouses featured street-front entrances with facades that resembled public buildings. Typically modelled on English clubhouses, they were finished in solid materials such as brick and stone where pretensions dictated and money allowed. The clubhouse incorporated changing, meeting, and reception rooms and sometimes provided windows overlooking the ice surface. It was in these rooms that the feasting and drinking took place that inevitably accompanied and followed matches. The constitution of the Royal Montreal Curling Club, founded in 1807, decreed, "The Losing Party of the day shall pay for a Bowl of Whisky Toddy to be placed in the middle of the table, for those who may choose it."[32]

The barn-like sheds, in back, housed from two to eight sheets of ice laid side to side. Windows along one or both of their long elevations helped illuminate the interiors. The method of spanning the ice surface might vary but construction was universally of wood. For example, a rink for the Thistle Curling Club of Montreal, erected in 1870, featured two sheets of ice covered by a flat roof, separated and supported throughout its length by wooden piers. As these buildings were meant primarily for the use of members, spectators were only nominally provided for, at rink's edge, at either end of the ice or on the narrow raised surface between the ice sheets. Reviewing the state of Canadian curling facilities in 1892, James Headly described the preparation of the ice: "The floors are made of boards, carefully levelled and jointed, on which ice is made by careful 'washing' and subsequent sprinkling. The rings, 'hog scores' and 'hack-lines' are cut in the ice, and to make them more distinct blue paint is put into them. Platforms are arranged at the ends, and there are rows and tiers of boxes to contain the curling rocks of which each club boasts from one to hundred pairs."[33]

Column-free interiors and wider spans were first realized through arched wooden trusses or traditional barn construction. The interior of the Royal Montreal Curling Club rink of 1889 featured spectacular wooden arches that sprang directly from the floor to span three sheets of ice. In "A Brief History of Toronto's Rinks and Curlers," originally published in the *Toronto Empire* newspaper, the Mutual Street (Caledonian) Rink is reported to have had "the largest clear surface of ice on the continent," with "a wood span 104 feet across the building, which is 165 feet long," a span "said to be the longest wooden one in the world except that of a railway depot in Leeds, England."[34] The Granite Curling and Skating Rink, also in Toronto and designed by architect Norman B. Dick in 1880, comprised six sheets of ice behind a two-storey Richardsonian Romanesque brick-faced clubhouse replete with a four-storey entrance tower. The pitched roof of its barn-like shed rose some fifty feet over an ice surface of over 20,000 square feet. Elevated balconies along the entire inner length of both walls allowed for additional spectators. With its basilical form, buttressing side aisles, clerestory windows, and six tall arched windows at one end,

1.6
Thistle Curling Club, Montreal, 1871. Early curling rinks
provided only minimal (accidental) space for spectators.

1.7
Granite Curling and Skating Rink, Toronto.

it presented an imposing form within nineteenth-century Toronto, which could then boast few buildings of comparable size and none that were essentially private.

Curling rinks were by no means limited to the major cities. When a team of Scottish curlers, the originators of the game, toured Canada and the United States during the winter of 1902–03, they were as surprised by the quality of the curlers they encountered as they were amazed at the ubiquity and impressiveness of the covered rinks in which these games were played.[35] By this date, Toronto could boast as many as eight enclosed curling rinks with a total of thirty-nine sheets of ice, "erected at a cost approaching $300,000,"[36] yet it was not unusual for even smaller towns, such as Stratford, Ontario, with a 1901 population of just under 10,000, to erect remarkably grand facilities.

Most early curling and skating rinks were multi-use buildings; in addition to being adaptable for both curling and ice skating, they hosted social events and, later, hockey matches. Owing to the seasonal limitations on natural-ice surfaces, and in order to maximize their use throughout the year, these buildings also often accommodated other functions. For example, an article in the *Ottawa Times* of 14 December 1867 announced plans for a new curling rink that would be "convert[ed] in Summer into parlor [i.e., roller] skating rooms, and archery galleries, and bowling alleys, all intended to be available to ladies as well as gentlemen."[37] Alan Metcalfe has shown that indoor rinks' very survival depended upon being patronized throughout the year. With increasing urbanization through the 1870s and 1880s, centrally located real estate became increasingly expensive, forcing many sports facilities to move to the suburbs or into bankruptcy. Metcalfe notes how Montreal's Victoria Skating Rink, faced with increased taxes and other costs, saw its profit margins decreasing in the early 1870s until rink management began promoting summer activities.[38]

Early ice rinks could be erected with remarkable speed. The curling rink described above by the *Ottawa Times* was expected to open on 1 January, less than three weeks after the start of construction.

Such speed reflects a simplicity of design and structure that parallels contemporary experience in the construction of baseball fields. Because of the economic uncertainty of North American professional baseball in the 1860s and 1870s, baseball grounds were built of wood both to minimize expenses and to ensure that they could be easily taken apart for transport to another city.[39]

Indoor skating rinks were quickly embraced as centres of nineteenth-century winter social life in Canada and the northeastern United States. Writing about sporting life in Canada in 1876, J.J. Rowan observed that "the rink is the great winter amusement and is to be found in every city. In these enormous wooden tents, well-lighted by day and by night, and fitted with every convenience for the skater, the bands play and young people meet to skate, to dance on skates and to amuse themselves."[40]

Nineteenth-century buildings for skating and curling developed in an ad hoc manner, following the design of simple barns and sheds, but by the 1860s two types of rinks could be discerned. The first was rectangular in plan, defined by long, tall, often free-span interiors. These spaces provided skaters with an ice surface large enough to approach the familiar experience of outdoor skating, and functioned well for curling, skating, and eventually hockey. Longitudinal skating rinks soon became the norm. They are now so ubiquitous and their use so tied to the sport of hockey that it is hard to imagine rinks of any other form. Yet early skating rinks were not built with hockey in mind, nor were they originally intended to accommodate paying spectators. The second type of rink occurring at this date was circular or octagonal in plan. This type did not survive past the nineteenth century and is now all but forgotten. But the sources underlying its design informed the form and function of all skating rinks and of their perception and use in the nineteenth century.

The Victoria Skating Rink, Montreal

The Quebec Skating Club Rink at Quebec City (see Image 1.1) represents the first type of ice rink. It was the first purpose-built indoor skating rink in the world when it opened in 1852. But the Victoria Skating Rink, constructed in Montreal ten years later, became the premiere venue of its kind, the most widely celebrated and the model for nearly all subsequent skating rinks. Built in 1862 and designed by Montreal architects Lawford and Nelson, the Victoria Skating Rink was a longitudinally oriented, two-storey brick building with a pitched roof, supported on the interior by elegantly curving wooden trusses that sprang 52 feet from the ground to span the entire width of the column-free interior (see Image 1.2). The natural-ice surface measured 200 × 85 feet, the dimensions subsequently adopted by the National Hockey League as the standard for all hockey arenas. A 10-foot-wide platform or promenade surrounded the ice, providing a space on which spectators could stand or skaters rest. Tall round-arched windows on three sides of the building illuminated the interior for daytime skating, while hundreds of gas, and later electric, light fixtures permitted evening events. The building opened for skating daily at eight o'clock and did not close its doors until ten in the evening.

The novelty of its architectural form and use may be gauged by the reaction of foreign observers, such as William Howard Russell, a reporter for *The Times* who visited the building soon after its opening. He likened it to a Methodist chapel, perhaps owing to the plainness of its exterior, and

1.9 *Right*
Victoria Skating Rink,
Montreal, 1862.

1.10 *Below*
Drill Shed, Hamilton, 1863.
The overarching frame roof
and viewing balcony make drill
sheds such as this functionally
indistinguishable from early
skating rinks.

1.11 *Opposite*
Yarmouth Skating Rink, 1878.

to "a large public bath-room" within, presumably having in mind contemporary bathing pavilions
with their tall, vaulted interiors.[41] For other observers, the rink called to mind contemporary
armouries or drill sheds, a building type that proliferated in the 1860s in the United States with
the onset of the Civil War and in Canada in response to perceived threats of American invasion.[42]
By the end of the third quarter of the century, this building type became characterized by a hulk-
ing, castellated form in Romanesque style, yet early examples were no more than large, wooden
sheds whose primary goal was the provision of spacious and dry interiors in which to shelter arms
and soldiers while allowing the latter space for military exercises.[43] Drill sheds and skating rinks
both required large unobstructed interiors and their designers turned to engineering solutions

already devised by European railway architects, who by mid-century had roofed spans of over 100 metres.[44] Skating rinks had also to withstand the accumulated weight of winter snowfalls, unless they wished to suffer the fate of Montreal's Craig Street Drill Shed whose roof collapsed in 1872 only five years after it had been built.[45] So similar are the requirements of drill sheds and skating rinks that the Canadian government erected a number of dual-service structures in the 1940s.[46] In April 2013 New York Mayor Michael Bloomberg announced the proposed transformation of the Kingsbridge Armory in the Bronx into the world's largest indoor-ice skating centre, expected to contain a suite of nine ice rinks, including one that could seat 5,000 spectators.[47]

Community and Commerce: Central-Plan Skating Rinks on Canada's East Coast

The second type of covered ice-skating rink could be found on the east coast of Canada between 1860 and 1890. These central-plan buildings were circular or octagonal in plan and topped with domes or cupolas. As the popularity of hockey grew toward the end of the nineteenth century, these circular skating surfaces proved inadaptable to that sport and they ceased being built. This now forgotten chapter in the design of buildings for skating is worth exploring, however, for the insights it reveals about the role of music in the design of these buildings and about the original social function of skating rinks as places of participation and social intercourse.

The Public Exhibition Hall and Skating Rink at Yarmouth, Nova Scotia, also known as the Phoenix, opened on 7 March 1878 with a promenade concert. The Milton Brass Band accompanied skaters. An advertisement in the *Yarmouth Herald* encouraged parents to attend with their children.[48] Yarmouth, located at the western coast of Nova Scotia, was a community of 18,550 inhabitants in 1871. By this date it had reached its peak as a shipbuilding centre, the second-largest port of registry, in tonnage, in Canada.[49] It was presumably this prosperity that encouraged its citizens to hire a New York architectural firm, Palliser, Palliser and Company, for the design

of a building that their community's modest size might otherwise have argued against.[50] Construction of the Phoenix signalled that Yarmouth was a player – a "world-class" centre in today's parlance – and the town's elite could now enjoy social events in a setting that matched anything that might be found in the provincial capital, Halifax.

In addition to annual exhibitions of cattle and produce, the Phoenix provided a venue for community and social events during the summer and autumn months. An advertisement in the *Yarmouth Herald* on 4 July 1878 announced an upcoming presentation

Skating Rink.

of Haydn's *Creation*, performed by the Yarmouth Choral Union.[51] And in winter, after long snow-bound work weeks in cold offices, colder and darker warehouses, and the boxy confines of their homes, the worthies of Yarmouth could look forward to an evening of exercise, entertainment, and good cheer among friends and neighbours in a brightly lit and sometimes festively decorated environment, a monument to their hard work and aspirations. The Phoenix also hosted the annual costume ball on ice, typically the most anticipated event of the year that was duly reported in all the newspapers.

The Phoenix was an imposing two-storey wood-frame building with a wide sheltering roof topped by an observation tower and cupola. Octagonal in plan, it was Palladian in inspiration, with four pavilions projecting from each of its major axes. Dark-stained exterior boards were enlivened by white-sash window trim and edging typical of the Queen Anne style. Two chimneys sprouted from the gable above the pilastered portico of the entrance pavilion. The bandstand, an essential and defining component of these buildings, was situated on the second-floor gallery, overlooking the ice. Following the common practice, live musicians accompanied skaters, a tradition that continued into the twentieth century and to which I will return. The "skating ring" was 110 feet in diameter and encircled by a promenade. To left and right of the promenade were staircases leading to the upper gallery. Directly across the ice from the entrance was a room for refreshments.

1.12
The Provincial Exhibition of Upper Canada, Hamilton, 1860.

THE ARENA, ST. LOUIS, MO.—55

1.13
"The Arena, St Louis, Mo." The first home of the NHL's St Louis Blues but originally constructed as the National Dairy Association Building in 1929.

The design of the Yarmouth rink shares many characteristics with provincial exhibition buildings constructed across Canada through the second half of the nineteenth century. These buildings, such as the one constructed at Hamilton, served as both temporary and permanent venues for annual exhibitions of cattle and produce while also providing space for community and social events. They varied in scale, from modest two-storey clapboard buildings to far grander four-story versions inspired by London's Crystal Palace, erected for the Great Exhibition of 1851. Nearly all these buildings began with a cruciform plan, the larger versions simply extending the wings and increasing the dimensions. The flexibility of this plan, which produced a central interior volume adaptable to many uses, made it a useful model for any municipality in need of a public space for community events.

Many of the central-plan exhibition buildings erected in Canada during the third quarter of the nineteenth century were converted to ice rinks in winter. None of these buildings survive today.[52] The Yarmouth rink burned to the ground in June 1893, by which date it would not have been replaced by another central-plan building. By contrast, cities continued to construct longitudinally oriented exposition halls that also served as skating rinks well into the twentieth century. For instance, the Calgary Arena was built in 1911 within that city's exhibition grounds as a home for horse shows and hockey, and the St Louis Arena, first home of the NHL's St Louis Blues, was originally constructed in 1929 as the National Dairy Association Building.[53] As recently as 1993 the San Jose

Sharks of the NHL played their home games beneath the concrete and steel roof of San Francisco's Cow Palace, built in 1941 and first known as the California State Livestock Pavilion.[54]

A second example of a central-plan skating rink, the Victoria Skating Rink at Saint John, New Brunswick, designed by Charles Walker and constructed 1864–65, may be the most spectacular example of its kind. Constructed of wood and more than 160 feet in diameter, the building's exterior was dominated by a monumental dome topped by a cupola and by a Palladian entrance portico forming a triumphal arch. A continuous band of round-arched windows punctuated the building at ground level. Its most astonishing feature, however, was inside, where a conical wooden structure, containing a bandstand and viewing platforms, ascended in a tapering spiral from the centre of the skating rink's floor to its cupolaed roof nearly eighty feet above.

An article published in the Saint John *Morning News* on 6 January 1865, the day after the building opened, offers a possible insight into one aspect of its unusual form. The author remarked upon the quality of the air within the building, observing that it was "by no means uncomfortable. The excellent ventilation and the style of the building is calculated to free the air from that dense, unpleasant atmosphere which sometimes pervades skating rinks constructed on a different principle."[55] Unlike more common low and flat-roofed rinks, the Victoria Skating Rink's high roof and vented cupola would have acted like a chimney, drawing up and expelling air that had been befouled by gas jets, wet woollens, and perspiring skaters. A neighbouring building may have provided Charles Walker, the Victoria Skating Rink's English-born engineer, with his solution.[56] Matthew Stead's 1858 Engine House for the European and North American Railway, also at Saint

1.14
Victoria Skating Rink, Saint John, NB, c. 1880.

1.15
Engine House for the European and North American Railway, Saint John, NB, elevation and plan, 1858. The building's tall convex dome acted like a chimney, drawing smoke up and out.

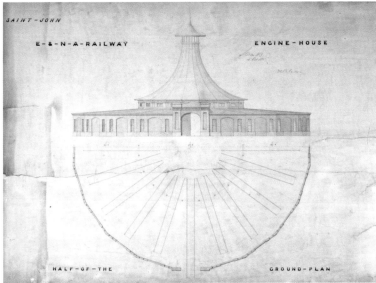

John, was a repair shop and "parking lot" for railway engines. The building was known as a round-house owing to its circular plan, and its central turntable featured nine radiating engine pits to house idle engines that could enter the engine house from one incoming rail line. The important feature for our purposes was its tall convex dome of wood construction, which would have helped eliminate the engines' smoke, making the interior bearable for the engineers who worked within.

But the solution of a technical problem was not by itself a factor adequate to define the architectural form of this building type. For this purpose, it is helpful to review the architectural program of nineteenth-century skating rinks. What were they built to accomplish, and whom did they serve? Skating was a physical and social activity, at which both sexes participated, often under the watchful eyes of a local audience. The sport also provided opportunities for social interaction and courtship. With the move indoors it was possible to add live music to the experience. Indoor rinks were usually encircled by platforms for promenading; the more elaborate ones, such as the

1.16
Victoria Skating Rink, Saint John, N B, 1870. The conical wooden structure at centre supported the bandstand.

Victoria Skating Rink, featured upper galleries from which non-skaters might take refreshment, observe the proceedings, and gossip about clothing, costumes, and pairings.[57]

What existing architectural models might a nineteenth-century architect turn to in arriving at an appropriate formal and spatial solution to these requirements? It was to England that early English Canadians consistently looked for cultural inspiration. A compelling source that served similar functions and clientele could be found in the mid-eighteenth-century summer pleasure grounds at Ranelagh and Vauxhall in England, with their centrally located orchestra pavilions.

Ranelagh and Vauxhall were the creation of "leisure entrepreneurs." They were elaborate pleasure gardens laid out with formal walkways and ornamented with statues and pavilions for entertainment and refreshment. London's fashionable and not-so-fashionable could enter for a shilling, to attend a masquerade, dine in decorated alcoves in the garden or in a Turkish Dining Tent, listen to an orchestra, watch fireworks, and even witness a parachute landing from a balloon.[58] The two venues vied with one another throughout the second half of the eighteenth century, while the

1.17
"A General Prospect of Vauxhall Gardens," 1880. Space for promenading and dining was organized around the centrally located, raised bandstand.

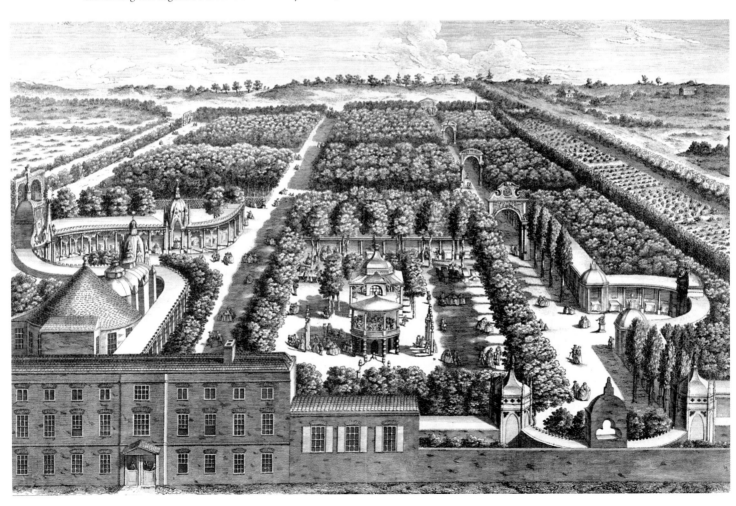

popularity of both declined toward century's end; Ranelagh closed in 1803 and Vauxhall struggled on until 1859.

One of the chief features of both gardens was the provision of music. At Vauxhall the orchestra pavilion was a roofed but otherwise open-air gallery, circular in plan, and raised from the ground on slender columns. It was centrally located on an open lawn, defined by a grove, and facing the Prince of Wales's pavilion. Patrons sat on chairs surrounding the pavilion to listen to music or simply strolled about. Although it was not situated "within" a building, the relationship of the circular, raised orchestra pavilion to its surrounding space and audience is analogous to the relationship of bandstand to encircling ice surface at the Victoria Skating Rink.

Still more compelling is a comparison with the spectacular music rotunda at Ranelagh. Designed by William Jones and opened in 1742, it was that garden's internationally celebrated focal point. An eight-year-old Mozart performed there in 1764. It was a three-storey circular building, 555 feet in circumference. An arcaded ground floor supported an open gallery on the exterior, but its prime attraction was the pavilion's lavish interior space that measured 150 feet in diameter. It was decorated with paintings, gilding, lamps, hanging chandeliers, and a painted rainbow over a part of its ceiling. Two tiers of fifty-two boxes, each holding eight persons, lined the inner walls. The octagonal bandstand at the centre of the room was the source of background music, for tea taking within the loges or polite conversation between promenading guests below. It was an open platform raised above the ground on sturdy piers that continued through the full height of the interior to help support the roof. By the time Ranelagh's music pavilion was painted by Canaletto, in the 1750s, the musicians had been relocated to a stepped and canopied position against the wall, to make way for a huge fireplace that enabled patronage in winter.

The notoriety of Ranelagh reached throughout England and to the continent, its splendours promoted by the aristocracy, described in guidebooks and novels, featured in engraved views, and literally sung; a song extolling its virtues was composed in 1780. Horace Walpole wrote to a friend in 1744: "Every night constantly I go to Ranelagh which has totally beaten Vauxhall. Nobody goes anywhere else." And then, pointing to a lack of exclusivity at these venues that further unites these spaces with North American skating rinks, Walpole noted that "the company is universal; there is from His Grace Grafton down to the children out of the Foundling Hospital."[59]

Ranelagh's widespread fame and social status led to a fashion for such pleasure gardens throughout England, France, and America that continued well into the nineteenth century. What connects Ranelagh in summer to seasonally challenged Saint John is the ways their patrons inhabited these spaces, as both spectators and participants. Whether they came to see or be seen, to dance or skate to music, in or out of costume, they attended not in order to receive entertainment passively but to create it. The interior spaces of these buildings thus have more in common with town squares and, like the outdoor rinks discussed above, with sociologist Ray Oldenburg's definition of "third places." It is this relationship between participation, community, and commerce that defines early buildings for curling, skating, and hockey. In 1865 the world was still more than thirty years away from the first purpose-built hockey arena that will definitively mark the transformation of buildings with ice into sites of spectatorship.

Skating Culture: Music and Women's Fashion

The central place of indoor skating rinks to the winter social life of nineteenth-century North Americans may be gauged from the diary kept by Frances Monck during a one-year stay in Quebec City from 1864 to 1865. Frances Monck was the sister-in-law of Charles Monck, Canada's first governor general.[60] Between mid-December and mid-March, she or her husband attended the Quebec City Skating Rink no fewer than eleven times, roughly one visit per week. Her description of the masked ball she and her husband attended on 14 January 1865 indicates how highly developed these events had become – extending to costumes, music, and decoration – and how integral to social life. "When we arrived I was struck with the very pretty and novel sight; the rink was lit with gas, and decorated with flags and ornaments; there were tables for refreshments on the ice, and the 25th band was playing. It looked like a fair in a Dutch picture."[61] By the end of the century, the audience for these events had become sophisticated enough that newspapers announcing upcoming skating masquerades even mention the name of the rink decorator. For the 4 January 1899 masquerade at the new Montagnard Rink in Montreal, "elaborate preparations are being made … and the decorations will be furnished and set by M. Beullac."[62] In Montreal, the *Gazette* newspaper regularly printed the coming evening's musical program at the Victoria Skating Rink under the heading "City Items." On the evening of 22 December 1864, for instance, the Prince Consort's Musical Brigade was to perform twelve pieces, including quadrilles, a mazurka, and the *Skater's Redowa*, an example of the many nineteenth-century compositions written especially for skaters.[63]

From its very beginnings, recreational skating was associated with music. The figures that early skaters attempted to master grew out of the natural movements that were possible on ice skates and soon developed into ballet-like choreography. The model for couples skating together was ballroom dancing. Both activities depended on music for the tempo, rhythm, and dynamics of their movements. Most indoor skating rinks engaged musicians who accompanied skaters with waltzes, quadrilles, polkas, and mazurkas. Especially composed music for both roller and ice skating soon followed. Many titles identify a dance style, often coupled with a location, sometimes a specific place: James E. Stewart's *Rink Waltz* (Detroit, 1868); A.F. Herwig's *St Louis Skating Rink Waltz*; John B. Smith's *Arena Waltz* (New York, 1883); Henry Schroeder's *Central Park Skating Quadrille Characteristic* (New York, 1862). But the most frequent themes concern gender relations, usually amorous. Titles like *Flirting on the Ice*, *Skating Beauty*, *Belle of the Rink*, and *Skating with the Girls* are typical, and even more anodyne pieces like *The Skaters Waltz* and *Skaters Festival* were printed with cover images of alluring young women.

Indoor skating rinks constructed as early as 1860 featured specially designed bandstands. The skating rink at Quincy, Illinois, erected in 1868 or 1869, featured "a gallery of appropriate dimensions for the use of musicians" at the east end of the building.[64] Bandstands were sometimes located directly on the ice, as was the case at the Chicago Skating Rink of 1860. Nineteenth-century skating rinks generally provided a large open area for skating, space around the perimeter for sitting, strolling, and socializing, and rooms for changing and refreshments. At Quincy the

1.19 *Opposite*
Ice Carnival at the Quebec City Skating Rink, 1878. Costumed skaters, decorations, music, refreshments, and gas lamps contributed to a fantasy environment.

1.20 *Overleaf*
"The Great Skating 'Rink' at Chicago," 1866. Note the centrally located bandstand and the man helping a woman into her skates.

promenade was seven feet wide, with two rows of seats that could accommodate some six hundred people.[65] Rinks were therefore used, if not actually conceived, along the familiar lines of ballrooms. The few available examples of ballrooms in most cities would have been domestic, rather than commercial or public, and considerably smaller in area than that required for skating. But skating rinks presented their designers with the added requirements of maintaining both the ice surface and a suitable temperature for skating within buildings adaptable to other functions during the rest of the year. Thus, the design of purpose-built skating rinks introduced an entirely new problem for architects to solve.

1.21
"Skaters Festival," 1869. Nineteenth-century skating introduced specialized music and customized dress for women, including raised skirts, exposed ankles, and fur trim.

In addition to the creation of specialized music, the popularity of skating led to the development of a couture for women. Female spectators at unheated rinks might prepare for an evening as Frances Monck did, "by putting on overstockings and warm boots, many warm things under my seal-skin coat, and my fur cap instead of a wreath!" But the young women skating on the ice needed clothes that permitted freedom of movement. They were also on display. Frances Monck again described how the women "wore 'very short' red petticoats and grey or black dresses; some wore scarlet, and some wore feathers in their fur caps."[66] William Howard Russell, *The Times* correspondent, noticed with approbation the "legs of every description, which were generally revealed to mortal gaze in proportion to their goodness," and feigned shock when a woman dusted the snow off her clothes, which consisted of a "dandy jacket and neat little breeches – yes, they wear breeches, a good many of them."[67]

Edwin Wilson Bullinger advised women, "The dress be short, reaching not below the ankles, and if possible shorter still," arguing that longer skirts were the cause of dangerous falls.[68] But, if freedom of movement was the goal, women's skating costumes soon became part of the "social foreplay" of an "essentially social and overtly sexual" activity, according to Adam Gopnik. "Men show off; women pretend to be impressed – the eternal circle of the selective lek."[69] Gopnik identifies the rise and fall of ice skating's popularity with society's growing acceptance of sex between unmarried partners, sometime in the 1920s. "This double move – away from sex and ever closer to it – is inevitable, as Freud would have said. We dam up the libido in wools and furs and steel and then release it in lengthened legs and heightened movement."[70] A nineteenth-century book of social etiquette steered women toward skating costumes of "rich, warm materials, fur trimmings, fur caps and warm furred gauntlets." But these trimmings were most often employed to draw attention to what was revealed.[71]

Patricia Campbell Warner tells us that, in the mid-nineteenth century, "tiny feet were the hallmark of beauty. Feet and ankles became erotic areas of the female body during this period, possibly because they were visible for the first time in generations."[72] American publications such as *Godey's Magazine and Lady's Book* and *Harper's Weekly* published regular features on skating fashion from the 1860s through the 1880s. A piece in *Harper's Weekly* included the poem "Twinkling Feet." "Small and neat / Peeping out from shy retreat; / Neatest ankle e'er was seen / Underneath a crinoline."[73]

Hiked skirts were popularized on the continent by the Empress Eugènie around 1862. This was made possible through the agency of "elevators," a "series of rings sewn into the underside of a skirt or petticoat through which strings were threaded, then pulled and tied into place to hike up the skirt in evenly spaced and artful flounces," thereby revealing the woman's underskirts.[74]

The artist who illustrated the sheet music cover for *Matilda Toots or You Should Have Seen Her Boots* pictures the moment after the heroine has fallen through the ice, with only her fur-topped boots, with their four rows of pearl buttons, visible above the water. "The water next came bubbling up! Crash! I saw the boots / alone, above the water where had gone down Tilda Toots."[75] The entire song revolves around the boots. They are the heroine's chief attraction, before which the hero kneels in fastening her skates, which he grasps in lifting her out of the water, and which she wears upon their wedding day.

MATILDA TOOTS.

"THE WATER NEXT CAME BUBBLING UP! CRASH! | SAW THE BOOTS,
ALONE, ABOVE THE WATER, WHERE HAD GONE DOWN TILDA TOOTS."

THE MAJOR & KNAPP, ENG. MF'G & LITH. CO. 449 BROADWAY, N.Y.

NEW YORK,
Published by **FREDERICK BLUME** 208 Bowery.

8½ *Plain*

Colored 5

1.22 *Opposite*
"Matilda Toots." Her fur-lined boots steal the hero's heart.

1.23 *Right*
William Notman's composite photograph of Captain Huyshe, posed in the studio, 1870.

In addition to the many lithographic and engraved images representing real or imagined skating scenes that were frequently published in contemporary newspapers and weekly journals in North America and abroad, wealthy Montrealers commemorated their love of skating by sitting for photographic skating portraits at the William Notman studio, frequently choosing to be depicted in a beloved outfit worn at a recent fancy costume skating ball, those social events that took place two or three times per season and were the highlights of the winter months.[76] Victorians from all walks of life loved to dress up in costume, or "fancy dress," for parlour games, theatricals, and balls. Assuming a fantasy character for an evening provided a form of escapism from otherwise rigidly conventional lives.[77] Popular magazines featuring illustrations of costumes and specialized books such as Ardern Holt's *Fancy Dresses Described or, What to Wear at Fancy Balls*

were widely available. Ardern Holt advised women that "there are few occasions when a woman has a better opportunity of showing her charms to advantage than at a Fancy Ball."[78]

Besides individual photographic portraits, taken in front of stock winter backgrounds, Notman's studio was recognized for its composite group photographs. These were produced by pasting individual photographic portraits onto a sketched background, photographing and reproducing the resulting collage, projecting the image onto canvas with a solar enlarger, and then painting it by

1.24 *Below*
William Notman, Skating Carnival, Victoria Skating Rink, Montreal, 1870.
The social event of the decade, in the presence of HRH Prince Arthur.

hand. Perhaps the most famous work of this type was also the studio's first, the monumental composite photograph depicting the fancy dress skating carnival held on 1 March 1870 at the Victoria Skating Rink, in honour of Prince Arthur, then stationed in Montreal as an officer in training.[79] As soon as Notman announced his intention to memorialize this event, one hundred and fifty intended guests responded, trooping into his studio with their costumes and skates, a testament to the lubricating lure of royalty but equally to the social status of skating and of the Victoria Skating Rink as society's grand locale.

Skating Carnivals

By the second half of the nineteenth century, festive skating carnivals had become ubiquitous. As early as 1865 the *Montreal Gazette* reported that, at the second fancy-dress entertainment of the season, "the costumes were of much the usual varieties that have become stock pieces at all masquerades."[80] Similarly, the author of an article in the *Canadian Illustrated News* discussing another festival could dispense with a general description of the event because "this was amply and ably done by writers on the daily press." Instead, the article offered a critique whose aim was "to make future entertainments of a like character even more successful."[81] The writer first took issue with "the monotony of the scene. However brilliant the costumes, and skilful the skating, it is after all always the same round and round." He argued instead for a prescribed program of exercises. The quality of the costumes was deemed "too common and cheap" and for the sake of consistency "a programme of these should be drawn up by a Committee. The choice should not be left to individual tastes." Children should be prohibited from participating; "they are better in bed." The writer further complained of the inadequate distinction made between Fancy Dress Entertainments and Masquerades; "a mingling of the two … is against all tradition." The former is "more stately, more aristocratic, more "*comme il faut*" while the latter "is jollier, more democratic, more *laissez aller*." Finally, the author complained of the spectator's lot. "Some way of seating them should be provided. Walking around the narrow passages from eight till eleven or twelve o'clock is no way of enjoying the Carnival." And this is the defining issue of the critique. What had begun as an entertainment for participants had become, at least for this writer, a spectacle to be watched. The critic's wish for a better spectatorship experience would not come to pass until the first purpose-built hockey arena was constructed in Montreal, in 1898. But this event also marked the end of the skating rink. Henceforth skaters would skate in hockey rinks and, in any event, by this date the fashion for such carnivals was already fading.

The First Hockey Game: How Architecture Changed the Sport

The skating carnival critiqued above was held on Easter Monday, 29 March 1875. Nearly four weeks earlier, on 3 March 1875, another event had been held at the Victoria Skating Rink that would have a more profound effect on the course of this history. All nineteenth-century skating rinks hosted a wide range of events during the winter months, including exhibitions by touring skating professionals and skating races. The directors of the Victoria Skating Rink were flexible enough also to admit the inclusion of snowshoe races, the first held in 1873, in order to benefit from the rising popularity of that sport.[82]

Before 1875 hockey was still a relatively unknown sport without agreed-upon rules, or rather the rules depended upon where you had been born and on what you called the game. Bandy (England), shinty (Scotland), hurley (Ireland), kolf (Holland), knattleikr (Iceland), and tooadijik and wolchamadijik (First Nations) were all stick and ball games, some played on ice. All of these games, in addition to field hockey, ricket or wicketts, shinny, lacrosse, and rugby, may have contributed to the contemporary international sport of ice hockey. Fortunately, I will sidestep the debate over the origins and birthplace of the sport since my concern here is with "rink hockey," and for this the facts are well established.[83]

Nineteenth-century English Canadians would have ranked hockey's popularity behind that of curling, snowshoeing, skating, and even tobogganing among winter sports.[84] In this they echoed the taste-making views of the home country, where a London writer in 1862 opined:

> The various games that are played on ice are most unworthy of a true skater's attention … Hockey, for example, ought to be sternly forbidden, as it is not only annoying (to leisurely skaters on a pond) but dangerous … The game is by no means what it ought to be, as it is impossible to enforce the rules in such a miscellaneous assembly … It is more than annoying to have the graceful evolutions of a charming quadrille broken up by the interruptions of a disorderly mob, armed with sticks and charging through the circle of skaters and spectators to the imminent danger of all. I should be truly glad to see the police interfere whenever hockey is commenced.[85]

Through the 1860s and 1870s, hockeyists had to vie with pleasure skaters, who far outnumbered them, for access to existing outdoor rinks. For example, free ice skating in Toronto, on Toronto Bay, the Don River, and Grenadier Pond, had become so popular by 1860 that the sport "went commercial," competing for patronage with uptown outdoor rinks that had to be surrounded by wooden fences to keep out non-paying kids.[86]

It was with evident trepidation then that Montreal's Victoria Skating Rink hosted a hockey game on 3 March 1875. The match was contested according to rules resembling today's by players attending McGill University and from local sporting clubs. An article announcing the game in that morning's Montreal *Gazette* alluded to fears that had been "expressed on the part of intending spectators that accidents were likely to occur through the ball flying about in too lively a manner." To overcome this perceived danger, the newspaper reassured its readers that "the game will be played with a flat circular piece of wood, thus preventing all danger of its leaving the surface of the ice."[87] Thus came to be one of the most important of the many changes that architecture and spectatorship would impose upon the game of hockey.

Other early changes to the sport already in place included a reduction in the number of players per side to seven, in deference to the more restricted dimensions of indoor rinks. There are records of matches contested by as many as one hundred skaters, at a time when hockey-like games were played on the near limitless space of frozen rivers and lakes. The first team to score three goals often won those early outdoor games, following the custom of the indigenous Canadian

1.25
Victoria Skating Rink, Toronto, 1863. Note the children (lower centre)
climbing the fence to get a view of the action.

game of lacrosse. Games played according to these rules might be concluded after ten minutes
or ten hours. Matches of fixed duration were therefore another consequence of the move indoors,
as demanded by spectators and rink owners alike. Yet there could be unintended consequences
when the technology necessary to mark time failed to work properly. A championship match
between the Montreal Shamrocks and Montreal Victorias was delayed more than an hour owing
to "the eccentricities of a chronometer" that "not only stopped at necessary intervals, but also
stopped apparently permanently on its own account," according to the report published in the
Montreal Gazette.[88]

While rubber balls continued to be used for outdoor games until 1885, it was not long before
representatives of the Crystal, Victoria, Montreal Amateur Athletic Association (MAAA), and
McGill hockey clubs of Montreal adopted a rule specifying the dimensions and material of pucks
to be used in their games ("one inch thick and three inches in diameter, and of vulcanized rubber"

– therefore a compromise between the rubber ball of outdoor play and the wooden disk first used at the Victoria *Skating* Rink).[89] This same rule was also adopted by the Amateur Hockey Association of Canada (AHAC) immediately after its founding in December 1886 and is now the standard internationally. Although initially introduced in order to provide for the physical and psychological comfort of spectators, and to limit the number of broken windows, the change from ball to puck also distinguished hockey, once and for all, from those other games from which it had derived and to which it previously had been compared. Furthermore, this rule allowed hockey to evolve in unique ways that would not have been possible otherwise, for example, by permitting greater control of the puck/ball and easier and more accurate passing.[90] J.W. Fitsell has also remarked upon the significance of another of the rules introduced by the AHAC in 1886 – Rule 7.

1.26
Alexander Henderson, photograph of hockey game, McGill University, 1884. The experience of early indoor hockey followed that of outdoor games, with spectators gathered at rink's edge or on wooden platforms.

It specified that a puck behind the goal line but still on the ice would be considered in play. Fitsell considers this the most significant development over previous hockey-like sports, one that "reflected the 'Canadianization' of the game, making it more like the newly organized game of lacrosse and less [like] British rugby-football."[91] This rule was especially suited to a game played on the fixed boundaries of an ice surface within a confined arena. It led to play characterized by speed and fluid non-stop action.

Another change that was gradually introduced to the design of skating rinks through the second half of the nineteenth century, as these buildings began to be employed more and more for hockey, was the placement of wooden boards around the perimeter of the ice surface. The earliest skating rinks offered no protection to spectators from flying balls and tumbling bodies. Those few spectators who did attend indoor matches stood literally at rink's edge, a spectatorship experience that paralleled the original, and still familiar, custom of watching hockey played on frozen lakes and streams.[92] While the boards protected spectators, they also enabled the game to proceed with fewer interruptions, by preventing the ball or puck from leaving the ice surface, and helped hockey evolve in ways that further distinguished it from its precursors, through the ingenuity of innovative players who used this new barrier for carom passes and punishing body checks.[93]

By 1894, when the first Stanley Cup game was played there, Montreal's Victoria Skating Rink had gained elevated balconies along both sides, to seat additional spectators, and a projecting loge, precursor of today's luxury boxes.[94] These features became increasingly necessary as hockey's popularity grew and as the building's role evolved to include spectatorship as a major component of its function.

In 1894, nearly fifty years after the first skating rink had been built, its chief characteristics were still almost exclusively utilitarian – a long rectangular plan, high-span roof of wood construction, and numerous tall windows. These buildings could boast no architectural style or particular set of features that might identify the skating rink as a unique and independent architectural form, as was true, say, for two other contemporary building types with similar technical requirements – military drill halls and railway stations. Crenelated towers, rough masonry facades, and prominent central entrances typified the former. Train sheds came to be fronted by facades featuring sweeping arches that suggested the long, tall train sheds behind.[95]

The reasons for this lack of independent architectural form are several and speak to the core of our subject as they continued to influence the design of buildings for skating and hockey through the twentieth century. Economics was a major factor. Writing about the rise of professional and commercial sport in Canada at the end of the nineteenth century, Alan Metcalfe notes: "One thing common to sport at all levels was money … For entrepreneurs it was the raison d'être for building facilities and promoting athletic competition."[96] Drill halls protected munitions and armaments that were of strategic military and economic value. Solid materials and airtight construction were wise investments. Transportation of goods and passengers by train developed into an essential service to the world economy and stations emerged as the new gateways to cities. By comparison, skating was a seasonal activity and, despite its increasing popularity through the nineteenth century, participants in northern locations could still indulge in the sport without recourse to indoor facilities. Cheaply thrown-together indoor rinks, constructed of wood and

3158—HOCKEY MATCH, VICTORIA RINK, MONTREAL.

1.27
William Notman and Son, photograph, hockey game, Victoria Skating Rink,
Montreal, 1893. "The game will be played with a flat circular piece of wood,
thus preventing all danger of its leaving the surface of the ice," reassured the
Montreal Gazette in advance of the game played on 3 March 1875.

adaptable to multiple uses during the off-season, and rinks set up within pre-existing buildings, while ubiquitous, were all of indeterminate lifespan and function. Neither could lead the way toward architectural definition. Private curling and skating facilities, though sometimes designed by architects and constructed of more enduring materials, were frequently conceived after the model of private clubs and functioned as such, with only the trailing shed covering the ice surface suggesting the unique nature of their purpose. When a client demanded an architectural veneer for a skating rink, as, for instance, at the Quebec Skating Club Rink, Quebec City (1877), designed by William Tutin Thomas, or the Granite Curling and Skating Rink, Toronto (1880) designed by Norman B. Dick (see Image 1.7), their facades were dressed up to resemble typical public buildings of their day, and from the street might be mistaken for Second Empire post offices or Romanesque Revival schools.

Skating Rinks in England

In spite of this lack of architectural definition, Canadian experience is remarkable for the sheer number of built examples, such that skating and hockey became available to all levels of society. By contrast, indoor facilities in the United States and Great Britain were still rare. Reporting on the first annual amateur championship of the National Skating Association, held in the vicinity of New York during February 1886, the *Montreal Gazette* informed readers that "there are no covered rinks in this vicinity, and that all the races will be out of doors."[97] In Great Britain indoor rinks remained the domain of a restricted elite until well into the twentieth century.[98] John Gamgee's

1.28
"Skating Rink of Real Ice at Chelsea," 1876. The first purpose-built ice-skating rink in London was only 40 × 24 feet, but it featured an elevated balcony for orchestra and walls painted with large murals of Alpine scenes.

Glaciarium at Chelsea introduced Britons to skating indoors in 1876. His was the first purpose-built ice-skating rink in London, the only one operating at that date and, according to Gamgee, the first in the world to successfully employ artificial ice.[99] The rink was tiny, only forty by twenty-four feet, but it featured an elevated balcony for orchestra and spectators and walls painted with large murals of Alpine scenes. According to the *Illustrated London News*, "the rink is not open to the public, but is subscribed to by noblemen and gentlemen, upon certain conditions."[100] The Glaciarium operated for no more than a year and it was not until twenty years later that another indoor ice rink was opened.[101] The lack of facilities certainly inhibited the sport's growth in Great Britain.

Prince's Skating Rink in Knightsbridge, of 1896, was still more exclusive. Patronized by royalty and the ultra-fashionable, it had a reputation for snobbery that led to rumours that "no lady could enter the club who had not been presented at Court."[102] Waist-high boards enclosed a rectangular ice surface and defined a perimeter space behind for standing with alcoves for seated spectators. The clerestory level featured a vast fresco of landscape views some fifteen feet in height and encircling the entire rink. A skylight provided natural light and the interior was also illuminated by dozens of hanging light fixtures. Slender columns supported a projecting and gently curved music loft to a height just below the level of the fresco. London was not alone in having such a refined space for ice skating. The Ice Palace at Nice, France, featured an Art Nouveau interior entered through sets of french doors with large overlights defined by curving Art Nouveau tracery, carved wooden side boards enclosing the ice surface, and a huge projecting balcony for the orchestra crowned by a grand arched opening.[103] These rinks have more in common with European riding schools such as the Spanish Riding School in Vienna, buildings that had similar dimensions, functional requirements for the accommodation, separation, and protection of spectators, and associations with aristocratic sport.

1.29 *Opposite*
Prince's Skating Rink, Knightsbridge, London, 1896. Rumour had it that
"no lady could enter the club who had not been presented at Court."

1.30 *Below*
Spanish Riding School, Vienna.

Writing in 1938, T.D. Richardson, author of numerous books on English figure skating, recalled the hallowed atmosphere that prevailed at Prince's Skating Rink in London: "Before the war at Prince's Skating Club, to waltz in the 'enclosure' … was the aim and object of all the habitués of that inimitable rendezvous. The professionals had a kind of unwritten law not to take beginners into the 'enclosure' until they had reached a certain mutually agreed standard. There was such a wonderful esprit de corps amongst the celebrated staff of teachers that rarely, if ever, did one see a real novice venture into that holy of holies."[104]

The formality, ritualized propriety, and absolute exclusivity of Prince's reflects not only the social standing of its elite clientele but the equally formal and controlled English style of skating known as "combination skating." This style favoured control over freedom, with precise movements performed in strict unison by four or more skaters who were also prohibited from any extraneous hand, arm, or leg movements. According to Mary Louise Adams, "it would have resembled more the internal workings of a clock or the smooth fit of cogs in a machine."[105] The relative lack of facilities in Great Britain contributed a further restriction and helped transform the activity of skating in London to near fetishism. By contrast, North America's climate and mores, along with its comparatively abundant indoor ice-skating facilities (especially in Canada), to say nothing of outdoor rinks, produced a far more democratic and forgiving skating experience. Nevertheless, it was the more restricted spaces of Canada's indoor rinks that led to the rise of a different style of skating in Canada. The nineteenth-century Scottish writer George Anderson noted that "the circumscribed space [of Canadian indoor rinks] has greatly dwarfed the bold sweeps and circles in which the British skater most delights, and has substituted small turns and intricate twists, such as the 'grape vine,' which though difficult of attainment, and in themselves very pretty, are not, at least in British opinion, the finest style of skating."[106] For Mary Louise Adams, "the complicated moves developed by Canadian skaters were, in part, a product of the limited space in the new enclosed rinks, but they were also a product of a lesser requirement for regal appearances and unwavering control."[107]

Competing Sports: Roller Skating, Roller Hockey, and Ice Polo

The last two decades of the nineteenth century, just prior to the construction of the first purpose-built hockey arenas, witnessed a rapid growth in the popularity of hockey, one that paralleled a more general fascination with sports and games throughout urban centres of the developed world. Hockey rules were codified and published, while leagues and competitive play began in nearly every region of Canada. From our present vantage point, the success of hockey often appears inevitable, so it is instructive to recreate the international sports landscape out of which hockey emerged. This sportscape included related games and activities like roller skating, roller hockey, and ice polo, as well as bizarre and short-lived inventions such as rink ball, baseball on ice, and bicycle skates.[108] Roller hockey and ice polo were played throughout Canada's Maritime provinces, the northeastern United States, and Minnesota during this period. These sports originated in the United States at Newport, Rhode Island, and spread from there to Ivy League colleges such as Brown, Harvard, Princeton, and Yale.[109]

1.31
"A Race on the Ice – Bicycles v. Skates," 1881. One of the many
short-lived ice sports that proliferated toward century's end.

Roller skating and roller hockey were popular enough to warrant custom-built facilities in
England, the United States, and Canada that easily rivalled contemporary skating rinks in terms
of scale and elegance. In London, the Denmark Hill Roller Skating Rink opened 30 May 1876, in
a high-ceilinged and well-ventilated building of iron construction that enclosed a skating surface
of about 11,200 square feet (comparable to the dimensions of early ice-skating rinks but far larger
than the 960 square feet available for ice skating at the exactly contemporary Glaciarium). In
addition to the provision of music there were comfortable, crimson-velvet easy chairs and a buffet
for the enjoyment of patrons. The following year the interior was redecorated with paintings
of Alpine and Oriental scenery interspersed with statues on bases. The original skating surface of
asphalt and powdered glass was replaced by one made of Vesuvian lava, prompting a name change
to Lava Rink.[110] By the early twentieth century, roller rinks were so ubiquitous in England that
Leeds alone boasted seven. And they attained monumental dimensions; the Maida Vale Rink in
London measured 375 × 106 feet, and in addition to rink-side tables for diners amid potted palms,
it contained a hairdressing salon and writing room.[111]

In the United States it was common for roller-skate manufacturers to operate their own rinks as a means to promote the sport and market their product.[112] By 1883, roller polo had become "a favorite pastime in Boston, Newport, and other cities where commodious rinks afford facilities for the game," according to *Harper's Weekly*. The 8 September 1883 issue illustrated a game being played at the Olympian Club Rink of Newport before a fashionable crowd seated within a tall wooden building decorated with US flags, potted plants, and painted fans and parasols *à la Japonais*. The game continued to be played into the 1930s in England but the craze for roller skating had already diminished by 1910 and the fashion for roller polo faded as well, the result, according to the *St. Paul Daily Globe*, of the "natural reaction after an unnatural craze."[113]

Ice polo appears to have been a cross between shinny and roller polo that flourished for about ten years, from the mid-1880s to the mid-1890s. The *Ice Hockey and Ice Polo Guide*, published in 1898 as part of Spalding's Athletic Library, informs us that the sport was often mistakenly referred to as American ice hockey: "Though this game has been largely indulged in in past winters, it is believed to be on the decline, due to the rapid increase of the much more scientific game of ice hockey. Harvard, Yale and Brown Universities, Boston and Tufts Colleges and Massachusetts Institute of Technology have played ice polo for several years, but last winter all took up the Canadian game, which Yale was the first to introduce."[114]

1.32
The Lava Skating Rink, Grove Lane, Camberwell, c. 1910. This roller rink featured a skating surface made of Vesuvian lava.

Not only did roller polo, ice polo, and ice hockey share similar rules and equipment, but their games were often played within the same facilities. At St Paul, Minnesota, four indoor roller rinks were outfitted with natural-ice surfaces in 1892.[115] Indoor skating rinks such as the Ice Palace and St Nicholas Rink in New York and Pittsburgh's Duquesne Gardens and Schenley Park Casino Rink likely hosted matches of all three sports and it was only natural for ice-skating rinks to serve as roller rinks after the winter season, as was the case at Calgary's Sherman Rink, and the reverse was no doubt true for roller-skating rinks.

Over the course of sixty years, the places where ice sports were practised evolved, from naturally occurring outdoor sites (frozen ponds and streams) to architecturally delimited outdoor spaces (Central Park Skating Rink) to indoor rinks within adapted vernacular structures (Dey's Skating Rink, Ottawa) to purpose-built skating rinks (Victoria Skating Rink, Montreal, and St Nicholas Rink, New York) and finally to arenas for the emerging spectator sport of commercial hockey (Westmount Arena).

A constant feature of skating sites throughout this period was their adaptability, from frozen surface to liquid pond, from skating rink to boat-building barn, from hockey arena to auditorium hosting a wide range of popular entertainments. This physical and functional flexibility suited the multiple exigencies of climate, economy, and users since it reflected an emerging and unstable sports landscape of competing and related activities and sports. In the following chapter we will see how these factors influenced the form and use of the first spectator arenas while continuing to stymie architects' attempts to define the skating rink in a distinctive manner.

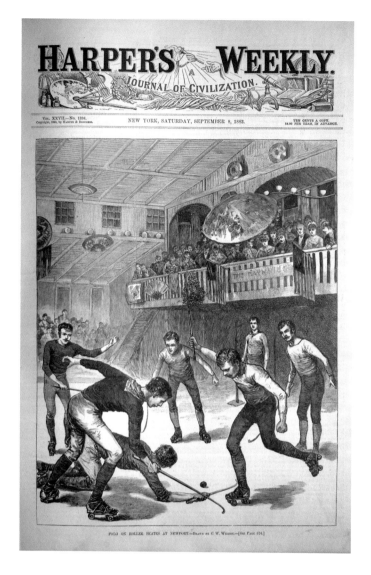

1.33
"Polo on Roller Skates at Newport," 1883.

2.1
"Grand Opening of the 'Arena.'" Advertisement appearing
in the *Montreal Gazette*, 31 December 1898. The first
"arena" functioned as a "hockey rink" and "auditorium."

2

Hockey as Entertainment: Spectatorship and the First Hockey Arenas, 1898–1912

"A box to contain a drama."
– Brian Nelson, "Baseball," in K.B. Raitz, ed., *The Theater of Sport*

The Origins of Spectator Hockey

By 1893 hockey was being described as Canada's "National Winter Game." A commentator writing in that year ascribed the game's success to "covered skating rinks, found in every city and town throughout the Dominion … and the introduction of electric lighting."[1] The spread of electric lighting (which replaced gas) was extremely rapid. In addition to the relative safety of electric lights, this system improved the comfort of patrons by substantially reducing the temperature of the interior being lit. For instance, in 1883 the Alliser Theatre in Havana replaced 342 gas burners with 193 Edison lamps, decreasing the temperature of the house by fourteen degrees Fahrenheit.[2] One can easily imagine how lower temperatures would have been appreciated by operators of both natural- and artificial-ice rinks.

In spite of the bounty of covered ice rinks in Canada, their inefficiency in meeting the changing needs of organized, spectator hockey was already being commented upon. Whereas championship matches between amateur teams could now attract as many as five thousand spectators, skating rinks on the model of Montreal's Victoria Skating Rink offered only minimal space for them (mainly standing room around the perimeter of the rink), limited views, and little protection from flying pucks and bodies. Eric Whitehead described the preparations at Dey's Skating Rink in Ottawa for an important match between the Montreal Wanderers and Ottawa Silver Seven in 1906. "Sold out to its normal capacity … the inside of the rink had been practically gutted in order to squeeze in as many bodies as possible without suffocation. Temporary seating platforms were erected at one end and double deck bleachers hoisted at the other. The grandstand press box had been torn out and a new one suspended from the rafters, a fact that brought howls of dismay, if not downright fear from the reporters."[3]

One contemporary commentator describing hockey in Ontario complained that "Hamilton is handicapped … by the further fact that 'The Thistle Curling Rink,' where the game is played, was designed simply for a curling rink" and that, generally, "the rinks are nearly all too small; new ice is almost unknown, even for matches; the lighting is only moderate, and practice hours scanty or inconvenient."[4] Other common complaints included the inevitable mounds of shaved ice that would build up over the course of a game, especially in the corners, slowing down the movement of the puck; parts of the surrounding boards that were prone to fall off; thin ice that might result in broken sticks or skates; and smoke produced by "human furnaces" that was so thick a reporter in 1912 claimed it almost stopped the puck.[5] Toward the end of the season, warm weather could produce large puddles on natural-ice surfaces, leading to messy spills. "One of the strategies still used in the 1920s was to shoot water into the goaltender's face before shooting the puck."[6] Warm air might even cause fog to settle over the ice surface, sometimes obscuring the puck from view altogether. A match between Montreal's MAAA and Dominion teams "would have been a really enjoyable match" but for "a roof like a sieve, through which a continual spray bath poured, and the clouds of damp, cold, unpleasant vapor that arose from the ice."[7]

The rink surfaces themselves could be of widely varying dimensions, and stories abound concerning the odd effects of hockey played in these rinks. According to one, possibly apocryphal story, early rinks could also be peculiarly shaped. Foster Hewitt, the early Toronto sports broadcaster, described a hockey match at Cobourg, Ontario, that might have been won by the visiting team but for their difficulty in accustoming themselves to the L-shaped rink.[8] And there are many instances of hockey players having to negotiate bandstands and other obstacles on the rink surface. At a match played at Montreal's Victoria Skating Rink, "play was rather tame for the first goal or two … in consequence of the ice grotto and snowshoe statue taking up a considerable space … but at last the boys woke up, and the dodging was very scientific and called forth the rounds of applause of the vast audience."[9]

In spite of these problems, playing and watching hockey inside was still preferable to being out-of-doors. Advantages included a more controlled environment, which meant games could be advertised; the availability of seats, at least for some; and protection from the elements. But beyond the physical conveniences and annoyances of early indoor hockey, spectators became aware of a qualitative difference in how they experienced the game. The charged atmosphere created by many fans within a confined location was exciting.

Hockey was still an amateur sport in 1893, and although there were organized leagues, games were much less frequent than in today's NHL.[10] Inter-league, inter-city, and even Stanley Cup games initially occurred in response to challenges by one team to another. If hockey had continued to be an amateur game, played by and for its enthusiasts, there would have been little need for purpose-built structures to hold spectators. Before the twentieth century, hockey teams rented ice time for games, either from privately run skating and curling clubs or from commercially run facilities. According to sports historian Bruce Kidd, the line between amateurism and professionalism was already beginning to blur: "By the 1870s, land costs, taxes, and the expense of uniforms, equipment, and travel had already led amateur baseball and lacrosse teams to pass the hat for donations. In spite of debates about the propriety of doing so, admission to games was soon charged without question. In the case of hockey, rink owners who rented the ice to amateur teams made the first ticket sales. When they discovered the great popularity of the new sport, they began booking games between successful teams, offering a percentage of the gate to the teams as inducement."[11] For instance, the Montreal Hockey Club, winner of the first Stanley Cup, was associated with the MAAA but had no home rink on which to play games or practise. Between 1893 and 1901 they rented the facilities of the Victoria Skating Rink, Duluth Avenue Rink, and Crystal Rink for games, netting from 33 to 50 per cent of the gate receipts.[12] The profit motive was therefore equally behind the decision of entrepreneurs who constructed the first purpose-built hockey arenas.

The First Hockey Arena: Westmount Arena, Montreal

The first purpose-built hockey arena in the world was Montreal's Westmount Arena, which opened in 1898.[13] An article appearing in the French-language Montreal newspaper *La Patrie*, soliciting investment prior to the building's completion, explained why it was needed. "For many years now the popularity of hockey, Canada's pre-eminent winter sport, has increased, so much that the rinks are too small for the crowds who attend the games."[14] The Westmount Arena was also purpose-built from an economic standpoint. A group of Montreal businessmen led by Ed Sheppard, president of the MAAA, joined to form the Montreal Arena Company specifically in order to profit from the growing interest in amateur hockey by constructing an arena that would serve as a venue for such games.

Its very name distinguished it from all predecessors. It is the first "arena." Up to this date, buildings constructed for curling or skating were named rinks, just like those outdoors, and in either case their primary function was to serve their users. What distinguished the Westmount Arena from all other ice rinks in the city, and in the world, was that it provided for spectators and did so as a defining aspect of its design. In 1900, two years after the Westmount Arena opened, there were ten skating rinks in Montreal (most of them enclosed), yet newspaper accounts and advertisements for games or events held there simply refer to it as the "Arena," no further distinction being required. When one of these ten rinks, the Montagnard, expanded in 1903, increasing its seating capacity from 1,200 to 5,000, it also announced a change in name, from "Rink" to "Stadium." The newspaper article in which this change was described confirms that the Westmount Arena had established the benchmark for all when it noted that the new stadium was now "similar to the Arena in every respect, it will comfortably hold 5,000 seated spectators who will be able to follow the action of all the games that will be played there this year unimpeded by any obstacles."[15] All subsequent buildings on this model, whether in Toronto or Vancouver, St Louis, or Seattle, will be named arenas.[16]

The building itself was unremarkable in appearance. A two-storey brick-faced block of wood construction with steel trusses arching over the ice surface enclosed the pitch-roofed auditorium. The principal facade featured three sets of round-arched entrances with the word "Arena" over the central doors. A simple pediment with crests at the corners and centre comprised the building's sole ornament. The interior consisted of a continuous graded amphitheatre rising in an uninterrupted span from the ground to the second-floor level. It could accommodate between 6,000 and

The Arena, Montreal

2.2
The (Westmount) Arena, Montreal, c. 1907. A simple brick box.

7,000 spectators for hockey around a natural-ice surface measuring 200 × 85 feet. Four-foot-high boards separated the ice from the amphitheatre, segregating spectator and player and once and for all distinguishing arena hockey from the outdoor game.

Twenty-five years earlier, when the first organized hockey game had been played at the Victoria Skating Rink, spectators huddled around the edge of the ice surface. This led to an episode described the following day in the *Montreal Daily Witness*: "Owing to some boys skating about during the play, an unfortunate disagreement arose; one little boy was struck across the head, and the man who did so was afterwards called to account, a regular fight taking place in which a bench was broken and other damage caused."[17] Anyone who has skated at a local outdoor rink has probably encountered a similar scenario, with skaters and hockey players dodging one another as they engage in their separate activities on a shared surface. While mischief on the part of the boys who interrupted the hockey match in 1875 cannot be ruled out, it is equally possible that they were simply acting as they would have had the game been played at their local pond. At the skating

VUE DE LA FAÇADE

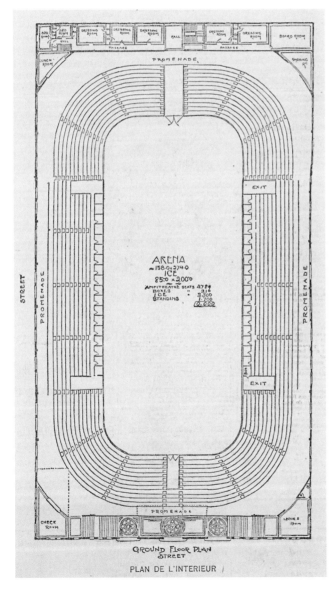

GROUND FLOOR PLAN
STREET

PLAN DE L'INTERIEUR

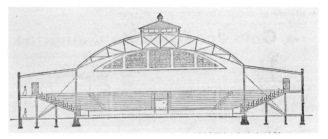

2.3
Westmount Arena, Montreal, elevation, plan, and section. A single tier of graded seats surrounding an 85 × 200-foot ice sheet.

pond the roles of skater and spectator were interchangeable, someone in conversation at rink's edge might at any moment skip onto the ice to take a turn and various games might all the while be underway. But at the arena the roles of spectator and participant became frozen. Architecture definitively established the spectators' realm, in tiered seats surrounding the ice surface, and that of the players, upon the ice, with the boards as the unbreachable border between them.

Thick wooden posts around the perimeter of the ice rink supported cross bracing for the roof structure and strings of electric lights that hung above the ice. Promenades surrounded the unheated stands, at ground level, and at the top of the grandstand level, where a sprinkling of windows afforded daytime illumination. Modest spaces for coat checking, ladies' room, players' dressing rooms, boardroom, and smoking room were also provided in the corners and at the back of the building.

Although over one hundred years old, the features of this rink – oval skating surface enclosed by boards and ringed by graded tiers of seats – seem both familiar and inevitable. But a transitional building that deserves some consideration as the first purpose-built arena indicates the contrary. In 1896 Ottawa's Dey Brothers opened a second skating rink after their first was demolished to make way for the tracks and depot of the Canada Atlantic Railway.[18] No image of this second building survives, but a 1901 fire-insurance map indicates that it had a simple rectangular form, pitched roof, and iron cladding up to its eaves.[19] Although described on the map and in newspaper accounts as a "Skating Rink," it was the first building anywhere to include galleries for spectators, although they were located only at each of the rink's short ends. A single row of raised seats was installed along the rink's long, south side. This less than optimal provision and disposition of seating (it could seat no more than about 3,500) may have been the result of a limited lot size and a corresponding wish to maximize the dimensions of the hockey-playing surface, which still only measured 81 × 200 feet. (Adding seats along the long sides of the rink would have further reduced the space available for the skating surface, making it too narrow for hockey.)

The Dey Brothers' second rink also included a bandstand for use during public skating, which was suspended fifteen feet over centre ice. That this bandstand doubled as a press box during hockey matches highlights the transitional status of the building. This intermediate quality, part place of participation and part place of spectatorship, was a characteristic of other ice rinks even into the twentieth century. In 1915 the Main Hall at Pittsburgh's Exposition Hall was transformed into the Winter Garden, an ice-skating and hockey venue. One year later, music specially composed for the venue was published as the *Winter Garden Glide* ("Listen jolly skaters to the band, It's grand.").[20] The cover illustration for the sheet music features an inset view of the rink's vast interior (the ice surface was 300 × 140 feet). Above this image dancing couples twist and turn but below, breaking through the picture frame, are two hockey players. They have nothing to do with the dance music found inside the cover but everything to do with the dual nature of the rink.

Early twentieth-century hockey rinks and arenas announce a change in focus, from sites of participation to places of spectatorship. As Brian Nelson has pointed out in reference to early enclosed baseball parks, the formal containment of the sport created "a box to contain a drama."[21] Throughout North America urban populations were growing, leisure time was increasing, and the expectation of paying for entertainment was becoming more common. According to Nelson,

2.4
"Winter Garden Glide," 1916. The Main
Hall at Pittsburgh's Exposition Hall
transformed into the Winter Garden,
with a 300 × 140-foot ice surface.

"baseball parks, movie theaters, and amusement parks were all part of a new city landscape generated by an equally new category of experience called 'leisure time' and the organization of that
time for commercial ends."[22] But how did this shift from participation to spectatorship affect the
design of skating rinks and hockey arenas?

    Skating and curling rinks of the 1860s, 1870s, and 1880s had been designed to serve additional
functions and this continued to be true for the hockey arena. In fact, everything you need to know
about the definition of this new building type can be gleaned from the advertisement in the
Montreal Gazette announcing the grand opening of the Westmount Arena on 31 December 1898
(see Image 2.1 above). The word "ARENA" appears in bold block letters at the top of this notice,

but to the right, in a much smaller font, its dual roles were described – "Hockey Rink and Auditorium." In this context the word "arena" announces the building type and proclaims its physical distinction from earlier skating rinks, characterized by graded tiers of seats for spectators surrounding a surface for performers. The additional terms help refine the owners' intentions for what will occur within that arena. But whereas "Hockey Rink" specifies a precisely defined and restricted function, "Auditoriums" are by nature flexible and imprecise in their intended uses, "a room, hall, or building used for public gatherings" according to Merriam-Webster. As nondescript containers for unrestricted and deliberately undefined forms of spectatorship, auditoriums do not (should not) express any purpose beyond that of containing crowds. It was in this latter capacity that the Westmount Arena hosted a wide range of events, from annual horse, flower, and later automobile shows to performances by world-famous celebrities like Enrico Caruso, on 18 May 1908, and the screening of films like D.W. Griffith's *The Birth of a Nation* in 1915.

The first rinks for skating and curling were constructed for the particular enjoyment of a privileged class and they reflected this patronage through designs that referenced private English clubhouses, even as no corresponding attempt was made to express their function. Other than the arched or peaked form of their roofs that sheltered the broad expanse of the ice surface, there was little in their architectural form or expression to identify them as skating rinks. They might easily be mistaken for barns, drill sheds, armouries, train sheds, exposition buildings, or warehouses, generic forms of sheltered space that could be, and were, converted to serve the simple needs of skating and curling. Toward the end of the nineteenth century, as hockey evolved into a commercialized entertainment product, entrepreneurs constructed the first covered ice rinks as profit-run venues for popular entertainment. To achieve financial viability, these entrepreneurs appealed to the widest possible economic range of constituents. Compared to the private skating clubs that preceded them, buildings for hockey were class-neutral. Men still comprised the largest part of the audience for hockey matches but this was beginning to change as well. In a comparable situation, Brian Nelson has noted that, by the early twentieth century, women began to attend baseball games, and that while saloons and pool halls remained strictly male preserves, baseball parks and cinemas were becoming gender neutral.[23] Should it be surprising, then, that as containers intended to serve an indeterminate range of mass entertainments, for an increasingly class-neutral, gender-neutral audience, early twentieth-century hockey arenas that originated as generic sheds might still lack a unique and clearly identifiable architectural form? And this was the case in spite of the innovative separation of athlete and spectator that these buildings introduced.

More and more, arenas came to be associated with the provision of commercialized entertainment. This was happening at the same time, the first quarter of the twentieth century, that hockey was undergoing its own transformation, from an amateur sport played by enthusiasts who were residents of a specific community and who played for their own enjoyment, to an entertainment product contested by geographically mobile, paid professionals, controlled by rink operators, and offered to the public for their consumption.[24] Bruce Kidd has pointed out that the transition from amateur to professional hockey was a gradual one. For instance, many amateur teams had for many years "employed" ringers who were "paid" through a variety of ruses.[25]

A distinct break with the pre-professional era can be dated, however, to the advent of the first spectator arenas. At issue is not the matter of closet versus open professionalism, but the public offering of a commercial product in a custom-built venue. For instance, before the advent of rink operators and shared gates in the 1890s, it is unlikely that hockey matches would have featured between-period entertainment. But operators of the new arenas felt impelled to maintain the interest of spectators between periods, to provide a show. Since they already employed live bands for public-skating sessions, arena managers simply adapted this familiar practice to hockey matches. For the opening of the Westmount Arena, a thirty-piece band played between periods. (It would be interesting to know whether the choice of music performed at hockey matches that were contested at arenas began to differ from the selection of music played to accompany skaters at rinks. Did the music at hockey games tend toward more popular selections, say Scott Joplin rags or Tin Pan Alley ditties versus Strauss waltzes?) At Ottawa, an intermission favourite in 1905 was Professor West, a magician who performed sword exercises, such as slicing potatoes through a handkerchief and on the neck of a young boy. The audience showed its appreciation by throwing coppers onto the ice, as they would have onto the stage at any vaudeville performance of the time, presented in a theatre.[26] For the audience at least, the increasingly indistinct line between sport and entertainment was being negotiated without difficulty.

The International Hockey League and Its Rinks

Openly professional hockey was played for the first time by teams within the International Hockey League (IHL), which operated from 1904 to 1907 out of five cities; Houghton, Calumet, and Sault Ste Marie (all tiny mining communities in northern Michigan), Sault Ste Marie, Ontario, and Pittsburgh. The features of IHL arenas and rinks and the role they played in the advancement of the game, and within their communities, serve as a microcosm for the issues affecting hockey arenas in the early era of spectator hockey during the first two decades of the twentieth century.[27]

Hockey gained popularity in the United States during the 1890s. According to Spalding's *Ice Hockey and Ice Polo Guide 1898*, "three winters ago Chicago, Minneapolis and Detroit were about the only scenes of the game's activity, but last winter wherever ice could be found, out of doors or inside, East and West, ice hockey was being played."[28] Organized hockey developed in three primary centres. In Pittsburgh, where ice polo, a hockey-like game, had already been popular, hockey took root after its introduction by visiting teams from Queen's University in Kingston.[29] In New York City a four-team amateur league played out of the St Nicholas Rink. It was in this league that Hobey Baker (the first American to be inducted to the Hockey Hall of Fame) played before becoming a fighter pilot in 1916. And in Houghton, Michigan – the so-called birthplace of US hockey – hockey developed beyond a game sporadically played by itinerant Canadian miners through the agency of Dr John L. Gibson, a transplanted Canadian dentist who had played intermediate hockey in his native Berlin, Ontario.[30]

Michigan's upper peninsula, pointing northeast into Lake Superior, was the copper-rich home to Houghton and Calumet. Mining wealth led to the creation of railway lines, which linked these towns together and also connected them to the outside world, by the end of the nineteenth century. The isolated location of Houghton and Calumet, combined with harsh winters offering few diversions, proved fertile ground for the development of winter sports, including hockey. The

2.5 Amphidrome, Houghton, Michigan, 1902. Its castellated design
was clearly inspired by contemporary military drill sheds.

railways made inter-city competition feasible. Players were imported from Canada and salaries were attractive enough that even major stars such as Fred "Cyclone" Taylor and "Hod" Stuart could be lured away from larger cities. But only Pittsburgh could boast an arena with adequate capacity to make its team financially viable, the 5,000-seat Duquesne Gardens.

Houghton's hockey team first played out of the Palace Ice Rink in neighbouring Hancock. It must have been anything but palatial. Its inadequate capacity led to plans to adapt the interior for more seating early in 1902, but fans wanting to attend championship matches that year were still turned away and, in the fall of 1902, a stock company was formed to build the new 2,500-seat Amphidrome at a cost of $16,000. In order to complete the building in time for the 1902–03 season, a small army of carpenters went to work and enough of it was standing by 26 December to allow the team to practice. Such short construction times for wood-frame buildings were not unusual. For instance, baseball parks constructed of wood in the early 1880s embodied the volatility and unpredictability of that game's early years; they were made of wood because wood was cheap and easily worked, expandable as required, and easily taken apart for transfer to a new locale. Early parks burnt easily and frequently but could be rebuilt within weeks or even days.[31]

The Amphidrome was strategically located within two blocks of the depots of two separate railway lines and of the local street railway. Special game-day trains featuring low, round-trip fares assisted neighbouring residents wanting to attend matches. This was of the utmost importance, since the Amphidrome depended on non-Houghton residents to fill its seats. Houghton's population was only 3,359 in 1902. Proximity to public transportation was equally important in larger urban centres. Ottawa's Dey Brothers could locate their second rink of 1896 farther from the city centre than its predecessor had been because of the new electric railway that ran along Gladstone Street, directly in front of the rink. And the importance of proximity of facilities to fans was likewise revealed in a study of the locations of Montreal rinks and arenas between 1895 and 1910. For example, in 1895 these facilities were located almost exclusively in the west end of the city, close to their English patrons. As the number of French Canadian hockey teams increased by about 1905, so too did the incidence of rinks situated in the city's east end, where the francophone population resided.[32]

Plans for the Amphidrome apparently also included a second floor intended to accommodate a 30-by-80-foot surface for ice dancing, although how such an expanse of solid ice could have been supported is not clear, nor what would happen below during the spring thaw.[33] The wish to increase the revenue potential of the building through the inclusion of additional facilities for leisure, recreation, and entertainment is typical, however.

The Sault Ste Marie teams of the IHL played out of their local curling rinks, and although the Michigan Soo later renamed its rink the Ridge Street Ice-A-Torium, a name change alone could not hide the fact that these buildings were inadequate for the function they were being asked to serve. The Calumet team, like Houghton's, played in a neighbouring rink before the completion of a 4,000-seat local arena, the Palestra, in 1904. Yet even this expanded capacity would not enable the IHL to compete with eastern teams once professionalism became the norm throughout North America, by about 1910.[34]

Architecture and the Economics of Early Professional Hockey

The larger populations of cities like Ottawa, Montreal, and Toronto, and the greater seating capacity of arenas there, enabled the hockey teams based in these centres to realize revenues that could be used to outbid IHL teams for talent. Yet capacity was a problem even for eastern teams wanting to "grow" the business of ice hockey. According to Bruce Kidd, "physical plant constituted one barrier to growth. Most arenas were cramped, cold, fire traps … built of wood and dangerously vulnerable to fire."[35] And burn they did. The Montagnard Stadium in Montreal burned in 1911. Four years later, Calgary's Sherman Rink burned down. And during 1918 and 1919 fire destroyed the Jubilee and Ontario rinks and the Westmount Arena, all in Montreal.

Little thought was given to spectator comfort in these early unheated arenas and it could be horribly cold inside. Recognizing this, Montreal's Westmount Arena rented blankets to spectators at ten cents apiece. "Seats were narrow and hard and many spectators had to stand. In Ottawa's Laurier Arena [which opened in 1907], for example, 2,500 of the 7,000 'places' for spectators were for 'standees.'"[36] The second Dey's Skating Rink in Ottawa was probably not unique in being

2.6
Sherman Rink Calgary, Alberta. Opened 1904, burned down 1915.

2.7
Dey's Arena, Ottawa, 1908.

unventilated, so that steam and tobacco smoke combined to make visibility increasingly difficult. Then there was the fact that the electric lights originally lacked reflectors, so that much of their illumination was lost to the ceiling.[37] If these buildings were cold and uncomfortable during the coldest of winter, they proved frustrating to players and patrons alike in early spring when a sudden thaw might turn to mush natural-ice surfaces that were typical of all but a few northern arenas until the 1920s. A 1920 Stanley Cup match between Ottawa and Seattle was played in Toronto after it was agreed that both teams would fare better on the artificial ice available at Toronto's Arena Gardens. And it was also an unexpected thaw that melted the ice at the Mount Royal Arena, which led the Montreal Canadiens to inaugurate the Montreal Forum in 1924, ahead of the Maroons for whom the Forum had been built.

While increased seating capacity could boost potential revenues for each game played, artificial ice presented the possibility of greater annual returns through a longer season.[38] In order to achieve this bounty, owners would need to construct new, more permanent facilities. But given the volatility of the hockey industry during the early twentieth century, few were willing to take this gamble until the early 1920s. Teams, and entire leagues, folded with alarming regularity. Even

2.8
Duquesne Garden, Pittsburgh, 1890.

after professionalism was openly acknowledged, amateur games could still outdraw professional games for attendance. And, if the professional teams were not constantly bickering among themselves, forming and reforming leagues every few years, they were competing with rival leagues that poached their players. Add to this the uncertainty of late-season weather, which might cause poor ice conditions or game cancellation, and frequent fires at rinks, and one wonders how professional hockey survived at all. When the Westmount Arena burned to the ground on 2 January 1918, it took with it $1,000 worth of equipment belonging to the Montreal Wanderers team. So precarious were the finances of early-twentieth-century hockey operations that the Wanderers never recovered from this double whammy and folded two days later.

One city that had artificial ice at an early date was Pittsburgh. The Schenley Park Casino Rink, a large hall of wood and glass constructed in the early 1890s at a cost of $300,000, apparently was equipped with an artificial-ice plant and has been credited with responsibility for encouraging the development of ice skating in that city.[39] Its 225-by-65-foot rink was illuminated by 500 incandescent bulbs. It was there, in 1895, that a team from Queen's University introduced hockey to Pittsburgh in front of more than 2,500 fans.[40] When the Casino burned down in 1896, a local developer of amusement parks approached C.L. Magee, the president of the Duquesne Traction Company, with the suggestion that one of his streetcar barns might be transformed into a skating rink. The building selected was well suited to its intended function. Constructed in 1890, it consisted of a two-storey office block of brick and sandstone in a faintly Richardsonian Romanesque manner in front of the massive car barn with its trussed, low-pitched roof. The stylishness of the design was partly owing to its location within one of Pittsburgh's finer residential districts. In addition to this neighbouring population of potential users, as a former streetcar barn, the Duquesne Gardens already had direct streetcar access from other points in the city. The office block could serve admirably for changing rooms, while the shed was easily adaptable to the relatively simple needs of skating and hockey. When it opened on 23 January 1899, it was the world's largest ice rink, with a surface of 26,000 square feet.[41] This huge interior contained graded stands for 5,000 spectators who were seated behind taller than usual boards that projected out slightly as they met the ice, providing a low bench that might have served as seating during public-skating sessions.

Pittsburgh, Pa., Ice Rink, Duquesne Garden.

Photo by R.W. Johnston.

2.9
Duquesne Garden, Pittsburgh, after 1895.

The Patrick Brothers' Arenas in Vancouver and Victoria

Physical plant also played a crucial role in the expansion of hockey to the west coast of North America. When brothers Frank and Lester Patrick conceived the unlikely idea of creating an entirely new hockey league on the west coast of Canada in 1911, they already knew that, after attracting players, their biggest problem would be the necessary construction of new buildings equipped with artificial ice, owing to the warm western climate. Both men had gained experience playing hockey in Montreal. Their venture was bankrolled by their father, a successful lumber baron who had made his money in Quebec before moving to British Columbia. According to Lester Patrick, they planned to model the arenas for their new Pacific Coast Hockey Association (PCHA) on New York's St Nicholas Rink, one of only a handful in North America with artificial ice and the only one they had visited.[42] But, since nobody in Canada knew anything about the construction of artificial-ice plants at that date, Frank Patrick decided to gain this knowledge first-hand. With his obviously devoted new bride, he took an unusual route to their intended honeymoon destination of Boston, one that just happened to lead through Detroit, Cleveland, and Pittsburgh, all cities with artificial-ice rinks.[43]

The Patricks were not only adventurous; they were also optimistic. When it opened early in 1912, the Denman Arena in Vancouver was advertised as "the globe's largest indoor sports emporium." It was 331 feet long and 200 feet wide and featured the largest artificial-ice surface in the world, at 90 × 220 feet.[44] The Denman Arena could seat 10,500 spectators, more than 10 per cent of the city's current population. The building cost their proud father $275,000. The Victoria Arena, which had opened two weeks earlier, on Christmas Day 1911, cost $110,000 and accommodated 4,000.[45] The hockey teams in the original three-team league received correspondingly affluent names – the Vancouver Millionaires, the Victoria Aristocrats, and the New Westminster Royals. The New Westminster franchise was subsequently transferred to Portland, Oregon, in 1914

2.10
Victoria Arena, 1911. Built at a cost of $110,000 and home to the Victoria Aristocrats.

and in 1915 a fourth team was added in Seattle. In 1917 the Seattle Metropolitans became the first team based in the United States to win the Stanley Cup.

The Vancouver building was anything but aristocratic in appearance. It was a bulky four-storey oblong block of brick-faced concrete, liberally pierced by windows and modulated by chamfered corners on its principal facade. In an effort to animate an otherwise monotonous and massive pile, Thomas Hooper, the building's architect, pulled forward the entrance bay on Georgia Street from the building's mass, included similarly projecting elements along each of the long sides, and extended the eaves on the Denman Street side. Otherwise devoid of ornament, the building presented a vaguely Edwardian appearance. But the importance of this building lay in its ambitious program and innovative features, not in its architectural form.

Another possible architectural model that Frank Patrick may have had in mind was Stanford White's Madison Square Garden in New York of 1889, according to the hockey player Fred "Cyclone" Taylor, one of the eastern stars the Patricks lured away to lend credibility to their new league.[46] While the thought of transplanting such an elegant and urbane building into the relative

2.11
Denman Street Arena, Vancouver, 1912. Constructed of concrete
and brick, with seating for over 10,000 and equipped with artificial
ice-making equipment.

wilds of Vancouver might seem mere pretension, in retrospect Frank Patrick was probably less interested in the Gardens' high style physical trappings than in its large seating capacity and its adaptability to a wide range of events.

The original plans for the Denman Arena called for dressing rooms capable of accommodating 3,000 public skaters, a large dining room that could also serve as a dance hall, a bowling alley, and additional surfaces below grade for curling and skating.[47] According to Eric Whitehead, there were also plans for a giant swimming pool in the basement but this was never realized owing to rising construction costs.[48] All of these supplementary uses would have been expected to boost the facility's financial viability, as was the plan to use the refrigeration plant to manufacture blocks of ice for public sale in summer.

The Denman Arena introduced a number of innovations to arena design. It was the first to be constructed of concrete and brick, sturdy materials intended to offer some protection against the fires that had destroyed so many earlier buildings. Thirteen exits were also incorporated for the safety of patrons in the event of fire.[49] The interior seating was disposed on two levels, making this the earliest arena designed with an upper tier of seats. A newspaper photograph taken soon after the building's completion shows a number of advertisements affixed to the second-floor balcony railing.[50] This may be the first instance of in-rink advertising and further demonstrates how shrewd the Patricks were at discovering new ways to maximize their revenue. Nevertheless, the PCHA struggled through ten years of operation before finally disbanding in 1924. The Denman Arena burned down in 1936. Though unsuccessful, the Patricks' west coast experiment did demonstrate that solidly built arenas equipped with artificial ice were the way of the future.

Artificial Ice and Its Origins

The invention of a system for making artificial ice arose out of experiments into refrigeration on three continents, beginning in the mid-eighteenth century. Early experiments were aimed at advancing methods related to the brewing industry, the transatlantic shipment of fresh produce and meat, and the production of ice and cooling for hospitals. The English fascination with ice skating, together with England's dominant position in manufacturing and technology during the nineteenth century, were factors that allowed England to lead the way in the development of artificial ice. As early as 1841 an indoor skating facility had been opened in London. The so-called Alpine Room, decorated with Alpine scenery and a Swiss cottage, was one of the many new attractions introduced at the Coloseum, an entertainment facility originally constructed to offer patrons 360-degree views of a vast painted panorama of London. Skaters could wear their usual ice skates with metal blades but the surface upon which they exercised was not in fact ice but a concoction made of hog's grease and soda that was laid over a bare wooden floor, a recipe that gave skaters the sensation of cutting through hard cheese.[51] Needless to say, falls were to be avoided. In spite of this the *Times* still pronounced the Alpine Room the place "for learning the art, and for viewing the performances of the best scaters [sic]."[52]

Between 1840 and 1876 no less than twenty patents for artificial or "real" ice were registered in England.[53] But it was not until John Gamgee opened his Glaciarium in 1876 that anyone succeeded.[54] While Gamgee's first Glaciarium was short-lived, in 1879 the city of Southport, England,

NOT-ICE!
WONDERFUL PHENOMENON!
MURPHY OUTDONE!—AWFUL PREDICTION!
GREAT THAW of the ARTIFICIAL ICE!
3000 SQUARE FEET IN EXTENT.

BAKER STREET BAZAAR,
KING STREET, PORTMAN SQUARE.

THE PROPRIETOR OF THE

GLACIARIUM

Feels it his duty to apprize the Public that, the Metropolis will assuredly be visited on Thursday, the 25th of January, 1844, with the most Extraordinary *Thaw* ever witnessed in this Country or any other; and he, therefore, takes the earliest opportunity of awakening the Public to the pending Calamity, and thus prevent disappointment to those who have not had the good fortune to see this admitted Wonder of Novelties—

THE ONLY ONE IN THE WORLD:
and, although the beautiful
LAKE OF LUCERNE

is now fast Frozen—the Mountains, Rocks and Trees, covered with Snow,—and the **GLACIER** of Ice, down which the venturous Skaters descend with astonishing rapidity, is solid, yet all must, on the fast approaching dreaded 25th of January, "*dissolve—and, like the baseless fabric of a vision, leave not a wreck behind.*" Skaters and astonished sceptics are therefore invited, whilst the opportunity offers, to witness this wonderful discovery, with its additional attractions of

Sledges on the Frozen Lake,

for the use of Ladies and Children, without additional Charge;—which is open daily from 10 in the Morning till 10 at Night, and beautifully Illuminated at Dusk.

A Band of Music will perform during the **Four Days** of the **Cattle Show,** viz. the 6th, 7th, 8th and 9th December—and, in the Evening, the usual **PROMENADE MUSICALE, Led by Mr. A. SEDGWICK.** And, with permission, it is announced that, Mornings and Evenings, the Members of the Glaciarium Skating Club will meet and perform their Elegant Evolutions to Music. ☞ For the accommodation of Visitors, there will be an Entrance from the CATTLE SHOW to the ARTIFICIAL ICE.

Admittance, 1s. — *Children, Half-Price,* — *Skating,* 1s.
S. G. Fairbrother, Printer, 31, Bow Street, Covent Garden.

2.12
The Alpine Room, Coloseum, London, 1844. The "ice" was actually a concoction made of hog's grease and soda, a recipe that gave skaters the sensation of cutting through hard cheese.

constructed a rink using his system that remained in operation for over a year. At only fourteen by fifty-four feet, space on the ice was limited and poor ventilation led to damp, misty conditions.[55] Gamgee's system is essentially the same as that in use today. A coolant was distributed via coiled pipes arranged on the ice floor, which produced cold temperatures that caused water above them to freeze, usually to a thickness of one inch for hockey. At the Glaciarium, a steam engine connected to an air pump, located in a nearby building, forced a refrigerated mixture of glycerine and water into an insulated store tank located about ten feet above ground. From there the mixture travelled by gravity some fifty-five feet to a looped network of copper piping installed beneath the skating floor where cold was transmitted to about two inches of water, turning it to ice. The glycerine mixture then returned to be refrigerated again.[56] In NHL-size rinks some eight to ten miles of ¼″ diameter coiled metal pipes are embedded beneath the ice floor.

The earliest installation of artificial ice-making equipment in North America was for pleasure skating in New York, at Gilmore's Gardens in 1879. By the 1890s artificial-ice rinks were common in Europe and the United States: Ice Palace, New York (1894); St Nicholas Rink, New York (1895); Schenly Park Casino, Pittsburgh (1895); Brooklyn Ice Palace (1896); and Duquesne Gardens, Pittsburgh (1899). The St Nicholas Rink originally employed the De La Vergne system, with the water being spread directly over the coiled pipes and then frozen. Canada was slower to adopt artificial-ice technology, because its climate typically guaranteed natural ice between December and March and the return on investment in such equipment could not initially be financially justified. Frank and Lester Patrick introduced artificial ice-making equipment in their two new arenas in Victoria (1911) and Vancouver (1912). Arena Gardens in Toronto was next in 1912, followed by Montreal's Westmount Arena in 1915. The availability of artificial ice, which promised longer seasons and therefore greater profit for rink owners, was an important factor leading to the construction of more permanent facilities beginning in the late 1920s.

All of the buildings discussed in this chapter were constructed in response to perceived needs. The growing popularity of hockey, and the willingness of people to pay to watch elite players perform, led entrepreneurs to finance the first hockey arena. No demand, no arena. No financial viability, no arena. Sport, architecture, and finance were inextricably linked. But did the clients for what became the Westmount Arena ask their architect to build an arena or did they describe a frustration with the status quo, a need to accommodate, and profit from, more spectators? The British architect Cedric Price defined a client as someone who comes to you in distress. They need something – a place to live, a place to treat sick patients, a space in which audiences may watch hockey – and they want the architect's help, first to help them understand exactly what they think they need and then to realize that idea in physical form. In defining these needs, architects and clients collaborate on establishing the architectural program. This recipe will then determine the building's form and expression. The Westmount Arena was a transformative, forward-looking building for architecture on ice even as it functioned with an eye to the past, maintaining continuities with a family of earlier ice rinks.

2.13 *Opposite*
St Nicholas Rink, New York, showing pipes for artificial ice before flooding.

2.14 *Left*
"De La Vergne Machine Co, 220-ton refrigeration machine."

Part Two

Hockey Arenas in the Golden Age of Sport, 1920–1931

3.1
Olympia Arena, Detroit. Opened in 1927, closed in 1979, photographed here in 1986.

3

Buildings for Mass Entertainment

"Nowadays the amusement of the public has become an industry and the
new Garden is nothing more or less than a specialized industrial building."
– Harold Sterner, *Madison Square Garden, Old and New*

The post–First World War era has been called the Golden Age of Sport, a period during which urban populations with rising amounts of leisure time and disposable income increased across North America. Cities could now produce large audiences eager for mass entertainments. But, with few exceptions, buildings to accommodate them did not yet exist. These circumstances led entrepreneurs to construct the first permanent baseball parks in the United States.[1] At the same time, the great popularity of "manly" sports and the legalization of boxing in the United Sates (following passage of the Walker Act in 1920, which allowed twelve-round matches) resulted in the construction of arenas in which this sport could be watched by many.[2] In 1927 Tex Rickard presented the Jack Dempsey-Gene Tunney rematch at Chicago's Soldier Field, at which 104,000 paid a record $2,658,660 to attend.[3]

To maximize income, building managers needed fully engaged schedules. New sports were introduced and once-popular ones revived. Basketball, for instance, which had lost its appeal as a spectator sport before the First World War, was re-established in the 1930s after interest in boxing began to fade. According to Benjamin Rader, "perhaps architecture more than anything else converted college basketball into a spectator sport."[4] Hockey was another sport that benefited from this environment.

Between 1920 and 1931 eight of the ten NHL franchises operating during this period moved into newly constructed permanent arenas, all equipped with artificial-ice plants and all accommodating substantially greater audiences. The average capacity of NHL arenas nearly doubled during this period, from 7,166 to 13,195 (see Table 2).[5] The universal availability of artificial ice removed the uncertainty of weather from the scheduling of games. The season doubled in length, from twenty-two games in 1917–18 to forty-four games from 1926 to 1931 (in between, twenty-four games were played in 1918–24, thirty in 1924–25, and thirty-six in 1925–26).

In the era before television revenues and other more recently introduced revenue streams, team income was derived almost exclusively from paid attendance. Increased capacity together with longer seasons produced a 200 per cent increase in maximum average attendance and a tenfold increase in hockey revenues over this period.[6]

In Montreal, Toronto, Boston, Chicago, Detroit, and New York, newly erected buildings remained home to their teams over the next forty to seventy years. This longevity transformed these buildings into icons revered by generations of loyal fans. Broadcast media expanded the base of devotion, enabling far-flung audiences to participate directly in events held at these "shrines" or "temples" of sport. Hockey games were broadcast to audiences across Canada from both Maple Leaf Gardens and the Montreal Forum, first by radio beginning in 1931 and twenty-one years later via nationally televised Saturday evening games. In the United States hockey and basketball fans revered Madison Square Garden, Boston Garden, Chicago Stadium, and the Detroit Olympia.

The buildings constructed in this era differ markedly from the hockey arenas that preceded them. Their common features indicate that the arena had come of age. For instance, in a 1931 article about Maple Leaf Gardens, the author stated that the seating "follows the usual tiered or banked arrangement employed in arenas and stadia."[7] Fans and commentators were amazed by

3.2
Madison Square Garden III, during construction, 1925. Completed in 192 days.

the technical wonders of the new arenas – their size, complexity, and comforts (heating, air conditioning, seats with backs) as well as the speed of their construction.[8] Without exception they were designed by architects, accommodated over 10,000 people, and featured artificial ice, modern construction techniques, and permanent materials, such as concrete, steel, and brick. "Madison Square Garden is completely fireproof and does not contain a single piece of lumber," trumpets the first lines of an article in the *Madison Square Garden Official Program and Guide* for 1927–28.[9] This was a fact worth boasting about. Earlier arenas and theatres had burned with ease and frequency. In 1903 a fire at the Iroquois Theatre in Chicago killed 602 people. Such disasters led to new building codes regarding semi-public buildings, including provisions that required the use of fire-resistant materials.[10]

3.3
The Forum, Montreal, during construction, 1924. Completed in 159 days.

Hockey arenas provided for the comfort of audiences as never before, with heating and air conditioning, more washrooms and food concessions, padded seats, restaurants, and bars. Speaking of the newly opened Maple Leaf Gardens, then Toronto Maple Leaf General Manager Frank Selke recalled that "the overall cleanliness and swank of the new building ushered in a new era for long suffering hockey patrons. It was only natural that women, who previously hated to dress for the stodgy old arenas of yesteryear, were glad to wear their best to see the Maple Leafs in their new arena. And just as the apparel of the lady fans stepped up in quality, that of the young men followed suit. Hockey crowds now had real class. They looked as glamorous and appeared to belong just as truly as the occupants of any box at the opera."[11] Catering for the comfort of hockey fans even led to a lawsuit in 1927 between T.P. Gorman, manager of the New York Americans hockey team, and Tex Rickard, president of Madison Square Garden Corporation. Gorman complained that Rickard kept the temperature inside the Garden so high (70 degrees during the first season) that his players could not compete. The *New York Times* reported, "Gorman said that his team had been compelled to play on nights when it was so warm in the Garden that women spectators in evening gowns sat with their wraps removed."[12] Gorman supported his lawsuit with an affidavit from a player attesting that he had lost as much as eight pounds during the course of a single game.

A different concern occasioned by the arrival of larger-capacity arenas in the 1920s was that smaller-market teams now found it increasingly difficult to compete at the elite professional level. A reporter for the *Hamilton Spectator* described the situation in 1925 in terms that sound remarkably familiar today:

> The manner in which the National Hockey League is expanding means that it will be only a matter of time until the largest cities will have the best teams, for with the greatest populations to draw from and the great seating capacity of their arenas they will be in a good position to pay top prices for players and will make better salary offers to the budding young stars. New York, with its six millions of population and an arena which will seat over 20,000 people, will have to have a winning team to keep the seats filled, while Boston, Montreal, Toronto, and Pittsburgh, if the latter is admitted, are all much larger than Hamilton and Ottawa … The expansion may be a good thing for the league, but it is only a matter of time until the smaller cities will have to look to other sources for their entertainment in professional sport.[13]

While statistics prove that dollars don't necessarily buy winners, they usually do guarantee that teams stay put.[14] Before the start of the 1925–26 season, the entire Hamilton Tigers team was sold, becoming the New York Americans, playing for that city's "six millions of population."

Of the eight new buildings, perhaps only Maple Leaf Gardens fully succeeds as a work of architecture – its streamlined form, Deco ornament, and massive dome alluding to great interior volume establish a grand street presence. But all the others made claims to architectural pretensions, if only by virtue of their scale; only the great nineteenth- and early-twentieth-century train terminals presented a more imposing appearance and saw greater foot traffic. Detroit's Olympia,

with its vast red-brick exterior, presents the image of a Romanesque cathedral while the massive sandstone blocks and muscular corner towers at Chicago Stadium helped that building dominate its surroundings. They are very much urban and urbane buildings, the first arenas that could be counted among the civic landmarks of their respective cities. Published prospectuses encouraging investment in these buildings all invoked civic ideals – and the fear of falling behind other metropolises. The prospectus for Maple Leaf Gardens argued: "Not only is the new building essential if big league hockey is to remain in Toronto, but it will fill a long-felt want in our civic life generally. For years, the need of such an amphitheatre for mass meetings, conventions, display shows, etc., has been apparent. In Maple Leaf Gardens we hope to create a centre that will not only cater to sports of one kind or another, but will prove to be a real asset in many other ways to our beloved city … Montreal, Boston, Detroit and Chicago have all built new arenas in recent years. Toronto dare not lag behind."[15]

These arenas continued to host diverse spectacles, from horse shows to opera, but they did so in a manner more openly commercial and theatrical than before. Their designs introduced increasingly flexible multi-functional spaces, including greater space for property storage and the stabling of circus animals and horses. Two of the arenas were designed by noted specialists in

3.4
Chicago Stadium, 1929.

3.5
Maple Leaf Gardens during a political rally, 1941.

3.6
Mount Royal Arena, Montreal, 1920.

theatre architecture – Thomas Lamb at New York, and Charles Howard Crane at Detroit. The buildings were typically located within their cities' central business districts, often close to designated theatre quarters. Ground-floor shops surrounded at least five of these buildings, augmenting income while more fully integrating their large volumes into downtown commercial centres.[16] Marquees projected outward to the street at most of these arenas. Additional illuminated external signs announced the entertainment function of these buildings, uniting them with theatres and cinemas that customarily employed such signage.

3.7
North Station and Boston Garden, 1930.

The importance of transportation was also a factor in site selection for all of these arenas. Boston Garden was built atop a passenger train station. Streetcar or bus service dropped spectators at the door of every other arena.

The fully fledged commercial spectator arena emerged during this period. Until about 1920, buildings for hockey still functioned equally as sites of community recreation – because there continued to be a demand for such activities, and because the revenues from public skating and other amateur participatory events were still economically important to the owners of these buildings. But the larger seating capacities of the new arenas, the greater financial outlay required to build them, and the increased value of the downtown sites on which they were built obliged them to realize a larger return per event than could ever have been possible from individuals paying to use the facility. Two classes of buildings for skating and hockey now emerge. Community rinks were usually erected beyond the city's central business district, at public expense. They offered minimal seating and were intended for public skating, amateur hockey, and other public events. Commercial recreational arenas were built with private funds and proffered professional sport and mass entertainment.[17]

It is precisely at this moment and under these conditions that one would expect the commercial hockey arena to emerge as a unique and fully realized building type, as had occurred for baseball stadiums. A professional, international hockey league was now firmly established, with teams located in major metropolitan centres. And there had been some twenty years of experimentation since the first purpose-built arena was constructed (in Montreal in 1898). Yet the very economic conditions that enabled hockey to successfully expand, and that encouraged promoters to construct spectator arenas, also militated against their realization as a single-purpose, identifiable building type.

All of the eight buildings for hockey constructed in this period feature huge interior volumes in which continuous grandstands surround ice surfaces of comparable dimensions. But little unites their exterior treatments, whether in materials, architectural style, or vocabulary. What these buildings do share is an overall massiveness clothed in conservative, even retardataire designs. And their architects share a common background, mainly in the service of corporate clients.

City dwellers recognized movie theatres, another new entertainment building type, by their exotic, even extravagantly bizarre designs. Their exteriors prepared moviegoers for what awaited them inside, the emotional and psychological transport to historically, geographically, or fantastically distant worlds. Other recently introduced building types, such as airports and gas stations, tended to sleek and stripped-down, "modern" designs, which reflected the speed and technological progress of air and automobile travel. Buildings with a single function – cinema, air travel, gas and car service – simplified the designer's task in arriving at an appropriate expressive form. But when is a hockey arena just a hockey arena? Is it still a hockey arena if the ice has been removed and a basketball game is in progress? By default, hockey arenas served so many functions that it might be more accurate to describe them as flexible containers for undefined mass spectacle. Such a definition was hardly likely to stir the blood of architects charged with forging a unique identity for them.

The architect's task was further complicated by the fact that so few buildings for professional hockey existed and those that did exist remained in use for so long. Looking for inspiration from previous buildings where hockey had been played, architects only discovered a similarly hybrid heritage – rinks for skating and curling and exposition buildings in Canada, circus tents and convention halls in the United States. Some clients simply preferred to adapt existing buildings for use as hockey arenas; in St Louis a dairy exposition building built in 1929 became the St Louis Arena. As recently as 1967 Pittsburgh's Civic Arena was modified from its original function as an auditorium for light opera (with a retractable dome). It served as the Pittsburgh Penguins' home until 2010. Wading through this muddied architectural landscape, architects of Golden Era arenas might be excused for getting mired. They were unable to produce hockey arenas in which one perceives the unique relationship between form, function, and expression that one expects to discover in buildings for a distinct purpose.

In one of the many nostalgic building histories published to commemorate the closing or destruction of Golden Age arenas, Maple Leaf Gardens' greatness was described as "never primarily about bricks or accoutrements or functionality but about mystique, nostalgia, and heroics – about the transporting quality of what went on there."[18] Discussing Madison Square Garden IV (1968) in an architectural guidebook to New York City, the author concluded that "sports arenas … are defined less by their architecture than by the collective memories they contain."[19] While both assessments may be true, one still wishes that architects of Golden Age arenas could have imbued their designs with an architectural identity that matched the emotional intensity of audiences, the heroics of athletes and performers, and "the transporting quality of what went on there."

4.1
"Darling, it's just a building," 1996.
Advertisement published in a special
section of the *Montreal Gazette*
commemorating the closing of
the Montreal Forum.

4

Canada's Secular Shrines: Myth, Memory, and Culture

"Fans coming to Toronto for the first time trooped like pilgrims to
 Maple Leaf Gardens."
 – Scott Young, *The Boys of Saturday Night*

"Ten thousand voices that only knew how to cheer a rubber puck past a goalie's
 pads, [were] now singing MERDE A LA REINE D'ANGLETERRE!"
 – Leonard Cohen *Beautiful Losers*

Maple Leaf Gardens: The First "Plugged-in" Arena

The iconic status of Golden Era arenas has virtually nothing to do with architecture and everything to do with myth, memory, and culture. Of all these buildings, Maple Leaf Gardens best epitomizes what it means to be mythic. As was true for the other professional hockey facilities of this
period, the Gardens' steadfast fans share a collective memory of historic moments and emotion-
ally intense encounters – with athletes, musicians, politicians – that became inseparable from the
physical place in which they were experienced. In Montreal, Toronto, Boston, Chicago, Detroit,
and New York, these buildings remained home to their teams for forty to seventy years, and this
longevity produced successive generations of devoted fans who all regarded their particular arena
as sacred ground. Such a strong sense of identification with a proud and exciting past only would
have been heightened at Maple Leaf Gardens, a building that changed little during sixty-eight
years of operation.

But in addition to these factors, Maple Leaf Gardens boasts the dramatic legend of its birth,
a Runyonesque saga from the depths of the Depression. The oft-told story of the cash-strapped
team led by Conn Smythe is a tale of mythic proportions that still inspires. It features a hockey-
mad war hero and gambler who raises money to purchase a stake in the team with a successful
outing at the racetrack. He then bends corporate financiers and union workers to the "higher"
purpose of realizing a sports temple.[1] The nicknames that Maple Leaf Gardens begat reflect the
awe it inspired – "The Taj Ma-Hockey," "Make-Believe Gardens," "Puckingham Palace." Even
seemingly critical epithets of the day such as "The Maple Leaf Mint" and "Carleton Street Cash-
box" convey notes of grudging admiration.[2] One indication of the distance we have travelled since
that time – from innocence to cynicism, from belief in heroes to their ritual destruction – may be

4.2
Foster Hewitt in his gondola broadcast booth, fifty-six feet above the ice,
at Maple Leaf Gardens, Toronto.

measured by the ironic nicknames applied to today's corporate-monikered arenas: "The Garage" for Vancouver's GM Place (now Rogers Arena), "The Hangar" for Toronto's Air Canada Centre, and "The Keg" for Montreal's Centre Molson (now Centre Bell). It is not that Golden Era arenas deserved worship, but that the people who frequented them still were capable of it.

The renown of Maple Leaf Gardens was broadened via another legendary medium, the voice of Foster Hewitt. Throughout the 1930s and 1940s, Hewitt's weekly radio broadcasts of Maple Leaf games created a virtual community of faithful listeners across Canada, people who felt an intimate connection to Maple Leaf Gardens without ever having set foot inside the place. According to journalist and author Scott Young:

> By the end of the 1930s, each game was reaching nearly two million people. Foster Hewitt's voice and, beginning in 1939, the popular intermission discussions featuring hockey experts on what was called the "Hot Stove League" became part of Canada's social history. Millions in all provinces came to treat Saturday night as Hockey Night, one of the few bright spots in a country facing war while still suffering the Great Depression. Fans coming to Toronto for the first time trooped like pilgrims to Maple Leaf Gardens, the only Toronto institution known across Canada with unquestioning respect. The same situation prevailed in Montreal, where fans flocked to see the Forum.[3]

4.3
R-100 Airship approaching Toronto, 1930.

It was Conn Smythe who recognized early on the power of radio to inspire fan interest and fuel attendance. After initial experiments beginning in 1923 at Arena Gardens on Mutual Street, the Maple Leafs' previous home, Hewitt discovered that the best location from which to observe the game and report the action was high above the ice. Another of the celebrated Maple Leaf Gardens yarns concerns Foster Hewitt's attempts to determine the optimum height from which to broadcast his game commentary. This involved mounting the stairs of a twelve-storey Eaton's department store and looking out the window at each floor. He deemed the fifth floor, fifty-six feet above grade, as ideal for surveying the widest extent while still distinguishing individual details in the crowd below.[4] The broadcast booth was constructed as a small pavilion, suspended over centre ice and originally accessed by a catwalk without safety railing. The heroic image of the lonely announcer perched on a plain wooden chair within its spartan confines further ensured Hewitt's place as a Maple Leaf legend.[5] The term "gondola," used to describe these booths even today, derived from the cabins carried beneath dirigibles (the appearance of which were still

cause for great wonder at this date). If anything at Maple Leaf Gardens suggested the modernity and excitement of the 1930s, it was this element of the building. It reminded spectators that what they were witnessing live others could only hear at home.

In 1931 Montreal was still Canada's leading city and business centre. Toronto, with a population of 631,000, had few tall buildings. Church spires continued to dominate the skyline. Maple Leaf Gardens' massive eleven-storey volume must have seemed a miraculous apparition to Torontonians as it rose amidst a predominantly low-rise, domestic neighbourhood at the height of the Depression.

At least three other quality hockey venues operated in Toronto in 1931: Ravina Gardens, Varsity Arena, and Arena Gardens. Ravina Gardens was a barn-like structure of concrete block, brick, and steel. It was equipped with artificial ice and situated in the city's west end. It replaced an earlier natural-ice facility that had been built in 1911.[6] Varsity Arena, opened five years earlier on the University of Toronto's campus, also featured artificial ice. Arena Gardens, also known as the Mutual Street Arena, opened in 1912 on the site of an earlier facility for curling and skating. Designed by Montreal architects Ross and MacFarlane, it had been the Toronto Maple Leafs' former home.

Upon completion, Arena Gardens was the most advanced and impressive hockey facility in the country, perhaps in the world. It had seating for 6,000 and space for another 1,500 standees. It was one of the earliest Canadian arenas to be equipped with artificial ice. Its steel and concrete structure clothed with buff brick in a stately Beaux-Arts manner presented a sophisticated and modern face to a world unaccustomed to associating such qualities with a hockey arena. But in the post-American-expansion era, after 1924, hockey teams could not compete economically in buildings accommodating less than 10,000 people. Just as the economic riches offered by "skyboxes" fuelled the construction of new facilities in the 1990s, forcing the closing and destruction of less well-endowed earlier buildings, by the mid-1920s small-capacity arenas were made redundant.

Shorn of its primary tenant and forced to compete for bookings with the bigger, newer, better, Maple Leaf Gardens, Arena Gardens soon faced financial difficulties. It was taken over by the City of Toronto in lieu of unpaid taxes and subsequently reopened as a roller rink.[7] Few cities have large enough populations to support more than one arena or auditorium.[8] Ironically, with the completion of the Air Canada Centre in 1999, Maple Leaf Gardens faced the same economic uncertainty to which it had consigned Arena Gardens in 1931. In 2011–12 the Loblaws grocery

4.4 *Opposite top*
Maple Leaf Gardens, 1931. A massive eleven-storey block.

4.5 *Opposite bottom*
Mutual Street Arena, Toronto, 1912. Surprising elegance for a hockey arena. Compare this with the Denman Street Arena in Vancouver, constructed the same year (Image 2.11).

chain partnered with Ryerson University to transform Maple Leaf Gardens into an 85,000-square-foot Loblaws superstore and Ryerson's new student athletic centre. The exterior of Maple Leaf Gardens remains intact as part of the renovated building, as do parts of the interior, notably the interior of the vast dome, which is now visible from a much closer vantage point. Ryerson's hockey rink was installed some fifty feet above the level of the original ice surface, placing it at about the same height as Foster Hewitt's gondola in the old Gardens.

Ross and Macdonald, architects of Maple Leaf Gardens, were a prolific early-twentieth-century corporate office. They were responsible for some of the most important buildings in Canada, notably office buildings, hotels, apartment buildings, and department stores. By 1931, their work was so prevalent that Sinaiticus, the anonymous reviewer of Maple Leaf Gardens for *Construction* magazine, noted that the firm "had already erected 'skyscrapers' upon every important corner in Montreal, and were [now] busily engaged in the task of filling in the intervening gaps."[9] Ross and Macdonald were a safe choice, architects with a proven track record who could be counted upon to get the job done, on time and on budget, no small accomplishment during the cash-starved Depression. Yet the firm also typified the architect-of-choice for arena clients, then as now. The

MAPLE LEAF GARDENS – TORONTO –

4.6 *Opposite*
Eaton's Department Store, College Street, Toronto, 1930. Maple Leaf Gardens was meant to harmonize with the classical refinement of Eaton's new store.

4.7 *Above*
Unexecuted proposal for Maple Leaf Gardens, Toronto, perspective, 1931. Note the stores and their awnings at street level on both facades.

technical complexity of these buildings require architectural firms with a strong grounding in engineering while the essential conservatism of corporate clients argues against flamboyance or experimentation in their design. With the exception of Olympic facilities, most sports architecture in North America has tended toward the safe, even banal. Only in the late twentieth century have major design architects – Peter Eisenman, Arquitectonica, Snøhetta – begun to get involved in the design of commercial sports facilities.

Another reason why Ross and Macdonald were a smart choice concerns conditions agreed to by Conn Smythe in securing the land on which Maple Leaf Gardens was built.[10] The land had been owned by the T. Eaton Company. Eaton's was Canada's largest retail department-store chain through the first half of the twentieth century, with stores across the country and a mail-order catalogue business that extended the company's reach still further. In 1930 Eaton's opened a huge 600,000-square-foot store at Yonge and College streets, half a block from the site of Maple Leaf Gardens. In doing so the company had two main goals. It wanted to shift the focus of the retail trade northwards and it sought to use modern design to transform and modernize shopping.[11]

The College Street store featured sleek Art Deco styling on the interior and a spectacular seventh floor, which included an auditorium and restaurant designed by French architect Jacques Carlu. In agreeing to sell the nearby land to Smythe, Eaton's executives insisted on two points: that the design of the new Maple Leaf Gardens "would not compromise Eaton's own efforts to create and attract the civilized bourgeois consumer" and that the company's goal of creating a new retail zone would not be detracted from by a building that would be dark most of the week.[12]

As a condition of the sale, Eaton's executives gained the right to review and comment on the drawings for Maple Leaf Gardens. Wishing to avoid unnecessary conflict or delay, Smythe chose Ross and Macdonald, the architect's of Eaton's College Street store, effectively mirroring the taste of those whom he wished to please. In a further nod to Eaton's, in particular its wish to establish a retail sector in the neighbourhood of its new flagship store, Ross and Macdonald proposed inserting a series of stores at street level. They argued in a letter that "the site in our judgement lends itself to the development of modern stores or specialty shops, both on the Carleton and Church frontages of the building. These modern shops would form a base to the Arena building and offer the opportunity of a splendid architectural treatment for the entire structure."[13] The number of shops proposed by Ross and Macdonald varies on the drawings, from a high of twenty-seven (ten each facing Carlton and Wood streets, five more facing Church, and one in each of the corners at Wood and Church and Carlton and Church) to the seventeen that appear on working drawings dated 15 May 1931. This is the number visible in a photograph taken on 28 November 1931, just after the building opened.[14] (On plans dated 20 February 1931 the number of shops was reduced to fifteen while a bowling alley and billiard room were introduced.) But the neighbourhood never developed into the shopping mecca that Eaton's had hoped for and the stretch of Carleton Street to either side of Maple Leaf Gardens remains a desultory site today.

During design development, the architects changed the orientation of the playing surface from east-west to north-south. From 14 February – when the as yet unnamed project was still titled "New Arena Toronto" on the drawings – until the end of March 1931, the ice rink was oriented east-west along Carlton Street. By shifting to a north-south orientation after this date, the architects were able to situate 90 per cent of the 13,000 seats along the more desirable long sides of the ice surface.[15] Ross and Macdonald also relocated the principal entrance to the centre of Carleton Street, a more prominent location where it faced an active transportation route.

Maple Leaf Gardens Limited issued a $700,000 stock offering on 15 May 1931.[16] The document is illustrated with a perspective rendering showing a pyramidal building composed of a sequence of stepped side bays rising in height toward the centre.[17] This drawing and two related perspectives are interesting for two reasons. First, although the dimensions of the site (350 × 282 feet) never changed throughout the design process, these early perspectives show a longitudinally oriented building, as compared with the cubic appearance of the built work. Second, the architects intended these perspectives to show how Maple Leaf Gardens related to the nearby Eaton's store. In the perspective drawing in the Conn Smythe Papers, the Eaton's store appears at the far left side of the drawing, but the architects made it appear closer than it actually was. They also depicted the Eaton's store with its never-completed, twenty-five-storey tower. As a final touch they introduced another skyscraper that did not exist, this one equipped with rooftop searchlights dramatically scanning the nighttime sky. These fanciful or wishful touches enhance the image but also serve a promotional function, encouraging potential investors through the vision of a dynamic site, one with growth potential promising a corresponding rise in share values.

Remarkably, Maple Leaf Gardens changed little over its sixty-eight years of continuous operation. Total seating increased from about 13,000 when the building opened in 1931 to more than 16,000 in 1968. But, because the building envelope was always respected, additional seating had to be squeezed into the space available, between the ice surface and the exterior walls. To maximize the number of seats, the architects gave the seating bowl an extremely steep gradient. Spectators enjoyed a viewing experience that was dizzying or exhilarating, depending on their susceptibility to vertigo.[18] Some seats were lost when private boxes were added, in 1979. The colour of the dome changed over the years, from black to white. The weight of this roof was supported entirely by four masonry piers, leaving the interior column-free and affording audiences excellent, unobstructed sightlines from the beginning.

4.8
Unexecuted proposal for Maple Leaf Gardens, Toronto, plan, 1931.

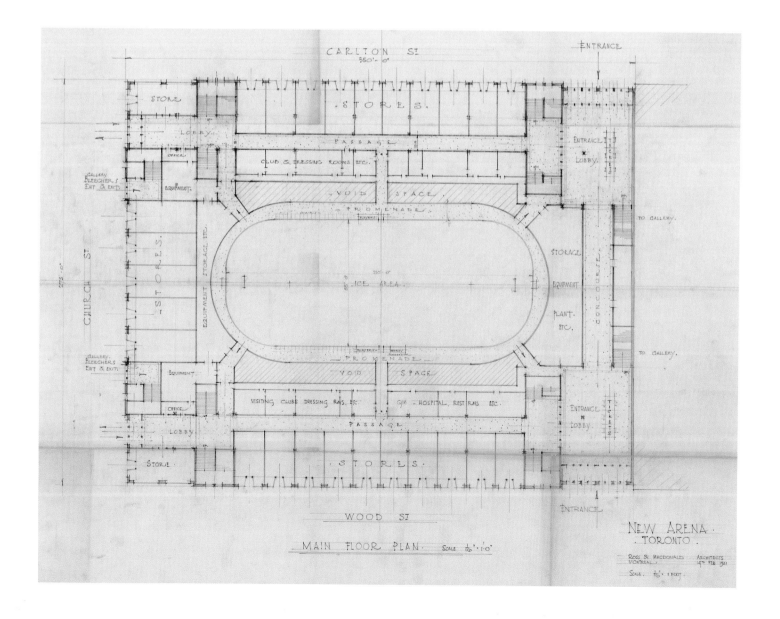

Northwest corner of Carlton and Church Sts.

MAPLE LEAF GARDENS

Toronto's New Sports Centre

4.9
Unexecuted proposal for Maple Leaf Gardens, Toronto, perspective, 1931. The cover of a stock offering aimed at raising construction funds.

4.10 *Below*
Unexecuted proposal for Maple Leaf Gardens, Toronto, perspective, 1931. Like the previous image, this one imagines the Eaton Centre (far left) with its never executed twenty-five-storey tower and adds another skyscraper at centre, complete with dramatic roof-top searchlight, that also never existed.

PROPOSED NEW ARENA TORONTO

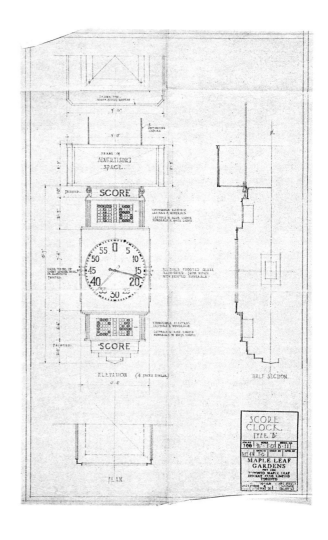

4.11
SporTimer Time clock for Maple Leaf Gardens, Toronto, 1932. The origin of the Jumbotron, a simple score and time clock.

In 1932 Maple Leaf Gardens introduced a further technological marvel, the four-sided SporTimer time clock. This architectural accessory had an impact on players and referees, allowing them to keep track of time remaining in each period. For spectators, the urgent presence of a ticking clock would only have intensified the drama of game play. Maple Leaf Gardens was also equipped with what was then believed to be the largest permanent indoor sound system. In addition to amplifying music and announcements within the building, it transmitted these to external listeners via radio broadcast. The system could also receive and transmit programming received from without. Maple Leaf Gardens was "plugged in." A massive frame suspended from the dome over centre ice carried twelve loudspeakers, the boxing-ring lights, and the time clock. They formed a focal point of advanced technology within the building. Together with Foster Hewitt's gondola, this visible technology lent a progressive dynamism to sport spectating at Maple Leaf Gardens that was entirely new.[19]

The Montreal Forum: At the Nexus of Sport, Religion, and Cultural Politics[20]

Like Maple Leaf Gardens, the Montreal Forum was one of the Original Six hockey arenas to achieve iconic status over the course of its seventy-two years of continuous operation. But, owing to Quebec's unique history and distinct culture within Canada, the Forum always symbolized more than just athletic struggle and triumph. The closing of the Forum in 1996 provides a rich point of entry to the extraordinary role this building has played in Québécois sport, culture, and politics.

On 15 March 1996 a parade made its way down Sainte Catherine Street, the primary shopping artery in downtown Montreal. Originating at the Forum, home to the Montreal Canadiens hockey team since 1926 (and to the Montreal Maroons, for whom it had been built in 1924), the parade's destination was the Canadiens' new home, the Molson (now Bell) Centre two miles away. Montreal hockey legends rode in vintage, open-topped cars of the 1950s to 1990s. A four-storey-tall inflated hockey player added a festive air to the procession, which nevertheless was tinged with the funereal – something gained and something lost. The parade marked the official opening of the Molson Centre, but its raison d'être was the transference of the Forum's ghosts, karma, and winning spirit to the new facility. In light of this underlying objective, even more important than

4.12 *Top*
Montreal Canadiens players parading from the Forum to the new Molson Centre, accompanied by a giant inflated hockey player.

4.13 *Bottom*
Opening ceremony at the Molson Centre on 16 March 1996. A meeting of sport and religion. Canadiens Captain Pierre Turgeon sanctifies the new Molson Centre ice with the storied torch.

those vintage hockey players decked out in the *bleu, blanc et rouge* was the presence of a simple torch.

In 1940 the then head coach of the Canadiens, Dick Irvin, Sr, conceived a brilliant tactic to motivate his players. Inspired by John McCrae's famous First World War poem, "In Flanders Fields," Irvin had painted high on the dressing room wall the following lines: "To you from failing hands we throw / The torch; be yours to hold it high."[21] The words remained in place for fifty-six years, during which time the team won a record twenty Stanley Cups, becoming the most successful franchise in team sport history. Guy Lafleur, a Canadiens great through the 1970s and early 1980s, recalled that "the first words that we learned when we first stepped into the room were about the torch. The first thing they show you is what's written on the wall."[22]

Four nights before the parade this torch had played the lead role in a public-relations extravaganza, a staged melodrama that was moving in spite of its calculated kitschiness. Prior to the start of the final hockey game at the Forum, on 11 March, twenty-three former Canadiens heroes trooped onto the ice to be cheered by an adoring crowd. Maurice "The Rocket" Richard elicited the greatest applause from the crowd, nearly ten-minutes' worth, including shouts of "Richard, Richard" and "Campbell, Campbell" (a reference that will be clarified further along). Then, the oldest surviving team captain, Émile "Butch" Bouchard, skated to centre ice carrying aloft a flaming torch. This incarnation of Montreal hockey tradition was passed from hand to successive hand of Canadiens captains in an allegorical re-enactment of the team's glorious history. Some eighteen thousand in attendance and thousands more watching on television witnessed the desanctification of the Forum.[23]

And now this torch was threading its way through Montreal streets, along with ice scraped from the surface of the old Forum. The twenty-four Stanley Cup banners that had hung from the Forum's rafters, inspiring local players and fans and striking fear among visiting teams, had been judged too small to be adequately visible within the more capacious confines of the Molson Centre. They had been sold off at a charity auction two nights earlier.[24] New, larger replicas rode with the players in the open cars, towering above them. These precious artifacts would soon consecrate their new home. The banners would be hoisted, and the Forum ice, now melted, would be sprinkled over a fresh sheet of Molson Centre ice in a ceremony of baptism and rebirth. Before the first game at the Molson Centre, captain Pierre Turgeon participated in yet another ceremony. Once again carrying the storied torch, he dipped it to touch the heart of the Canadiens' logo, the CH inscribed at centre ice, thereby dedicating the Canadiens' new home.

The overtly religious dimension of these ceremonies echoed the medieval tradition of "translation," according to which a saint's remains, or other holy relic was transferred from one church or holy resting place to another.[25] The sacred aspect of the parade could not have been lost on French Quebecers, especially those old enough to remember the common occurrence of local and province-wide religious processions, such as the parades organized for Corpus Christi, Sacred Heart, and Saint Jean Baptiste.[26] While the hold of the Catholic Church within Québécois culture was not so strong in 1996 as it had been fifty years earlier, its impact is still evident, in the language of profanity (*câlisse*, *tabarnak*), in the popularity of communion wafers sold as snack food in grocery stores, and even in the nicknames for the Canadiens hockey team (*les Glorieux*, *la Sainte-Flanelle*).[27]

Since the beginning of organized hockey in Montreal in the 1870s, teams had often been established along ethnic lines. This was one way for recent immigrants to a melting-pot society to express pride in what made them different. The Shamrock and Wanderer teams were Irish, the Montagnard and the National were French, and the Victorias were Scots.[28] With the advent of

4.14
Corpus Christi parade, Notre Dame Street, Montreal, 1914.

open professionalism in the early twentieth century and the rise of civic-based teams competing in inter-city leagues, such early vestiges of the game largely were left behind, although promoters might still try to use the (sometimes manufactured) ethnicity of players to drum up fan support from specific communities.[29] But in Quebec the rivalry between French and English hockey clubs, which continued at the NHL level through to 1938, was always more than just a struggle to establish ethnic bragging rights. It carried on its back long-simmering, irreconcilable differences over language, religion, economics, politics, and cultural values, to say nothing of the open sore produced by military defeat and the co-habitation of victor and vanquished. An article published in the Montreal French-language daily *La Patrie* on the eve of the 1924–25 hockey season described the Montreal Canadiens upcoming match against the Toronto Saint Patricks as that between the glorious world champions and their formidable enemy, the Irish club from the Queen City.[30]

After fire destroyed the Westmount Arena in 1918, the Montreal Wanderers ceased operations, leaving the Montreal Canadiens as the sole club representing Montreal in the National Hockey League. The Montreal Canadiens Hockey Club had been formed in 1909, "to add a French face to hockey in Montreal," which then included English teams such as the Shamrocks, Wanderers, and Victorias.[31] The name "Canadiens," as well as the team's nickname, "Les Habitants" or Habs, made reference to specifically French Canadian traditions.[32] After playing at the less than satisfactory Jubilee Rink during 1918–19, located far from the city centre and with seating for just over 3,000, the team moved to the Mount Royal Arena in 1920. With room for 10,000 fans (6,000 seated and 4,000 standing), this venue was an improvement over all previous rinks in the city but the lack of artificial ice continued to be a problem. While certain hockey rinks in the city were home to specific French or English teams, the major city arenas, such as the Westmount Arena and the Mount Royal Arena, had always been operated as profit-making businesses and the managers of these facilities spoke the language of money, renting their premises to teams representing both linguistic groups.[33] A newspaper article commenting on the inauguration of the Mount Royal Arena in 1920 noted the small turnout of only 1,800 but explained that "since the four clubs on the programme were English the number of French-Canadian fans was not very high but they will be there in greater numbers when the National compete against the other clubs of the league."[34]

When the National Hockey League expanded from three to ten teams, between 1924 and 1926, Montreal gained a second franchise. From the very start, the Maroons were intended to draw support from Montreal's English community and to restore a rivalry with the Canadiens that had lapsed after the Montreal Wanderers folded. The Maroon's new building, the Montreal Forum, was located on the border of Westmount, bastion of English Montreal society, and a stone's throw from the site of the now-destroyed Westmount Arena, former home to the now-defunct Wanderers. The site was already associated with popular entertainment, having served since 1908 as home to a roller rink that enclosed an open-air skating rink, also called the Forum. The new arena's board of directors represented a who's who of Montreal's English corporate elite, including two Molsons, of brewery and bank fame; Edward Beatty, president of the Canadian Pacific Railway; Sir Herbert Holt, president of the Royal Bank; Sir Charles Gordon, president of the Bank of Montreal; and J.W. McConnell of St Lawrence Sugar.

French-English relations in Quebec ever have been subject to often inexplicable and ironic anomalies and hockey is no stranger to these. The fact that it was the Canadiens who played the

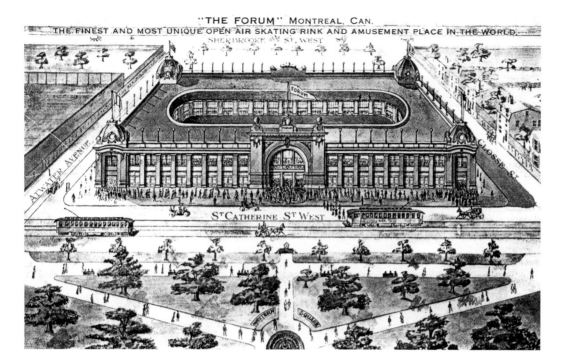

4.15
The Forum Open Air Skating Rink, Montreal, 1908.

inaugural game in the new Forum, rather than the Maroons, is merely one of these incongruities. That the Forum would soon become the sole home of the Canadiens, emerging as a symbol of French Canadian pride in the excellence of their hockey team and a rallying site for a rising wave of French-Quebec nationalism, is merely a continuation of this irony.[35]

Prior to 1963, every NHL franchise sponsored amateur teams as a means to groom junior-aged players who might eventually play for the parent club. The franchise owned the rights of these young players. Canadiens teams were guaranteed a steady stream of local, French Canadian talent for fans to identify with and rally behind. Even when this system was dismantled in 1963 with the introduction of the NHL Amateur Draft, a system that guaranteed each NHL club equal access to amateur players, the Canadiens were awarded a special dispensation. "Due to the unique situation of the Montreal Canadiens, it was agreed to protect the French-Canadian flavour of the team. Therefore, the Canadiens were granted the option to select up to two players of French-Canadian heritage before any other team could exercise its first selections in the Amateur Draft."[36] In spite of this tradition, Canadiens teams were never ethnically pure, and Canadiens fans (who, after the Maroons folded in 1938, included both French and English citizens) have always been proud to cheer equally for a Morenz or a Blake as for a Richard or a Plante.

According to William Brown, Canadiens management welcomed the arrival of a new "English" team in Montreal and the greater capacity of their new artificial-ice rink. Léo Dandurand, the Canadiens' manager and co-owner, "liked the idea of a new arena and had visions of installing the Canadiens there. After all, he had just gone through the humiliating experience of having to play the Stanley Cup winning game on Ottawa's brand-new artificial ice surface because an early spring had melted the ice in Montreal. And besides, the combination of a bigger arena and a cross-town rivalry might be good for business."[37]

Sensing trouble, Thomas Duggan and Hector Racine, co-owners of the Mount Royal Arena, arranged to install artificial ice for the 1924–25 season, and it was difficulties with its performance that led the Canadiens to inaugurate the Forum ahead of the Maroons.[38] Duggan and Racine next hired local architect Raoul Gariépy in 1925 to prepare plans for a new 12,000-seat arena, in an effort to stop the Canadiens from moving to the newly completed Montreal Forum, as seemed likely.[39] Although plans were prepared for this new Mount Royal Arena, it was never constructed. The Canadiens broke their lease with the Mount Royal Arena in 1926, joining the Maroons at the Forum and gladly paying court costs of $83,000 that they fully expected to recoup from the facility's increased seating capacity. The two teams competed for fourteen years through 1938, until the effects of the Depression finally caused the Maroons to end their operations.

Between 1924 and 1938 Montreal's two hockey teams combined for five Stanley Cups, four of them won at the Forum.[40] The two teams produced a succession of stars, from the goaltending heroics of three-time Vezina trophy winner George Hainsworth to the scoring prowess of Nels Stewart, Herb Gardiner, Aurel Joliat, and the "Stratford Streak," Howie Morenz. It was the tragic events surrounding the death of Morenz, named Canada Press "hockey player of the first half-century," that first, and forever, marked the Forum as more than a simple sports auditorium. Rushing toward the net during a match against Chicago on the evening of 28 January 1937, Morenz was checked and fell awkwardly into the boards with a Chicago defenceman on top of him, breaking his leg. Still in hospital two months later, he suffered a heart attack and died. His funeral service, held at the Forum, was the largest ever arranged for an athlete in Canada. After thousands had paid their respects at the funeral chapel, Morenz's casket was brought to the Forum on the morning of 11 March. Laid at centre ice, surrounded by four truckloads of flowers and an honour guard of teammates, some fifty thousand mourners filed past to bid farewell to Morenz in the four hours preceding the ceremony. Ten thousand fans remained behind for the funeral service itself, which was broadcast to a still larger radio audience.[41]

4.16
The Montreal Forum becomes a memorial site. The casket of Howie Morenz enters the Forum on the shoulders of his teammates. Fifty thousand mourners filed past and ten thousand remained for his funeral service in 1937.

4.17
Maurice Richard appeals for calm from the Forum dressing room a day after fans rioted
to protest his suspension, 1955.

Throughout the 1940s and 1950s, a period during which French Quebecers were subjugated by both church and state and economically subservient to English bosses, the success of their hockey team provided an important and visible source of pride and positive self-identification. It was during these two decades that the Canadiens began their ascendancy as the most successful franchise in team sport history by winning eight Stanley Cups. The Forum began to be recognized as a shrine where homegrown heroes could be worshipped with raucous abandon. But the events of 17 March 1955 proved that hockey sometimes could be more than a sport, and that a hockey arena sometimes could be more than bricks and mortar. The Forum, formerly a site of athletic brilliance and entertainment, became a national stage for the unfolding of a cultural and political drama.[42]

On 16 March NHL President Clarence Campbell suspended the greatest of the Forum's heroes, fiery-eyed Maurice (the Rocket) Richard, for the remainder of the hockey season and all of the playoffs for having attacked an official. When Campbell attended the following night's hockey game at the Forum, he was pelted with debris and physically jostled by indignant fans. A tear-gas canister erupted within the arena, and as an angry crowd left the building, the game now forfeit, protesters who had gathered outside joined them. Together they rioted and looted through the night. The next evening, a shaken Maurice Richard spoke to Montreal fans over the airwaves in French and in English from the Forum dressing room. Asking for calm, he said: "I'll take my punishment and come back next year."

Newspapers called the rioting the worst the city had seen since the anti-conscription battles during the Second World War, an earlier flashpoint that had highlighted the distance separating Canada's two solitudes.[43] The incident was more than an outburst of hooliganism, as Montreal's English-language newspapers described it.[44] In Roch Carrier's poetic retelling of the story, Richard's unfair suspension caused the riot and unleashed the natural force of Quebecers' repressed dissatisfaction with the status quo: "Clarence Campbell is trying to crush a little French Canadian who has wings. That's what people are saying. Anger is rumbling in the province of Quebec like the water held captive in the rivers by the winter ice."[45] Many people regarded Clarence Campbell as an agent of James Norris, head of the powerful family that effectively controlled the NHL and whose team, the Detroit Red Wings, was then in a struggle with the Canadiens for first place.[46] But for Quebec's francophones, Campbell also represented the anglo establishment that for too long had dominated the little guy, for whom Richard was a symbolic champion. One year earlier Richard had accused Campbell of being anti-French in his ghostwritten sports column, "Le Tour du Chapeau," in the French-language Montreal newspaper *Samedi-Dimanche* and was forced to apologize.[47] And even twenty years later, in a biography of Richard, bitterness over Campbell's handling of the affair and his identification with anglo authority remained absolute: "Mr. Campbell, from the height of his magnificence, crushed Maurice Richard under his English boot and, in so doing, every French-Canadian felt crushed."[48]

As if Richard's suspension was not enough to draw attention to the grievances of French-speaking Quebecers against their English masters, an ongoing controversy over the naming of the new Canadian National Railway (CNR) hotel then nearing completion on downtown Dorchester (now René Lévesque) Boulevard exploded onto the front pages of Montreal newspapers. Sharing the front page of *Le Devoir* with the news of Richard's suspension on 17 March was an article subtitled "Le royalisme et Donald Gordon." Francophones, championed by then mayor Jean Drapeau, were offended by CNR President Donald Gordon's plan to name the hotel the Queen Elizabeth. They preferred the Château Maisonneuve. Drapeau had also spoken out against Clarence Campbell, condemning him for his harsh suspension of Richard. After the riot, Drapeau blamed

4.18
"Toutes mes excuses." Editorial cartoon showing Maurice Richard humbled and forced to apologize to Clarence Campbell, 1954.

Campbell for having incited the crowd through his presence at the game and advised him to stay away in future.[49]

There is divided opinion on when to date the start of Quebec's Quiet Revolution. Did it begin as early as 1949 with the Asbestos Strike, when the church gave its support to workers and their union rather than to the corporation and the government of Maurice Duplessis? Or, as many commentators believe, did it begin with the election of Jean Lesage's Liberal Party in 1960? Some have even suggested that the Richard Riot, five years earlier, deserves credit.[50] Whatever one believes, there can be no argument that the Montreal Forum played a pivotal role at the politically charged centre of a people's movement from oppression toward self-definition. In his 1966 novel *Beautiful Losers*, Leonard Cohen explicitly connects the Quiet Revolution to hockey when he recalls how "ten thousand voices that only knew how to cheer a rubber puck past a goalie's pads, [were] now singing MERDE A LA REINE D'ANGLETERRE!"[51]

Over the course of its seventy-two-year history, the Forum witnessed many extraordinary events that contributed to its status as a revered shrine. Yet little of this veneration redounded from the quality of the Forum's architecture, which has remained never more than ordinary through a series of additions and transformations. Completed in 1924 to a design by John S. Archibald, the structure had a three-storey neo-Renaissance exterior, composed of red brick with sandstone trim, that repeated the rhythms, punctuating corner pavilions, and central arched main entrance on Sainte Catherine Street of the 1909 roller rink it replaced. The encompassing girdle of small shops at street level, marked by signs and marquees, endowed the Forum with a commercial aspect intended to harmonize its great bulk within its downtown location. Only the Forum's massive footprint, occupying the entire block bounded by de Maisonneuve Boulevard and Atwater, Sainte Catherine, and Closse streets, and its huge, simple shed roof, visible from above or at a distance of several blocks, betrayed the scale of the building's interior volume, its reason for being.

By the time of the Richard Riot, the Forum already had been renovated once, in 1949, at which time a second floor and 3,163 seats were added along the long east and west flanks of the building, bringing the total seating to just under 14,000. Although this expansion had been long overdue, delayed first by the Depression and then by the Second World War, newspapers still claimed that the additional seats were needed to accommodate the popularity of Maurice Richard. They even suggested that the Forum be renamed "The House that Richard Rebuilt."[52] Unfortunately, the roof was still supported by internal supports, and the expansion only increased the proportion of seats in the auditorium with partially obstructed views. The 1949 renovation also introduced a new suspended catwalk – home to journalists, an organist, and some two hundred spectators who were immediately dubbed *plafonneurs* (ceiling dwellers). One sportswriter commented waggishly, "The fact is that if this continues the organist will soon be playing more for the Good Lord than for the Forum's fans."[53]

The more substantial renovation of 1968, by architect Ken Sedleigh, increased seating to about 18,000 and eliminated the interior columns that had supported the roof but obstructed views. This makeover completely transformed the exterior, unifying and accentuating its mass by sheathing it in a composition of concrete panels and glass. Though otherwise undistinguished, this final renovation did succeed in branding the building with the iconic and televisually punchy image of

4.19
The Montreal Forum in 1947. As at Maple Leaf Gardens, shops occupied two sides of the Forum's ground level. Streetcars deliver fans to the door.

4.20
Montreal Forum, after its renovation in 1968.
Note the massive piers supporting the roof
frame, enabling a column-free interior.

4.21
Montreal Forum, 1995–96. The illuminated
escalators added during the 1968 renovation
branded the Forum, and Montreal hockey,
for the next thirty years.

crossed hockey sticks, actually side-illuminated escalators, visible through the glazed facade along
Sainte Catherine Street. This repeatedly televised image of the building has been seen by far more
people than have actually entered the Forum.[54]

The closing of the Forum and the move to the Molson Centre in 1996 were therefore events
requiring careful handling for both economic and political reasons. Those fans greeting Maurice
Richard with shouts of "Richard, Richard" and "Campbell, Campbell" indicate the long memories
of Quebecers but also the political and cultural resonance of the Richard Riot. (Many in attendance at the Forum's final game probably had not even been born when the riot occurred.)
Quebec society had undergone massive changes in the intervening years, striking evidence of
which could be found in Montreal's remaining English-language newspaper. The *Montreal*

Gazette's front page on 12 March 1996 featured a headline and photograph describing the closing of the Forum along with an article titled "We are all Quebeckers – Bouchard," reporting on a speech in which the Quebec premier, Lucien Bouchard, sought to reassure anglophones that they "belong in Quebec because it's their home, too." The game of hockey and the economic and social environment encompassing it had also undergone substantial changes in the intervening years since the Richard Riot. Players were now less loyal to teams, in the face of million-dollar salaries, and fans were less loyal to hockey, in the face of an expanding universe of competing entertainment possibilities. In spite of those fans with long memories, capable of connecting the dots between Maurice Richard, the Forum, and a struggle over politics and language, the Forum succumbed to economic realities. Though not demolished, the fate of Golden Age arenas in Boston, Chicago, Detroit, and New York, it was gutted and otherwise disfigured on the way to its reincarnation as the Pepsi Forum, a multiplex cinema with shops and restaurants. An ersatz re-creation of the Forum's interior, complete with tiers of rescued seats, provides a sanitized and Disneyfied experience for visiting tourists.

Although of no consolation to those devoted fans mourning the loss of such cherished shrines and the memories they embodied, it is nonetheless useful to recall that Americans and Canadians have become less observant of religion through the twentieth century while they have placed greater emphasis on wealth and consumption. According to statistics gathered by the Fondation du patrimoine religieux du Québec, some two hundred and fifty religious buildings in the province have closed their doors since 1976.[55] Nearly half of these buildings gained new life in the service of different religious faiths, but the remainder have been demolished or transformed, often serving functions far removed from the spiritual roles they once played. If one such example, the 1893 Valleyfield Presbyterian Church, could be rechristened the Centre d'Escalade Vertige, an indoor rock-climbing centre, as it was in November 2005, we can hardly be surprised by the fate of the Forum.[56] The deconsecration and destruction of so many religious buildings, over such a long period, elicited very little public response, individually or collectively. Conversely, the overwhelming outpouring of sadness and regret surrounding the Forum's closing and subsequent transformation potently illustrates that building's deep hold on the popular imagination and serves as stirring evidence for its claim to apotheosis within some future pantheon devoted to buildings of Canadian culture.

No architect designs a building expecting it will achieve the notoriety attained by Maple Leaf Gardens and the Montreal Forum. That these hockey arenas became revered touchstones for so many people speaks not to the power of architecture or the intentions of clients but to the authority of users in taking cultural ownership of these buildings. The downside of such popular appropriation is that not everyone may agree. One man's shrine may be another's prison. It's unlikely that the one hundred boys and girls who were sexually abused at the hands of Maple Leaf Gardens ushers will recall that building in worshipful terms.[57] Protests during construction of Pittsburgh's Three-River Stadium in the late 1960s, which centred on the construction industry's discriminatory hiring practices, led one prominent community and civil-rights leader to describe the

4.22
Molson Centre, Montreal in 1999.

stadium as a symbol for bigotry.[58] The point is that, whether we place our belief in religion, politics, or sport, it is users who get to decide the meaning of the buildings in which they manifest their allegiances. The English corporate elite who financed construction of the Montreal Forum may have thought they were building a home for the Maroons and for that team's English-speaking fans. History decided otherwise. Golden Age arenas were embraced by fans who correspond to those whom sports sociologist Richard Giullianotti designates as "supporters," individuals with "inextricable biographical and emotional ties to the club's ground [or stadium]."[59] The arena does not create the fans; the fans adopt and sanctify the arena.

5.1
Opening night at Madison Square Garden III, New York, 15 December 1925.
Montreal Canadiens vs. New York Americans, each team accompanied by its
own brass band.

5

Hockey Night in America: The First NHL Hockey Arenas in the United States

"I went to a boxing match last night and a hockey game broke out."
– Traditional joke

Introduction

In 1917, the year the National Hockey League was formed, hockey was already well established in eastern Canada. The NHL consisted of four Canadian teams: the Toronto Arenas, playing out of the 6,000-seat Mutual Street Arena; the Montreal Canadiens, playing their games at Westmount Arena, with a capacity of about 6,000–7,000 seats, until they moved to the much smaller Jubilee Rink after the Westmount Arena burned in 1918; the Ottawa Senators, whose Laurier Arena could accommodate 7,000 fans; and the Montreal Wanderers, who also played at Westmount Arena but who ceased operations after the 1918 fire. A number of other professional leagues vied for the allegiance of hockey fans across the country. There was the Pacific Coast Hockey Association, which operated teams in Vancouver, Victoria, New Westminster, Portland, and Seattle, between 1912 and 1924, and whose Seattle Metropolitans won the Stanley Cup in 1917.[1] The Western Canada Hockey League iced teams from 1921 to 1925 in Calgary, Edmonton, Regina, and Saskatoon. Numerous senior amateur leagues also operated from coast to coast, with clubs such as the Toronto Granites, winner of the 1924 Olympic games, who were equally, if not more, popular than their professional counterparts.

In 1917 hockey existed in only isolated pockets in the United States. When the short-lived International Hockey League operated from 1904 to 1907 in the Great Lakes region, it was manned almost exclusively with transplanted Canadians. The two purpose-built arenas constructed there, in Houghton and Calumet, were relatively small, and these cities' isolated locations and small populations argued against their ever participating in a national league with teams located in major metropolitan centres. Amateur leagues had been established in Boston and New York early in the twentieth century, but teams there played out of small, inadequate facilities that had been constructed for pleasure skating (a situation that paralleled Canadian experience twenty years earlier).

In 1917 the United States had many skating rinks, quite a few of which featured artificial ice, but not one that could be called an arena. Without adequate facilities, those that provided enough seating to promise promoters an acceptable return on their investment, professional hockey could not achieve success in the United States. In 1917 only Pittsburgh's Duquesne Gardens had enough seats to suggest that city as a potential NHL expansion site. In New York, the St Nicholas Rink had just 6,200 seats while Madison Square Garden, though it could accommodate over 8,000, had no artificial ice. Boston Arena and Chicago Coliseum had less than 6,000 seats and Detroit, even when it entered the league in 1926, played its first season at the Border Cities Arena in neighbouring Windsor, Ontario, with fewer than 5,000 seats. A 1914 article published in the Montreal newspaper *Le Devoir* discussed the possibility of New York being included in a new International Hockey League. The only problems to resolve were the limited dimensions of the playing surface and small capacity of the St Nicholas Rink.[2]

With the end of the First World War, the outlook brightened. According to John Chi-Kit Wong, "as economic prosperity in the 1920s contributed to the blossoming of sporting spectacles in the United States, hockey entrepreneurs such as Tom Duggan and Eddie Livingstone wanted to exploit the opportunity by selling hockey as an entertainment commodity."[3] The great popularity of exhibition matches played over the years between visiting Canadian teams in both Boston and New York suggested that professional hockey could be successful in the United States.[4] Two conditions were necessary for success: players and facilities. The experience of the IHL and PCHA proved that hockey players were now mobile commodities and that, with clever management and generous pocketbooks, high-calibre teams could be assembled. Adequate facilities were a more difficult impediment given the huge capital investment required.

Tom Duggan and His Architect: How the NHL Expanded to the United States

At the January 1923 NHL league meeting, Leo Dandurand, owner of the Montreal Canadiens, introduced Thomas Duggan, a sports and entertainment promoter and part owner of Montreal's Mount Royal Arena, where the Canadiens then played. Duggan proposed that the NHL expand into the United States and he sought options on two franchises to be located in Boston, New York, or Brooklyn. In consenting to his request, the NHL hoped to benefit from expansion into the rich American market while also heading off the establishment of a rival league by Eddie Livingstone, the disgruntled former owner of the Toronto Ontarios of the National Hockey Association (NHA). In 1917 the NHA owners had met without Livingstone to establish the NHL with the express goal of excluding Livingstone, who had for years battled the other owners while threatening to establish rival leagues in Canada and across North America.[5] Duggan expected to profit by brokering the sale of the franchises and he may have hoped to serve as manager of one or both new teams.

Duggan's surviving correspondence from this period, some of it privately held and previously unpublished, provides fascinating insights into the obstacles that he negotiated in successfully achieving expansion into the United States, particularly the behind-the-scenes machinations of his competitors, opponents, and business associates.[6] Duggan allied himself early on with the

Boston architectural and engineering firm of Funk and Wilcox (architects of the 1911 Boston Arena), and one of its principals, George C. Funk, served Duggan as architectural adviser, business counsellor, and spy.[7] In a letter to Duggan about introducing professional hockey to Boston, George C. Funk outlined the difficulties facing Duggan and Charles F. Adams, the grocery-chain millionaire who eventually purchased the Boston franchise and established the Boston Bruins.

> It seems to us that every director of the Boston Arena is lined up against Mr. Adams at the present time on this proposition … This so-called amateur crowd of hockey moguls known as the United States Amateur Hockey Association, consisting of Schooley, Haddock and Brown, will fight to prevent pro-hockey overshadowing them completely as they know it will when it comes into the United States. At the present time they are the big toads in the puddle … if there was any possible way for them to horn in on a professional franchise, they might leave you standing at the church unless you have some club to hold over them and keep them in line.[8]

The "club" that Duggan reached for was George "Tex" Rickard, the New York City event promoter par excellence who had single-handedly turned around the fortunes of a financially ailing Madison Square Garden ii (1889–91), with a little help from the alleviation of restrictions on boxing in the post-First World War era. In another letter, George C. Funk suggested to Duggan that "if professional hockey starts in New York … it will force the Boston crowd to get in it all the quicker, as they cannot continue to dish out amateur hockey in Boston when the public is getting professional hockey in New York."[9] To that end, Duggan had already contacted Rickard toward the end of 1923 and on 20 December Rickard replied that he was "much interested in your proposal."[10]

From the very beginning, the correspondence between Duggan and both Tex Rickard and Charles F. Adams is filled with references to physical plant. The very fact that Duggan chose an architect as his US confederate underscores the central role that architecture played in hockey's expansion to the United States. The architectural scenario was similar in both cities. First came attempts to modify existing buildings, to add seating at Boston Arena (1910) and to install artificial ice at Madison Square Garden ii (1889–91). Only when these failed was the decision made to build new arenas.

The Boston Arena, which had opened to the public early in 1910, was a transitional hockey building, in the mould of the 1907 Dey's Arena in Ottawa. Inaugurated just prior to the period of open professionalism and the founding of the nhl, it was built to serve the winter needs of amateur curling and hockey enthusiasts and pleasure skaters, in addition to the usual roster of circuses, carnivals, and conventions in summer. The artificial-ice plant produced ice surfaces for sport enthusiasts and also blocks of ice for domestic consumption. The building's seating capacity of only 4,000, disposed on three sides of the interior, attests to the still nascent state of hockey as a spectator sport. The fourth side of the interior included a large bandstand, some forty feet wide, and this feature, together with the changing rooms for men and women and the generous dimensions of the ice surface (90 × 242 feet), enough to accommodate 1,800 skaters, suggests that the Boston Arena Company, which commissioned the arena, continued to favour pleasure skaters in the conception of their building.

5.2 *Above*
Boston Arena, 1910. The grand, three-storey-tall arched entrance
with marquee contrasts with the more utilitarian treatment
of the arena's recessed long facade.

5.3 *Opposite*
Boston Arena, 1910. With seating for only 4,000, the arena was
too small to accommodate professional hockey crowds.

The Boston Arena Company regarded the arena as an entertainment centre. The site they chose for it, on St Botolph Street near Massachusetts Avenue, was at the centre of Boston's new entertainment district. The Museum of Fine Arts, Boston Opera House, Symphony Hall, Horticultural Hall, and other attractions were close by and trolley lines from all points in the city passed close by the arena's entrance. In keeping with the spirit of this new entertainment district, the arena's architects, Funk and Wilcox of Boston, paid special attention to the principal entrance, which they fashioned after the manner of contemporary Edwardian cinemas. Twin towers topped by cupolas framed a three-storied arched opening that was bisected at ground level by a horizontal marquee, brightly lit at night with exposed light bulbs. Except for a projecting entrance bay, with five round-arched doors, the architects left the arena's long shed unadorned and it might have been mistaken for a warehouse or factory.

Early in 1924 Charles Adams wrote to Duggan concerning the need to procure an engineer's estimate for the addition of a balcony to Boston Arena.[11] By 10 April, it was clear that the cost of doing so would be prohibitive and would, in any event, add only 1,100 seats to the existing 3,800. In view of this, Adams wrote to NHL President Frank Calder that "a very substantial group of men in the city are proposing … to construct a large Exposition Building … which will have a seating capacity of at least 15,000 people … [and] be able to house a professional hockey team to good advantage."[12] Adams explained further that the building would also handle other events such as large conventions, prizefights, and automobile shows. On the same day Adams wrote to Duggan, asking "for copies of plans, if available, of the Montreal proposition which you mentioned," possibly referring to Duggan's own plans to enlarge the Mount Royal Arena.[13] Whether or not Duggan supplied these, Adams wrote to Duggan on 15 May that he had seen plans for the new Boston Exposition Building, "and if they can finance this proposition, it certainly is going to be a wonder."[14] Two weeks later Adams remained enthusiastic: "The new building plans are coming along very well here and it looks very much as though next year, we will have a fine place."[15] But Adams's optimism was misplaced and the proposed building never materialized. The Bruins entered the NHL for the 1924–25 season and would play at Boston Arena for four more years. Duggan's relationship with Adams subsequently deteriorated over disagreements about compensation and ended in a lawsuit in 1929.[16] In 1928 Boston Garden opened after a design by Funk and Wilcox. It was the second of an intended seven Madison Square Gardens (the original name was Boston Madison Square Garden) that Tex Rickard had planned to construct throughout the United States.[17]

Madison Square Gardens III and Its Sources: Hockey as Entertainment, Part I

In his efforts to introduce professional hockey to Boston, Charles Adams had had to contend with rival forces that supported amateur hockey and initially sought to bar him from presenting the professional game at the only existing venue that could accommodate adequate numbers of fans at that date – Boston Arena. But in New York Tex Rickard was focused on boxing. Rickard knew little of hockey, referring to it as "that durned furrin game."[18] Yet if hockey could bring people in, filling seats on otherwise dark nights, Rickard was not going to argue. The different motivations behind the introduction of hockey to these two American cities, and the factors that led to the construction of buildings in which to present the sport in New York versus Boston, Toronto, and Montreal, are fundamental to a schism that occurs at this date in the history of the hockey arena.

Hockey was first played outdoors, then within skating and curling rinks until the first purpose-built hockey arenas were constructed. But the construction of Madison Square Garden III marks the first time that hockey would be played within a building primarily designed to host other events. These two related but distinct building types – the hockey arena and the entertainment venue – would continue to operate together in North America for another sixty years, until the 1990s when the NHL made a wholesale change of its venues, after which the professional hockey arena would disappear and the entertainment-venue model succeed.

While Tex Rickard quickly grasped the financial potential of regularly scheduled hockey matches, he shrewdly calculated that a key ingredient to success centred on the time needed to change his building from event mode to hockey mode and back again. In answer to a request from Thomas Duggan, George Funk addressed this issue in the most specific terms.

> With a crew of 12 to 14 labourers, the ice can be removed from 11 o'clock in the night to 8 o'clock in the morning. In order to do this, it is necessary, however, to have a small Ford truck that can carry the ice out of the building or into the melting pit. What water remains on the floor at 8 o'clock in the morning can be dried up in an hour or two and the building can be arranged for whatever other event is necessary, such as prize fights, etc. After the prize fight, we have been able to put on ice surface when the floor has been swept clean by starting at 6 o'clock in the morning, and one man with a hose can have about an inch of ice ready for skating at 2:30 in the afternoon.[19]

A brief changeover period was critical to building managers everywhere but nowhere more so than at Madison Square Garden, which to this day is one of the busiest venues in the world. Professional hockey was untried in New York in 1925 and its financial impact was initially expected to be small relative to the returns from other programmed events at Madison Square Garden. A Class A share offering for the New Madison Square Garden Corporation boasted that gross receipts from boxing alone in the eighteen months up to 31 December 1921 had been over $3 million, while those from swimming-pool rentals and other exhibitions for the same period amounted to over $1.5 million.[20] By contrast, gross revenue from hockey was expected to be in the range of $300,000 to $600,000 per year.[21] Even after the start of professional hockey at Madison Square Garden in

1926, the absolute identification of the Garden with boxing, and the comparative obscurity of hockey, was immortalized in the joke, "I went to a boxing match last night and a hockey game broke out," although this quip was probably also a wry commentary on hockey's violence.[22]

The relative unimportance of hockey to the overall financial picture of Madison Square Garden III becomes still clearer from the following evidence. Whetting the appetites of potential investors, the above-mentioned Class A share offering explained that boxing and swimming would form only a small part of the new building's activities. The published list of projected events includes dog shows, motorboat shows, and even poultry shows; hockey is not even mentioned.[23] A year after opening, Madison Square Garden Corporation's 1926 annual report showed gross profits of $1,473,276. The report explained that this had been achieved through "exhibitions of diversified entertainment, such as boxing, six-day bicycle races, track meets, the circus, Horse Show and other features." Hockey is only mentioned later, as one of many long-term contracts entered into to assure future success.[24] Even when the New York Rangers made it to the Stanley Cup finals against the powerful Montreal Canadiens in 1928, they were forced to play all five games in Montreal because Madison Square Garden was unavailable – the circus was in town. John Ringling was chairman of the board of Madison Square Garden Corporation. While he might be expected to favour his circus in scheduling bookings, the expulsion of the Stanley Cup finals nonetheless speaks volumes about the lowly place of hockey within the Madison Square Garden pecking order at this date.

All NHL arenas constructed in this era earned money from a variety of events that included boxing, wrestling, the circus, and hockey, in addition to whatever else people might pay to see. But whereas hockey revenues were only expected to make up about 10 per cent of gross income at Madison Square Garden, a 1924 report prepared by John S. Archibald, architect of the Montreal Forum, indicates that predicted annual hockey revenues of $100,000 would amount to nearly 75 per cent of total arena rental receipts in Montreal.[25] Unlike Madison Square Garden, which hosted events throughout the year, an earlier report prepared by John S. Archibald, for an unexecuted Montreal arena, proposed that letting the building as an automobile showroom and garage could augment off-season revenue.[26] While this helps explain why the Forum was so strongly, even uniquely, identified with hockey, it also highlights fundamental differences between hockey arenas like the Montreal Forum and entertainment venues like Madison Square Garden.

In Montreal and Toronto, and to a lesser degree Boston, businessmen constructed arenas with the express purpose of hosting professional hockey matches. The Forum, Maple Leaf Gardens, and Boston Garden replaced existing buildings that had likewise served this purpose (in Boston's case it had been amateur hockey). For example, in Montreal the Forum was home to the Montreal Maroons and initially operated in tandem with the Mount Royal Arena, where the Canadiens played. These two arenas replaced a long line of buildings that the public identified with hockey, whatever other functions they also may have served, including the Montagnard Skating Rink (1898), Westmount Arena (1898), and Jubilee Arena (1908). But Madison Square Garden III was built as an entertainment venue, with boxing the prime entertainment through the 1920s. The Garden evolved out of earlier incarnations also built as venues for entertainment. Let's see how this came to be.

Skating out-of-doors in New York's Central Park had been a tradition since the park opened in 1860. The popularity of this exercise in New York, Boston, and other northeastern American cities led to the construction of covered rinks by the late 1860s. The St Nicholas Rink, which opened in 1896, followed the tradition of indoor skating rinks that had been built in both Europe and North America by this date. These rinks featured an ice surface of small dimensions enclosed by low boards and with minimal seating or standing room at ice level. Balconies along the two long sides of the rink, often lit by large, round-arched windows, contained additional seating space. A raised bandstand was generally situated on one of the building's short ends. The two other contemporary New York area rinks with artificial ice followed this mould; New York's Ice Palace Rink (at Lexington and 107th Street), which opened in 1894; and Brooklyn's Clermont Avenue Rink, home to the Crescent Athletic Club and Skating Club of Brooklyn, which opened in 1896. Hockey-like games had been played in the American northeast before the twentieth century, and amateur hockey leagues were organized after that date, but no rinks specific to the game were constructed in the United States, save those built in northern Michigan for the IHL.

Although Madison Square Garden III (1925) was designed to accommodate hockey from its earliest planning stages, the building had been constructed for and was defined by other events, notably boxing and the circus. And this was in keeping with the architectural heritage out of which it arose. The ancestors of Madison Square Garden III were not arenas for skating or hockey. Its predecessors were the circus and entertainment buildings that previously bore its name.[27] When construction plans for Madison Square Garden II were announced in 1887, *Harper's Weekly* commented that "Madison Square Garden, owing to its happy location and what may be termed the 'good will' of the spot, arising from the habit of citizens to go there for amusements of various kinds, has been marked these many years as the place for some building of public entertainment," and it noted that the new building would constitute "a sort of central palace of pleasure."[28]

The first Madison Square Garden began life as Barnum's Master Classical and Geological Hippodrome when it opened for business in the spring of 1874. The site was the former Union Railroad Station and depot, originally constructed in 1857. Images of the building before and after its repurposing make clear that Barnum simply reused entire sections of the railway station for his new building, including the long low walls and corner towers, covering the open central space with a vast canvas big top. In addition to equestrian entertainments and religious revival meetings,

5.4
St Nicholas Rink, New York, 1896. As at Montreal's Victoria Skating Rink (Image 1.2), spectators stood at rink's edge. The St Nicholas Rink provided additional space for viewing from an upper-balcony level.

5.5 *Above*
Madison Square Garden 1, 1874.
The big-top tent covered the
open volume formed by the
four walls of the pre-existing
surrounding structure.

5.6 *Left*
P.T. Barnum's Grand Roman
Hippodrome, Madison Square
Garden 1, 1874. Chariot races
with lady drivers.

the Hippodrome hosted performances by Barnum's circus. Patrick Gilmore took over the site in 1876 and ran it as a concert ground under the name Gilmore's Garden, in which guise it hosted the American debut of French composer and conductor Jacques Offenbach. In 1879 a vast skating rink was installed in Gilmore's Garden; at 18,000 square feet it was the largest artificial-ice rink yet formed.[29] With Gilmore's financial failure, following Barnum's, William Vanderbilt took over the building in May 1879 and renamed it Madison Square Garden.

The authors of *New York 1880 Architecture and Urbanism in the Gilded Age* discuss this first Madison Square Garden as a "pleasure garden," "another building type designed to contain public entertainments … [but which] tended to have interiors that were more spatially flexible than those other kinds of theatres and halls and … aimed at less highbrow attractions and events."[30] Another such building, George B. Post's Metropolitan Concert Hall (1880), even featured a retractable roof for open-air summer concerts or theatre.[31] Surprisingly, then, these buildings, and the subsequent Madison Square Garden II of 1889, share with the circular skating rinks discussed earlier a common ancestry in the eighteenth-century summer pleasure gardens of Great Britain such as Vauxhall and Ranelagh.

McKim, Mead and White's Madison Square Garden II of 1889–91 grew out of an 1880 proposal by Barnum for "a new mixed-use facility, a veritable coliseum that would transcend the constraints of conventional building types, including pleasure gardens, containing within a single structure large and small concert rooms, an opera house … an arena for horse shows, a winter garden, an aquarium, a skating rink, stores, offices, and a 250-foot-tall observatory."[32]

Stanford White's design approached this ideal; its main amphitheatre with seating for 8,000 accommodated large events, a 1,250-seat theatre and 1,500-seat concert hall catered to smaller gatherings, and restaurants and a roof garden atop the building's massive tower encouraged people to stay. There was no ice rink. Over the next twenty years it became established as one of New York's architectural landmarks, even though financially it fared no better than its predecessor, in part owing to the horrendous debt incurred from the original three-million-dollar cost of its construction. As early as 1900, the New York Life Insurance Company, which owned the land on which it stood, considered selling the building to the government for use as a post office, prompting the *New York Times* to urge "the rich men of New York to retain for public uses the place which has so admirably served those uses ever since it was built."[33] This would not be the last threat to the building. In 1911 the New York Central Railroad proposed a $2,500,000 building intended to supplant Madison Garden. Designed by their house architects, Reed and Stem, the building featured an arena measuring 130 × 13 feet, which would have made it unusable for hockey in any event.[34] Still seeking new ways to remain financially viable in 1915, ownership planned to transform Madison Square Garden into an ice rink, as had been attempted earlier at Gilmore's Garden. The unrealized plans called for three rinks decorated after arctic themes, one for exhibition skating and ice ballet, another for hockey, curling and other ice sports, and the final for public skating.[35]

Madison Square Garden II finally began to show a profit after the arrival of Tex Rickard, who in 1920 secured the rights to promote boxing matches there.[36] In five months Rickard promoted one hundred fights, earning one million dollars for the Garden with a total attendance of 275,000.[37] The next year he installed a white-tiled pool for public swimming. It was 250 × 110 feet large, held one and a half million gallons of water, and featured a cascading waterfall.[38] Early in 1923 Rickard

5.7
Madison Square Garden II, New York, 1889–91. This exotic pile
is the forebear of today's corporate-entertainment complexes.

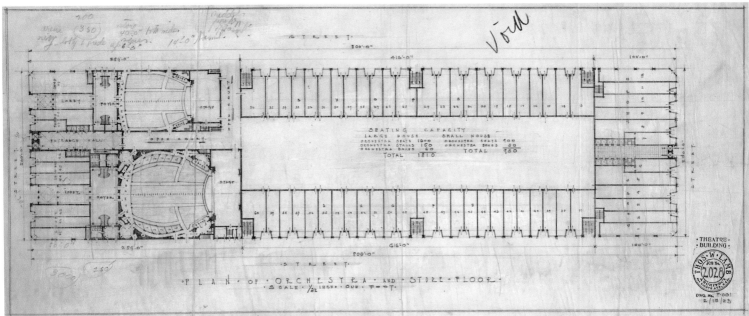

5.8 *Top*
Unexecuted proposal for "The New Garden," Madison Square Garden III, New York. This proposal anticipates today's sports-anchored-developments (SADs). Office towers, theatres, and shops augment the arena.

5.9 *Bottom*
Unexecuted proposal for Madison Square Garden III, New York, 1923. Two theatres seating 1,810 and 950, each with its own lobby and foyer, and 60 individual shops at ground level.

was already planning his own replacement for Madison Square Garden II. He wanted a larger amphitheatre and he wanted it located closer to the entertainment centre of Manhattan, which had moved uptown since the 1890s.

In February 1923 cinema architect Thomas Lamb was at work on a project called "Theatre Building," labelled as job # 2028 on the plans at Avery Library, which holds Lamb's complete archive. (On drawings dated May and June 1923 the project is called "Arena and Office Building.")[39] No site is indicated on these drawings, which are interspersed among those for Madison Square Garden III, job # 2248. But on 28 June 1924 the *New York Times* announced that Rickard, with John Ringling and other associates, planned to purchase a lot owned by the New York Railway Company for the erection of "the largest indoor arena in the world."[40] The lot was situated between 6th and 7th avenues from 50th to 51st streets, and its dimensions – 200 × 800 feet – are consistent with those of Lamb's drawings, which also answer their description in the *New York Times*.

The few surviving plans for this unexecuted design reveal a grandiose project comprising twin, twenty-six-storey office towers flanking five-storey sections that house theatres and the central seven-storey arena, with seating for 26,515 according to the *New York Times*. The entire block is girdled with shops at ground level. The project was valued at $11,500,000, with $5 million for the land alone. The program repeats that employed at Madison Square Garden II, with a main auditorium and a pair of smaller theatres.[41]

Rickard's purchase of the plot at 7th Avenue and 50th Street was delayed by disagreement among the bond and stockholders of the New York Railway Company. It was shortly after this that Duggan approached Rickard about introducing hockey at Madison Square Garden II. Though Rickard knew that he would be leaving the old Garden, he reasoned that introducing the sport there might "lay the groundwork for stimulating interest in hockey."[42] But there was one major problem. Madison Square Garden II lacked an artificial-ice plant. According to Duggan's correspondence, Rickard expected Duggan to arrange and pay for the installation of ice-making equipment at Madison Square Garden II, in addition to stocking and managing a team that could play there. To this end, Duggan commissioned drawings from Funk and Wilcox, and the correspondence and surviving blueprints show that by 27 May 1924 preliminary plans had been completed.[43] To keep costs down, since the equipment might only be used for one year, George Funk wrote to Duggan that he was pricing "second hand ice machines, condensers, brine coolers."[44]

But before these plans could be implemented, another emergency erupted. In April 1924 executives of the New York Life Insurance Company, owner of Madison Square Garden II (they had purchased it at auction for $2 million in 1916), announced their intention of razing the building and constructing a skyscraper for their offices, to be designed by Cass Gilbert. Anticipating that he would soon be out of a home, Rickard could no longer afford to wait for the New York Railway Company to resolve its minority stakeholders' issues and authorize sale of the property at 7th Avenue and 50th Street.[45] He moved swiftly. On 17 June 1924 Rickard announced the purchase of a new plot of land, between 7th and 8th avenues from 49th to 50th streets, on which he would erect "the largest building in the world devoted exclusively to amusements."[46]

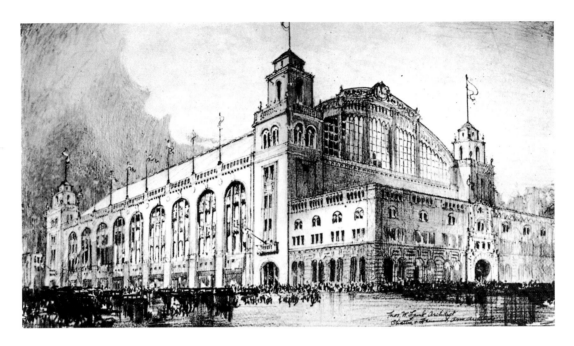

5.10
Unexecuted proposal for Madison Square Garden III, New York, perspective.
Compare this to what was built (next three images), described by one contemporary
critic as "nothing more or less than a specialized industrial building."

Thomas Lamb's drawings for this building, dated July 1924, reveal a scaled-back program – no office buildings, no smaller theatres – just the main arena, measuring 400 × 200 feet with a 76,000-square-foot Exposition Hall in the basement. In a perspective drawing for this scheme, published in the *New York Times* on 10 January 1925, after site demolition had already begun and reproduced in a share offering, Thomas Lamb presented a grandiose vision of the theatre.[47] It was a vast structure, entered through a lower, three-storey entrance block, that resembles the massive New York City train terminals erected earlier in the century, such as Pennsylvania Station and Grand Central Terminal. With its arcaded facades framing three-storey windows along 49th and 50th streets, corners defined by Campanile-like towers, and the great interior space suggested by the overarching roof and a large semi-circular window facing 8th Avenue, this would have been a stately if not exactly cutting-edge design in 1925. But as executed Madison Square Garden III was far less grand.

It was only in June 1925 that Rickard acquired the adjoining 200 × 125-foot lot fronting 8th Avenue. This was not developed as part of the arena project (as Lamb had imagined in the perspective). In a construction photograph taken on 10 December 1925, just prior to the inaugural hockey match, the facade opposite 8th Avenue was no more than a blunt brick wall with an unobtrusive entrance. But because Rickard had negotiated an easement, Madison Square Garden III eventually gained the desired entrance on 8th Avenue. The bland, four-storey block of offices and shops that was soon built on the 8th Avenue frontage featured a canopied entrance to Madison

Square Garden. Upon entering, visitors followed an ascending corridor running one hundred and twenty-five feet through the centre of the block to the main auditorium. In fact, this was a standard strategy employed by cinema architects and their clients, one that Lamb would have been well aware of. It allowed the theatre to gain a front door on a more expensive main street while the actual theatre was situated on cheaper side-street space.[48]

5.11
Madison Square Garden III, New York, 8th Avenue entrance before construction of shops, as it looked five days before opening on 10 December 1925. Note the illuminated signs at upper left and right promoting boxing.

5.12 *Above*
Madison Square Garden III, New York, view along 50th Street, 1925.
"[The new Garden] might well be an enormous storage warehouse or garage."

5.13 *Opposite*
Madison Square Garden III, New York, 1925.

In the perspective, four-storey-tall arcaded openings animate the facades along 49th and 50th streets, lending them lightness while bringing daylight to the interior. As executed, the arcaded openings are only suggested by a raised pattern on the brick surface. Most of the windows have been eliminated, as has the great semi-circular window opposite 8th Avenue, and the arching roof has been flattened and is no longer visible. In any event, the street facades would never be as visible from within the narrow street grid of Manhattan as Lamb shows them in his drawing. The fame and misfortune of Madison Square Garden ɪɪ influenced its successor in two important ways. The widespread association of the name Madison Square Garden with spectacular entertainment led Tex Rickard to retain this name for the new building, even though its location, at 50th Street and 8th Avenue, was nowhere near Madison Square. And could it have been the financial difficulties experienced by the earlier building that led to a more restricted program and a simpler structure with far less ornament?

Attempting to put a positive spin on the utilitarian, box-like results, one promotional article praised the building's engineering qualities (honest, no-nonsense) in contradistinction to its obviously lacking artistic merits, claiming that "the New Madison Square Garden tho severely simple in interior decoration, impresses one immediately by the vast practicality of its conception and the brilliant technical perfection of its design. Supplanting the ornate falsity of decorative

144.:— NEW MADISON SQUARE GARDEN. NEW YORK CITY.

40783

plaster-work and colouring the New Madison Square Garden presents the beauty of faultless technical proportion and the undisguised presence of steel and ceramics – imperishable, sturdy, and appropriate."[49]

A contemporary critic was less gracious. His prescient comments laid bare the underlying economics of sports architecture, revealing factors that have influenced its design to the present day. "From a glance at its barren exterior, [the new Garden] might well be an enormous storage warehouse or garage. Not a cent has been spent upon decorating the exterior beyond the necessary electric light signs to tell one that here is a place of entertainment, for nowadays the amusement of the public has become an industry and the new Garden is nothing more or less than a specialized industrial building."[50]

Thomas Lamb's architecture has received scant critical or scholarly attention, but even the author of a master's thesis devoted to Lamb's New York theatres could muster no love for Madison Square Garden III, describing the building as "a large rectangular block in an Italianate mode, an uninteresting academic interpretation with clumsy detailing."[51] When, in 1961, plans were announced for the replacement of Madison Square Garden III by a new incarnation, proposed for the site of Pennsylvania Station, there was dismay and outrage at the anticipated loss of McKim, Mead and White's great architectural landmark. No one lost sleep over the loss of Thomas Lamb's building.

But what of the plan to install artificial ice at Madison Square Garden II? By late July 1924, Tex Rickard was still keen to move ahead but Thomas Duggan was having second thoughts. To be sure, Duggan's expenses in installing the system would be repaid should the new Garden open as expected,[52] and the building's greater seating capacity would yield significant profits. But what if it didn't open on schedule? To protect himself, Duggan asked Rickard to post a $200,000 bond against losses Duggan might incur if the new building was not completed in time for hockey the following year (1925–26).[53] Rickard refused and both sides determined that it would be wiser to wait and see. So an ice plant was never installed, and professional hockey was never played, at McKim, Mead and White's Madison Square Garden II.

This episode might appear to be no more than a footnote to the history of Madison Square Garden II except that it speaks to the core of our subject. Late in October 1925, only six weeks before the inaugural hockey match at Madison Square Garden III, Funk and Wilcox wrote to Tex Rickard concerning the need for time clocks. In addition to providing details about their number, placement, dimensions, and other physical characteristics, the writers stated: "We do not see why the Owners of the building should pay for the clock installation for the hockey games. We think it just as much a part of the hockey equipment as the hockeys [hockey sticks] that the players use as a part of the hockey equipment, and that the cost of installing these clocks should be paid for by the hockey company."[54] On first glance, this seems a minor point: the clocks only cost nine hundred dollars. But when viewed alongside the fact that Thomas Duggan was asked to cover the cost of installing artificial-ice-making equipment at Madison Square Garden II, it reveals anew the difference between entertainment centres, like Madison Square Garden, and hockey arenas, like the Montreal Forum or Maple Leaf Gardens. Ownership of the latter would have understood implicitly that such "equipment" was integral to the building, essential for it to carry out its primary function. Thomas Duggan made this point three years later when he advised an entrepreneur who was considering investing in an NHL franchise in Cleveland. In describing "the costs and revenues that can be obtained from a sports arena coupled with a professional hockey team," Duggan enumerated the desirable features of an arena, beginning with seating capacity ("not less than 12,000"), plot size ("250 × 370 to 400 feet"), and an artificial-ice plant capable of making an ice surface in four to six hours. He then listed additional equipment: dashers, clocks, goals, bells and indicators, electric lights, plumbing, heating, and refrigeration, ventilation, telephones, and loud speakers.[55]

In spite of its dowdy design, Madison Square Garden III was hugely successful as a stage for sporting, entertainment, and political events; it was there that Marilyn Monroe purred "Happy Birthday" to John F. Kennedy. But the range of rooms it provided for the staging of spectacle was considerably diminished by comparison with the palace of pleasure, Stanford White's Madison Square Garden II. New Yorkers would have to wait until Madison Square Garden IV was completed in 1968 for a building complex that approached the programmatic versatility and sense of occasion that characterized its nineteenth-century forebear. Madison Square Garden IV will return to the genetic roots of New York buildings for spectacular entertainment, in the circus big tops and hippodromes of Barnum and Gilmore.

In this chapter the dialogue between sport and architecture was of paramount importance. Without adequate physical plant – arenas equipped with artificial ice and capable of seating enough fans to turn a profit – professional hockey could not have succeeded in the United States. But in this chapter we also reached a fork in our story's path; one road led to the continued construction of arenas whose primary role and identification was hockey while the other road, the one we are on today, led to entertainment centres whose primary role and identification was spectacle. Just as a heritage of masked balls and skating music, common to early skating culture, influenced the design and use of the earliest hockey arenas, so too have ancestral circus buildings and pleasure palaces shaped the program and image of today's corporate entertainment complexes, the preferred venues of cities that construct facilities where professional hockey is played and consumed.

Part III.1
The (Great Western) Forum, Los Angeles, 1967. The Roman Forum gets the Hollywood treatment.

Part Three

The Spanning of Space versus the Spectacle of Place: Urban and Suburban Post-War Arenas, 1960–1983

Between 1938, when the Montreal Maroons folded, and 1967, when the NHL expanded to twelve teams, the league consisted of only six teams – in Boston, Chicago, Detroit, Montreal, New York, and Toronto which continued to play in arenas that had been erected during the 1920s and 1930s. While these buildings were periodically updated, including the addition of seating, escalators, and other amenities for the comfort of fans, their building envelopes remained virtually untouched. The six owners who controlled the league saw no reason to change the status quo, which was extremely lucrative; their teams played in buildings that were paid for and frequently sold out, and with no competition,

labour costs could be maintained at remarkably low levels.[1]

The worldwide economic depression followed by the Second World War acted as a brake on new construction across North America through the 1930s and 1940s. Pressure to reduce construction costs through this period resulted in new arena designs that were at best efficient and streamlined (Memorial Auditorium, Buffalo – 1940; Le Colisée, Quebec – 1949) and at worst severe and barren (Calgary Corral – 1950; Maurice Richard Arena, Montreal – 1961).

In 1948, as Calgary was preparing to replace the Victoria Park Arena (1911), architect John M. Stevenson was touring existing

Part III.2
Arena at Owen Sound, Ontario.
What you could get for $80,000
in 1938. Described as the "cheapest
possible job."

hockey arenas in eastern Canada and the United States. His report, submitted to C. Yule, manager of the Calgary Exhibition Board and Stampede, on 9 September 1948, provides a snapshot of arena construction during the 1930s and 1940s.[2] Stevenson visited about a dozen arenas that can be classed as small, medium, and large, based on their seating capacities and the populations of the communities they served. The arenas at Owen Sound (1938), Collingwood (under construction), Barrie (1938), St Catharines (1938), and Welland (1947), all in Ontario, provided seating for between 1,500 and 3,000 spectators. Stevenson characterized these arenas, constructed primarily of steel and timber, as cheap and crude. They were built for $90,000 to $240,000. Lighting was poor, heating non-existent, and mechanical ventilation lacking. One senses that Stevenson described these structures only in order to convince his clients of what they did not want. He visited mid-size buildings, with seating for 5,500 to 7,200, in Hershey (1936), Toledo (1947), and Minneapolis (1924), built for $600,000 to $1 million. The arenas at Hershey and Toledo were more pleasing to

Stevenson and offered themselves as more appropriate models for his client. The Hershey arena had special suspended lighting and pipes under the seats that delivered heat. Sound equipment and a cork-covered ceiling made this the only arena with good acoustics, a subject to which I will return in the next chapter. Stevenson considered Hershey to be "a very fine building" but he suggested that it might cost "several millions to duplicate." His Calgary clients hoped to spend $750,000. The largest-capacity buildings that Stevenson visited were in Buffalo and Toronto. Memorial Auditorium (1938) and Maple Leaf Gardens (1931) provided seating for 9,800 and 13,100 and cost $6 million and $1.5 million respectively. Yet even these buildings, at the "high" end of the scale, could be surprisingly deficient; Maple Leaf Gardens had no heating and simple finishes throughout, while there was no acoustic treatment at Memorial Auditorium and the acoustics were consequently bad. Stevenson's survey indicates that hockey spectating was still not up to the standards of theatre- and concert-goers at this date. Materials were generally cheap or merely adequate and architectural finish or ornament was rare. The experience for players was no better. Stevenson reported that, among the architects and arena managers he talked to, "no one felt that hockey players' rooms should be at ice level. The attitude was, if they can't walk up a few steps they shouldn't be players."[3]

Before 1960 new cities got major league sports franchises only when an existing team relocated, but between 1967 and 1983 the NHL expanded to twenty-one teams and fifteen new arenas were constructed.[4] The three other major league sports also expanded at this time, adding twenty-two new teams. From 1960 to 1985 forty-two new buildings were constructed for the National Basketball Association (NBA), the National Football League (NFL), and Major League Baseball (MLB).[5] This was also a period of growth and construction of new universities across North America, as the baby boom generation reached college age, and many new arenas and stadium buildings were constructed on college campuses.[6] The design of all these new sports facilities benefited from post-war advances in architectural design and engineering, the wide availability of reinforced concrete, steel, and glass, and the example of buildings constructed for Olympic games. All of these factors led to improved means for spanning large surfaces and providing unobstructed views. Architectural firms specializing in sports architecture emerged.

Political pressures stemming from the threat of anti-trust legislation and competition from rival leagues were among the negative forces that stimulated this sudden expansion of professional sports franchises across North America. Positive factors, such as anticipated profits from franchise fees and higher media rates for owners of established

teams, also played a role.[7] By 1968, NHL teams had spent over $130 million on the construction of new hockey buildings at New York, Philadelphia, Bloomington, Atlanta, Vancouver, Los Angeles, and Oakland, and on the renovation of existing ones at Montreal, Boston, Detroit, and St Louis.[8] The new and renovated buildings were remarkable for their architectural designs, their means of financing, and their geographical locations and siting in relation to their population bases.

In 1967 the NHL was still a regional league, with all six franchises located in the northeast and north-central quadrant of North America. Improved and cheaper air transportation now made a transcontinental league possible.[9] In considering potential expansion sites, NHL governors hoped to locate new franchises in geographically dispersed major population bases. Of the twenty largest US cities, nine were then located in the Sunbelt. According to Steven Riess, the main reason for adding teams in cities like Atlanta, Los Angeles, and San Francisco, which had no tradition of winter sports, was to take advantage of their valuable television markets. The NHL believed that, with teams located in major cities spread across the country, the league would present a more attractive package to national television networks.[10] The NHL reasserted its monopoly status after the creation of the rival World Hockey Association (WHA), in 1972, through further expansion and an eventual merger with the WHA.

Sports architecture of the late 1960s and early 1970s is most often remembered, and critiqued, for the introduction of dual-facility (baseball/football) stadiums, the so-called "cookie cutter" or "doughnut" structures that were often situated on remote suburban tracts of land surrounded by acres of asphalt.

But this reality has overshadowed the defining moment in the development of the hockey arena, when it momentarily emerged as an identifiable building type. Two competing visions of the arena reached maturity in this period. One saw the brief realization of a fully expressed, even heroic, arena while the other provided the model for the corporate-entertainment complexes that would reign in the 1990s. The opposition of these two conceptions pits the spanning of space against the spectacle of place.

In the 1960s Skidmore, Owings and Merrill (SOM) at Portland and Oakland, Charles Luckman Associates at Los Angeles, and Ken Sedleigh at Montreal (redesign of the Forum)

designed arenas that matched the expressive qualities of classic American baseball parks. SOM's buildings married a Modernist engineering sensibility with a perfection of form and proportion to produce sparkling monuments. At the Oakland-Alameda County Coliseum Arena and Portland Coliseum, SOM's architects revealed the seating bowl, enclosing it within transparent glass envelopes, distinctly separate enclosing walls and roofs. For the first time the seating bowl, and the unseen but implied playing surface that it surrounds, was visible from without. At Portland, passing pedestrians could see the bleachers, while spectators in the upper rows not only enjoyed unobstructed views of the

Part III.3
Portland Memorial Coliseum, 1960. "A great cube of light." Structure in the service of function.

playing surface but also 360-degree views of the surrounding cityscape, across the Willamette River. Expressing the building's function, making it visible to passers-by, and connecting spectators to the surrounding city are qualities that unite these arenas with classic American ballparks.

At Los Angeles and Montreal the architects boldly and triumphantly expressed their buildings' functions as centres of sport/entertainment on the exteriors. For Jack Kent Cooke's expansion team, the Los Angeles Kings, Charles Luckman Associates created a sense of occasion by marrying the Roman Forum with the refined elegance of Wallace K. Harrison's Metropolitan Opera House (1966) and the pizzazz of rat-pack era Hollywood. At the Los Angeles Forum (1967), an arcaded screen composed of eighty pre-cast concrete columns girdles the exterior of the building. Each tapering column is sixty feet in height and weighs fifty-seven tons. The columns end at the gently scalloped roofline where they support the compression ring from which the cable roof is suspended. This diaphanous curtain conveys monumentality and transparency, grandeur and accessibility. Visible just behind it, the arena's slightly protruding shell rises and curves, suggesting the profile of the grandstand within and thus announcing the building's function.

At Montreal, the redesigned Forum was nowhere near as compelling but the massive, muscular vertical piers at either end of the building's length did express the effort required to support the roof that now spans the breadth of the interior space. This new structure enabled the removal of interior columns that had previously blocked patrons' views; spectators now enjoyed unobstructed views

of the playing surface (see Image 4.21 above). On the Forum's principal facade, along Sainte Catherine Street, the architects introduced a three-story section of glazing that opened the inside of the building to view. Here the new Forum achieved its moment of transcendence. Just inside the glazed entrance a series of paired escalators snaked their way from ground floor to the building's upper reaches. Illuminated panels covered the sides of these criss-crossing escalators so that at night passersby encountered the vivid spectacle of fans rising like spirits to their seats. Owing to a happy accident, the horizontal access and angled rise of each escalator resembled the blade and shaft of a hockey stick. This image of illuminated crossed hockey sticks became synonymous with hockey in Montreal for thirty years.

In buildings of this period, modern engineering is the unseen element that frees the interiors, permitting unobstructed views from any seat, whether through giant space frames (Portland Memorial Coliseum, Los Angeles Memorial Coliseum) or by deploying cable-hung structures (Oakland-Alameda County Coliseum, Madison Square Garden IV, New York, Great Western Forum, Los Angeles).

6.1
Portland Memorial Coliseum, 1960.

6

Suburban Arenas and the Spanning of Space

"A great cube of light … one of the purest and most powerful arenas
of the twentieth century."
– Allan Temko, *Architectural Forum*

The New Suburban Sportscape

As already mentioned, strategic, economic, and geographic factors helped determine the sites for
NHL expansion but demographics played the determining role in establishing where these new
buildings would be situated in relation to their host cities. In the post-war era the middle-class
abandoned the central core of US cities for the suburbs and relied increasingly on automobile
travel. Consequently, sports promoters located many new stadiums and arenas within reach of
this primary audience, where land costs were lower and ample parking space existed. Brian Nelson
has noted the effects of this shift on the "geographic landscape" of baseball stadiums and his
observations apply equally to arenas. Whereas early baseball parks became tightly enmeshed in
their cities' urban fabric and could be serviced by public transport or reached on foot, the new
suburban facilities were now "set on, not in, an exploded suburban landscape of parking lots,
expressways, commercial strips, and low-density sprawl … defined by speed, mobility, an
expansive horizontality, and a consequent dissociation from the urban matrix."[1]

Typical postcard or promotional views of sports facilities reveal this changing geographic
landscape. Photographers of earlier, urban arenas and stadiums favoured dynamic street-level
views. Pedestrians can be seen entering these buildings, having arrived on foot or by bus or
tramway. Sports facilities of the 1960s and 1970s are more likely to be depicted in bird's-eye
views that emphasize their insular detachment and their reliance on technology (the car)
and engineering (the turnpike).

The isolated siting of these facilities lent them a quality of placelessness that was often accentu-
ated by their literal dissociation from any specific place. Brian Nelson points out that Arlington
Stadium, built in 1965 in Arlington, Texas, was "first and most truly named Turnpike Stadium,
[as it] lay adjacent to the freeway connecting Dallas and Fort Worth, midway between them. Its

6.2
Aerial view of Veteran's Stadium, the Spectrum, and John F. Kennedy Stadium, Philadelphia, in 1971.

location thus reflected a reality more statistical than historical."[2] The team's name – the Texas Rangers – reflected this geographical "no place," identifying the team with an entire state rather than a specific city. Hockey produced a parallel experience – Minnesota North Stars, New Jersey Devils, Colorado Rockies, and one team even named for an entire region – the New England Whalers. Hockey's California Golden Seals played at the Oakland-Alameda County Coliseum, a facility located "at the geographic center of Northern California's most populous area" and only "a few minutes via Freeway from downtown Oakland … 3 minutes from Oakland International Airport," according to a promotional statement prepared by the facility's architects, Skidmore, Owings and Merrill.[3]

The experience of attending events at suburban facilities differed markedly from doing so at earlier, urban buildings. In exchange for the downtown hubbub of noises, smells, lights, and accidental encounters, the suburban spectator would have encountered the eerie hum of turnpike traffic and the spectral glow of receding tail lights. Not to be denied, however, sports audiences proceeded to transform these desolate parking lots into sites of lively human interaction, introducing the "tailgate party" to the cultural landscape of North America. Arriving hours before game time, caravans of spectators opened the trunks of their cars and the tailgates of their station wagons, disgorging picnic baskets and barbecues, instantly translating an otherwise barren asphalt vista into a bustling oasis of animated humanity and transforming themselves "from relatively passive spectators to relatively active participants."[4]

Cultural anthropologists Tonya Williams Bradford and John Sherry liken tailgate parties to ancient harvest festivals. They characterize them as "vestavals," in reference to Vesta, the Roman goddess of hearth and home. At the tailgate party the home is turned inside out so that it embraces and transforms public space.[5] For Bradford and Sherry, these "consumption encampments" represent "the transformative power of domesticity to remake our conception of … civility, in the postmodern era."[6]

Tailgate parties may be a sociological phenomenon representing mankind's need for community but they also express modernity and, more specifically, architectural modernity.[7] The spontaneity and pure, unnecessary joy of these ephemeral gatherings, along with their dependence on technology and mobility, make them the closest realization of the "instant" and "pop-up" cities being fantasized by contemporary architects such as Cedric Price and the British group Archigram. At the same time, they reveal a distant echo of ancient Greek society; at the tailgate party a community of free citizens communes within a parking lot (agora) and proffers barbecued meats (sacrifices) to their sports heroes (gods) at the foot of the stadium (temple).

6.3
Tailgate party – NCAA football, Florida at Miami, 7 September 2013. Cars and station wagons disgorge picnic baskets and barbecues, translating a barren asphalt vista into a bustling oasis of animated humanity.

Dual-sport superstadiums (baseball/football) erected through the 1960s were characterized by round bowls, steel and concrete construction, public financing, regional rather than municipal orientation, and siting adjacent to expressways and parking lots. Critics began to recognize these buildings as civic symbols. In an increasingly competitive market for sports franchises, they represented the necessary cost of membership in the select club of big-time cities.

Brian Nelson views the architectural blandness and indistinguishability of these stadiums as deliberate and consistent with the design of "other interchangeable, utilitarian places such as airport lounges, motels, and convention halls … They are meant to be judged as 'facilities,' pragmatically conceived containers of entertainment functions."[8]

Nelson sees a "cultural discontinuity" between earlier pre-war stadiums and their post-war successors, which have assumed "the values of a homogenized, nationwide entertainment culture," one that belongs to "the nationwide television grid," wherein these stadiums are meant to be seen "in the atomized fragments of reality that the screen presents to us."[9] Economics may explain this cultural discontinuity. As television- advertising revenues for sports broadcasts increased dramatically through the 1960s and 1970s, athletes demanded a growing share of this income, resulting in an escalation of player salaries. According to Allen Guttman, "no matter how many fans thronged to see the [Philadelphia] Phillies, no matter how many hot dogs they consumed, they alone were too few to pay Mike Schmidt's $2,130,000 [salary]. At best, ballpark spectators have become the equivalent of studio guests; at worst, they are background, mere television props."[10] While less applicable to hockey at this date, where team revenues still depended largely upon attendance, rising NHL salaries were partly behind the drive to discover ever more sources of venue income.

If arenas and stadiums adopted a corporate aesthetic in the 1960s and 1970s, might this also reflect the changing profile of franchise ownership? As professional spectator sport became a national, as opposed to regional, industry, the cost of sports franchises and of their requisite buildings rose dramatically. According to Andrew Zimbalist, "the days of family ownership of franchises are fading. As franchise prices have skyrocketed from less than $5 million in the 1950s to $10 million–$20 million in the 1970s to in excess of $100 million today [2006], there are fewer families who can afford to be sole proprietors. Instead there has been a gradual process that began with CBS's purchase of the [New York] Yankees in 1964 for $14 million toward corporate partnerships and joint-stock company ownership."[11] And Zimbalist believes that "corporate ownership is more likely to be professional and proficient; less likely to be eccentric and errant."[12] Many authors have explained the idiosyncratic shapes of early- twentieth-century baseball parks as a response to the limits set by confined urban sites. But the diversity of hockey-arena designs in the 1920s and 1930s is more likely attributable to the individualism of owners, self-made men like Conn Smythe, Charles Adams, and Tex Rickard who demanded and got buildings that reflected their personal tastes and aspirations. A natural consequence of corporatism was the banishment of irregularity and a convergence toward orthodoxy.

Along with the justifiable complaints levelled at 1960s and 1970s era sports facilities, one sometimes finds an uncritical dismissiveness of their designs that conflates architectural Modernism with consumer and corporate culture, mixed with nostalgia for a bygone age. Certainly, many dual-purpose, "doughnut-shaped" stadiums were unimaginative, repetitive, and functionally ill-considered, inadequately serving both baseball and football. But the decision to build on barren, context-less sites cannot be blamed on the architect alone, nor the fact that such sites produced stand-alone monuments by default.

Architectural Modernism could be, and was, used to celebrate and promote the technocratic tendencies of corporate America. But in the hands of skilful and sensitive architects, Modernism's reductivist geometric rigour and engineering sensibility could result in buildings of the highest order. Such qualities were especially appropriate to the design of arenas, which I have already characterized as containers for a wide variety of unspecified sport and entertainment activities. Generic criticism of architectural Modernism has prevented the merits of hockey arenas constructed during this period from being more widely recognized.

Discussing baseball's Oakland-Alameda County Coliseum in 1974, *Los Angeles Times* architecture critic John Pastier noted the professional vacuum that then existed concerning criticism of sports architecture. He bemoaned the fact that "theoreticians and scholars have given this characteristically American building form roughly 1% of the attention that they have lavished upon a handful of secluded neo-Corbusian private residences."[13] But Pastier's own criticism of the Oakland-Alameda stadium illustrates a widespread generational prejudice against 1960s Modernism, as the above-quoted passage makes clear, with its dismissive reference to "a handful of secluded neo-Corbusian private residences." Pastier's comments also highlight the changing critical fortunes of this building and of its pendant arena.

Oakland-Alameda County Coliseum: Part I, The First "Classic" Arena?

Located just outside of Oakland, adjacent to the Nimitz Freeway, and within a forty-five-minute drive of 4.2 million people, the Oakland-Alameda County Coliseum complex, designed by Skidmore, Owings and Merrill, comprises a stadium for baseball, football, and soccer, an arena for hockey, basketball, and other events, and exhibition space totalling 120,000 square feet, all set within a 120-acre site with over 8,000 parking spaces and served by Bay Area rapid transit. When the complex opened in 1966, *Architectural Record* hailed it as "strikingly handsome, bold, sophisticated" and noted that its dramatic expression derived directly from structural conditions.[14] But just eight years later, John Pastier (discussing the stadium only) complained that the very architectural purity that distinguished this building from other baseball stadiums was precisely what made it a flop. He conceded that the problems inherent in the Oakland stadium (seats too far from the field for football, poor sightlines for baseball) applied in varying degrees to all contemporary, dual-purpose circular stadiums, all of which he found inferior to their early-twentieth-century counterparts. He interpreted these failings as symptomatic of changes occurring within American society. The greater distance between players and fans and the increasing scale of stadiums paralleled for Pastier "other alienating influences in our culture," while the reductivist geometric palette employed by stadium designers struck him as "only natural in the age of McDonald's and Holiday Inn."[15]

By 1993, however, when the California Council of the American Institute of Architects (AIA) awarded it their 25-Year Award, it was again possible to appreciate the qualities remarked upon

in 1966 (economy of construction, structural clarity, and straightforward use of materials) and to identify the particularities that distinguished the Oakland-Alameda complex from its contemporaries. The jury commended it for innovations in planning, engineering, and cost efficiency, noting, for instance, its construction within a sunken landscaped earth form, which minimized its visible bulk while allowing ground-level access to the middle of the seating bowl, decreasing the distance to seats upon entering.[16] Suddenly the simplicity of its exposed structure, good proportions, consistency and devotion to an uncompromising idea, and even its quality as a monument ("a wonderful thing to drive by on the freeway") were seen as virtues, particularly "in the context of the incredibly ugly retro-neohistorical stadiums being built today."[17] (It seems you cannot praise one thing without bashing another.)

6.4 *Above*
Oakland-Alameda County Coliseum, aerial view of the entire complex. Adjacent to the Nimitz Freeway and within a forty-five-minute drive of 4.2 million people.

6.5 *Opposite*
Oakland-Alameda County Coliseum, arena, 1966.

The sculptural and technological qualities of 1960s and 1970s arenas, such as the Oakland-Alameda County Coliseum complex, were heightened by abstract architectural designs that relied on the frank expression of exposed materials and their proportional relationship in modular, gridded patterns. Located as they were on the natural "tabula rasa" of their undeveloped suburban sites, they became instant monuments. While many are still named "Arena," there are increasingly more named "Coliseum" and "Coloseum," the former referencing the circular form, expression of structure, and technological grandeur of the Roman arena, the latter suggesting the magnitude of the ancient colossus. Also contributing to the industrial qualities of these arenas was the choice and articulation of construction materials; an earlier generation of buildings had been surfaced in "soft" materials, such as brick, or sculpted terra cotta, stone, and concrete, while the newer facilities were clad in "hard" materials, like steel, glass, and pre-fabricated concrete panels.

Post-war advances in architectural technology, particularly in the spanning of long distances, and the inspirational architectural/engineering feats of Pier Luigi Nervi in the use of concrete and

6.6
Palazzetto dello Sport, built for the Rome Olympics, 1960. The dome is
completely independent of the grandstands it shelters.

of Buckminster Fuller in the design of geodesic domes had a marked impact on the designers
of these arenas. Longer spans, free of internal supports, could now be achieved with lighter,
more transparent walls, not to mention a dynamism and elegance not seen since late-nineteenth-
century experiments with iron and steel construction. Particularly noteworthy was Nervi's contributions to two facilities constructed for the 1960 Olympics in Rome. The Palazzetto dello Sport
that Nervi designed in association with the architect Annibale Vitellozzi comprised a dome of
criss-crossing ferro-concrete ribs supported by Y-shaped buttresses. The dome is completely
independent of the grandstands it shelters. Not only did the architects scoop out the earth beneath the dome, so that one entered at the mid-point of the seating bowl, thus decreasing the
distance to be mounted or descended to reach one's seats, but their design also enabled natural
light to enter the arena.

A still earlier examplar was the J.S. Dorton Arena at Raleigh, North Carolina, designed by the
Russian-born architect Matthew Nowicki in association with the office of William Henley Dietrick
and the structural engineering firm of Severud-Elsted-Krueger. When it opened in 1952 as a home
for the annual livestock-judging competition (the building was known as the Cow Palace), it was
the first building to have been designed with a saddledome roof structure. The Dorton Arena's
cable-supported roof hung from two intersecting ninety-foot parabolic concrete arches. The

cables slope down toward the spine of the building, giving the roof its distinctive saddle form. The structural solution was the means to achieving Nowicki's goal of providing every spectator with both an unobstructed view and a sense of openness. The exterior walls were entirely glazed, allowing natural light to enter the building, and the gentle rise of the bleachers was expressed as a sinewy concrete band along the exterior. Approaching fans could also detect from a distance the sawtooth form of the underside of the bleachers so that the building's function was made manifest before entering. Though not widely known, the arena achieved great notoriety in architectural

6.7 *Top*
J.S. Dorton Arena, Raleigh, NC, c. 1952. The precursor to many subsequent saddledome arenas.

6.8 *Bottom*
David S. Ingalls Rink, Yale University, Hew Haven, CT, 1961. Perhaps the most elegant hockey arena ever constructed.

and engineering circles and was the precursor to many subsequent saddledome arenas. Severud-Elsted-Krueger would subsequently apply the lessons learned at the Dorton Arena to structures such as Eero Saarinen's David S. Ingalls Rink at Yale University, New Haven, of 1958 and Madison Square Garden, New York, of 1968.[18]

Architects were eager to try out these new technological and architectural possibilities and were competitive in pushing the limits of what might be achieved. The architect/engineer Myron Goldsmith was one practitioner who devoted his career to exploring both vertical and horizontal long spans.[19] As a student of Ludwig Mies van der Rohe at Chicago's Illinois Institute of Technology in the late 1940s, Goldsmith investigated the effects of scale on tall buildings, synthesizing these studies in his master's thesis of 1953. A Fulbright scholarship enabled him to spend the next two years in Italy studying under Nervi. Working in the offices of Skidmore, Owings and Merrill upon his return to the United States, Goldsmith designed the 1958 United Air Lines Wash and Maintenance Hangar at San Francisco, the 1959–62 Solar Telescope at Kitt Peak, Arizona, and the unrealized Ruck-a-Chucky Bridge at Auburn, California, of 1978, works that demonstrated how engineering structures could achieve the purity of poetry.

Working with the architect Chuck Bassett on the Oakland-Alameda County Coliseum, Goldsmith employed a cable-suspended roof system, a technique that produced an inverted concrete dome weighing nearly two thousand tons.[20] This roof was held in tension and hung from a massive 420-foot-diameter concrete ring, supported on the perimeter by elegantly thin X-columns. As in the design of contemporary curtain-wall skyscraper construction, the glass walls of the arena were self-supporting elements, independent of the cross-braced beams that supported the roof. Similar to a Fuller dome, the walls and roof at Oakland were treated as a single unit, a shell that encompassed the free-standing bleachers, concessions, and other amenities, and protected them from the elements.

This was the goal for many architects at this date, to create massive free-standing, long-span canopies under which individual programmatic components could be disposed in whatever fashion was required, without compromise by internal vertical supports. It was an architecture of freedom, defined by space, volume, and natural light, rather than of containment, delimited by solid walls, vertical supports, and roofs. At his most utopian, Buckminster Fuller imagined an entire city protected from the elements under a glass dome. Applied to the design of arenas, this system permitted the unobstructed interiors that had eluded previous designers of sports facilities. And it allowed them to achieve this result with great verve and style. These achievements were particularly important for the development of the arena as an identifiable building type. In arenas designed on these structural principles, the grandstand was revealed to view from the outside for the first time. In this way passersby could "read" the arena's function before entering, in a way that hearkened back to classic American ballparks. If buildings for sport create "a box to contain a drama," then transparent arenas focus attention on the drama, rather than the box. The excitement experienced within them was now broadcast through their designs.

Portland Memorial Coliseum

For the Portland Memorial Coliseum, Goldsmith proposed a design that clearly reflects the influence of his Italian mentor Pier Luigi Nervi. A catenary roof of pre-cast concrete elements, resembling a giant abstract chrysanthemum according to architectural critic Allan Temko, was to have been supported around its perimeter by eighty-foot-high X-frames (producing an exterior elevation similar to that of the later Oakland-Alameda County Coliseum arena).[21] Unfortunately, Goldsmith's 1961 design was rejected by the client in the face of objections from the lumber industry, which argued in favour of a building constructed using wood in order to promote the abundant wares of the Pacific Northwest.

6.9 *Opposite*
Oakland-Alameda County Coliseum, 1966. The cable-suspended roof, an inverted concrete dome weighing nearly 2,000 tons, was held in tension and hung from a massive 420-foot-diameter concrete ring.

With the rejection of Goldsmith's proposal, a new design emerged from the Portland office of SOM, which then included William Rouzie, David Pugh, Edward Kirschbaum, and Joachim Grube. Gordon Bunshaft, one of the leading designers of this period at SOM's New York office, also contributed to the project, according to William Rouzie.[22] They produced a design at once completely different from Goldsmith's and yet intimately related to the effects it would have achieved. Where Goldsmith began with a circular plan, the new design was based on a 360-foot-square and 120-foot-high structure comprising a glazed exterior shell that enclosed circulation space and a seating bowl for up to thirteen thousand spectators.[23] The entire enclosing structure is supported on only four reinforced concrete piers, located within the corners of the glass box. The result is a massive transparent canopy that seems to float above the space it encloses.[24] In consequence, the seating bowl became a free-standing sculptural object within this space, distinctly visible from outside the building. The resulting juxtaposition of solid and transparent, curvilinear versus rectilinear, is one of the building's joys, especially at night, when, lit from within, it appeared to Allan Temko as "a great cube of light."

Bringing light into the building and establishing a connection with the outside world was one of the architects' goals. Fans seated in the upper ranges of seats can see out to the surrounding cityscape. For daytime events requiring a dark house, a 1,060-foot, flame-proofed blackout curtain could shroud the entire seating bowl.[25] According to William Rouzie: "We were thinking, we've got this oval bowl that is going to sit in a glass box. When you're in the bowl looking at something happening, you can either have light or not with the control of the curtain. The thing we hated was the mouselike approach to the seats in most stadiums, where you walk blindly through these dark corridors. To get out of [the Portland Memorial Coliseum], or at halftime,

6.10 *Opposite*
Portland Memorial Coliseum, 1960. The enclosing structure is supported on only four reinforced concrete piers.

6.11 *Above*
Portland Memorial Coliseum, 1960. Light, space, and views out to the landscape.

6.12
Portland Memorial Coliseum, 1960. An oval bowl within a glass box.

you walk out into a space and instead of being in some blind corridor, you come out and you've got glass and you can see the city. You know where you are whether it's day or night. You never feel lost there."[26] When the Portland Coliseum was threatened with demolition in 2009, discussion began on ways to remodel the building. Asked to comment on that possibility, Rouzie revealed the essence of som's design. "I worry about it, because it's very simple the way it is. Simplicity is hard to come by."[27]

Portland's wood lobby was mollified by the visible use of wood on the building's exterior. The continuous twenty-two-foot-high band that caps the building is made of plywood overlaid with acrylic-plastic and eighty-three-foot-high heavy glulam timber mullions support the curtain wall of clear grey glass. With its narrow, plinth-like base, glulam columns, and plywood entablature, the Coliseum resembles a modern Greek temple. In place of the cella or naos (the sacred inner chamber at the centre of Greek temples), this arena housed a seating bowl for mass entertainment. Perhaps it was this quasi-sacred quality that inspired Allen Ginsberg after he attended a Beatles concert there in 1965. Ginsberg composed the poem "Portland Coliseum." In it he refers to a "Leviathan auditorium" in which

> A single whistling sound of ten thousand children's
> larynxes asinging
> pierce the ears
> and following up the belly
> bliss the moment arrived

And he described how the audience

> Scream again & claphand
> become one Animal
> in the New World Auditorium
> – hands waving myriad
> snakes of thought
> screetch beyond hearing[28]

Arena Rock: How The Beatles Redefined the Arena's Program

The Beatles are important to this story. According to Laurel Sercombe, "the Beatles' appearance on *The Ed Sullivan Show* on the evening of Sunday, 9 February 1964, marked the beginning of a new era in American popular music and culture as well as a new standard for its promotion and marketing."[29] Their first US tours coincided with a period of vast social change in the West, brought about in part by a baby boom generation that was just then reaching maturity and making demands. Music became an important vehicle for self-expression, protest against the status quo, and generational solidarity. Not only did the music differ stylistically from that of previous generations, its mass appeal also required new, larger venues to accommodate its young audiences. The Beatles are often credited with introducing this new era of music concerts to the world. Sometimes referred to simply as "arena rock," the genre became associated with a loud, amplified sound and with spectacular effects such as fireworks. Its great popularity could best be served, and not always even then, by the new sports arenas that were only beginning to be built.

Over the course of their 1964 and 1965 North American tours, the Beatles played fifty-two shows at thirty-four venues with an average attendance of nearly sixteen thousand.[30] Yet, of the thirty-four venues at which they performed, only twelve had been built after the Second World War.[31] The Beatles played their first concert on 11 February 1964 at the Washington Coliseum. Built in 1941 as a home for ice hockey, basketball, and other events, it was constructed using the Zeiss-Dywidag (ZD) system that employed stiffening ribs to give load-carrying capacity to curved, thin-shelled reinforced concrete roofs, resulting in a column-free interior. The direct model was the Hershey Sports Arena (1936) but the system had been used in the United States since the early

6.13
Uline Arena (Washington Coliseum), Washington, DC, opened 1941. "A vast echoing cavern,"
according to a *New York Times* critic.

1930s, notably for the 1934 Hayden Planetarium in New York.[32] The Washington Coliseum featured a long barrel-vaulted roof over brick exterior walls, which served well the needs of sports
and other entertainments such as the Ice Capades and wrestling matches through the 1950s.

The Washington Coliseum could seat 7,000–9,000 people. Attendance for the Beatles concert
was 8,092 and in consequence the only space left for the performers was on an improvised stage
at the centre of the arena's playing surface. Photos, and especially video, of this concert make two
things clear. First, because the band was perched on the surface of the boxing ring (minus the
ropes), they were forced to reorient themselves every few numbers, even rotating the position of
the drum kit, so they could face audience members in all four quadrants of the arena.[33] And second, the band's sound was being delivered via three suitcase-sized amplifiers on the stage. This
level of amplification might have been adequate to reach the few dozens or hundreds of audience
members at the clubs and cellar venues the Beatles had performed at in London and Hamburg a
few years earlier but proved totally inadequate inside a vast arena filled with screaming fans, to say
nothing of outdoor venues like Shea Stadium where 55,600 saw, but likely never heard, the Beatles
perform on 15 August 1965. One year earlier, Democratic Senator Hubert H. Humphrey had bemoaned the lack of a proper auditorium in Washington, likening the acoustics at Washington Coliseum to "talking down a salt mine."[34] And a 1962 jazz festival held partly at Washington Coliseum
prompted a reviewer for the *New York Times* to describe that venue as "a vast echoing cavern" that
"completely drown[ed] out any possible understanding of what was being played or sung." And he
reported, "Under the circumstances there is nothing that can be said of the musicians' performances except that they were there."[35]

6.14
The Beatles performing at the
Washington Coliseum on 11 February
1964. Perched upon the surface of the
boxing ring, the Beatles reoriented
themselves every few numbers in
order to face audience members
on all four sides.

Poor sound had plagued the tours of other bands in this era, to such an extent that sound became a key issue in the selection of venues for the Rolling Stones' US tour in November 1969. (It is worth noting that the Beatles ceased touring altogether after 1966, at least in part because of frustration with poor arena acoustics. John Lennon was widely quoted as saying: "I reckon we could send out four waxwork dummies of ourselves and that would satisfy the crowds. Beatles concerts are nothing to do with music any more. They're just bloody tribal rites.") The Rolling Stones hired lighting designer Chip Monck, who had gained notoriety by handling this role at the Woodstock Festival, and the band agreed to perform only at arenas that could accommodate their more exacting standards for sound and lighting equipment. Of the fifteen venues where the Rolling Stones played twenty-two shows, only three had been built before the Second World War and more than half had not existed when the Beatles had visited North America just four years earlier.[36]

The demands of touring rock bands only increased through the 1970s, in concert with their growing popularity and economic impact. Michael Ethan points out two such instances in his dissertation *A Spatial History of Arena Rock 1964–79*. For their 1970 performance at the Los Angeles Forum, Grand Funk Railroad's crew needed two full days to set up the stage and sound equipment, as compared with the forty-five minutes it would take for a typical concert.[37] And at Anaheim, concert revenue at Angels Stadium was so lucrative, nearly $100,000 per event by the mid-1970s, that five such concerts earned the facility as much as it did from the entire eighty-one-game schedule of the California Angels.[38] During the 1960s and 1970s new and existing arenas could either keep pace or be left off the lucrative grid of touring rock bands.

The phenomenon of Beatlemania has been exhaustively studied elsewhere but one aspect, the changing relationship of audience to spectacle, is relevant here. At the Beatles' early performances in the United States, the musicians were pelted with jelly beans, an apparently friendly gesture in response to an interview in which George Harrison had expressed a fondness for "jelly babies." George Harrison recalled their first concert in Washington: "That night, we were absolutely pelted by the fuckin' things. They don't have soft jelly babies there; they have hard jelly beans. To make matters worse, we were on a circular stage, so they hit us from all sides … We don't mind them throwing streamers, but jelly beans are a bit dangerous, you see! Every now and again, one would hit a string on my guitar and plonk off a bad note as I was trying to play."[39]

But dangerous as the flying candies must have been, the adoring fans who arrived laden with jelly beans and then screamed through most of the Beatles' thirty-minute set may actually have been exhibiting the first signs of a reorientation of the relationship between audience and performer. In place of the typical unidirectional performance model, according to which audiences "receive" the performance, Laurel Sercombe describes the Beatles appearance on the *The Ed Sullivan Show* as "a set of nested performances" that included a "performance by the studio audience, whose actions and reactions to what was happening both onstage and on the television monitors

6.15
The Beatles rehearsing for the *Ed Sullivan Television Show*, New York, on 9 February 1964. "A set of nested performances."

ran parallel to the stage performance."[40] She quotes a reviewer for the *New Yorker* who attended a rehearsal for the show and noted that "the kids weren't actually looking at the Beatles themselves but at the TV pictures of the Beatles that appeared on the nine or ten monitors scattered around the studio. I noticed this because the kids also began screaming louder every time a different Beatle appeared on the TV screen." And Sercombe observes how during the live, televised show, "the television cameras frequently cut to this parallel performance, and it was the subject of much of the media coverage of the event."[41]

The audience's participation in the Beatles' performance and their impact on how the band was perceived by the wider North American television audience, estimated at some seventy-three-million viewers, was still more direct. The reviewer for the *New Yorker* noted that, during the rehearsal performance, "the ones they screamed loudest for were Ringo, the drummer, and Paul, who was doing most of the singing."[42] Laurel Sercombe compiled a detailed, minute-by-minute performance log of the Beatles' appearance on *The Ed Sullivan Show*, which reveals that "the total onstage time for the Beatles was 12 minutes, 19 seconds. (The breakdown of solo close-ups was ten for Paul McCartney, nine for Ringo Starr, five for George Harrison and five for John Lennon.)"[43] In other words, the director of the "live" television show seems to have taken his cue from the preferences of the rehearsal audience by favouring with close-ups those Beatles who had elicited the greatest studio response. As a proxy for the wider TV audience, the rehearsal audience's responses fed a feedback loop that filtered the show and shaped how the Beatles would be re-presented and received by the larger audience.

In their 2009 publication *Modes of Spectating*, Alison Oddey and Christine White ask, "What is radically different about how we spectate now?" They note, "in live spectatorship, the spectator's frame of spectating focuses on their own self in relationship to what they view." And they wonder whether "'liveness' is simply a mode of entering the live event; a means of display? The audience is watching the screens installed in the Regency Theatre, not the actors on stage; the large-scale plasma screens at the music concert, not the performers. Is this the end of the 'live' event? Life captured on screen?"[44]

By the 1990s and 2000s, sports fans would find their own ways of reorienting the experience of spectatorship, by doing the wave, by hamming it up for the Jumbotron camera and then watching their "live" performances on the hundreds of monitors hung throughout the arena, by enjoying a drink or a meal with the sports contest as backdrop, and by using personal electronic devices to individualize their experience. When facility managers and team owners argued in the 1990s for the need to provide buildings with the kinds of amenities that their fans wanted, they were in fact responding to a recalibrated relationship of spectator to spectacle that had begun in 1964 with a shower of jelly beans.[45] Yet another consequence of the Beatles North American tour for sports spectating was that a new generation of urban youth, regardless of their interest in sport, now associated their civic arenas with music.

As ambiguous grounds for mass entertainment, arenas have always been many things to many people but in the 1960s, an era of burgeoning pop culture and its attendant cult of celebrity, the lines between the worlds of sports and entertainment became increasingly blurred. The defining moment of this phenomenon may have occurred during the Beatles' 1964 US tour. After appearances on *The Ed Sullivan Show*, in New York, and live performances at the Washington Coliseum

6.16
The Beatles and Cassius Clay meet in Miami on 18 February 1964.
The confluence of sports and music.

and New York's Carnegie Hall, the Beatles left for Miami, where they appeared live and taped another show for Ed Sullivan on 16 February. Two days later, a photo opportunity was arranged at the Fifth Street Gym, where a twenty-two-year-old Cassius Clay was working out in advance of his championship heavyweight bout with Sonny Liston on 25 February. The five young performers clowned for the photographers, with Clay at one point knocking out all four Beatles, domino-style, with one punch. Clay, media savvy and prescient, having been inspired by the showmanship of wrestler Gorgeous George, quipped, "Hello, there, Beatles. We oughta do some road shows together. We'll get rich."[46] This iconic event, described by David Remnick as "a meeting of the new, two acts that would surely mark the sixties," highlights the confluence of sports and music like no other at this date.[47] Clay has been described as "a 'crossover' artist before the term found its application in youth culture and the music world; he was the "'Fifth Beatle,' a deracinated, classless, alien, antiestablishment figure of broad appeal."[48] The Beatles had more in common with Clay than beauty, youth, and brash, boastful manners; they could be considered crossover artists of another sort. One week earlier, at their inaugural US concert, they had performed at the centre of a sports arena, upon a boxing ring similar to the one on which Clay would soon perform in claiming world attention. The Beatles were agents in the crossover of arenas, from their identification as sports facilities to their employment and appreciation as venues for both sports and music, now better understood as mass spectacle.

This process of identification is now complete. As Brooklyn's new Barclays Center prepared to open on 27 September 2012, with the first of eight sold-out shows by Jay-Z, an article published in the music section of the *New York Times*, described the facility, now home to the NBA's Brooklyn Nets and the NHL's New York Islanders, as "an 18,000-seat performance space that will fundamentally transform the music scene in New York City."[49] The Barclays Center will effect this transformation by directly competing with Madison Square Garden as a venue for touring music acts. Jay-Z followed up his involvement with the Barclays Center by opening his own sports agency, an indication of the degree to which "the borders among music, film and sports [are] growing ever blurrier."[50] Before the Beatles, elite athletes, actors, and musicians performed in separate venues. Today these performers are recognized as celebrities who participate in the presentation of mass spectacle that is presented in corporate-entertainment complexes.

In the next chapter I will discuss Madison Square Garden in New York and other sport/entertainment facilities that wholeheartedly embraced their role as sites of mass spectacle.

Oakland-Alameda County Coliseum: Part II, Neutered

The continuously glazed exterior of the Oakland-Alameda County Coliseum arena, like the arena at Portland, permitted views into and out of the interior and allowed natural light to fill the public spaces and even enter the auditorium. The broad public concourse at Oakland-Alameda allowed patrons to circulate freely around the interior and to perceive the curving profile of the seating bowl. The expansiveness of the concourse distinguished this building from earlier arenas with their usually cramped and crowded public spaces.

The two SOM-designed arenas of the 1960s at Portland and Oakland achieved what no other building for hockey had managed to that date. They are classic designs, the first to unabashedly express their function, the first to define this building type. The Portland and Oakland arenas might have served as models for the future, yet even as the Oakland-Alameda Coliseum was being awarded the AIA's 25-Year Award for excellence, in 1993, plans for its renovation and expansion were already under discussion.[51] Work began in 1996 by the engineering and architecture firm HNTB. More than 4,000 seats were added as well as seventy-two luxury suites, three clubs, retail outlets, two new entrances, and many other features. These changes severely compromised the architectural integrity of the original design, within and without.

In the next section of this book I will show how sports facilities constructed in the 1990s were conceived as multi-purpose entertainment facilities, whose primary goal was the maximization of revenue streams. All that one needs to know about the attitude of ownership toward the original Oakland-Alameda County Coliseum arena can be gleaned from the fact that they chose to renovate because it saved them $75 million dollars, and more than a year of construction time, over demolishing the building and erecting a new building.[52] The driving force behind the $102-million redesign was the inclusion of seventy-two luxury suites, which sold for an average

$100,000 per year. Together with the sale of personal seat licences (psls) to 3,000 preferred club seat holders, these seating classes could increase revenues by millions of dollars. In addition to added revenue from seating, new and renovated arenas in the 1990s were crammed with a multitude of income-producing features. When completed in 1997, the renovations of the Oakland-Alameda arena had virtually gutted the original interior. A state-of-the-art video scoreboard, high-resolution video boards, new lighting, enhanced sound system, and laser-lighting effects were installed. [53]

The 4,000 extra seats were accommodated by a new and completely reconfigured seating bowl that featured a third tier of seats, achieved by lowering the playing surface four feet. As originally designed with two tiers, fans entered the building at the midpoint of the seating bowl and thus had but a short walk up or down to their seats, but with three tiers of seats it was now necessary to provide elevators. On the main concourse this precipitated the inclusion of enclosed elevator shafts, one of many new elements that now blocked the continuous flow of space and views through the interior that had been a hallmark of the original design. The reconfigured octagonal seating bowl now required vertical supports, where none had been necessary before when it was oval-shaped, and these also protruded into what had been the free-flowing space of the concourse. Finally, two new emergency exit stairs included in the redesign are accessed at concourse level through ungainly blue structures that also impinge on the purity of the former interior.

The beauty of the building's exterior had derived from the simplicity of its materials and proportions – two 420-foot-diameter pre-cast concrete rings separated by thirty-two pairs of concrete X-columns. Behind this stood the independent self-supporting glass curtain wall. In 1966 one entered the building via stairs that mounted the surrounding berm wall and brought patrons to a series of doors at the concourse level, just below the lower of the pre-cast concrete rings. Nothing interfered with the purity and transparency of the exterior, which could be appreciated from any viewpoint. The 1996–97 renovations introduced two new (so-called "grand") entrance structures at the north and south sides of the building and an eastern extension housing a sports bar, retail outlet, and administrative offices. The new entrances rise almost the full height of the building and extend across nearly one-quarter of its surface. Not only do these tacked-on entrances block views into and out of the interior, but they also introduce decorative detailing that is unsympathetic to the original building. One of the standard critiques of 1960s Modern buildings was that you could never find their entrances. The revenge of bad post-modern architects was to brand the entrances with large ungainly elements that do nothing more than call attention to them. The eastern extension begins at grade level and obscures only the lowest part of the original building's curtain wall. Its lightly curving canopy clashes with the rectilinear regularity of the original structure.

In 2006, when the arena was renamed Oracle Arena, the original exterior was further compromised by the installation of bright red signs announcing the arena's name: two of these spell it out in ten-foot-tall letters at the level of the upper concrete compression ring, while others extend across the tops of the north, south, and east entrances. The centre of the roof was also branded with an Oracle sign, roughly 250 feet in diameter.

The Oakland-Alameda County Coliseum Arena was home to the nhl's California Golden Seals, from 1967 to 1976, and to the nba's Golden State Warriors, from 1971 until the time of this

6.17
Oakland-Alameda County Coliseum arena, after renovation by HNTB, 2006.

writing.[54] The 1996 renovation of the Oakland-Alameda arena coincided with the renewal of the Golden State Warriors' lease. With that lease set to expire again, in 2017, the Warriors' new owners announced their intention, in September 2012, to move the team to San Francisco and to build a new arena there, to be designed by star Norwegian architectural firm Snøhetta.[55]

In this chapter we saw how sports facilities at Oakland and Portland responded to economic, geographic, and urbanistic factors as well as to new programmatic requirements that reflected a changed sport/entertainment landscape. These buildings emerged as the first arenas worthy of the name through their employment of an architectural Modernism composed of simple forms and advanced engineering that expressed structure and function. But their victory was short-lived. The fate of Oakland-Alameda County Coliseum mirrors the fate of the hockey arena as a building type. Although still capable of fulfilling the program for which it had been built, by 1993 that program had changed. Not only was the building obsolete, so was the entire building type, defined and identified as it had been by a single function.

Arena Rises Atop Buried Rail Terminal

ILLUSTRATION BY RAY PIOCH

A great engineering project moves New York's famed Penn Station underground—and erects new Madison Square Garden above it

A cable-suspended roof 425 feet in diameter, largest of its kind in the U.S., will dispense with supporting pillars and give spectators an unobstructed view from every seat of New York's new Madison Square Garden. Express escalators four feet wide will empty the arena of a capacity crowd in 22 minutes. Those are outstanding features of the $44 million sports center, shown in the cutaway view below, now rising on the Pennsylvania Station's 8½-acre site.

Meanwhile the earth is swallowing up the rail terminal. Being razed to the ground is a famous New York landmark, the Pennsylvania Station's Roman-columned marble building. Six street-level entrances will admit commuters and intercity travelers to a new underground station, enlarged and air-conditioned—its capacity actually increased by the $10 million transformation. Thus P.R.R. and L.I.R.R. trains will run as usual, while the Pennsylvania Railroad receives rent from the Garden for above-ground use of the handy-to-transit site.

Due for completion in the fall of 1967, the new drum-shaped Garden will provide a main arena seating 20,500 for major boxing matches, hockey and basketball games, bike racing, conventions, and circuses; and, among other facilities, a 5,000-seat "forum" suited to a tennis game or concert.

7.1
Madison Square Garden IV, cutaway perspective. A "machine that makes the land pay," architect Cass Gilbert's classic definition of a skyscraper, aptly describes Madison Square Garden IV.

7

Urban Revitalization and the Spectacle of Place

"If they had a maternity ward and a cemetery, you'd never have to leave."
– Bob Hope on the Houston Astrodome

Introduction

Architecture is a negotiation between form and function. A successful building might be described as one in which the architect conceives novel or expressive forms while accommodating a distinct set of functional requirements. In arenas constructed before the 1960s, function was satisfied but form left to languish. But the designers of 1960s arenas like the Oakland-Alameda and Portland coliseums gave expressive, even poetic form to this building type for the first time by focusing on the arena's primary function as a vast auditorium for spectator sport and through the agency of advanced engineering and design. In doing so, they established a benchmark and it seemed possible to imagine that architects were poised to produce additional examples that might further establish the hockey arena as an identifiable building type, where previously it could at best have been described as a miscellaneous collection of large, roofed buildings.

Madison Square Garden IV: The First "Center"

But the construction of Madison Square Garden IV in 1968 presented an entirely different model for buildings in which hockey could be played, expressive in its own way but responding to a revised mandate that included enhanced urban and economic programmatic requirements. The expanded architectural program for such buildings required them to be "more than" arenas and stadiums. They were now expected to be economic engines to revitalize their neighbourhoods; anchors for ancillary development; enhanced sources of owner profit; oversize studios for the production of television broadcasting; and producers of big-business entertainment spectacle. Madison Square Garden IV established a model that would be followed, beginning in the late 1980s, by designers of the next generation of buildings in which professional hockey would be played.

In the design of these buildings, vast scale replaced form as the most appropriate expression of their updated functional program.

In Part Four of the book I will look at this next generation of hockey buildings. So fundamentally different are they from the rinks, arenas, and forums in which hockey was formerly played that they represent a distinct and separate building type, one that I have called the corporate-entertainment complex. The evolution toward this next generation of hockey building also led to the devolution of the professional hockey arena. Madison Square Garden IV stands as a vital link in the eventual disappearance of the hockey arena.

Madison Square Garden IV, or MSG Center as it came to be known, is the first "center." What does this designation imply? First, it tells us what the building is not. It is no longer just an arena or coliseum, that is to say, a building defined programmatically by a single function and physically by a large central auditorium. American Seating, the company that supplied Madison Square Garden IV, addressed this characteristic in a 1968 advertisement. The ad copy notes a perceived movement away from sports arenas and toward what it calls family-centred entertainment facilities: "Many architects anticipate a nationwide trend in communities of every size – a trend away from limited-use arenas and auditoriums, toward the more versatile family 'center' in which many different events can be held simultaneously, as in the new Madison Square Garden Center."[1]

Second, the name "center" informs us that this is more than a building; it is intended as a geographical place, an urban focal point akin to civic and shopping centres. Like the latter, which also came to prominence during the 1960s, Madison Square Garden IV and its followers were meant to be worlds unto themselves. Referring to this all-inclusive quality at the Houston Astrodome, another of the sports centres that would redefine post-1960s sports architecture, and about which there will be more to say, comedian Bob Hope reportedly quipped at that stadium's opening in 1964: "If they had a maternity ward and a cemetery, you'd never have to leave."[2] And third, the word "center" tells us that this is a place in its own right. No longer just an unspecified background, "a box to contain a drama," Madison Square Garden IV thrusts itself forward as an active participant, a new ingredient that shapes and expands the spectator's experience beyond mere attendance at an event. Together these three new characteristics will define all subsequent sports facilities.

Madison Square Garden IV was also held out as an example of how large urban developments could trigger new construction and economic activity in the surrounding area. And it could even be pointed to as an agent of wholesale urban revitalization, a tabula rasa development where an existing site is razed, often as part of a slum-clearance initiative, to be replaced by an entirely new complex that is dropped onto the site. Typically set upon a podium or platform that sets the new complex apart from the rest of the city, the individual building components of such developments often turn their backs on the surrounding city; they are dislocated from the city's street grid and look inward upon self-contained landscapes.

In 1948, well before the current Madison Square Garden IV broke ground, plans had been developed for a new Garden intended for a site on Columbus Circle between 58th and 60th streets. Initiated by John Reed Kilpatrick, then president of Madison Square Garden Corporation, the project was supported by Governor Thomas E. Dewey who signed a financing bill authorizing $25 million in municipal bonds toward its construction.[3] The massive project called for two attached

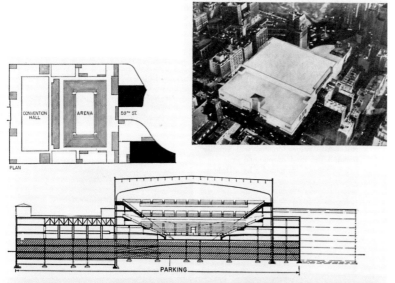

7.2 *Left*
Unexecuted proposal for Madison Square Garden,
Arena and Convention Center, plan, aerial perspective,
longitudinal section, and perspective, 1948.

7.3 *Below*
New York Coliseum, 1950s.

buildings, a 25,000-seat auditorium and the world's largest convention hall. The architects for this unrealized project were Lionel and Leon Levy and the monstrosity that would have resulted may be gauged from what they succeeded in building on the site eight years later, after Robert Moses condemned the west side of Columbus Circle.[4] The scale of the New York Coliseum and its brutal effectiveness in transforming a formerly derelict neighbourhood epitomizes the urban-planning goals and strategies of municipalities across North America in this period. The architects themselves were under no illusions concerning the artistic merit of their own design for the New York Coliseum, explaining that "it is a solution to the operating problems of the business, not a design produced in an atelier."[5] The scale of the 1948 project and its conjoining of sports auditorium and convention hall anticipate MSG IV.

The genesis of Madison Square Garden IV began in 1957 with an anti-trust suit brought against the International Boxing Club (IBC) by the United States federal government. At that time the IBC enjoyed a virtual monopoly over all boxing matches, controlling the sport at several major arenas including New York's Madison Square Garden, Chicago Stadium, and the Detroit Olympia. James D. Norris and Arthur Wirtz ran the IBC. In the late 1920s Norris's father, James Norris Sr (1879–1952), had begun acquiring control of NHL teams and buildings so that, by the late 1940s and continuing through the early 1950s, he owned half of the league, a state of affairs described by James Quirk and Rodney Fort as "one of the most bizarre links between arena corporations and NHL teams."[6] Norris Sr was a clever businessman who made his fortune in grain, cattle, railways, and land acquisition before, during, and after the Depression, at which time he was one of the richest men in the United States with a net worth of over $250 million.[7] Norris, Sr purchased the Detroit Red Wings and their building, the Olympia, in 1933. By the early 1940s, he had purchased controlling shares in Madison Square Garden, which in turn owned the New York Rangers hockey team. And in 1945 he became the silent partner in the purchase of Chicago Stadium, owner of the Chicago Blackhawks hockey team.[8] According to David Cruise and Alison Griffiths, James Norris Sr "quickly came to understand something that many modern hockey owners have tumbled to only recently. While hockey teams can be immensely lucrative if run well, the key to real riches is owning the rink itself."[9]

One of the court rulings resulting from the federal government's successful anti-trust prosecution of James D. Norris and Arthur Wirtz in 1957 required that they divest themselves of all stock in Madison Square Garden within five years.[10] The need to release so much stock onto the market within so short a time must have acted to reduce its price. It was at this moment that Irving Felt, president of Graham-Paige Corporation, entered the scene. Graham-Paige began as an automobile manufacturer in 1927. When Irving Felt joined the company, sometime in the 1930s, he helped to reorganize Graham-Paige as an investment and real estate firm, soon becoming its president. Felt jumped at the chance to invest in Madison Square Garden and by January 1959 had gained a controlling interest. In 1962 Graham-Paige changed its name to Madison Square Garden Corporation.

In 1959 Madison Square Garden III was thirty-five years old and Felt understood that its investment value was declining and its days were numbered. He was not in the business of hockey or hockey arenas. As an investment and real estate expert, Felt recognized that his job was to maximize the potential profit to be gained from the relocation of Madison Square Garden. In 1960 he reached out to architect Charles Luckman, asking his firm to produce a "dream scheme" for a new Madison Square Garden that could be used to fuel interest in the project and to elicit offers of potential sites.

Charles Luckman, the "Boy Wonder of American Business" (he appeared on the 10 June 1946 cover of *Time* magazine in recognition of his accomplishments as president of Pepsodent and Lever Brothers), returned to architecture in 1950, forming a partnership with his fellow University of Illinois architecture student William Pereira. Together, Pereira and Luckman collaborated on high-profile projects such as CBS Television City in Hollywood (1952), the Hilton Hotel in Berlin (1955–59), the Disneyland Hotel (1955), and the "Theme Building" at Los Angeles International Airport (1959–61). In 1958 they split to form separate agencies. Pereira and Luckman also produced an unexecuted 1956 plan for Lincoln Center, another of the mammoth urban-development/slum-clearance projects that reshaped New York City through the 1960s.[11]

Luckman's genius was as a businessman, a first-rate problem solver and motivator of men, someone who could be counted on to get the job done on time and on budget. These abilities brought him to the attention of at least two United States presidents. In 1947 Harry S. Truman appointed Luckman chair of the "Citizens' Food Committee" that was charged with conserving one hundred million bushels of American grain supplies and using them to prevent the starvation of post-war Europe's population. Luckman had three months to complete the task.[12] And in 1961 Luckman's firm was selected for the master planning and design of the Manned Spacecraft Center (now the Johnson Space Center) in Houston, the first step toward John F. Kennedy's goal of putting a man on the moon. Charles Luckman Associates had forty-eight days in which to design forty-nine buildings.[13] The skills that he brought to the successful management of these Herculean labours would serve him well in negotiating the complex task of raising a massive building, 425 feet in diameter and 153 feet high, over the top of an active train station in the centre of Manhattan without interrupting the ongoing commuter rail traffic of the Pennsylvania Railroad and Long Island Rail Road, which together carried two hundred thousand passengers daily.

On 4 November 1960 the *New York Times* featured a front-page article illustrated with an annotated perspective view of Charles Luckman Associates' proposed Madison Square Garden, a 25,000-seat "modernistic sports center" to cost an anticipated $38 million and expected to open in time for the New York World's Fair in 1964.[14] At the press conference announcing the plans, Irving Felt proclaimed that the new Madison Square Garden would combine with Lincoln Center and the Flushing Meadows World's Fair site to establish "a great triumvirate for the World's Fair of 1964."[15] The *New York Times* article noted that the new Garden would be "far more splendorous than the present Garden." It would encompass "the major arena, two smaller arenas, a theatre and auditorium, two restaurants, an indoor swimming pool and two outdoor pools, an outdoor skating rink, bowling alleys and indoor parking space for 3,000 cars."[16]

Charles Luckman Associates' initial scheme for Madison Square Garden covered three city blocks. The saddledomed arena perched atop a one-storey podium stretched across two blocks, while pedestrian and automobile traffic continued uninterrupted at street level. This two-block unit connected to a third block, containing a 2,500-seat theatre, smaller arenas with 1,000 and 2,000 seats, and restaurants housed in individual circular pavilions, via a promenade that encircled and interconnected the entire site while providing open landscaped spaces. It was a dynamic

7.4
Unexecuted proposal for Madison
Square Garden IV, perspective, 1960.
The proposed "modernistic sports
center" for an as-yet undisclosed site.

7.5
Unexecuted proposal for Madison
Square Garden IV, 1960, plan. The
scheme covered three city blocks and
rested atop a one-storey podium.

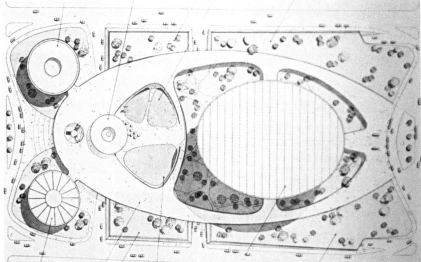

plan but one that would have di-
vorced users from the encompassing city as a result of the stepped
podium and self-contained circulation along the raised promenade.
A site did not yet exist for this
ambitious plan.

   The forces that led to the selection of Pennsylvania Station as the
site for Madison Square Garden
IV gathered strength through the
1940s as increased car and airplane use siphoned passengers and reduced train travel. By 1951, the
Pennsylvania Railroad was running a serious deficit and the station had deteriorated owing to
decreased maintenance and poor design decisions.[17] The deal between the Pennsylvania Railroad
and Graham-Paige that would seal Pennsylvania Station's fate was prefigured in 1954 when developer William Zeckendorf purchased the station's air rights and proposed replacing the building
with a thirty-two-storey merchandise mart to be designed by I.M. Pei.[18] The project did not go
forward but the concept remained of razing the site and transferring the waiting room and ticket-
ing operations below grade. At its annual meeting in May 1961, the Pennsylvania Railroad announced that engineering studies for using the station's air rights had been received along with
proposals for the station's use that included "'the construction of a group of modern buildings.'"[19]

   At the November 1960 announcement of a new Madison Square Garden, Irving Felt explained
that three sites were then under consideration. On 25 July 1961 the *New York Times* revealed that
the site of what was now called "an entertainment complex" would be Pennsylvania Station.[20]
At a press conference the following day, James M. Symes of the Pennsylvania Railroad and Irving
Felt and John Bergen of Graham-Paige disclosed a revised proposal and an increased budget of
$75 million. Graham-Paige also announced the formation of a new company, Madison Square
Garden Center Inc., that would build and operate the project and of which they would own 75 per
cent. In payment for the nine-acre site, the Pennsylvania Station would receive the remaining 25

7.6
Unexecuted proposal for Madison Square Garden Center IV, 1961, now called "an entertainment complex."

per cent stock in the company along with "a substantial rental for the site on a long-term lease that, with options, would extend for ninety-nine years."[21] As illustrated in the *New York Times*, the revised project now featured two slab towers, a twenty-eight-storey hotel, and a thirty-four-storey office building, in addition to the 25,000-seat saddledome arena and the smaller 4,000-seat arena. All of this rested upon a three-storey landscaped platform that provided access to the railway platforms, reconfigured concourses, and parking space for 3,000 cars.

By September 1962, the project had changed again.[22] It still featured the two towers facing one another at Seventh Avenue but the ovoid saddledome had now given way to a drum-shaped arena with a cable-hung roof. The perspective view shows an arena encircled by a screen of lithe columns and transparent glass that rises to the building's full height and through which the interior is visible. Was Charles Luckman Associates referencing the high-style facades of Lincoln Center, the recently opened Philharmonic (now Avery Fisher) Hall by Max Abramowitz, or the soon-to-be-completed Metropolitan Opera House by Wallace K. Harrison? In any event, this scheme was abandoned but Charles Luckman Associates recycled the concept in modified form four years later in their design for the Los Angeles Forum (see Image Part III. 1).

In April 1964 a model of the definitive project was presented as part of *Our Town 1970*, an exhibition organized by the Municipal Arts Society of "major New York City projects, currently being prepared by government bodies, institutions and private interests."[23] In addition to MSG IV, the show featured the twin towers of Minoru Yamasaki's World Trade Center, for which construction was to begin in 1966, and an unrealized mixed-use development called "Litho City" that called for 12,000 apartments on a site including landfill in the Hudson River. The exhibited model for MSG IV Center included the circular, drum-shaped Garden, now sheathed in solid panels and with its four protruding escalator towers, and the single, pendant twenty-nine-storey office tower. Demolition of Penn Station had already commenced, in October 1963, and construction of MSG IV began on 29 October 1964 when the first of 207 steel grills, each weighing five tons, was lowered onto the site.[24]

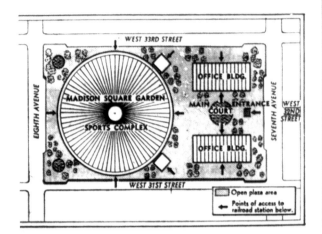

7.7
Unexecuted proposal for Madison Square Garden IV, 1962, perspective and plan.
Charles Luckman subsequently recycled this design, minus the towers, for the
Great Western Forum in Los Angeles (see Part Three, Introduction, Image 1, above).

As built, Madison Square Garden IV featured an exterior composed of large precast concrete
panels alternating with forty-eight truss columns, whose location corresponded to the forty-eight
spokes of its cable-supported roof structure. The truss columns extend some forty to fifty feet
below grade and helped transfer the building's load.[25] At the roofline the truss columns extended
above the height of the concrete panels to support the 404-foot-diameter outer compression ring.
With previously constructed cable-roof systems the roof rested immediately on top of the cables
that extended from the outer compression ring to the tension ring at the centre of the roof structure. But at MSG IV the architects filled the space created by the sloping cables with a two-storey
steel structure housing lighting and mechanical equipment and a cooling tower.[26] It was the
building's stacked construction of auditorium, theatres, and other spaces that drew so much
admiring attention at the time, especially the location of the arena floor, four storeys above grade.
The sense of transparency envisioned by the September 1962 scheme was reintroduced to the built
project through four glass-enclosed escalator towers that rise nearly the full height of the building
and that were expected to empty the building within twenty minutes while offering a bit of street
theatre to passing pedestrians and motorists. The forty-eight truss columns likewise recalled the
columns of the 1962 scheme.

The building that was demolished to make way for Madison Square Garden IV, McKim, Mead
and White's Pennsylvania Station, had been completed in 1910 as a majestic gateway to the city.
It was considered a masterpiece of grand Beaux-Arts architecture, its exterior set off by a massive
colonnade of pink granite Doric columns while inside its soaring waiting room, based on the
Baths of Caracalla in Rome, was New York's largest indoor space. Its proposed demolition ignited
fierce and widespread condemnation and led to organized protest in August 1961, a month after

7.8
Aerial view of Madison Square
Garden and Penn Station,
Manhattan.

7.9
Bird's-eye view of Pennsylvania Station, New York, between 1910 and 1920. Pennsylvania Station
"went not with a bang or a whimper, but to the rustle of real estate shares."

its demolition was announced. Though unable to save it, the local heritage movement was
galvanized by Penn Station's destruction,

Architectural critics reviled Madison Square Garden IV (and continue to do so), calling it banal
or "at best [of] execrable banality" and complaining in equal parts about its poor artistic merit
and negative urban impact.[27] A 2016 *New York Times* editorial described how Madison Square
Garden "sits upon Penn Station like a manhole cover, blocking light and air."[28] The memory of
what was lost to give it life surely has not helped its reception. Even fifty years later, assessment
of the centre's architectural qualities and significance are still intertwined with what it destroyed.[29]
But what is especially interesting for our purposes is the degree to which the terms used to
critique the building for its artistic and urbanistic failings are equally applicable to the impact
it would have on sports architecture. Ada Louise Huxtable, writing in the *New York Times*, saw

beyond Madison Square Garden's appearance to the power and the money that had demanded it. For Huxtable, Pennsylvania Station "went not with a bang or a whimper, but to the rustle of real estate shares" and she lamented that the new style of its replacement "would not be Imperial Roman but Investment Modern." "The passing of Penn Station is more than the end of a landmark. It makes the priority of real estate values over preservation conclusively clear. It confirms the demise of an age of opulent elegance, of conspicuous, magnificent spaces, rich and enduring materials, the monumental civic gesture, and extravagant expenditure for esthetic ends. Obsolescence is not limited to land use and building function in New York."[30]

It may be accurate to date the disappearance of the professional hockey arena to the moment that Madison Square Garden III was bought by Graham-Paige. What Graham-Paige purchased was not a hockey arena and its team but a real-estate development opportunity. The air rights to Pennsylvania Station and the cost of building on that site were so great that Graham-Paige could maximize its profits only by maximizing the entire development. A promotional brochure seeking potential tenants for Madison Square Garden IV calls the site "one of the most valuable pieces of land in the world" before going on to extoll the many virtues of the complex.[31] As a result, the arena itself became just one element within a much larger complex that included a twenty-nine-storey office tower; a forty-eight-lane bowling alley; a 5,000-seat forum; an exposition rotunda; an art gallery; cinemas; and a sports museum. According to Alvin Cooperman, "the Garden had evolved into a 'happening.'"[32] Two years before its completion, collateral development in the immediate neighbourhood was already spiking. An August 1966 article in the *New York Times* summarized the ongoing and proposed changes, which included a fifty-two-storey office building (1 Penn Plaza by Kahn and Jacobs); a fifteen-storey distribution centre; a 1,650-unit apartment building with underground parking for 1,650 cars; a large complex of middle-income housing; the modernization of the Governor Clinton Hotel; and the renovation and seven-storey extension of the former Saks–34th Street building.[33]

By the late 1960s, sports facilities were already being championed as engines for the economic recovery of ailing metropolitan areas across the United States. Municipalities hoping to justify public subsidies in support of new sports facilities could therefore point to the development around Madison Square Garden IV. (Madison Square Garden IV was constructed using private funds only.) It would take another twenty-five years before the developers of sports complexes themselves took full advantage of the potential for economic gain offered by developing the area around the complex.

In spite of its pared-down style and great scale, Madison Square Garden IV actually hearkens back to Madison Square Garden II, the building designed by McKim, Mead and White in 1889 as a palace of wonder. Like its 1960s version, the nineteenth-century Garden featured a programmatically diverse set of individual spaces within a single shell – a primary auditorium along with a smaller theatre and concert hall – that were to position it as the centre for entertainment in the city. Madison Square Garden II was also famous for its restaurants and roof garden, attractions that lured visitors and enticed them to extend their visit upon arrival. It was these features, concentrated within a single building, together with the extravagance of its tower and the exoticism of its ornament that generated enchantment and a sense of wonder.

Madison Square Garden IV also was composed of vertically stacked theatres that could accommodate a range of audience sizes. While it lacked the high-style exoticism of its nineteenth-century forebear, MSG IV was nonetheless identified as a centre of pleasure. The British *Architectural Review* titled its short preview of Madison Square Garden IV "Fun Palace," a reference to an unrealized but highly influential project by Cedric Price.[34] Price's Fun Palace (1961–64) was intended as a "laboratory of fun," a twenty-four-hour entertainment centre, with flexible and wide-ranging educational and recreational facilities for dance, music, drama, and fireworks. Price was responding to transformations within post-war British society, including predictions of decreased work weeks and increased leisure time. He was also inspired by the egalitarian philosophy of eighteenth-century English pleasure grounds, such as Vauxhall and Ranelagh, with their sprawling spaces for strolling, amusement, and gossip.[35] Madison Square Garden IV could be considered the commercialized bastard cousin of this scheme.

7.10
Bull Ring Centre, Birmingham, 1964. One critic compared it to
Madison Square Garden IV for its lack of aesthetic charm.

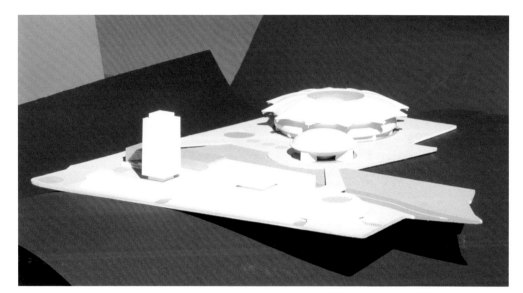

7.11
Model for an unexecuted proposal
for Fort Point Channel stadium/
arena project, Boston, 1965. The
domed stadium, for football and
baseball, and the smaller, circular
stadium rest on a continuous
podium, with parking across
the channel.

The critic at the *Architectural Review* anticipated that Madison Square Garden IV, though "vulgar," "low-class," and "corny," might end up with more architectural honours than its high-born counterpart Lincoln Center, in spite of aesthetic qualities that "will probably not be greater than that of the Bull Ring at Birmingham."[36] The Bull Ring had been Birmingham's marketplace since the twelfth century. In the late 1950s it was redeveloped to include a traditional open-air market and Britain's first city-centre, indoor shopping mall, now renamed the Bull Ring Centre.[37] The shopping centre's Brutalist design, featuring broad expanses of raw concrete, may constitute the "aesthetic qualities" that the reviewer believed MSG IV would not exceed. But there are further and more interesting parallels between the two projects. The Bull Ring Centre has been described as an early example of a megastructure, "in which a range of functions were brought together within the same container."[38] Like Madison Square Garden IV, the Bull Ring Centre featured multi-level shopping and concourses and direct connection to urban and inter-urban transportation. John R. Gold's assessment of the Bull Ring Centre as owing "less to avant-garde theorising than to the economics of property development, in particular the desire to maximize available floor area," could equally describe Madison Square Garden IV.[39]

Megastructures such as MSG IV, Lincoln Center, and Birmingham's Bull Ring Centre were rising throughout North America through the 1960s, often instigated as a form of remedial post-war urban amelioration. The scale of sports facilities individually, but especially when combined with like amenities and expanded by additional commercial, entertainment, and residential structures, made them ideal vehicles through which to achieve this goal. Their realization was assisted by the practice of providing public subsidies for their construction, which became common at this date. One such scheme, an unrealized $80-million proposal intended for Boston's Fort Point Channel, called for a retractable-domed dual football/baseball stadium, an 18,000-seat arena for hockey, basketball, and other events, and a 5,400-car garage with direct access to the Massachusetts Turnpike.[40] The intended location was rail lands of the New York, New Haven and Hartford Railroad Company, which, like the Pennsylvania Railroad in New York, had been forced into bankruptcy in 1961 as a result of dramatic decreases in ridership. In 1965 South Station was sold to the Boston Redevelopment Authority. The Fort Point Channel stadium development was proposed that same year. Governor John A. Volpe supported the project and financing was to come from state bonds and state funds for credit.[41] Vincent G. Kling and Associates were the architects. The forty-five-acre site comprised the stadium and arena, which rested on a single podium. Parking facilities located across the channel were accessible by a bridge.

The Houston Astrodome: Size Matters

While sprawling sports complexes such as the proposed Fort Point Channel stadium might affect urban development through scale alone, they did not introduce anything new to the field of sports architecture. (The first operable retractable dome, SkyDome in Toronto, was still some twenty-five years off.) But the Houston Astrodome, when it opened in 1965, affected a paradigm shift in sports architecture the significance of which is still being exploited today. The Astrodome inaugurated many "firsts" and "biggests" that are today standard features at every arena and stadium. But the true achievement of Ray Hofheinz, who conceived the Astrodome and saw it through completion, was that he unabashedly and decisively altered the focus of such buildings – from sport to sport-entertainment. The impact of this altered focus can be discovered in every aspect of the building's design and operation.

Never afraid to blow his own horn, developer/promoter Judge Ray Hofheinz designated the Astrodome the "Eighth Wonder of the World," claiming that "we are building something that will set the pattern for the 21st century. It will antiquate every structure of this type in the world."[42] And he was right. Hofheinz implicitly understood that the success of his venture depended on creating a stadium that was more than a sports facility. Through a combination of clever business

7.12 *Right*
Aerial view of the Houston Astrodome, downtown Houston in the upper distance.

7.13 *Opposite*
Houston Astrodome. The so-called "Eighth Wonder of the World," it had to be, and was, more than a simple sports facility.

skills, superior public-relations acumen (instead of shovels, participants at the groundbreaking ceremony fired Colt .45s into the earth[43]), and sheer chutzpah, he redefined the nature and role of sports facilities. Every innovation at the Astrodome from financing and ancillary development to the experience of spectators was related to its scale.

Hofheinz's first move, once an expansion franchise had been awarded, was to arrange financing for the enclosed, air-conditioned stadium that he understood would be a requirement in the hot, humid, mosquito-infested climate of south Texas. But the site on which he proposed to build, 495 acres of swampland located six miles south of Houston's central business district, was not promising. Hofheinz drained the site, sold 180 acres to Harris County for $5 million (the price he had paid for the entire site), and proceeded to develop the remaining 315 acres.[44] He next got Harris County voters to approve a $42-million-bond issue to finance the stadium, in part by enlisting the aid of Quentin R. Mease, a locally respected African American community leader and civil-rights pioneer and by agreeing to his condition that the new stadium be opened as an integrated facility.[45] Hofheinz then raised further funds by introducing fifty-three skyboxes ($15,000 per year on a five-year lease for a twenty-four seater), making the Astrodome the first sports facility to provide luxury suites.[46] Roger Angell, writing in the *New Yorker*, pointed out that the most expensive seats in the house were also the worst, "entitl[ing] the boxholder to approximately the same view of the ballplayers as he might have of a herd of prize cattle seen from a private plane."[47] But the die was cast.

Following the example of Disneyland, which had opened in Anaheim in 1955, Hofheinz planned to lure Texans to his patch of reclaimed swampland by offering them a wide range of amusements. His prospective audience was therefore a mass audience and not only limited to fans of professional baseball. "If we've established grandeur we've done it for the bleacher fan and the country club member. Baseball people will tell you that they don't need all that, just give them a crackerbarrel seat and a stale frankfurter and they'll be happy. Maybe you can do that with a real baseball fan but we're just educating the people to baseball here."[48] But Hofheinz was doing far more than educating his audience; he was actually tilting the playing field so that he could not lose. With the Astrodome, Hofheinz unabashedly embraced and celebrated the relationship between sports and entertainment, which henceforth became synonymous and symbiotic. Sport became part, but not all, of the show that audiences paid for.

People came to see the building about which they had heard so much, the first and largest domed stadium in the world; the eighteen-storey structure covered nine acres, could seat 42,217, and had an outer diameter of 710 feet, a clear span of 642 feet, and a roof that was 202 feet above the field.[49] The parking lot, also the world's largest, held 30,000 cars. Referring to the Coloseum in Rome, Hofheinz had boasted, "We'll build a stadium that will make Emperor Titus' playhouse look like an abandoned brickyard."[50] Some ten years after it opened, nearly half a million people still visited just in order to tour the building.[51]

The sports facilities at both MSG Center and the Astrodome were always intended as only one element within much grander development schemes. At New York the location was some of the most expensive real estate in North America. In Houston, Judge Hofheinz hoped to make it so. Hofheinz surrounded his "eighth wonder of the world" with the Astrodomain (now known as Reliant Park). Spread over 350 acres and connected to the Astrodome by a bridge across Loop 610, the thirty-eight-mile-long Interstate highway that encircles downtown Houston, it comprises the Astrohall, an exhibition and livestock arena (1966); Astroworld, a fifty-seven-acre amusement park (1968); Astrovillage, a complex of four motels (1969); and Astro Arena (1975), all of which "reinforc[ed] the argument that baseball is but one of many forms of entertainment available in this air-conditioned instant city."[52]

Six years later, Houston gave the world another "air-conditioned instant city" when the Galleria was completed, the first of the mega-shopping malls. [53] This 420,000- square-foot, $20-million, mixed-use development stretched over thirty-three acres. In addition to the expected retail shops and department stores, it originally included commercial and office space, a hotel complex, and even an ice-skating rink. Gerald D. Hines, the man who built it, claimed that "a shopping center it is not. It will be a new downtown."[54] MSG Center and the Astrodome provide the model that will be exploited in the design of the sports-anchored developments of the 1990s that will be discussed in the next section. These urban-scaled sports-anchored campuses were the children born of the coupling of the Astrodome and Galleria.

Catering to first-time fans and families as much as to hard-core baseball enthusiasts, Hofheinz determined that everyone should get what they wanted from their experience. For his wealthiest patrons, Hofheinz introduced the first luxury suites. Each of the fifty-three skyboxes was equipped with a bar, icemaker, refrigerator, telephone, radio, closed-circuit television, and Dow-Jones stock service. Suites were serviced by a butler and individually decorated, from Aztec to Ship Captain's Cabin. Suite holders also enjoyed exclusive access to the SkyDome Restaurant, with its 210-foot glass-walled view of Houston's skyline, and a personalized gold spatula with which to serve themselves from the gourmet tray.[55] Understanding that the best way to encourage visitors to remain and spend money was to entertain and enthrall them, Hofheinz provided a wide range of restaurants and bars. At the Domeskeller, a beer hall seating 6,000 beneath the centre-field seats with windows looking onto the playing field, waitresses in Bavarian-styled costumes served patrons. The Astrodome's club bars would not have looked out of place on the Las Vegas strip.

To lend further excitement to the event experience, Hofheinz exploited the buzz generated by NASA's space program, located just twenty-four miles away at the Manned Spacecraft (now Lyndon B. Johnson Space) Center. Not only were the building (Astrodome) and the team (Astros) named in honour of the space age, but ushers and groundskeepers reinforced the theme through specially designed costumes. Spacettes in gold-lamé miniskirts and blue boots helped patrons to their seats while Earthmen in orange space suits and white helmets managed the grounds. (These are the precursors of todays "Ice girls," scantily clad in team colours, who clear the ice during commercial breaks and interact with the crowd – see Image 8.9 below.) Audience members could also eat in the Countdown Cafeteria, served by Blast-off Girls.

Dominating the overall game-day experience at the Astrodome was the massive, $2-million, three-panel electronic scoreboard, located above centre field. Dubbed the Astrolite, it measured more than four storeys tall and 474 feet long, weighed 300 tons, required some 1,200 miles of wiring, and called for a producer and six technicians to operate. It was, of course, the largest

7.14 *Opposite* Aerial view of the Astrodomain site, including Houston Astrodome and Astroworld. An "air-conditioned instant city."

7.15 *Above*
One of the fifty-three luxury suites at the Houston Astrodome, each serviced by a butler and individually decorated, from Aztec to Ship Captain's Cabin.

7.16 *Left*
Spacettes (ushers) and Earthmen (groundskeepers) in costume at the Houston Astrodome, 7 April 1965. Sport spectating as theatre.

scoreboard ever erected. In addition to the usual game-day line-ups and statistics, it could simultaneously display out-of-town results, messages of welcome to groups of fans, ads for souvenirs on sale in the ballpark, and animated commercials accompanied by sound effects.

But it was the cartoon animations that responded to on-field action and exhorted the audience to respond that attracted the most attention. Roger Angell marvelled that "the giant set is impossible not to look at, and there's no 'off' switch. By the middle of the game I was giving the game only half my attention; along with everyone else, I kept lifting my eyes to that immense, waiting presence above the players."[56] A home run by the Astros occasioned an orgasm of pyrotechnics, a forty-five-second-long sequence featuring fire-snorting bulls, American and Texan flags, cowboys with lariats, more cowboys firing guns, fireworks, and skyrockets.

The broad popularity of the scoreboard was immediately recognized as the game-changer it would become. Roger Angell observed that "the scoreboard and its busy screen seemed anxious to improve on baseball," and he noted how few fans at the Astrodome kept score in the traditional way, with pencil and scorecard. Hofheinz was less interested in traditional fans than in freshly minted ones, but he was not at all interested in improving the game on the field; his goal was to improve the fan's overall game-day experience. Hofheinz makes it clear that he is not even en-gaged in the sports industry but in what he refers to as "sports entertainment": "This park keeps 'em interested enough so they don't *have* to keep busy with a pencil and scorecard. Why in most other parks you got nothing to do but watch the game, keep score, and sit on a hard wooden seat. This place was built to keep the fans happy … They don't have to make a personal sacrifice to like baseball. We have removed baseball from the rough-and-tumble era … We're in the business of sports entertainment. Baseball isn't a game to which your individuals come alone just to watch the game. They come for social enjoyment. They like to entertain and *be* entertained at the ballpark."[57] Twenty-five years later, the architecture critic Douglas Pegues Harvey lamented the transformation of fully engaged sports fans into passive recipients of entertainment. "The first spectators in the Astrodome became the live audience in the world's largest television studio, fur-nished with *theater seats*, not bleachers, with a scoreboard that lit up like a game in an arcade."[58]

Like Madison Square Garden Center, the Astrodome could survive financially only with a fully booked calendar of events. In its first year that meant Judy Garland, the Ringling Brothers circus, a rodeo, a boat show, a polo match, the home football games of the University of Houston, a bloodless bullfight, and a Billy Graham crusade.[59] But, unlike previous arenas and stadiums where the accommodation of such events were an afterthought, where the performers were forced to adjust to the venue, the Astrodome had been built and programmed from the first in order to stage the widest range of entertainments. Though less flashy than the great scoreboard and the costumed attendants, sound and lighting had been given particular consideration. The sound system was "the most modern ever created for a public building," one designed to produce "stereo-quality" sound. The dome itself had been "acoustically deadened with absorbent fibre-board, acoustical plastic, and 1,078 miniscule perforations on the bottom of each seat."[60] And in another first, the Astrodome was the first stadium equipped with three-hundred-foot candles of light, the necessary level for an optimum picture in colour television.[61]

In the previous chapter we noted how rock music affected the design of arenas at the same mo-ment that entertainment and sport had begun to merge, becoming spectacle. In this chapter we saw how two new buildings were conceived and designed not only to stage such spectacular events but to play a leading role themselves in the spectacle on offer. As conceived by Ray Hoffheinz, the Astrodome offered ticket holders more than an opportunity to be spectators at a particular event. People arrived at the Astrodome with the expectation of being wowed. Their experience would be memorable not only because of what happened on the stage or playing field but also because of the excitement provided by the building, indeed by the entire site. By expanding the experience of sports spectatorship beyond the match, to include other aspects of entertainment culture (costumed attendants, video scoreboard, themed restaurants), Hoffheinz effectively marginalized the sporting event while he simultaneously expanded its locus beyond the playing field. In the last section of this book I will explain how this fundamentally altered conception of sports spectating affected the buildings in which professional hockey is presented today.

Part IV.1
Individual TV screens and concession keypad system proposed for Pacific Bell Park, San Francisco, 1996. Expanding the live experience.

STATE-OF-THE-ART STADIUMS

Many cities across the country are either planning or building new stadiums. Most of these facilities, which will cost between $150 million and $1 billion each, will employ cutting-edge technology. With wired seats, digital scoreboards and lightweight retractable roofs, the high-tech stadiums will mean more fun for fans–and more money for team owners.

In a new league

One of the most technologically advanced stadiums now on the drawing boards will rise in San Francisco, where baseball's Giants are constructing a new home. The facility, which will be called Pacific Bell Park, will offer a number of audio and video options for spectators. Other new stadiums are sure to follow San Francisco's lead.

Money game

Many ticket holders will have their own stadium credit cards, which will provide an itemized bill of concession and souvenir purchases made at the ballpark.

High-tech hot dogs

1. Fans may soon be able to order snacks during the game by using a credit card swiper, which will be located on each seat.

Swiper

2. After entering their credit cards, spectators will log in their orders, as well as their seat, row and section number, on a keypad connected to a concession stand.

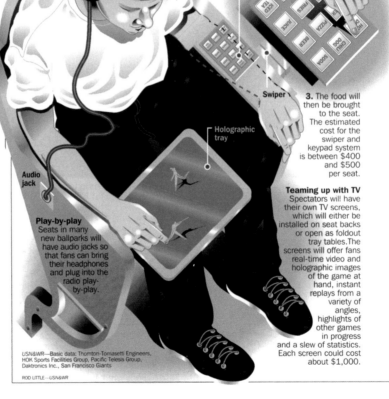

Concession keypad

Swiper

3. The food will then be brought to the seat. The estimated cost for the swiper and keypad system is between $400 and $500 per seat.

Teaming up with TV

Spectators will have their own TV screens, which will either be installed on seat backs or open as foldout tray tables. The screens will offer fans real-time video and holographic images of the game at hand, instant replays from a variety of angles, highlights of other games in progress and a slew of statistics. Each screen could cost about $1,000.

Holographic tray

Audio jack

Play-by-play

Seats in many new ballparks will have audio jacks so that fans can bring their headphones and plug into the radio play-by-play.

USN&WR—Basic data: Thornton-Tomasetti Engineers, HOK Sports Facilities Group, Pacific Telesis Group, Daktronics Inc., San Francisco Giants

ROD LITTLE—USN&WR

Part Four

From Place to Space: The Corporate-Entertainment Complex, 1990–2010

"Simply watching a sports event is no longer sufficient to attract adequate numbers of spectators."
– Michael Lischer, HOK Sports

"It's not a baseball stadium anymore. It's a pleasure palace, it's a place to go have fun."
– Rod Robbie, SkyDome architect

Introduction

Between 1990 and 2010 the professional hockey arena disappeared. To be sure, NHL teams continued to compete against one another but the spaces in which these events took place had devolved, from buildings once identified as hockey arenas to sheets of ice within "Places" and "Centers," massive corporate-entertainment complexes. During this period twenty-eight new facilities were constructed across North America by cities hosting NHL teams at a total cost of over $5 billion.[1] This remarkable construction boom produced a nearly complete sea change in the places where professional hockey is played. Mammoth, multi-purpose, many costing in excess of $200 million, and without exception named for multinational corporate sponsors such as Pepsi, General

Motors, and United Airlines, these buildings potently symbolize the transformation of professional sports into big business, the business of providing diversified mass entertainment.

Four interdependent factors shaped the corporate-entertainment complex: financing; the desire of owners to squeeze greater profits from their buildings; a changed fan base for professional sporting events; and new approaches to technology and marketing. In the following chapters I will show how these issues affected the design of buildings in which professional hockey is played, the experience of spectators within them, and the relationship of these facilities to their cities. The corporate-entertainment complex reshaped the dynamic by which patrons engage with events today. According to David M. Carter: "Historically, stadiums and arenas were built solely so fans could attend sporting and entertainment events … However, in our modern technological world this is not enough."[2]

The 1960s construction boom that ushered in a new era of major-league expansion arenas represented the last opportunity for the hockey arena to achieve a distinctive, recognizable architectural form. This hope was partly and only momentarily realized through buildings such as the Oakland-Alameda County Coliseum and the Great Western Forum. But by the late 1980s, when the next generation of hockey facilities began to be built, the major league sports landscape had shifted dramatically.

Sports commentators viewed this new crop of corporate-entertainment complexes as fundamentally different from the buildings in which the sport had been played formerly. For instance, they contended that the new arenas were not built for the loyal, knowledge-

able fan of a bygone age but for a mobile, affluent, and thrill-seeking consumer who could not skate.[3] Sports sociologist Richard Giulianotti described this consumer as a "flâneur."[4] Furthermore, they found homogeneity of experience in these new buildings. This is hardly surprising. Of the twenty-eight new buildings constructed between 1990 and 2010, most were designed by a handful of large, corporate architectural firms, in particular Ellerbe Becket (eight) and HOK Sports (now Populous) (eleven) (see Table 1).

These firms have constructed hundreds of sports facilities around the world and have achieved expertise in satisfying the "hard" architectural components that contribute to the success of these buildings: spanning huge

spaces, air conditioning and ventilation, maximization of circulation. But equally important is their mastery of those "soft" architectural features that enable owners to maximize their arena's revenue streams, such as increased space for concessions and restaurants, concert-quality sound and light systems, and maximized opportunities for in-arena advertising.

The size of these architectural firms, some employing several hundred architects as well as engineers and other specialists, make them uniquely suited to deal with the complexities of such large and detailed construction projects. But their experience over time in shepherding through to completion what are often politically sensitive projects, especially in regard to public funding and urbanism, is no less crucial to their success. These firms' access to lobbyists, political advisers, and public-relations firms with tried and true strategies for promoting arena and stadium initiatives provides clients with extraordinary advantages. Winning tax subsidies and overcoming community opposition often seems a foregone conclusion.[5]

The most eye-catching feature within these buildings is the omnipresence of in-arena advertising and entertainment systems. They dominate a visitor's experience and most contribute to these buildings resembling one another. A small number of specialized companies such as ANC Sports Enterprises and Daktronics supply NHL arenas with video scoreboards, fascia and dashboard rotational monitors, giant continuous bands of LED displays, and other digital signage systems.[6]

Together these architectural firms and digital-signage companies have designed and contributed to hundreds of arenas and stadiums around the world, facilities that are increasingly owned and managed by a shrinking number of diversified trans-national sport-entertainment companies. For example, SMG, the company that runs Pittsburgh's Consol Energy Center, also manages sixty-eight arenas and civic centres as well as convention centres, exhibition halls and trade centres, stadiums, performing arts centres, theatres, and specific-use venues such as equestrian centres.[7] Global Spectrum, the company that runs Philadelphia's Wells Fargo Center, also manages a further thirty-eight arenas, while AEG owns, operates, and consults with over one hundred venues on five continents, including the Staples Center in Los Angeles.[8] According to Tim Leiweke, AEG's president and CEO, "We've built more arenas and stadiums than anyone in the world, ever – including the Romans!"[9]

The perceived homogeneity of these sport and entertainment facilities parallels a more generally remarked upon detachment of sport from both place and civic history. This disconnect occurred gradually over the course of the twentieth century as the impact of television as a mass media led major league sports from regulated to unregulated professionalism.[10] With the advent of free agency, players became mobile, autonomous agents moving freely and regularly from team to team and from league to league in an increasingly international market for player's services.[11] And teams themselves proved no less mobile: relocating to new cities or to regional locations (the so-called "turnpike" teams); disappearing altogether; and sometimes reappearing, occasionally in the same city.

Then, beginning in the 1970s, the demand for televised sport grew phenomenally alongside significant changes to the telecommunications and media industries, notably the expansion of delivery systems (cable, digital, satellite). For example, National Football League broadcast rights rose from $4.7 million in 1960 to $2 billion in 2004. But in what has been termed the "prune juice" effect, much of this flow of revenues, into teams, uncontrollably flowed out again to players in the form of increased salaries.[12] Although impressive, this unprecedented increase in media revenues tells only a part of the story. Major-league sports owners have

profited from broadcast revenues but sport is even more important to owners of cable, digital, and satellite delivery systems. Across the globe, access to sports is the chief reason that consumers purchase media subscriptions. Media owners have invested heavily in sports franchises and leagues, to satisfy their viewers' appetites and to guarantee themselves a steady stream of product that they control.[13] A 2000 survey of North American major league sports found that nineteen different media groups owned twenty-nine teams wholly or partly. In 2000 Time Warner had stakes in the Atlanta Braves (MLB), Atlanta Hawks (NBA), and Atlanta Thrashers (NHL).[14] In Toronto, the number of commercial sports teams increased from five to twenty-five between 1995 and 2003 yet just two media corporations – Rogers Communications (RCI) and Maple Leafs Sports and Entertainment (MLSE) – owned them all.[15] According to S. Miller, "'software' is what media empires call the teams they own. Fans may see the Los Angeles Dodgers or the New York Knicks as home teams with illustrious histories, but the new breed of owners – Rupert Murdoch's News Corp., Time Warner, Disney, Cablevision, Comcast – view them as content, programming fodder for the insatiable beast called television."[16]

As the ownership of major league sports teams shifted over this period, from individual owners to vertically integrated corporations, frequently with large media and entertainment holdings, the corporate objectives of these owners also shifted. At mid-century owners had sought to maximize sporting performance, by spending more on talent, so long as they broke even or suffered minimal losses. But later in the century corporate owners shifted to a new model. They approached their teams as profit-led businesses and sought to increase shareholder value, regardless of team performance.[17] Sport was further homogenized in the process, transformed into one more interchangeable module of global entertainment.[18]

Sports sociologists and urban geographers interpreted these changes within the larger context of post-modernism, that period of late capitalism in which we still live. Whether referred to as "Consumer Society," "Media Society," or "Society of Spectacle," these critics agree that capitalism, consumption, media, and new technologies of communication and computerization dominate the present era. As public space and individual experience were commercialized, the result was the "serial reproduction" of universal homogenous "non-places" – malls, pedestrian city centres, plazas, and waterfronts – in which globalization erased distinctive local identity, replacing it with a mix of shopping and leisure experiences that varied little from one city to another.[19] Sociologist John Hannigan identified six defining features of such spaces or urban entertainment centres (UECs): they are themed, usually with reference to sports, history, or popular entertainment; they are branded, most often by drawing upon existing consumer and show-business brands (Coca-Cola, Nike); they operate day and night; they are modular, incorporating a collection of chain stores and restaurants; they are solipsistic, "physically, economically and culturally isolated from surrounding neighbourhoods"; and they are post-modern.[20]

The most dramatic changes to sport spectating over the past twenty years have been urban and technological. In both cases these changes have been directed toward achieving a totally immersive experience, in particular by expanding the limits of participation in sporting events. According to this new immersive model, a fan's sports experience is no longer limited to the time spent watching a game within a sports facility. Spectators attending a match can now begin their experience online, continue to access information digitally throughout a match, and extend their visit by patronizing themed restaurants, bars, and hotels within the sports-facility precinct. In the near future, people will "live" the events, instead of just showing up for them. Within these densely packed environments, known as sports-anchored developments,, living, shopping, working, and dining intermingle with the play aspects of sports and entertainment as part of a total immersion experience.[21]

Urbanistically, designers speak of the "street-to-seat" experience to define the broader spatial range of influence offered by contemporary sports/entertainment facilities. Physically attending the sporting event within the facility may comprise only one element of a fan's wider game-day experience. Today fans can customize their spectating experiences, through technological advances in handheld digital devices and more fully wired sports facilities.[22] As corporate-entertainment complexes replaced arenas across North America, the professional hockey arena ceased to exist as a distinct identifiable building type. Once a physical place, the hockey arena has been reduced to a space or, more accurately, a surface, buried within massive and more economically powerful facilities.

8.1
Aerial view of the United Center, with Chicago Stadium (below) before demolition in 1995.

8

Mediated Experience and the "Fansumer"

"This is no longer a mom-and-pop business. We're in the entertainment and
communications business, not just the sports business, so we are trying to
tap into all the resources that are available to us."
– Matt Levin, vice-president of marketing, San Jose Sharks

Hockey's New Fan Base

Until NHL hockey expanded, in the late 1960s, hockey's core audience comprised traditional fans
who regarded hockey as a unique form of entertainment, often bordering on religious experience.
For many years, loyal fans watching hockey in arenas willingly endured hard narrow seats, bad
food, and smoky corridors. Such conditions were even embraced as a rite of passage. It united
fellow sufferers while establishing a threshold for the true believer. The game on the ice was the
main attraction, and these spectators craved little more. Owners gladly maintained the status quo;
until 1968 the original six NHL teams competed in arenas constructed in the 1920s, and only
minimally altered since.

Through the last quarter of the twentieth century, however, hockey's core fans – its supporters –
were gradually replaced, or at least outnumbered, by a more fickle, less devout audience. This
new brand of spectator – urban, upscale, bred on television – regard a pair of NHL tickets as just
another consumable product, providing access to one of many entertainment possibilities in an
ever-expanding universe of choices. Writing about English soccer fans, sports sociologist Richard
Giulianotti has theorized four ideal types of spectator identity – supporters, followers, fans,
and flâneurs – that apply equally to North American hockey. He sees the broad trend in sports
identification moving away from the supporter model, with its hot, traditional identification with
local clubs, toward the more detached, cool, consumer-orientated identification of the flâneur.[1]
Giulianotti defines the supporter model as comprising fans with long-term personal and emotional investment in the club and "inextricable biographical and emotional ties to the club's
ground [or stadium]," where the stadium itself "is a key cultural emblem of the surrounding
community."[2] By contrast, the flâneur is a mobile cosmopolitan consumer with no personal

attachment to a club as a locally defined institution; the flâneur is more likely to sport club signi-fiers (caps, jerseys, crests) "in a cool, market-oriented style," as fashion statement as opposed to club adherence.[3] Giulianotti believes that this shift occurred in the context of sport's commodifi-cation, which he defines as that gradual process by which an object or social practice acquires an exchange value or market-centred meaning.[4] In the case of sports, the shift involves affluent spectators supplanting less wealthy ones.

In a parallel development, interest in hockey has been declining in Canada, especially among young people who register for soccer in greater numbers than for hockey. "Hockey, like artificial ice, is not 'natural' at all," argue David Whitson and Richard Gruneau. "It is a human social and cultural product, something that we Canadians have 'made' over a period of years."[5] The authors note how youth culture is now global in reach and, like Richard Giullianotti's flâneur, young people's interests and allegiances are matters of choice rather than national loyalties.[6] They observe that Canadian youths attracted by anti-authority or "cool" role models turn to the NBA rather than the NHL. The NBA has been especially successful in tying its game (and star players) to other aspects of consumer culture that attract contemporary youth, such as popular music, videos, and clothing.[7] Hip-hop performer Jay Z exemplifies this trend. Though only a minority shareholder in the New Jersey Nets basketball team, and in their new facility, the Barclays Center in Brooklyn, Jay Z's celebrity status, popularity, and cool image were exploited to promote the new building. He also intervened in the design of team logos and clothing and in the selection of music played during games.[8]

This demographic shift transformed hockey's fan base in traditional hockey cities, such as those in Canada and the northeastern US states, as it did in expansion, Sunbelt cities with no pre-existing or naturally occurring tradition of the sport, such as Anaheim, Tampa, Phoenix, and Dallas. To compete in this environment, NHL hockey has adapted, marketing itself in new ways aimed at attracting and maintaining audiences for whom fidelity to hockey is no longer a given.

But team owners and managers have themselves contributed to the makeover of their fan base. As revenue streams became the mantra of team owners beginning in the 1980s, they pursued up-scale and corporate audiences with their more plentiful dollars. Wealthier patrons pay more for their seats and can be counted upon to spend more on new services and products, from private parking to Perrier. The same logic guided the award of new NHL franchises, which were granted to cities sharing two characteristics: high per-capita income and expanding population bases. All of these factors transformed the late-twentieth-century arena inside and out. They now function primarily as sites of consumption instead of sport spectatorship.

Revenue Streams and the Design of the Corporate-Entertainment Complex

The financial bottom line of major-league hockey depends to a greater degree upon ticket revenues than do other major-league sports.[9] Baseball, football, and basketball earn profits from hugely lucrative national television contracts that are capable of generating incomes far in excess of anything they might realize from game-day admissions. In 2010 NFL and NBA teams each earned more than $140 million and $30 million respectively from broadcast revenues. By contrast, NHL teams received about $8 million each.[10] But without a national television contract, and with labour costs spiralling out of control through the 1980s, NHL owners in particular looked for ways to maximize their existing income streams. According to Stephen Taub, writing in 1995, the largest increase in revenue for NHL teams would come from the construction of new arenas. "What's the significance of a new arena? Well, in virtually every case, they become licences to print money. That's because they are armed with all of the modern revenue streams, including scores of sky-boxes, huge concession stands and lots of strategic nooks and crannies to cram in all the adver-tisements."[11] According to information published in *Financial World* magazine, "NHL clubs skating in new rinks increased in value 133 percent, compared with a league average of 105 percent."[12] And in a list of team valuations reported in the December 1998 issue of *Forbes Magazine*, seven of the top ten NHL teams skated in new rinks opened during the 1990s.[13]

According to Andy Dolich, vice-president of marketing for the Oakland Athletics, "teams are starting to understand that they're not just competing against other teams. Teams that understand they are part of the whole entertainment firmament seem to generate the most success."[14] And for Matt Levin, vice-president of marketing for the San Jose Sharks, "this is no longer a mom-and-pop business. We're in the entertainment and communications business, not just the sports business, so we are trying to tap into all the resources that are available to us."[15] Those resources comprise seating (including luxury suites, club boxes, and PSLS), merchandising, refreshments (including concessions, catering, bars, and restaurants), and advertising. A 1991 article in *Fortune* states that "as the cost of new or purchased [sports] franchises rises, owners are coming to realize that it's not whether you win or lose, but how you raise the cash flow per seat that counts."[16] One way to achieve this has been to demand more and more concessions from the host city and state. According to Jay Coakely, "the main reason so many new stadiums have been built since the late-1980s is that owners now see venue revenues as an income category that they can increase without going into debt themselves. This is the reason a new stadium looks like a combination shopping mall and food court, with a playing field in the middle."[17] This observation was neatly underlined by NBA commissioner David Stern in assessing the transformation of his league's playing facilities: "We went from a league playing in beat-up buildings to this model of video boards and sound systems and restaurants and suites and clubs and, oh yes, there's a basketball game in here somewhere!"[18]

Merchandising of NHL-licensed products rose to $1.1 billion in 1994, up 37 per cent from 1993 and nearly double the amount earned in 1992, translating to $1 million per team, while in-arena advertising can earn arenas between $3 million and $5 million per year.[19] For example, San Jose posted $15 million in profit on only $45 million in revenues after its new building opened, just over half of which was derived from gate receipts.[20] But, of all the revenue streams to which teams availed themselves, none had a greater impact on the interior design of arenas as concessions selling refreshments and merchandise. Where were the existing models to instruct team owners and their architects in effecting this reformation? Their eyes turned upward for inspiration, and what did they see? They saw airplanes landing at airports and witnessed the conversion of jaded travellers into avid consumers.

Beginning in the 1980s, airport administrators cottoned on to the potential cash cow repre-sented by millions of idle upscale travellers. They transformed their terminal buildings into shopping malls, altering the world's experience of air travel in the process. Air terminals are now

8.2
Marine Midland Center,
Buffalo, 1997. More and
wider concourses allowing
greater space for restaurants,
bars, and shops.

designed for more than departure and arrival. According to Jan Jansen, general manager of Terminal 4 at John F. Kennedy International Airport in New York, the airport resembles a "shopping mall with planes leaving from it."[21] Sports-facility architects followed suit, increasing the size and converting the function of their open and underused spaces in the image of food courts and boutiques. In his book *Landscapes of Modern Sport*, sociologist John Bale argued that the globalization of modern sport was realized through the established "spatial parameters" within which sports take place. "It is this explicitly spatial character of the globally applied rules of sport which has such an important impact on the sports environment since it facilitates global 'body trading.'"[22] Bale's observation applies to all of sport, that is to athletes, athletic performance, and the playing fields where the action takes place. What owners, facility managers, and sports architects came to understand through the 1980s was that the action on the playing field was only a part of the total experience of attending a sporting event; they came to see that their facilities were "more than" just arenas or stadiums. Bale's "spatial parameters" when applied to the contemporary experience of sport spectating encompass an expanded sports environment that now includes parking, outdoor plazas, concourses, and, in a plugged-in world, an extended, virtual field of action.

Arenas acquired many of the features of shopping malls – so-called "points of sale" such as boutiques, restaurants, and even food courts – in attempts to maximize profit by offering their affluent, captive audiences no respite from the urge to buy. According to HOK architect Rick Martin, this is known as "extending the duration of the visit."[23] Ellerbe Beckett architect Steve Hotujac explained that "the whole goal is to have people come early and stay late. The more you can offer fans outside the game itself pushes a lot of the design now." Hotujac noted that fans coming to Ellerbe Beckett's Canseco (now Bankers Life) Fieldhouse, which opened in 1999, spend ninety minutes longer at the stadium than they had at its predecessor.[24] To make sure that specta-tors lose no time to non-shopping activities, current facilities are designed with a greater number of wider concourses and nearly twice the number of restrooms called for in the building code. According to Donald Eyeberg of Ellerbe Beckett, "by making it easier and less time consuming to use restroom facilities, per capita expenditures at concessions has increased."[25]

There is more than a passing relationship to the new multiplex cinemas, which employ a simi-lar strategy. Describing the burgeoning in Canada of multiplex cinemas, or megaplexes, *Toronto Star* architecture critic Christopher Hume noted that movie admissions barely cover the cost of their rental by movie theatres and that the real profit comes from the sale of refreshments, where the mark-up can be as high as 85 per cent.[26] Thomas W. Stephenson Jr, the owner of Hollywood Theatres, a Dallas-based chain with over 77 theatres containing 474 screens, explained that he lost $8.2 million on ticket revenues of $50 million but still turned a profit, raking in $22.4 million on sales of $26.7 million from concession stands.[27] Cineplex architect Richard Young (his firm designed the transformation of the Montreal Forum into a Cineplex) explains that "we hope to take advantage of the synergies that occur when people go out to see a movie."[28] The synergies he refers to are those between affluent patrons and merchandise for sale. "The whole design princi-ple," says Young, "is to keep the concessions in sight. They are lined up on the visual axes."[29] "This is no ordinary moviehouse," notes Hume, "[it] is an *entertainment centre*. As such, the environment must be equally as engaging as what's on the screen."[30]

The most financially lucrative new revenue stream, which by itself powered the demand by owners for new sports and entertainment complexes, was the addition of private boxes and luxury suites that promised huge rental revenues from their wealthy, primarily corporate sponsors.[31] Returning from a 1988 visit to the Palace of Auburn Hills, the venue in which the NBA's Detroit

8.3
Private suites at Marine Midland Center, Buffalo, 1997.

8.4
View from a private
suite to the ice surface at
United Center, Chicago.

Pistons began to play that year, Chicago Blackhawks owner Bill Wirtz remarked that the facility "obsoletes every arena in the country." The object of his enthusiasm was its 180 suites, a record at that date.[32] Income from seat licences, club seats, and suite tickets produce more than half the total attendance income at sports facilities. It was the allure of luxury-suite profits that spurred the construction frenzy of the 1990s. All six Golden Age arenas were replaced, including Witz's Chicago Stadium. Not even relatively new facilities were immune. The Calgary Saddledome, completed in 1983, underwent a $35-million renovation just ten years later, in spite of being "a first class structure that has been well maintained and is in little need of significant repair," according to a 1993 report.[33] The goal of the renovation was a new concourse level fifteen feet above the ice on which forty-five more executive suites and 1,200 club seats were added. The upgrade was demanded by the hockey team to "optimize their operations" and in order to "ensure the viability of the Saddledome into the next century."[34]

Luxury suites are often accessed via separate concourses. Many of the new sports and entertainment complexes are designed with private entrances and escalators, as well as private restaurants and bars. These features protect corporate customers from mingling with the common fan. (One of the many valid arguments against public subsidies for these buildings is this segregation of publics and the creation of private space within facilities financed by the public.) According to Rick Martin, a senior architect with HOK Sports, increasing the number of concourse levels has led to the phenomenal expansion in the size of new sports facilities, and of their unprecedented cost.[35] HOK architect Chris Carver explained that, while a typical single-concourse arena of the 1960s might enclose about 400,000 square feet, the 1990s multiple-concourse version ranges from 650,000 to 700,000 square feet.[36] The Staples Center in Los Angeles covers 950,000 square feet while Chicago's United Center encompasses 1,000,000 square feet. The latter's roof serves as the world's largest advertising sign, used by airline pilots as a navigation landmark (see Table 5).

Facility-naming rights have developed into another boon for building owners. These sponsorship agreements range from about $1 million to as much as $6 or 7 million per year. Deals generally last ten to twenty years. In 2007, 94 of 122 major-league sports teams played in corporate-named venues.[37] Advertising pervades these facilities, from the ice surface and dasherboards that encircle the ice to the Zambonis that ride upon it, from the Jumbotron to the flashing LED fascia lights around each tier of the building. Even individual parts of a building can be branded. In October 2011 the Nashville Predators announced that the main entrance to the Bridgestone Arena and the space just within would be renamed the Nissan Entrance and the Nissan Atrium. Nissan also acquired rights to one of the Zambonis and to other signage within the building.[38] In a 1992 article published in the *Hockey News*, Toronto Maple Leafs director of marketing Bill Cluff explained how he had "talked to an advertiser about buying the space on the goalposts and the crossbar. "We've also looked into the possibility of stamping a logo into the mesh of the net. The NHL doesn't permit that now, but it's a possibility."[39]

Mediated Experience: Hockey as Spectacle

In the 1920s artificial ice was introduced into solidly built new arenas. These architectural and technological enhancements ensured the financial stability of individual owners, encouraged NHL expansion, and guaranteed the long-term financial viability of professional hockey. Games took place regardless of the weather and buildings did not burn. In today's increasingly complex and competitive sport-entertainment world, hockey owners again turned to architecture to preserve their financial security. They constructed facilities capable of generating income from a growing array of non-hockey sources while delivering a more stable entertainment experience – one that is less dependent upon the game on the ice.

If you have attended a televised hockey game, you are familiar with the many ways that television has altered the live game and its experience by spectators. These include altered start times to suit prime time or Sunday afternoon east coast television broadcasts and stoppages in play to accommodate advertisements. Equally significant has been the subtle alteration of the live-hockey experience to mirror its televised version, including television and scoreboard monitors showing replays, advertisements, and images of dancing fans and the over-stimulation of rock music inserted at every stoppage in play. (My eight-year-old son was so overwhelmed and unsettled by his first live hockey match at the Molson Centre that he spent most of his time watching the television monitors. They presented a more orderly and controllable world, with images he had already learned to decode.) Such enhancements of the live game and diversions from it further blur the line between sport and entertainment, eroding and transforming hockey spectatorship into a new category of experience.

The stated aim of EA Sports, the manufacturers of *Vice Squad NHL 99*, an interactive, simulated hockey video game, was to model this product as much as possible on televised hockey. It features play-by-play commentary, broadcast-style features, real advertising, real-time replays, a choice of eight "camera angles," and a deafening heavy-metal soundtrack. "Where most video games create fictional worlds, sports games aim to replicate real people and places. Realism is an important selling point," states EA producer Todd Batty. "We're constantly compared to reality, and the reality is on TV every single night."[40] A reviewer of *Vice Squad NHL 99* noted that "the game is as much a media simulation as a sports simulation. In other words, EA wants the game to look as much like televised hockey as possible. Why not be satisfied with the game itself?"[41] The answer, I believe, is that the audience for such video games is drawn from television viewers whose understanding and experience of hockey has been completely shaped by that medium. And, just as these toys are tailored to the expectations of television viewers, so too is the experience of live hockey at your local NHL arena. Peter Moore, president of EA Sports, confirms this observation in reference to viewers of NFL football: "There's now a tipping point where fans get their knowledge of the game from video games. In fact, polling has shown that *Madden* video gamers have a greater knowledge about football and its strategies, history, and structure than people that play the game in real life. We are now a mainstream staple in the way people consume sports."[42]

There is no better place to witness the detachment of sport from place and the embrace of commerce and entertainment that are characteristic of recent hockey facilities, and of sport spectating generally, than southern California. At Anaheim, twenty-five miles southeast of Los Angeles, a new NHL hockey team was born. The Walt Disney Company, which first owned the Anaheim Mighty Ducks, named them after a successful Hollywood movie.[43] HOK Sports designed the Ducks' new facility, the Arrowhead Pond (now Honda Center), which opened in 1993. Michael Lischer, a vice-president with HOK Sports Facilities Group, states that this "arena is the latest in the new generation of sports facilities designed to exploit the entertainment value that modern marketing and corporate sponsorship has injected into sports."[44]

Anaheim is a suburb of Los Angeles with a 1993 population of 285,000. It is situated within affluent Orange County and the Mighty Ducks hockey team planned to draw fans from its wealthy regional population of 2.4 million. Orange County boasts swank shopping malls, such as South Coast Plaza in Costa Mesa. According to its advertising, South Coast Plaza is

8.5
Arrowhead Pond, Anaheim. "The latest in the new generation of sports facilities designed to exploit the entertainment value that modern marketing and corporate sponsorship has injected into sports."

8.6
Interior view of the entrance lobby at the Arrowhead Pond, Anaheim,
with "Video Arch" sculpture by Nam June Paik.

the highest-grossing planned retail centre in the United States, visited annually by 22 million
people.[45] Noting this fact, Brad Mayne, general manager of the Arrowhead Pond in 1993, explained
that HOK had "created what Orange County expects."[46]

As a consequence of a construction lull in southern California in the early 1990s, the building
came in $10 million under budget. The owners used this money for enhancements that yielded
highly finished exterior and interior surfaces. While remarkable for a sports facility (one journalist
asked, "Is this a sports and entertainment arena or the Ritz-Carlton?"[47]), the result is comparable
to the detailing of high-rent malls like South Coast Plaza. Granite imported from Sweden and
fabricated in Italy encircles a twelve-foot-wide stretch of the building's exterior. Inside, 200,000
square feet of marble covers the floors and wainscoting of all three concourses. Four different
hues of pink and beige marble were selected from the mountains of Spain, Taiwan, and the
Philippines. The marble even extends through service stairways that connect the levels. The club
level is carpeted. A "one percent art program" – a common strategy at the municipal level in
North America, aimed at forcing developers to spend at least 1 per cent of their construction
budget on art – partially funded the purchase of three works of art. Was it only coincidence that
one of these was "Video Arch," an installation by Nam June Paik comprising multiple television
sets? It was located just inside the main doors.

Characteristic of the new corporate sport/entertainment facilities constructed in the 1990s are
bowl-like interiors with less steeply graded stands. Jumbotrons, hung high over the centre of the

playing surface, and hundreds of televisions monitors, suspended throughout the interior, deliver instant replays and more to live spectators. (Toronto's Air Canada Centre provides 650 televisions, many in the washrooms.) Other improvements introduced in the 1990s include superior acoustical designs and concert sound systems that enable one to hear the "sweet clean sound of silence with 20,000 people in the room," according to one music critic describing a concert at Vancouver's GM Place. Air-conditioning allows shirt-sleeved spectators.[48] The television monitors and sound system create a seamless entertainment experience by providing images and music to distract spectators from lulls in the action, especially during commercial breaks during televised games or between periods. Jumbotron screens even inform spectators when to cheer. Just like television audiences, nothing is left to chance.

The multitude of television monitors and the Jumbotron screen serve many purposes. On a practical level, spectators will leave their seats during a game to purchase refreshments or merchandise at concessions if they can remain in touch with the game on the ice. But the presence of so many televisions within the auditorium also performs a crucial function in achieving the new, mediated experience within these facilities.

Live entertainment and sports events compete for audiences against television- and computer-based programming. Why leave the comforts of your home and pay large sums of money to watch a hockey game that you can access free on your television screen or digital device? In certain respects, televised sport delivers a better product than the live version. Its multiple camera angles, close-ups, and replays guarantee that television viewers are always at the centre of the action.

Advances in sound technology have vastly improved the aural quality of televised hockey. According to Stanley Allen, "in hockey the sound of the game itself is vital to the excitement of the pace of action: skate sounds, puck slaps, players crashing against the boards, and sticks hitting the ice, the puck and other sticks."[49] To capture these sounds for television, sound technicians place a variety of microphones throughout the facility. Boundary mics on transparent plastic plates are mounted on the inside of the glass surrounding the ice surface. Shotgun mics are handheld or attached to cameras. Wireless mics are attached to the bars of each goal post. Mics are even embedded in the ice surface.[50]

Replays are especially important to television viewers considering the speed at which hockey is played. For spectators new to hockey, one of the greatest barriers to comprehension is the game's speed and the difficulty of following the puck. Notoriously, this led the Fox Sports network to introduce a digitally enhanced flaming puck to its televised broadcasts of hockey games from 1994 to 1998. The system, named FoxTrax, worked by highlighting and tracking the puck's position. Hockey pucks were first split in half, embedded with a tracking device, and glued back together. Its inventor, Stan Honey, explains: "Once you're an experienced hockey fan, watching the game is all about the gestalt of where all the players are and the flow of the game. It's not really that important that you see the puck all the time because you see the big picture and you kind of know where the puck is anyway. But for somebody who's not a hockey fan, the game doesn't make any sense if they can't see the puck. There's just all these guys skating around, and it's hard for an inexperienced, potential hockey fan to figure it out. It then becomes hard for them to become a hockey fan without having the initial ability to see the puck."[51] If novice spectators find the puck

8.7
"Superpuck," FoxTrax electronic puck. It left a blue comet tail on the TV screen when struck, a red tail if travelling faster than seventy miles per hour.

hard to follow on television, they will find it harder still at a live match, without the benefit of cameras zeroing in on the primary action. The many televisions hung throughout arenas help bridge the gap for new fans by providing numerous opportunities to see, or to re-see, a goal, a save, a fight, or other notable event.

Televised sport is one of the only unscripted programming available; anything might happen. Producers of televised sports shows became aware that this was good so long as something did happen. But what if the game was dull and scoreless or a foregone conclusion between mismatched opponents? To protect against such eventualities, announcers and commentators actively shape televised sports broadcasts, infusing them with narrative arcs, sometimes referred to as "empathy-inducing personal narratives."[52] How will Player X perform after returning from injury/suspension/drug rehab/being sent to the minors/his fight with Player Y the last time their teams met? Such narratives, agreed upon in advance by producers, directors, and commentators, are then reinforced with camera close-ups of the protagonists and special attention paid to their presence on and off the ice. Broadcasters hope that such enhancements will engage, invest, and retain viewers no matter what happens during the game.

At the live game, spectators cannot be engaged through storytelling. Yet the live-sports experience is no less a carefully constructed product. At the live hockey match, spectators consume the game as part of a larger spectacle. Architect Michael Lischer of HOK Sports noted in 1993 that "in order to compete with other forms of entertainment the modern sports facility has to cater to the spectators' demands. Simply watching a sports event is no longer sufficient to attract adequate numbers of spectators."[53] Attendance at a sports event (the product) must deliver acceptable entertainment value. This is achieved by inscribing the game within a larger spectacular experience (the enhanced product). "You can't control the outcome of a game," acknowledges Russ Simons, a senior principal at HOK Sports, "but you can control an environment, so that the business client or the family of four leaves the facility and thinks, 'That really was worth the money and time spent.'"[54]

At Anaheim, home games once began with a bevy of young women, dressed in the team colours of purple, jade, silver, and white, circling the ice amidst swirling coloured lights. These cheerleaders on skates, known as the "Decoys," conjured the arrival of "Wild Wing," a part-human, part-animal team mascot. "Wild Wing" descended from the rafters to welcome the team, whose members skated onto the ice through smoke and coloured lights. (At San Jose the Sharks start each home game by skating onto the ice through the gaping jaws of a massive shark's head. At Nashville they use the head of a sabre-toothed tiger.) Rock music fills lulls in the action such as television commercial breaks and digital-light shows transform the entire ice surface into a movie screen. Animated images are projected onto the playing surface, from waving flags for the singing of national anthems to local landscapes or regional landmarks. The Jumbotron monitor and continuous bands of flashing LED displays that encircle the seating bowl at several levels shout messages, exhorting fans to cheer or do the wave. But still more remarkable, the Jumbotron serves as a giant screen on which spectators can watch themselves. Just as Roger Angell found the Astrolite, the

8.8
Nashville Predators hockey player entering ice surface through the jaws of an inflated sabre-toothed tiger at the Sommett Center, Nashville, TN.

8.9
Bruins Ice Girl with smoking T-shirt cannon, 2003.

giant scoreboard at the Astrodome, "impossible not to look at" in 1965, the Jumbotron has become an integral part of the live hockey experience.

Television cameras originally intended to capture the game on the ice for broadcast beyond the facility now film spectators for simultaneous broadcast within the building. Audience members instinctively know what is expected of them when they discover that they are being filmed. Like participants on a reality show, they wave, stand up and dance, kiss their partners, and sometimes even lift their shirts over their heads. The larger audience may then be invited to "vote," through their applause, for the best dancer or kisser or most enthusiastic fan. Roving camera teams stage impromptu interviews or trivia contests that are likewise broadcast live on the Jumbotron. On the ice, activities between periods might include contests in which fans attempt to score a goal from centre ice or mini-Zambonis outfitted with cannons that propel packaged team T-shirts into the hands of lucky fans. Audiences have been turned into actors, performing for themselves while simultaneously watching their own performances.

But spectators are not the only participants engrossed by the Jumbotron. Look at the posture of hockey players on the bench during a break in action, after a goal or a crucial play, and you will find them with their heads tilted back and their eyes fixed on the giant screen. They are studying the replay of their own recent accomplishment. Like film actors watching dailies of their perform-ances, hockey players can now review and assess their own athletic feats instantaneously. In the process, the Jumbotron transforms their game play into a televised spectacle. Beamed back to them, and to every spectator, it is re-consumed as a mediated, televised product. Post-modern philosophers such as Jean Baudrillard describe this experience as hyperreality, the substitution of the real by a simulated and intensified version of itself.[55] Geneviève Rail, writing in *Sport and Postmodern Times*, defines the experience as one in which the "real" is absorbed by televisual screens. The cybernetic images reproduced on them become reality. Representation, not direct experience, comes to determine all meaning.[56] Richard Giullianotti has noted how the media are integral to this process of confusion whereby virtual technologies reformulate our sporting experiences.[57]

With an article published in *The Walrus* in 2011, Stephen Marche joined a long list of authors arguing for the ultimate Canadianness of hockey. Marche's position is essentially a nostalgic one. He perceives deep within the sport aspects of a rough-and-tumble frontier spirit – an amalgam of violence and speed where voyageur meets aboriginal – that characterizes the country and shaped the sport. For Marche, players enact these qualities every time hockey is played.[58] Marche's analysis reveals primal truths about the sport but he omits aspects of the contemporary game that do not agree with his romantic vision. Today science, technology, finance, and media have infiltrated and transformed all aspects of contemporary sport to the extent that nothing happens by itself or by chance. Today the professional game is a spectacle that is performed. For example, two kinds of violence exist in the current game. "Natural" violence occurs when large players moving at high speeds within a confined space collide or when legal bodychecks strategically alter the flow of a play or an entire match. Marche discovers the origins of the game in this type of hockey violence.

But a second type of hockey violence also exists – staged combats between designated brawlers. In these nothing is natural. Such choreographed fights are performed as part of the entertainment spectacle of contemporary professional hockey. In a 2008 article about the resurgence of fighting in the NHL, sports columnist Michael Farber referred to fighting as "the NHL's dirty secret," without

which there would be empty buildings, according to one coach.[59] He wrote: "In some ways …
[fights] … serve a similar role to that of the chorus in Greek drama, offering a pause in, and a
commentary on, the narrative that drives the play. In this sense, fighting is scripted. 'The biggest
misconception is that fighters are mad at each other,' [then Tampa Bay Lightning coach Barry]
Melrose says. 'In fact, fighters are very much in control … like [players] taking a slap shot. They
do it for a reason.'"[60] Would these kinds of fights occur without audiences to consume them?

Other changes to the spectator's experience within corporate-entertainment complexes have
distanced the fan from the event and from one another. These adjustments include greater
distances between spectators on opposite sides of the auditorium, and the physical separation
of fans by economic class. Discussing the Staples Center soon after its opening, *Los Angeles Times*
architecture critic Nicolai Ouroussoff described it as the opposite of former "venues of popular
interaction" where the mingling of classes was an inevitable by-product. "Each strata of the
Staples Center has its own separate space – it's not just the seats. You go in separate entries, you
go to separate bars – it's extreme."[61]

The overlay of an insistent mediated and prescriptive soundtrack competes with the crowd's
roar. John Bale has noted how the "sport-induced sounds" of sports landscapes contribute to their
particular ambience, enriching the spectator's experience. But he believes that, as electronically
amplified sound increases, it will "reduce the spontaneity of the crowd's songs and chants."[62]
Audience's increasing reliance on video monitors and personal electronic devices acts to isolate
spectators. In an age of mass customization brought about by the marriage of mass production
and digital technology, spectators have come to expect individualized experience, even in the
context of collective events. Brought up on portable electronic devices, a 1,000-channel universe,
and the immediate gratification of Google searches, we have grown accustomed to shaping our
own experience, participating in and even controlling our entertainment. Locked as we are
inside our individual experience, our connection to the collective audience is diminished.

The above-mentioned technological changes acted to distance spectators from the live event
compared with the ways sports had been consumed historically. But these advances also introduced new ways for fans to interact with sports. In the past we experienced collective events physically and in real time. New approaches to the marketing and presentation of mass entertainment
and sports are re-engaging spectators by mobilizing them in interactive, participatory, and fully
immersive experiences. New digital technologies are transforming the ways in which sports are
consumed today, both live and via alternative platforms. "The vast array of sports-related Internet
options has enabled fans to fully immerse themselves in all aspects of the sporting experience. No
longer relegated to merely 'consuming' sports by watching games in person or on television, fans
now participate in the dialogue and even produce their own content. With the advent of sports
blogs, fans are an integral part of the sports entertainment experience – active participants in the
process rather than just interested bystanders."[63] Paul Swangard points out that the traditional

8.10 *Opposite*
Buffalo Sabres hockey players on bench watching replay on Jumbotron screen.
A simulated and intensified version of experience.

experience of attending a game from start to finish is now only one among a range of options available to fans.[64]

In *The Elusive Fan* the authors divide fan interaction into three periods over the twentieth century: the Monopoly Generation (1900–50); the Television Generation (1950–90); and the Highlight Generation (1990–).[65] In the present era audiences increasingly control their own communication environments. These new avenues for interaction are particularly vital for the NHL, given its historically poor television ratings in the United States and low income from that media relative to other major-league sports. Paul Swangard cites an ESPN poll that concluded that hockey fans were most likely to turn to the Internet for sports information. He noted that in 2007 the NHL signed a large number of digital-related agreements that established new ways for fans to access content, to interact with each other, and possibly to record and share broadcasts, turning fans into "brand ambassadors."[66] (See Image Part. IV. 1.)

In 2000 Madison Square Garden installed 557 ChoiceSeats, so-called "wired seats," that allowed spectators to individualize their entire spectating experience. The seats were equipped with ten-inch computer screens that enabled spectators to view live action and replays from eight camera angles, call up statistics, and order refreshments and souvenirs from their touchscreen (an earlier version used a wireless concession keypad on the seat arm). They paid with a swipe of their credit card. Purchases were delivered directly to their seats.[67] Fans in other cities resisted the devices and some facilities balked at the high cost of wiring the seats (about $1,000 per seat, according to Ellerbe Beckett's Steve Hotujac) and at difficulties with adequate bandwidth. At Anaheim's Honda Center, premium seat holders benefit from an electronic food-ordering system. Spectators order their hot dogs and soft drinks (or sushi and imported beer) from a wireless concession keypad and receive delivery at their seats.

A company near Montreal launched Kangaroo TV, a "hand-held, wireless, audiovisual, multi-functional, entertainment system" that delivers user-selected instant replays, multiple camera feeds, access to other live games, dynamic statistics and analysis, and the ability to track fantasy teams. The device features call-to-action alerts, multi-language game audio, and in-stadium information. Initially conceived for Formula One and NASCAR races, where there are long gaps between action, it has also been employed for Professional Golf Association (PGA) and NFL matches. In 2010 the Miami Dolphins supplied 25,000 of the devices to season ticket holders. Dolphins CEO Mike Dee explained that "this device provides our fans with the best of both worlds – the unparalleled live experience with the benefits of seeing the replays and angles previously reserved for in-home viewing. We are finding that the way fans watch and experience sports is constantly changing, and we want to be on the forefront of bringing technology to the fan experience at Sun Life Stadium."[68]

Sports facilities providing spectators with new technological devices are part of a move toward an increasingly immersive viewing experience. But, even without such gadgets, spectators now have access to their own arsenal of personal devices. Smartphones and tablets individualize but also extend each spectator's experience, permitting them to interact with a virtual audience of enthusiasts. Such enhancements to spectating experience further transform the real into the hyperreal. They blur the line between live and simulated, or reformatted, sporting experience.

David M. Carter believes that, over time, the transition between consumption in-home and away-from-home will become seamless. "Fans will have access to exceedingly close relationships with their preferred sports and athletes – even if the connection is more perception than reality."[69]

Nostalgia and the "Ur" Hockey Arena

As the NHL expanded from six to twenty-one teams between 1967 and 1983, and then to thirty teams over the 1990s, the number of Canadian teams increased from two to seven but declined as an overall percentage. Canada's self-perception as the world's dominant hockey power was seriously challenged over the past four decades. Beginning in 1972, when Canada narrowly defeated the Soviet Union, subsequent world championships revealed the growing strength of hockey programs in the United States, Russia, Sweden, Czechoslovakia, and Finland. Since 1972 players from all these countries joined NHL teams in increasing numbers. By the 2011–12 season, the percentage of Canadian-born players in the NHL had declined to 53.3 per cent from 97.2 per cent in 1966–67.

Through the 1990s many Canadians interpreted a range of events as signs of the NHL's growing commercialization. These included: expansion into predominantly US Sunbelt cities; the loss of Canadian teams in Quebec City and Winnipeg and their removal to Denver and Phoenix; the construction of new sports complexes in all cities; and the corresponding closing and destruction of beloved earlier hockey arenas.

For many in Canada, commercialization was code for American and caused wringing of hands and gnashing of teeth. "What was happening to 'our' game?" was the question underlying this obsessive worry.[70] Hand-in-hand with this national angst, heard in bars, call-in shows, and even within the halls of Canada's Parliament, went nostalgia for an earlier time when hockey was apparently innocent, simple, and Canadian.

Jason Blake's excellent study of Canadian hockey literature is filled with examples of this soul-searching, a mingling of anger and longing for a lost and glorious past.[71] In his 2001 book *Tropic of Hockey: My Search for the Game in Unlikely Places*, Dave Bidini describes his search for "real" hockey, in Transylvania, Mongolia, and even Dubai. He asked himself: "Would I glimpse our game being born? Would I see it as it had existed at the dawn of the last century? See hockey before it was complicated by economics, corporate lust."[72] Blake cites numerous stories and books in which the game has gone wrong owing to greed or drug use. He cites Mordecai Richler's 1997 novel *Barney's Version*, in which the lead character, a diehard Montreal Canadiens fan, bemoans the current state of hockey with the "no-talent, chicken-shit Canadiens" and the "ear-piercing rock music played at 10,000 decibels while a face-off was held up for a TV commercial."[73] These instances stand beside others in which hockey is employed as a symbol of nationhood. For Blake, the "rosiest depictions of hockey in literature" are those that "occur when people play shinny instead of regulation hockey. As we so often hear, hockey is best enjoyed outside, beyond the indoor arena's confining walls."[74] In a non-fiction piece by radio broadcaster Tom Allen, the author stands in the cold to watch his son play hockey, "what we'd been told was the true Canadian hockey experience." Blake notes, "In Canadian hockey mythology, the sanitized game in heated indoor arenas does not count as the true hockey experience."[75]

Advertisers and the NHL itself were quick to exploit these sentiments. An advertising campaign for Molson Canadian beer with the tag line "I Am Canadian" trumpeted, not without a sense of irony, simple Canadian virtues that aligned patriotism, hockey, and Molson beer with a dollop of anti-Americanism.[76] And beginning in 2003 the NHL introduced the Heritage Classic and the Winter Classic, series of annual regular season matches played outdoors in Canada and the northern United States. Against all reason these games became a huge hit with spectators and television viewers, with an average 52,000 fans attending each game and some four million more watching on television, making these the most watched hockey matches in the United States. What would possess 57,167 people to attend a hockey game in temperatures of minus 30 degrees Centigrade, as fans in Edmonton did in 2003, except a misplaced sense of nostalgia, as though there was some inherent virtue in transposing the indoor, arena game to an outdoor setting?[77]

With the hiring of John Collins as chief operating officer of the NHL in 2006, the Winter Classic began to be recast as hockey's Super Bowl. The advertising firm Collins hired to assess the strengths and weaknesses of hockey's brand concluded that hockey fans were innately tribal in their allegiances. If their team was not playing they rarely paid attention, even to post-season games. "What we wanted to do was create a halo over the top of the whole business that would get our fans not to trade their passion for a team, but at least watch more hockey."[78]

The first and strangest of all NHL outdoor games, played at the other extreme of the climatic scale, and with biblical undertones, was that between the New York Rangers and Los Angeles Kings in 1991. The site of this pre-season match was a rink and grandstands constructed in the parking lot of Caesars Palace in Las Vegas. The Zamboni driver was dressed as a centurion. In spite

of 85-degree weather and a pre-game rainfall, the ice held throughout the game, thanks to the use of three times more coolant than is usual at NHL rinks. But no one could have predicted the swarms of grasshoppers that would invade the ice surface. (Perhaps this provides the ultimate proof that the Almighty is a hockey fan and unamused by this unnatural, hubristic act.) Attracted by the lights and the reflections off the ice, the grasshoppers descended and fans swatted them away. The game was delayed twice. According to Los Angeles player Luc Robitaille: "There were these big giant grasshoppers jumping on the ice. They would land on the ice and freeze right there, so by the end of the second period they were everywhere on the ice and it was kind of funny."[79] Rink attendants, also dressed as centurions, used shovels to sweep them away. The nostalgia represented by such games (the frozen pond of yore) may be the NHL's response to the retro-themed stadiums of Major League Baseball. In both cases, according to Gregory Ramshaw, there is an attempt to revisit antiquated sports landscapes and to construct new/old sporting spaces through "a pastiche of images and impressions of the past."[80]

Around the same time, in the early 1990s, that the NHL was busily expanding across North America, shedding its old, outdared arenas and constructing new, larger, glitzier facilities, Major League Baseball was rethinking its own building strategy and moving in the opposite direction, away from its larger, suburban, sometimes dual-facility fields to more intimate downtown locations. Baltimore's Oriole Park at Camden Yards, which opened in 1992, was the first example of this shift and it became the poster child for a series of retro ballparks, almost all of them designed by HOK Sports, that consciously sought to evoke the qualities of early twentieth-century baseball fields. Just as the terms used to describe hockey buildings evolved at each stage of their development, this was also the case for baseball stadiums. Designated "Grounds," "Park," and "Field" from the 1870s to the 1910s, "Stadium" and "Dome" from the 1920s through the 1970s, beginning in the 1990s baseball facilities reverted to the use of "Park" and "Field," preceded by the name of a corporate sponsor. Whether or not the building was designed in a retro style, the name at least recalled baseball's pastoral origins in the late nineteenth and early twentieth centuries.

This nostalgic tendency was partly a backlash against the so-called "cookie-cutter" or "doughnut" stadiums of the 1960s and 1970s. Many of these had been dual-sport facilities seating 60,000–70,000. The most common result of endeavouring to encompass the dimensions of baseball and football fields in one building was a circular, enclosed stadium, domed or open to the sky at the centre. Without exception these buildings provided poor viewing conditions for fans of both sports. Often constructed from modular units of reinforced concrete, they projected a monolithic, heavy appearance redolent of the certainties of a Modernism that by the 1980s had been discredited. By the 1990s, when downtowns across North America were being rediscovered and gentrified, these earlier sports facilities were a case of the wrong building in the wrong place.

Fans returning to the city wanted also to return to the spectating experience enjoyed by their fathers and grandfathers, as represented by classic, still-functioning ballparks in New York, Boston, Detroit, and Chicago – Yankee Stadium, Fenway Park, Tiger Stadium, Comiskey Park, and Wrigley Field. Those more traditional buildings were deemed "fan-friendly" owing to quirky, asymmetrical designs, a result, it was believed, of accommodating pre-existing city street grids. They were open to the surrounding city, sometimes incorporating neighbouring buildings into their designs, and they offered views of the city from the spectator's seat.

HOK tapped into this deep vein of dissatisfaction and nostalgia in its 1992 design for Camden Yards, producing a ballpark that hearkened back to an earlier fan experience and to a more innocent time, an age before anabolic steroids, player unions, labour disputes, and multi-milliondollar contracts. This same wave of nostalgia fuelled the wish-fulfillment fantasy of the 1989 Hollywood film *Field of Dreams* ("If you build it they will come"), in which the disgraced Chicago Black Sox team – implicated in match fixing – is conjured and redeemed in order to restore the relationship between a son and his dead father. According to film critic Steve Vineberg, who interprets the film as a legacy of the Reagan era, the film "tells us that not only can we pretend the past we don't like never happened, but we can go back and change it to one we like better."[81]

HOK Sports could indulge the whims of team owners in replicating features of bygone ballparks thanks to flexibility on the part of league officials in applying the Official Baseball Rules governing the design of playing fields.[82] Old-fashioned bleachers, iron gates, and red-brick arcaded facades all recalled earlier ballparks. Camden Yards harmonizes with the existing B&O Warehouse that was incorporated into the design.[83] Even the billboards at Camden Yards were retro-inspired, with Coke ads featuring stubby bottles rather than the more prevalent cans.[84] But this retro veneer in no way conflicted with the inclusion at Camden Yards, as at other sports facilities opened in the

8.11 *Opposite*
Los Angeles Kings vs New York Rangers at Caesar's Palace, Las Vegas, 27 September 1991. The first, and strangest, of the outdoor "classic" hockey games.

8.12
Oriole Park at Camden Yards, Baltimore. The first retro baseball park.
It enables us to "pretend the past we don't like never happened."

1990s, of that vast array of income-generating features such as private suites, club seats, and other elements that had become standard equipment by this date. In fact, like a sleight-of-hand act, the feel-good retro surface of these facilities helped bury the lead.

The reason for describing this phenomenon in such detail is to ask the question: Why did this not also happen for hockey arena design in the 1990s? The answer can be found at the core of nostalgia, its object. Dreaming of their ideal baseball stadium, team owners, fans, and architects, from Seattle to Miami, could all agree upon those characteristics that make a ballpark classic. They would possess a common frame of reference, a ballpark vocabulary, and could be counted upon to compile an agreed-upon list of specific models, many of them still standing. Not so for hockey. Chicago fans might yearn for a heart-pounding Barton pipe organ inside an arena with lively sound-deflecting surfaces. Boston fans might opt for the steep, nosebleed-inducing rise of bleachers that offer a nearly vertical view of the ice surface. But there were only six "original" hockey buildings that could be referred back to and they shared few common features. The Ur-hockey arena does not exist. Yet, even if consensus could have been achieved, it is unlikely that the agreed-upon features of a classic hockey arena would have meant much to spectators in Atlanta, Tampa, or Phoenix with no sense-memory of former hockey sportscapes. It is difficult to feel nostalgia for something you never experienced. What most fans in these cities knew of hockey arenas they had learned from television and video games.

Although nostalgia was not a direct factor in the designs for new sports facilities for "original six" teams in Montreal, Toronto, Boston, and Chicago, it was still an issue to be reckoned with. As these teams abandoned, and razed, their older buildings they hoped that fans would not abandon them. The economic rationales for the construction of these new buildings, ubiquitously represented by their corporate-sponsored names, caused many hard-core fans to question their allegiances while providing fodder for sports editorialists and cartoonists who came up with disparaging nicknames that specifically targeted these buildings' corporate monikers – "The Garage" for Vancouver's GM Place (now Rogers Arena), "The Hangar" for Toronto's Air Canada Centre. The Montreal Forum, once regarded as a "hockey shrine," was replaced by the Centre Molson (now Centre Bell), a "basilica of beer," also known as "The Keg."

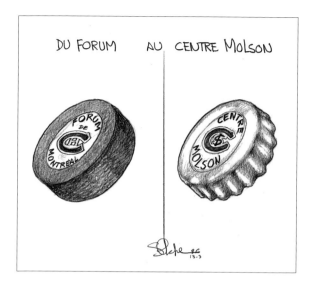

8.13
Serge Chapleau,
"Du Forum au Centre
Molson." The "hockey
shrine" replaced by
"The Keg," a "basilica
of beer."

Many artifacts recovered from their former homes have been remounted in plexiglass displays within the new facilities, along with framed vintage photographs, witnesses of a proud and, team owners hoped, continuing, heritage. For the one hundredth anniversary of the Montreal Canadiens, the team inaugurated a ceremonial plaza at one entrance to the Bell Centre, complete with oversize statues of past hockey greats. But within the new buildings recovered artifacts must compete for attention with television monitors, flashing advertisements, and neon-lit signs for refreshments, souvenirs, seating, washrooms, and exits. In such a simulated atmosphere, the presence of these "authentic" heirlooms may appear merely quaint, further distancing the traditions and history they represent from the hyper-reality of their surroundings.

Signed jerseys and sticks, framed photographs, and even the actual seats and bricks of Golden Age arenas now provide the decor for every downtown sports bar and suburban rec room. If players, teams, and buildings can be bought and sold, then why not history? In 1991–92 the NHL introduced replica retro jerseys in honour of the league's seventy-fifth anniversary. Players wear these so-called throwback jerseys in select games, sometimes called *Turn Back the Clock Nights*, or during entire individual seasons. (Some teams also introduced "fauxback" versions featuring designs that never existed.) But the real reason for introducing retro jerseys is their popularity with fans; "if you mark it, they will buy," notes journalist Phil Patton.[85] In 2000 the sale of baseball caps was a $1-billion industry, at a time when the average North American teenage boy owned at least half a dozen. According to Patton, new teams now confer with design consultants before selecting their colours and logos (teal is popular with women and men, black is popular in urban markets). "Often a new franchise's choice of logo is more important than its first draft pick."[86]

In an earlier chapter I showed how the move by the Montreal Canadiens from the Forum to their new home, the Bell (Molson) Centre, was handled with the utmost regard for history, politics, and the sensibilities of local fans. Anouk Bélanger points out how the Molson company, owner of the team and building, understood that the shift in venues, called "Le Grand Déménagement" (the Great Move), should be a participatory event in the life of the city. Some two hundred thousand citizens lined the streets to witness the parade that symbolized this move.[87] Each of the "original six" teams followed a similar process in changing arenas in the 1990s. The accompanying discourse of marketers and team officials tiptoed a line between good and bad news, often going to extremes in arguing that the winning spirit and magic feeling of the former building would be transferred to the new facility. In Chicago the owners of Comiskey Park (1910) and Chicago

8.14
Original unrestored double seat from Boston Garden. Auctioned by Sotheby's New York, 10 June 2005. Lot #151. Estimate: $2,500–3,500. Nostalgia as commodity.

Stadium (1929) employed the same public-relations and marketing communications firm – Public Communications Inc. – in 1990 and 1992 respectively, to successfully smooth public perception of their transition to new buildings. In typical PR-speak, this was achieved with catchy, yet oxymoronic expressions like "BRAND NEW OLD FASHIONED FUN."[88] In a commemorative magazine about Chicago Stadium, Blackhawks owner William W. Wirtz described his own sadness at the move from Chicago Stadium, a building in which he and his family had grown up. He nevertheless listed some of the old building's failings: narrow hallways, tight washrooms, steep stairways. "Modern luxuries are not found here," he wrote. "When we go to the Stadium, it's not about convenience and luxury. It's about emotion." And then he shifted gears to call upon civic pride for what he modestly claimed would be "the most phenomenal entertainment facility in the world."[89]

Mediated Community

In *The Elusive Fan: Reinventing Sports in a Crowded Marketplace*, the authors describe what they see as an increasingly fragmented contemporary sports market, one in which fans are more elusive – harder to reach, to engage, and to sustain.[90] They propose six "drivers" of successful sports brands, stressing the importance of individualizing each fan's experience. To achieve this, teams must connect with fans directly in personal relationships and on an emotional level, not only at the venue on game days but on a daily basis.[91] One method by which hockey teams have sought to effect such a connection has been through marketing strategies that promote the centrality of the team to its city and its citizens. John Hannigan builds on the concept of "mediated nostalgia," a term coined by sports historians John Nauright and Phil White to describe the conflation of nationalism, recollections of a happier time, and the success of Canadian professional sports teams.[92] Hannigan constructs the term "mediated community" to refer to the discourse employed by teams and media that posit "a 'nation' of fans who are united in their collective devotion to the team as both a cultural touchstone and a lifestyle."[93] Leafs Nation (Toronto), Habs Nation (Montreal), and Hockeytown (Detroit) are all designations created in order to unite fans in a community of believers, whether or not they attend matches or even live in the city where the team plays. It is precisely because these communities are virtual that there is a need to ground them in geographic terms.

Unlike the tradition of the tailgate party, which generally takes place at or near the sports facility, the geographical locus of such urban-based marketing campaigns may be situated at a distance from the team's venue; it may comprise the length of a street or the entire city. In an article titled "La ville est hockey," Jonathan Cha describes examples of such marketing in which teams and their fans have colonized parts of their cities. In Calgary during the Flames' 2004 Stanley Cup run, some fifty-five thousand fans, the so-called "Sea of Red" (after the colour of the Flames' jerseys), celebrated their team's success in a festive atmosphere along a stretch of several city blocks, from inside the arena to 17th Avenue. Now trademarked as the "Red Mile," this is still the place to go to show support for the team. A recent municipal initiative even proposed installing webcams along the street so that fans could participate in the excitement virtually. Similar situations followed: in 2006, during Edmonton's attempt for the Stanley Cup, a media and Web campaign helped transform Whyte Avenue into the "Blue Mile"; during Ottawa's 2007 Cup run, a nineteen-year old launched a Facebook campaign that resulted in the creation of "Sens Mile" along Elgin Street at the corner of McLaren in downtown Ottawa, about fifteen miles from Scotiabank Place where the Senators play; and in Buffalo, Sabres fans created "Party in the Plaza" at the corner of Perry and Illinois Street, near the HSBC Arena (now First Niagara Center).[94]

In 2006 the Montreal Canadiens launched a city-wide publicity campaign called "La ville est hockey." Its goal was to communicate the degree to which the team and its players were embedded in the very fabric of the city. Posters and banners hung throughout the city paired a player's portrait with a famous Montreal building. For Cha, such efforts suggest that hockey is more than a sport; it has become a mark of cultural identity evolving at the heart and at the scale of the city.[95] Two years later, also in Montreal and following the example set in Toronto, people began placing pennants with the Canadiens' logo on their cars. Approximately two hundred thousand of these were sold so that the entire city was overtaken by mobile symbols of fan support. Finally, in 2014, the Catholic Church got into the act, acknowledging what everyone already knew, that hockey is akin to religious devotion for fans of the Montreal Canadiens. As part of their annual drive for funds, the church inaugurated a virtual campaign, inviting Habs fans via its website – www.laflammedesseries.ca – to light a red, white, or blue candle for a one-dollar donation and to add a personal message in support of the Canadiens playoff hopes.[96] The website explains that the church "decided to connect the two types of faith that most enliven Quebecers." While the ability of the Catholic faith to enliven Quebecers may be debatable, it is nevertheless clear that the Canadiens' faithful extend well beyond the borders of Quebec; candles of support were lit by fans from across Canada, from Hantsport, Nova Scotia, to Thunder Bay, Ontario, to North Vancouver, British Columbia.

The corporate-entertainment complex was conceived for a new breed of "fansumer." At nearly twice the size of its earlier relative, the late-twentieth-century hockey arena, its bulk was swelled by the addition of private suites and added concourses, while its interior was further transformed through the inclusion of food courts and shops, digital signage, Jumbotron screens, and hundreds of televisions. These changes gave rise to a new genre of mediated spectatorship, an experiential mode that acknowledged that spectators were not necessarily loyal fans and that took into account their consumer-oriented identification and shorter attention spans. For nearly 150 years, architecture on ice had reflected the entangled relationship of sport and architecture. The construction of corporate-entertainment complexes in the 1990s marks the moment at which hockey no longer directed this conversation.

THE TORONTO STAR

Partly sunny. High -2C. Friday, February 13, 1998 www.thestar.com Metro Edition

$500 million blockbuster: Maple Leafs buy Raptors

The Leafs' new home

BAY ST.

GARDINER EXPRESSWAY

The Air Canada Centre

Cost:	■ $288 million
Seating:	■ 19,000 hockey
	■ 20,000 basketball
Corporate boxes:	■ Number will increase from 104 to 164
	■ Original price of $160,000 per box will increase
Entrances:	■ Bay St.
	■ Bremner Blvd.
	■ Union Station: The station will be the main entrance and tickets will be sold in the station's great hall. The Go concourse will be extended to allow access to the stadium.

One arena for both teams as Stavro reverses field

BY BRUCE DEMARA,
PAUL MOLONEY
AND DALE BRAZAO
STAFF REPORTERS

In a blockbuster deal that will change forever the face of sports in this city, the Toronto Maple Leafs have bought the Toronto Raptors.

The deal, believed to be worth $500 million, includes the purchase of the historic Union Station and the Air Canada Centre, now under construction at Bay St. and Lake Shore Blvd.

Announced yesterday in the Great Hall at Union Station, the deal ends a period of intense rivalry and bickering between the two franchises.

It also marks a stunning reversal for Leafs chairman Steve Stavro, who barely two months ago said the Leafs would be building a new home at Exhibition Place.

"Toronto sports fans have been telling us that they want both of their teams to play in one building. Single ownership makes all of this possible."

'Toronto sports fans have been telling us that they want both of their teams to play in one building. Single ownership makes all of this possible'

LEAFS BOSS STEVE STAVRO

undisclosed amount. The Bank of Nova Scotia also sold its 10 per cent interest.

9.1
"$500 million blockbuster: Maple Leafs buy Raptors." Maple Leaf Sport and Entertainment acquired the Air Canada Centre (then unfinished) as part of the purchase.

9

The Corporate-Entertainment Complex and the City

"Providing a major league arena or stadium is the way places demonstrate
they are ready for the big time."
– Michael N. Danielson, *Home Team*

"Increasingly, sports venues are being positioned simultaneously as a draw
for a particular event and as a gateway to consumer entertainment in the
surrounding area."
– David M. Carter, *Money Games*

Introduction

In the previous chapter I showed how architects and clients reconceived professional hockey
facilities through the 1990s, leading to far larger buildings in which the spectator's experience
was transformed through merchandising and media. This chapter takes a macro approach. It
examines the impact of corporate-entertainment complexes on the cities that build them and the
citizens who fund them. The accommodation of new revenue streams transformed the insides
of these new facilities and also reshaped their exterior appearances, siting, and scale.

Public versus Private Financing and the Location of the Corporate-Entertainment Complex

NHL corporate-entertainment complexes constructed during the 1990s were financed primarily
by public funds, as was the case for other major-league sports. Steven Riess notes that, before the
1950s, most sports franchises played in privately owned buildings. But during the early 1960s this
began to change and by 1970 nearly 70 per cent of all major-league sports facilities were publicly
owned.[1] By 1995, just under 80 per cent of major-league sports stadiums had been financed by
government, including 73.5 per cent of NHL facilities.[2] Michael N. Danielson believes that public
development of arenas and stadiums fundamentally changed the relationship between professional sports and places. "Teams became tenants of governments that owned arenas and stadiums,
creating a new set of relationships affecting everything from scheduling of games to relocation
of teams."[3]

New major-league facilities were predominantly located in downtown locations, even though this was actually counterintuitive. Land costs had only risen since the last round of construction. Baltimore sited its new, individual stadiums – for baseball and football – downtown in spite of consultants' reports that urged sites closer to highway connections and more ample parking.[4] But the civic boosters promoting the construction of new sports facilities, and lobbying in favour of public subsidies in their support, did so because they conceived of them as engines of hoped-for economic recovery. They believed that their cities' central business districts would benefit through new jobs and an influx of people wanting to live downtown. Defending his state's 1999 decision to commit $445 million of taxpayers' money to a new NFL stadium, Connecticut Governor John Rowland argued that "it's more about urban revitalization than it is about football. What we are trying to do is attract young people in the next generation to our community. It's going to have a huge spiritual impact. It's going to have an urban impact."[5] But, according to Michael N. Danielson, "without public development, there would be hardly any stadiums down-town, fewer arenas in the center of the city, and a smaller number of professional sports facilities within the city limits."[6]

Initially the arguments in favour of building new facilities for existing teams or for the hoped-for relocation of franchises, and for their subsidization by the state, centred on three main points. First, it was argued that the new facility would jump-start development of a moribund down-town; people attending events would spend money at the facility and on other activities while en route. It was also maintained that a new facility would attract national events (sporting, enter-tainment, conventions) that would draw people from outside the region. This economic activity would start a chain reaction, leading to collateral development, such as shopping malls, restau-rants, and bars that would entice people to move back to this now revitalized area, resulting in the further construction of new housing and generating new jobs. Second, it was contended that the mere presence of a team and its facility elevate a community to the major leagues, thereby garner-ing free publicity and drawing new businesses to the region. And third, proponents claimed that additional tax revenues and lease payments would offset any costs incurred by the city in attract-ing or retaining a team. In other words, subsidizing the facility would be a good investment.[7]

All of these points were definitively refuted by a virtual outpouring of books and articles writ-ten by academics and journalists throughout the 1990s.[8] The arguments against public subsidies were neatly summarized in a report prepared in 2010 by economist Andrew Zimbalist, one of the most vigorous opponents of economic subsidies for major-league sports. Zimbalist restates the fact that new sports facilities alone do not raise employment or per-capita income levels in a community or otherwise lead to positive economic development. He supports his position with four primary arguments. First, in spite of their large cultural presence, sports teams are modestly sized businesses. They employ between 60 and 160 full-time workers (about the same as a medium-size department store). Team revenues vary from $100 million to $400 million. Second, there exists a fixed pie of entertainment dollars in any local economy. Dollars spent on hockey are dollars not spent at local theatres, concerts, bowling alleys, or restaurants. One form of entertain-ment expenditure substitutes for another. Third, a significant proportion of sports revenues gath-ered in a local economy is invested or spent elsewhere. Athletes earn a major proportion of league revenues (57 per cent in the case of NBA players), but they do not generally live in the city where they play. A city retains more money spent at non-sport, entertainment venues. Fourth, in the vast majority of cases, sports facilities create a budgetary gap. Over the last twenty years, approximately two-thirds of their development costs have been publicly funded but little of the facility revenue has been shared with local government. Cities respond to budgetary gaps by raising taxes or reducing services, either of which puts a drag on the local economy.[9]

There is another explanation for the decision to situate new facilities downtown, as opposed to outside the city where land is cheaper. It concerns the increasing economic impact of private-suite sales and personal-seat licences. The corporate clients, who overwhelmingly purchase these, tend to work downtown. Tim Chapin believes that "with the identification of corporations as the new 'core fan base,' sports franchises have been more than willing to accept the location of new facilities in central city areas."[10] A select segment of the spectating audience has influenced every aspect of the design, operation, and location of new facilities.

Public versus Private Financing and the Design of the Corporate-Entertainment Complex

Throughout the 1990s teams and civic boosters promoted professional hockey facilities as civic institutions that belonged to a local community and reflected its pride and national standing. In their designs for new corporate-entertainment facilities, architects embodied and reflected this public ideal by emphasizing their openness and accessibility. At Nashville, the architectural brief for the Gaylord Entertainment Center (now Bridgestone Arena) required that the building achieve urban and economic goals. It was expected to relate to and revitalize its urban context while establishing an iconic architectural presence, one by which the city could be recognized. Although difficult to achieve, these are completely reasonable ambitions for an urban building on the scale of an arena, particularly one paid for by the people. But the impact of such requirements remade contemporary facilities in which hockey is played into another type of building; they are no longer hockey arenas.

Corporate-entertainment complexes are private enterprises (even though publicly funded) but clients prefer that they are designed to appear public. Steve Hotujac of Ellerbe Beckett explained that most sports facilities are at least partially public/private enterprises and this means that the architects must deal with two sets of owners, even though the team usually controls the agenda as "they have the product that everybody wants." For Ellerbe Beckett's design of the National Car Rental Center (now BB&T Center) outside of Fort Lauderdale, it was the city that wanted a more civic building. The team agreed to buy into this idea.[11]

Design elements that enhance visibility and apparent accessibility include large "public" entrance plazas, extensive expanses of exterior glass, especially along their principal facades, and towers or other visible, though often non-functional, design elements. At Boston's FleetCenter the architects included an illuminated glass tower that "emphasizes the arena as an urban beacon, giving it visibility from a distance," according to Ellerbe Becket's promotional literature. For Nashville, HOK designed a twenty-two-storey broadcast tower. It was meant to recall Grand Ole Opry radio broadcasts and to mark the facility district within the Nashville skyline.[12] You would expect to find such design characteristics at city halls, libraries, and other public, institutional buildings. Transparency conveys openness. Even the non-paying fan gets a look inside. Patrons

9.2 *Above*
Xcel Energy Center, Saint Paul, Minnesota, 2000. Extensive expanses of exterior glass along principal facades suggests public accessibility.

9.3 *Right*
BB&T Center, Sunrise, Florida. Large entrance plazas convey "public" openness to private facilities.

on the inside feel connected to the surrounding city. Entrance plazas and clock towers act as civic signifiers. They define these buildings as public landmarks even though they are decidedly private, commercial enterprises. Commentators have noted these qualities in warning against the confounding of public and private space in such commercial developments.[13]

Programmatically, sports/entertainment complexes are increasingly multi-functional. The primary auditorium serves the needs of diverse events while additional spaces can further extend the possible range of functions. MSG IV includes movie theatres, theatres, and a bowling alley while at the Gaylord Entertainment Center in Nashville additional rehearsal halls were added to support the music industry.

John Bale describes modern sports landscapes as "monocultural." "In its purest form," he says, "sportscapes can be used for nothing but sport." The modern sportscape can be indoor or outdoor, natural or artificial, public or private, mono-functional or multi-functional. But in Bale's view the post-modern sport landscape rejects these polarities, tending instead toward ambiguity, ambivalence, and contradiction.[14] From their origins, buildings for skating and hockey have embraced ambivalence and ambiguity regarding their function. The corporate-entertainment complex extends this ambiguity to other facets of its conception, design, and operation.

Today major-league sports facilities have become indistinguishable, in form and function, from other publicly funded civic enhancements, from convention halls to cultural centres. The curators for *Building Culture Downtown: New Ways of Revitalizing the American City*, a 1998–99 exhibition at the National Building Museum in Washington, DC, explained that "since World War II, American cities have searched for ways to revitalize their aging downtowns … Now cities are capitalizing on their traditional assets – art and culture … In addition to their primary mission as cultural magnets, today's museums, theatres, and performance halls … demonstrate that the arts still can provide creative possibilities in solving the urban challenges now facing American cities."[15] The projects selected by the curators addressed these urban challenges through multi-functional designs that mix cultural and commercial activities. In the effort to revitalize downtowns, the "public" becomes commercial and the commercial becomes "public."

The Sports-Anchored Development

By the late 1990s through 2010, new NHL facilities were still being promoted as engines of downtown economic recovery but by the end of this period team owners had modified their development strategy. Instead of building stand-alone facilities that were expected to generate nearby economic growth in trickle-down fashion, new NHL facilities were developed as so-called arena-anchored integrated development projects. The surrounding areas of previously built facilities were likewise being exploited along these lines. Also known as sports-anchored developments, or SADs, these multi-facility urban campuses typically include hotels, condominiums, restaurants, and other urban entertainment activities in addition to the sports facility.[16] David M. Carter explains: "Historically, stadiums and arenas were built solely so fans could attend sporting and entertainment events … However, in our modern technological world this is not enough. The evolution of the sports venue has reached a point at which the consumer is no longer seen as a single-purpose visitor to a destination. Increasingly, sports venues are being positioned simultaneously as a draw for a particular event and as a gateway to consumer entertainment in the surrounding area."[17] One effect of such large-scale urban developments is to diminish the importance of hockey within the overall scheme. This has contributed to the disappearance of the hockey arena, of which there will be more to say farther along.

Toronto's SkyDome, which opened in 1989, may be the first example of this new approach. Michael Danielson argues that SkyDome "ushered in a new era of megastadiums, with major league sport facilities designed to provide diversified amusements in attractive settings while serving as the focal point for entertainment, tourism, shopping, and business development."[18] Writing in *Time* magazine, Walter Shapiro observed how "the SkyDome became a monument to itself,

9.4
Guests watch a ballgame from their
SkyDome hotel room in Toronto.
How we spectate in the 1990s.

with baseball reduced to a minor sideline."[19] John Bale goes further still. He describes SkyDome as "a classic example of an ambiguous landscape," noting that a publicity brochure calls it "the world's greatest entertainment centre."[20] For Bale, "SkyDome is to sport what McDonald's is to food … an environment where sport is reduced to packaged consumption in an antiseptic, safe and totally controlled landscape. In other words, the SkyDome is akin to a shopping mall."[21] But how did it get that way? SkyDome architect Rod Robbie recalled that it was Charles Magwood, president and CEO of the Stadium Corporation of Ontario, who came up with the idea of adding functions to the project. "Magwood would say to us, 'What do you think of putting a something-or-other in this building?' So we put a hotel in it. No one's ever put a hotel in a stadium before … He kept on adding things – a health club, more floor space, a television station, a sports and enter-tainment area … And I don't think they understood that what he was doing was turning it into an all-time, all-weather, all-season destination. It's not a baseball stadium anymore. It's a pleasure palace, it's a place to go have fun."[22]

An early example of this broader development approach for a hockey-related facility was Manitoba Gardens. This unexecuted 1992 proposal for a $300-million development would have included a new home for the Winnipeg Jets on a site near the Convention Centre. The proposal comprised a 250-room luxury hotel and twin office towers. The deal was being brokered by Edgecombe Properties, the real estate arm of North American Life, the company that owned part of the proposed site. Pointing to the underlying issues motivating its proponents, Thin Ice, the local group that opposed the deal, argued that "the arena is really just a vehicle for a massive speculative land grab. One cannot even discern the outlines of the arena facility in the drawing, so freighted down is it with high rise office towers."[23] At least two other arena proposals were sub-sequently put forward as part of a larger "entertainment, exhibition, and convention centre com-plex" centred on a casino. The government rejected these schemes since they included financing provisions whereby gambling profits would be used to support the arena, profits the government was reliant upon and therefore unwilling to forego.[24]

The three-year saga that resulted in the NHL's Maple Leafs and the NBA's Raptors sharing a single facility, the Air Canada Centre in Toronto, underlines the great financial stakes associated with ownership of major-league sports facilities and the paramount importance placed by owners on the potential for development of the area surrounding the facility. For the Toronto Maple Leafs, it seemed to be the sole motivating factor in their search for a suitable site on which to build a replacement for Maple Leaf Gardens (1931). Throughout this search, beginning in 1996, Toronto Maple Leafs owner and Maple Leaf Gardens chairman Steve Stavro and others associated with this project insisted that they needed a site with room for expansion. The circumstances in Toronto were complicated by the fact that the Raptors had already broken ground on their own facility. (They had been playing in the less than ideal SkyDome since entering the league in 1995 and were under pressure from the NBA to construct a new facility.) The situation presented further difficulties because the Raptors were then embroiled in an ownership battle.

From the outset, Steve Stavro insisted that he had no interest in sharing the Raptors' new building once it was completed. Stavro wasn't opposed to sharing any building with the Raptors, but only one controlled by the Leafs and in which the Raptors were tenants.[25] In May 1997 the Maple Leafs announced plans for their own project, a sports facility flanked by two office towers on a site at Union Station, Toronto's downtown rail terminal. The site was literally a stone's throw from the foundations for the Raptors' new home, on a site just east of the CN Tower and south of Union Station. By mid-May it looked as though the Raptors would indeed join the Leafs at the Union Station facility and talks began about finding a use for the massive hole in the ground where the Raptors had begun to dig.[26] But by 25 June 1997 the Union Station deal had collapsed, with the city, which owned the land, unable to agree with the Leafs on the market

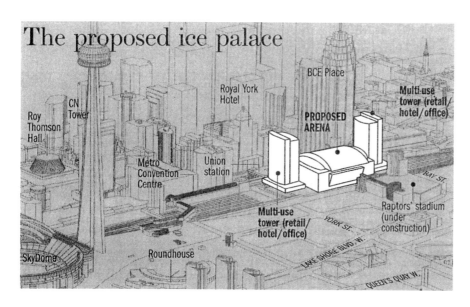

9.5
Unexecuted proposal for a new Maple Leaf Gardens project at Union Station. Even on this "hemmed-in" site there was room for two towers for retail, hotel, and/or office use. Note the proximity of the "Raptor's stadium," which would become the Air Canada Centre.

value for this prime real estate; the value would be used to establish rent payments. According to the *Toronto Star*, the Leafs offered $1 million a year while the city wanted $6 million, prompting City Councillor Tom Jakobek to describe the Leafs' offer as "tantamount to theft and we can't let you steal public property."[27]

With the deal for a shared facility ended and construction at the Raptors' site past the point where it could be converted to other uses, Leafs and Raptors ownership returned to their original negotiating positions, with the Leafs refusing to share the Raptors' building.[28] The Maple Leafs repeatedly complained that the Raptors' site was hemmed in and therefore limited as a base for larger development possibilities. What does this mean? Maple Leafs vice president Tom Anselmi explains: "We see sports changing so dramatically right now. We see a need to have flexibility in the long term, to add ancillary buildings and businesses and other amenities the fans will want. To be land-locked is a big issue."[29]

Six months after the Union Station negotiations had collapsed, the Maple Leafs were negotiating a fifty-year lease on a new site on the grounds of the Canadian National Exhibition (CNE). This site included an additional twelve acres that could be developed as a year-round retail/entertainment facility with hotel. Once again Maple Leafs Vice-President Tom Anselmi was abundantly clear on what was wanted: "There is a new wave of arena that seems to be happening in pro sports now that is not just plunking an arena in a downtown block that already has its infrastructure built around it. We want to use this arena as a catalyst for other developments."[30]

Everyone in Toronto agreed that building separate hockey and basketball facilities was economically unworkable but the anticipated windfall from single ownership of a sports facility and its surrounding site galvanized the Leafs. It should be clear by now that what motivated the Leafs had nothing to do with fans watching hockey. Harry Ornest, former owner of the Canadian Football League's Toronto Argonauts, succinctly summarized the issue: "If you own your arena and you own the major tenant, it's the next best thing to having sex, if you're having sex. If you're not having sex, it's the best thing."[31] In February 1998 the standoff of duelling facilities was finally settled when the Maple Leafs concluded a $500-million deal, purchasing the Toronto Raptors and their building.[32]

When the Air Canada Centre opened in 1999, it already included a twelve-storey, 140,000 square-foot office tower on the northeast corner of the site. (It provides offices for Air Canada and Maple Leaf Sports and Entertainment Ltd.) Maple Leafs ownership proceeded to develop the site. It constructed the Galleria, a covered, climate-controlled public walkway at the north end of Air Canada Centre to house the ticket office, a food court, and retail outlets; an atrium space, Maple Leaf Square, that can accommodate five thousand fans and includes a 50 × 80-foot video screen on its outside wall, a television studio, restaurants, and bars; and, in 2010, the $500-million Residences of Maple Leaf Square. Jointly developed with MLSE by the real estate firm Cadillac Fairview and the condominium developer Lanterra, it comprises two condominium towers

9.6 *Opposite*
Fans watch a basketball game on the 50 x 80-foot video screen in Maple Leaf Square adjacent to the Air Canada Centre.

of 44 and 40 storeys with 872 units. The towers rise from a nine-storey podium containing the 170-room, luxury Hotel Le Germain, 200,000 square feet of office space, and over 100,000 square feet of retail space.

In Los Angeles, Tim Leiweke president and CEO of Anschutz Entertainment Group (AEG), owners of the Staples Center, were quick to follow Toronto's example. Before the Staples Center opened in 1999, AEG had already assembled nearby land, adding more later to a total of four million square feet. It began developing L.A. Live, a $2.5-billion sports, residential, and entertainment campus. The first of three phases saw the inauguration, in 2007, of a nearly two-acre plaza directly outside the Staples Center. Then, in December 2008, AEG opened a series of sports and entertainment restaurants and bars, the Grammy Museum, and the 2,300-seat Club Nokia. Finally, in 2010, AEG opened the Regal Cinema (14 screens,) the 54-floor JW Marriott and Ritz-Carlton hotel (over 1,000 rooms and 224 luxury condos), and the five-storey ESPN building, which houses ESPN Zone (a restaurant with over 150 television screens and more than 45 interactive games and attractions) and a full-fledged broadcast facility. Tim Leiweke described the origins of the scheme: "When we started thinking this up, we went to Universal Studios and Disneyland. The theme parks have a very brilliant concept. If twenty million people go through Disneyland, why can't we build hotels, restaurants, and retail that service the twenty million people? That's all we did here."[33]

9.7
L.A. Live. A $2.5-billion sports, residential, and entertainment campus adjacent to the Staples Center.

The granddaddy of all SADS, if it ever gets completed, is Dubai Sports City. Begun in 2003, it is projected to cover fifty million square feet, cost $4 billion, and include four major stadiums and arenas seating over 100,000 people, a golf course designed by Ernie Els, housing in residential towers and villas, and two retail complexes.[34] The goal is total immersion, according to Malcolm Thorpe, the director of marketing for sports business at Dubai Sports City: "Live Sport is what we're all about. People will live here, spend time here, send their kids to programs here, and be immersed in sport."[35] But immersion is only a means to expand the money-making potential of sports facilities. "I think every new sports facility will have some other element to it in the future to drive revenue. You can't put more and more use on the sports element. You need to have the opportunity to create revenue. Selling real estate or leasing shop space is a great way to do that."[36] We are a long way from the single-concourse arena of the 1960s selling hot dogs, beer, and souvenir programs.

SADS are the wave of the future. Why let the wealth "trickle down" when the sports team can have a piece of it all, with no requirement to share the profits with players, other teams, or the league? Bruce Ratner's $4-billion Atlantic Yards development on a twenty-two-acre site in central Brooklyn was originally projected to include sixteen residential towers with 6,400 apartments and office towers in addition to a Frank Gehry-designed $1-billion glass-walled basketball arena.[37] According to the *New York Times*, "Atlantic Yards emerged late in 2003 when Mr. Ratner bought the Nets for $300 million and announced plans to move the team to Brooklyn. Although he was not a basketball fan, Mr. Ratner saw the arena as a lever for a much larger development of housing, parks and office space directly across from a major transit center."[38] As economic conditions worsened, Gehry was removed as architect of the Barclays Center and Ratner's larger development plans for the site were put on hold.

The same poor economic forecast has delayed Edmonton's planned replacement of the Edmonton Oilers home, the 1974 Rexall Place (formerly Northlands Coliseum). Local business-man and Oilers owner Daryl Katz, whose Rexall pharmacy company already owns naming rights on the current Edmonton facility, is spearheading the new project there. Katz had pledged $100 million to the $450 million cost of the new facility and also promised to invest a further

9.8
Aerial view of Edmonton's proposed Rogers Place and surrounding "Ice District," scheduled to open 2016.

$100 million into development around the arena. And that's the key. The Katz Group is teaming up with WAM Development Group to develop what is being touted as the biggest local development since West Edmonton Mall, an expected $1.5 billion worth of neighbouring projects called the "Ice District." It is expected to include an office tower, 800 housing units, two hotels, bars, shops, restaurants, a parkade, and a casino.[39] Edmonton City Council reached an agreement to share the costs of the arena in October 2011, but with expected costs rising to $475 million and the team demanding millions in new tax concessions, the project stalled (though, at the time of writing, it is underway).

Team owners who can buy up and develop land adjacent to their existing downtown sports facilities will continue to do so, following the example of Los Angeles and Toronto. Rogers Arena in Vancouver (1995) and the Bell Centre in Montreal (1996) have added real estate developments on adjacent land. In Vancouver Aquilini Developments and Construction, the same family that owns the Canucks, developed a $300-million project. Completed in 2016, it provides a total of 614 rental units and offices in three towers ranging in height from twenty-three to thirty-two storeys.[40] In Montreal the forty-eight-storey, $175-million Tour des Canadiens condo project provides 534 units and the opportunity for residents to skate at the Bell Centre once a year.[41]

Build It ... Or Else

During the massive expansion that took place in all four major league sports beginning in 1960, the number of teams nearly doubled, with the addition of fifty-five new franchises through 1998. Hockey saw the most dramatic change over this period, rising from a six-team league in 1967 to thirty teams. The primary reasons for this growth have been demographic and economic. With growing urbanization over this period, more and more cities achieved a size that could support a major-league team. Positive economic advantages such as rising prices for new franchises were also a factor, as were negative considerations: political pressure and potential anti-trust legislation, and fear of rival leagues.[42] The NHL in particular embraced expansion only under duress, as a means to eliminate competition from the rival World Hockey Association, which operated from 1972 to 1979.

In spite of significant growth in the number of franchises, more cities desire a professional sports franchise than are available. Naturally, this demand increases the value of existing franchises and the power of franchise owners in their negotiations with cities and governments. According to political scientist and urban historian Charles Euchner: "Until there is reform of the structure of major league sports in the United States, cities will always be confronting the dilemma of subsidizing or losing itinerant teams. The teams hold all the advantages in negotiations with cities, chief among them being a highly desirable product in artificially short supply ... the major leagues of baseball and football in the United States enjoy monopoly status as the

9.9 *Opposite*
Tour des Canadiens condominium tower, next to the Centre Bell.
Residents get to skate at the Bell Centre once a year.

superior brand of competition. This gives the leagues extraordinary power in their relations with cities, because it makes them unique and impossible to duplicate."[43]

The only option for many cities hoping to nab a major-league franchise has been to lure away an existing one. According to Danielson, "providing a major league arena or stadium is the way places demonstrate they are ready for the big time. New buildings and attractive deals are the means by which places tempt teams to relocate and compete for expansion franchises."[44] Team owners have played on this fear to extract ever-larger economic concessions from their home cities, demanding everything from new arenas and stadiums to larger tax breaks. In fact, threatening to move their teams to another city unless such public subsidies are received became so common that it was given a name – "sportmail."[45] For Richard Gruneau and David Whitson: "It is simply through the negotiation of the financial interests of team owners (that is, in maximizing the profitability of their franchises) and the co-ordination of these interests with the growth strategies of local political and business elites that new arenas are built or not, and that teams come to and threaten to leave cities like Edmonton, Winnipeg, or Quebec. Indeed the pursuit of major-league franchises and 'world class' events today is now best understood as part of a larger project in which corporate and civic elites struggle to establish and maintain their cities' status in a transnational economic and cultural hierarchy of cities."[46]

This economic environment does not directly affect the design of sports facilities but it does determine whether they get built, where, and with what frequency. Danielson claims that "the relationship between places and professional sports is increasingly driven by the desire of teams and leagues for new arenas and stadiums. Underlying these demands is the accelerating obsolescence of existing facilities."[47] But the definition of obsolescence in this context and the reasons for the speed of its arrival need clarification.

In 1967 the average age of the six NHL buildings was forty years. A year later, with the addition of six teams in new buildings, that average had dropped to about twenty-two but by 1990 it had risen again, to thirty-two. In 2010, after the construction of twenty-eight new facilities, the average age of NHL facilities was now 15.6 years. Yet many sports facilities that were replaced in the 1990s were not architecturally obsolete, in the sense of depleted batteries. They were superseded because they could no longer compete economically. In 1995, shortly after Gary Bettman was installed as the NHL's first commissioner, he took aim at those critics who complained that teams were blackmailing cities by threatening to relocate unless new arenas were forthcoming. According to Jonathon Gatehouse, Bettman "delivered the same message he had been peddling to governments in Quebec, Manitoba, and Hartford, Connecticut: Those who wanted to keep their NHL teams into the next century had better find a way to house them 'appropriately.'"[48] While his comments might still sound threatening to cities with existing NHL franchises, Bettman's position should also be understood as establishing a very significant entry condition for any city hoping to join the NHL club.

It was in this context of flux and uncertainty enveloping the sports world that one architectural firm proposed an ingenious and playful solution to the problem of itinerant teams and franchise relocation. In 1997 the Los Angeles-based Academy of Architecture, Arts and Sciences sponsored an ideas competition for the design of a football stadium for a proposed site on Santa Monica beach. The competition's underlying premise was that a new stadium might help lure an NFL

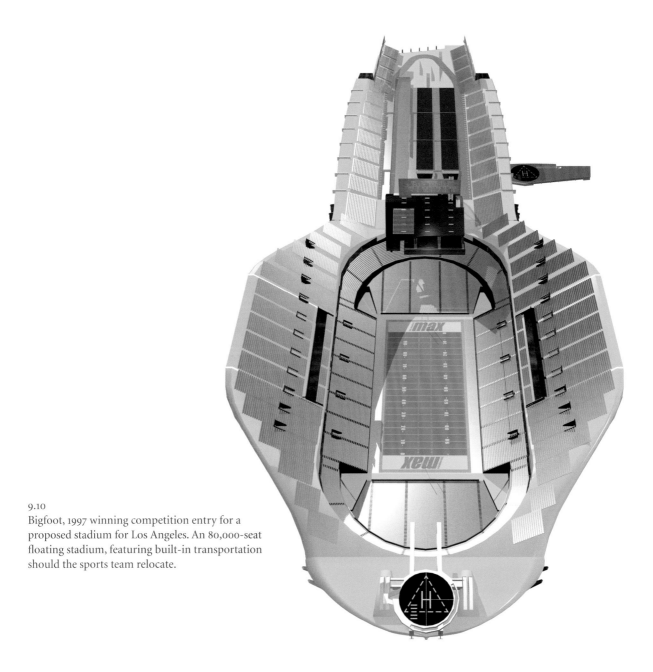

9.10
Bigfoot, 1997 winning competition entry for a
proposed stadium for Los Angeles. An 80,000-seat
floating stadium, featuring built-in transportation
should the sports team relocate.

football team back to Los Angeles. Two football teams had recently abandoned the city – the Rams
left for St Louis in 1994 and the Raiders departed for Oakland in 1995. The competition-winning
design, by New York-based heneghan peng architects (hparc), implicitly posed the question: "But
what if the new team moves again?" They called their response Bigfoot. In place of a traditional,
land-based brick-and-mortar building, heneghan peng proposed an 80,000-seat floating stadium,
housed within the hull of a repurposed super tanker. The stadium would be docked at Santa

Monica pier during the football season and could easily sail away with the team should the siren song of a new port of call lure it away.

The architects promoted the project's viability by pointing out that twenty-five of thirty NFL teams were then sited in cities with waterway access and further argued that their floating stadium would enable its owners to bypass the political and commercial aspects associated with siting such a large facility on dry land. And, well aware of what they called "the peripheral commercial conditions surrounding the game," they conceived their stadium project as a shopping mall, with the football stadium serving as an anchor store. Finally, lest diehard fans fear that such a novel solution might do away with traditional forms of participation, heneghan peng proposed accommodating tailgate parties on the parking lot/deck of the ship and also on the adjacent beach, where tailgaters could watch simultaneous broadcasts of the game on large, ship-mounted screens.[49]

The architectural heritage for this project is deep; it shares elements of ephemerality, flexibility, mobility, and humour with the 1960s pop-up cities imagined by the British Archigram group and Cedric Price.[50] And it recalls Louis Kahn's floating concert hall *Point Counterpoint* (1964–67) while also harkening back to Le Corbusier's fascination with ocean liners, and specifically to his *Asile Flottant*, a 130-bed floating dormitory that he realized for the Salvation Army in Paris in 1929 by converting a 260-foot-long concrete barge. A floating stadium may seem at once fanciful and pessimistic; like a pre-nuptial agreement, it suggests a relationship that may only be temporary while establishing the terms or at least the means of departure at the outset. Yet, if the relationship between cities and sports franchises can be compared to marriage, it is all too often a union of partners with mismatched levels of commitment. Twenty years after this competition, Los Angeles may finally have attracted a willing suitor. Early in 2016 Stanley Kroenke announced plans to move his St Louis Rams NFL team to Inglewood, California. According to the *New York Times*, "St. Louis never had the real estate possibilities that Inglewood does. In St. Louis, Kroenke was the owner of the Rams. In Inglewood, Kroenke will be the owner of the Rams plus the developer of a retail and entertainment complex that [Dallas Cowboys owner Jerry] Jones has described as Disneyland for professional football."[51]

This is not a new story nor is it exclusive to football. Between 1976 and 1998 nine NHL teams changed locations.[52] Yet, of the nine cities that lost teams during this period, four eventually regained them, either by the award of a new franchise or through the acquisition and relocation of another existing team.[53] Two examples highlight this game of musical franchises. In 1976, after only two years of operation, the Kansas City Scouts were relocated to Denver, becoming the Colorado Rockies. Six years later the Rockies moved again, to New Jersey. Then in 1995 Denver regained its NHL franchise when the Quebec Nordiques team was sold and relocated there. Atlanta, Georgia, has the distinction of winning and then losing two NHL franchises, both to Canadian cities. In 1980 the Flames moved to Calgary after eight years of operation in Atlanta and in 2011 the Thrashers relocated to Winnipeg. While many of these relocations were a consequence of small-market cities unable to sustain an NHL team, in every instance the relocated team moved directly into a new building in their new home city or did so within a few years.

On the other side of the ledger are those cities left standing at the altar. Hamilton (Copps Coliseum, 1983), Kansas City (Sprint Center, 2007), Quebec City (Videotron Centre, 2015), and Seattle (Sonics Arena Project) all have built or are moving toward construction of arenas in the absence of major-league franchises and in the hopes of attracting them. Meanwhile, NHL teams in Sunrise (Florida) and Phoenix are regularly mentioned as potential candidates for relocation. The New York Islanders moved from their home on Long Island to the new Barclays Center in Brooklyn for the start of the 2015–16 season.

On 24 September 2012 Seattle City Council voted 6–2 to approve a financing agreement with principal investor Chris Hansen for a new $490-million multi-purpose sports arena, a major step in the city's effort to attract a professional sports franchise, preferably an NBA team. (Seattle lost its NBA team, the Sonics, to Oklahoma City in 2008.) Meanwhile, back in Edmonton, Oilers owner Daryl Katz and the City of Edmonton continued to disagree over how much each should contribute to the rising cost of a new home for the Oilers. What's a billionaire owner to do? Katz followed a well-worn script according to which team owners threaten to move or sell the team if suitable financial concessions are not forthcoming from the municipality. On the very day that Seattle City Council moved their city closer to realizing their own arena, Katz was in Seattle, accompanied by Oilers' president Patrick LaForge and team executives Craig MacTavish and Kevin Lowe, "where he met with unspecified officials about the possibility of relocating the club."[54] When word of his trip became public, Katz was forced to apologize to enraged fans, taking out full-page ads in the *Edmonton Journal* and *Edmonton Sun* newspapers.[55] Yet even his apology contained an implied threat: "I did it [travelled to Seattle] because I'm fighting for a deal that will enable the team to stay in Edmonton – and not because I want them to be anywhere else."[56]

Spectators attending events at the corporate-entertainment complex differed significantly from their earlier twentieth-century counterparts and their mode of spectating was also entirely new. The ownership, financing, and urban strategies contributing to the construction, siting, and design of corporate-entertainment complexes had changed as well. These facilities were brought back to the downtown core with the goal of jump-starting urban regeneration; they were sited within plazas to suggest openness and accessibility; and they featured transparent exteriors and landmarks such as towers to simulate public buildings. Such changes were not undertaken in response to changes in the game of hockey. Sport no longer drove the design of these buildings because professional sport had been reconceived as a unique brand of spectacular entertainment, slotted into these facilities' performance schedules.

In the Conclusion that follows we will see how owners looked upon these facilities less as venues for hockey teams than as opportunities for profit making, within the facility itself and by colonizing the facility's surrounding territory to create urban entertainment districts.

Conclusion

The Disappearance of the Hockey Arena

"I asked the Zebra,
  are you black with white stripes?
  Or white with black stripes?"
  – Shel Silverstein, *A Light in the Attic*[1]

"Simply put, the 'arena' is dead."
  – Brian Brisbin, Brisbin Brooks Beynon Architects

Each development in the design and use of buildings for skating and hockey brought corresponding changes to their names. The first covered structures for skating in the 1860s were called rinks. These were followed, beginning in the late 1890s, by buildings specifically intended to accommodate spectator hockey, called arenas. In the 1920s, as the NHL asserted itself as the dominant provider of major-league hockey, a series of new buildings were constructed in permanent materials. They were named Forum and Garden or Gardens. And with NHL expansion in the 1960s the names Coloseum, Coliseum, and Colisée were added, in reference to the grandeur and scale of these facilities. Since the 1990s the majority of sports facilities in which major-league hockey is played have been called Center (Centre) and Place.[2] What does this change in name mean? How and why did it come about?

On the one hand, the inclination to name these facilities Center and Place could be seen as a reaction to the buildings that preceded them, those geographically placeless and context-less turnpike facilities of the 1960s and 1970s that were situated in the middle of asphalt parking lots. They lacked geographic specificity or attachment to a particular community. The Centers and Places of the 1990s were located, or relocated, in city centres, and their names announce that they are "some-place" as opposed to "no-place." But being "in" the city is not necessarily to be "of" the city. These large complexes do not necessarily integrate with their urban settings; many still retain their former suburban character as self-contained destinations. Following John Hannigan, the Centers and Places of the 1990s can be characterized as solipsistic, detached from their surroundings, inward looking, and self-referential.[3]

But what if the new designation actually reflects a fundamental change in the nature of these buildings as compared to their predecessors? What if hockey arenas, gardens, forums, and coliseums all belong to one family or building type while the new Centers and Places belong to another? What I am suggesting is that through 100 years of development, from rinks to arenas and then to gardens, forums and coliseums, buildings for hockey shared a common DNA – call it the "arena" gene, which gave rise to buildings whose primary function was to bring large numbers of spectators in proximity to an ice surface. But the Centers and Places of the 1990s were conceived according to another model; they represent an evolutionary break in the development of buildings where professional hockey is played. In hindsight, what at first looked like evolution turns out to have been devolution; the arrival of the Center marked the disappearance, the extinction of the professional hockey arena.

Regardless of their designations, buildings for hockey have always been defined by multi-functionality. From the early nineteenth century, buildings for skating and hockey served more than skaters and hockey players. By economic necessity they were transformable to other functions. In the days before artificial ice, this change occurred seasonally. In a poetic sense the process mirrored the ephemeral nature of the original spaces for skating and hockey, frozen ponds that literally disappeared with the spring thaw. The echoes of this seasonal change can still be heard today in the grim suggestion, come spring playoff time, that the losers will soon be playing golf (the professional hockey equivalent of "pushing up daisies").

With the advent of artificial ice, the changeovers – from skating and hockey to almost any other activity – could occur daily throughout the year, although ice quality often suffered. Hockey players complained bitterly about poor ice quality after the circus had come to town or, worse still, about the presence of buzzing flies after a livestock fair, a situation with which the San Jose Sharks had to contend from 1991 to 1993 when they played at the Cow Palace (officially the 1-A District Agricultural Association).

Over the past 150 years these rinks, arenas, gardens, and forums – generically, large indoor spaces with seats for spectators – hosted a multiplicity of events. This has been true no matter what sport was played by the building's primary tenant – hockey or basketball. Which leads to the sort of philosophical conundrum epitomized by the riddle: Is a zebra white with black stripes or black with white stripes? Was Madison Square Garden III (1925–68) a boxing arena where hockey was played or a hockey arena that hosted multiple other events? Was Boston Garden the home of the Celtics or the Bruins? Is the place where local youths play hockey a hockey arena that hosts community events, or a community centre where hockey is sometimes played? Has some pure form of the hockey arena ever existed?

In his seminal study *A History of Building Types*, architectural historian Nikolaus Pevsner chose to focus on the nineteenth century, which he identified as the crucial century for the development of new types, a consequence of the Industrial Revolution and rapid urbanization that together created an unprecedented demand for new building forms to house the expanding requirements of business, leisure, and civic life.[4]

Railway stations, factories, and skating rinks are but three of the building types introduced during the nineteenth century. Each of these building types evolved over the course of subsequent decades, adapting to technological and social change. But in the cases of railway stations and factories, as for many other building types, they continued to serve the basic set of functional requirements for which they were originally conceived and built. Trains became faster and sleeker in design but passengers still needed to purchase tickets, confirm itineraries, check bags, board trains, and greet friends and family, all while protected from the weather. Buildings for hockey also underwent massive changes throughout the twentieth century: they became larger in order to accommodate more fans; they provided heating, air conditioning, and restaurants for fan comfort; and they introduced lighting and sound systems and additional space for the staging of diverse events, from the Barnum and Bailey circus to Beatles concerts. Yet, after all these changes, a Coliseum or Forum still maintained a functional relationship, a family resemblance, with the arenas that preceded them, call it "arena-ness."

But with the end of the twentieth century a new slate of NHL buildings broke ground and in the process broke company with their predecessors in fundamental ways. Building types are defined by their functions. These functions are determined by clients who dictate their requirements to architects in what is collectively referred to as the architectural brief. The arenas constructed for expansion teams in the late 1960s and 1970s were the last NHL buildings for which hockey defined the architectural brief. At Bloomington, Denver, Long Island, Los Angeles, Philadelphia, and Washington, new arenas were built in direct response to the need for facilities to accommodate expansion or transferred NHL teams, to provide a space in which hockey teams could compete and spectators could watch them. These buildings would have been identified as hockey or sports arenas no matter what other additional, secondary functions they were asked to serve.

The new Centers and Places constructed in the 1990s differ from these expansion-era arenas because the architectural brief that defines them changed. Clients no longer wanted buildings limited by a specific activity, "hockey" or "basketball" – John Bale's "monocultural" sports landscapes. They deliberately sought facilities that were functionally indeterminate or ambiguous. The clients for these facilities were no longer in the business of a particular sport. Instead, they were engaged in real estate development, in the staging of spectacle for mass audiences, and in ensuring that there were ample opportunities for those attending to consume a wide range of other services and products within the facility or nearby. The building itself was now required to serve as a component of that spectacle and an increasingly important actor in the overall spectatorship experience. The subject or flavour of a particular spectacle could change regularly, from hockey to wrestling to boxing to Céline Dion, but no individual activity could be permitted to define the identity of the Center.

The new Centers and Places were not a functional response to changes within the game of hockey. Rather, as I have shown, they were a response to changing social and economic realities surrounding the staging of spectacle and its consumption, in part as demanded by a new set of spectators. The presentation of professional hockey had broadened in the 1990s to include increasing elements of entertainment, media, and luxury consumption. For venue operators, hockey matches were now equivalent to other forms of spectacular entertainment, treated as content or "product" and slotted into performance schedules. Hockey, as hockey, was no longer a defining element in the architectural brief for the new Centers and Places, nor is it a factor in the identification of most such facilities. Once a sport watched by fans in arenas designed for this purpose, hockey is now repackaged and staged as spectacular experience, consumed by audiences in Centers and Places also designed for that purpose.

A consequence of the devolution of arenas and Gardens to Centers and Places has been the disappearance of the hockey arena. The new Centers subsume the hockey arena's function, as well as that of the basketball arena, the concert hall, the circus venue, et al. All of these former "places" survive but only as a set of underclothes or stage props (different playing surfaces, altered seating configurations) that the Centers and Places change into to suit the event. The professional hockey arena as a distinct, physical place has become extinct.

Diehard hockey fans may continue to regard the TD Garden as the "home of the Bruins" but those who own and manage such facilities cannot afford to define their buildings so narrowly. Clients get the buildings they demand. And corporate owners in the 1990s did not want hockey arenas. What they needed were generic, shape-shifting "no-places," buildings that could accommodate anything and everyone while generating excitement in their own right. The reason for marketing campaigns, like the ones discussed earlier, that sought to identify and reconnect hockey fans to their teams' new facilities, was to retain those diehard fans by convincing them that the new, corporate-entertainment centres were coeval with the mythic hockey grounds of their memories. The arrival of the Place/Center in the 1990s marked the final step in the devolution of the hockey arena. To appreciate the fundamental ways in which these new facilities differed from their predecessors, I turn to a final example, the planning of a new facility constructed in the 1990s for a city with no pre-existing hockey tradition, indeed there was not yet even a franchise.

In 1993 Nashville, Tennessee, was desperate to attract a major-league sports franchise. The City Council understood that the best way to lure an existing team, or of improving the likelihood of their being awarded a new franchise, was to construct a brand-new facility. Following the recent example of Anaheim, Nashville employed a "build it and they will come" philosophy.[5] Council approved a property-tax increase in 1993 that enabled the city to sell $120 million in bonds while

10.1
Nashville (now Bridgestone) Arena.

announcing a design competition that resulted in the selection of HOK Sport as the arena's architect. So anxious was the city to bag an NBA or NHL team that Nashville's mayor, Phil Bredesen, offered an additional $20 million to the owners of any team that would relocate to Nashville, an offer that was refused by team owners in New Jersey, Miami, Winnipeg, and Hartford. The mayor subsequently withdrew his offer when, in 1997, Nashville was awarded an NHL expansion franchise. Mayor Bredesen announced: "The animal has been tagged."[6]

Although a major-league sports team was deemed important to the city's status, as it was to the economic viability of the new facility, it was never the primary factor in the building's design. Announcing the winning scheme, the journal *Progressive Architecture* noted how the competition for what it called a "sports and concert arena" "demonstrates the difficulty of addressing urban context, the functional requirements of a 20,000-seat hall, and a city's urban aspirations all in one building."[7] According to this article, the brief to which competing architects responded stressed the importance of the arena's function as a concert hall, likening the arena to "a concert hall that they also play basketball in."[8] This focus is also evident from the make-up of the competition jury for the Nashville arena, which included, in addition to the expected architects, country music star Vince Gill and New York Knicks basketball player Anthony Mason.

HOK senior vice-president Ben Barnert noted that the city wanted a landmark that people could identify with, like the Sydney Opera House. HOK's design for the Nashville (now Bridgestone) Arena, which opened in 1996, attempted to satisfy this wish by emphasizing the building's relationship to music, on the exterior and on the interior.[9] One element of the project, a 1,400-square foot rehearsal hall, described as a "sound stage quality space," includes a full concert stage; it has accommodated pay-per-view concerts, video shoots, and full tour rehearsals. HOK designed this space to resemble a French horn in plan. A proposed but

10.2
Nashville (now Bridgestone) Arena.

unexecuted design for a parking lot across from the rehearsal hall was to have been graded like a drive-in theatre, in order to evoke, in plan, the radiating sound waves emitted from the horn/rehearsal hall.[10]

Continuing the music analogy, the architects conceived the arena's roof as a music box lid, raised slightly to allow the sound to escape, while the terrazzo floor pattern of the main concourse was meant to resemble the neck of a guitar, with bronze dividing strips representing the strings and white discs serving as fret markers. At the lower suite level, balcony recesses were designed to resemble a piano keyboard. Artificial lighting in different parts of the arena was deployed in order to evoke the experience of being on stage or backstage. Whatever you may think of HOK's ham-fisted attempts, it is clear that the building's primary focus is music, not basketball, and certainly not hockey.

The seating arrangement and acoustics also were designed to serve the auditorium's function as a concert hall. While the seating in sports arenas is usually organized in symmetrical, oval-shaped seating bowls, at Nashville HOK opted for a horseshoe-shaped seating plan, with far fewer seats on one of the arena's short ends, a configuration that favours stage events. HOK worked with acoustical consultants Wrightson Johnson Haddon and Williams to ensure optimal acoustics for concerts. Noting that sport and concert venues require different sound configurations, HOK on-site representative Bob Jalilvand explained that "in sporting venues you typically want a lot of live sound – echoes and roars – but in concerts you want clear, crisp sound without too much reflection or reverberation."[11] To ensure the best concert sound for the Nashville arena, the consultants specified sound-absorptive materials such as upholstered seats, a sprayed-on acoustical treatment over the stage, fin baffles to improve bass sounds, a perforated metal halo ceiling with a sound blanket and baffles within the roof structure, and sound blankets in walls at the back of the upper seating. HOK's efforts to forge a first-class music facility clearly paid off; in 2012 Nashville's Bridgestone Arena ranked sixth in the United States in terms of concert attendance and in 2011 it was the eighth busiest facility in North America and the twentieth busiest in the world.[12]

It would be easy to dismiss Nashville's experience as exceptional, outside the norm of designs for hockey buildings, were it not for evidence to the contrary. By any standard, Toronto is a hockey city with a long history of teams playing at the professional level and a long line of buildings specifically designed to accommodate the sport. Yet, in describing his firm's design for the Air Canada Centre, Brian Brisbin of Brisbin Brooks Beynon Architects explained: "It's a theatre of sport and entertainment … One of our objectives at ACC has been to adapt the arena to the concert venue. It has to embody aspects of sports … but also function in a much greater capacity."[13] "Simply put, the 'arena' is dead. Sport is entertainment; entertainment occurs in theatres; we design theatres of sport and entertainment, not arenas."[14]

In 2014 Populous (formerly HOK) released a design for a proposed new facility for the Calgary Flames of the NHL. Designed by Brian Mirakian, the project points to the future of sports-entertainment centres, now made possible through the agency of digital design and smart technology. These advances allow architects to produce dynamic buildings that can change states. No longer will clients have to choose between facility designs that favour either sport or entertainment. The Calgary design features a responsive, transformable ceiling concept that adapts the interior to the event. In hockey mode the interior presents the familiar spectacle of tiered platforms of seating conforming to the oval ice surface with views up to the hanging Jumbotron screen. In entertainment mode the Jumbotron screen retracts into the roof cavity while sound baffles and wall sections descend to enclose a smaller, three-sided seating configuration, providing the appropriately intimate and sound absorptive environment more suited to theatre and music performances. This project definitively solves the problem of multi-functionality that has bedevilled designers of skating and hockey facilities since the 1860s. So is the proposed Calgary facility a theatre or an arena? It's neither. It's a zebra.

This book has described a move from adaptability to ambiguity. Architecture on ice has proved a slippery building type for a slippery surface. The difficulty in defining this building type, even of determining if it ever existed, reflects a continually shifting response by clients and architects to changing economic realities. Over the twentieth century, perhaps only banking and shopping buildings have experienced equally dramatic changes. The vast, ornate banking halls and massive, multi-storey department stores constructed early in the century have given way to wall-mounted ATMs or disappeared entirely into the ether of online computer terminals. In the future people will skate and play hockey wherever ice surfaces can be found but the commercial game and its venues will continue to evolve, as always, in response to economics, urbanism, and technology.

Tables

Table 1
Chronological listing of selected skating rinks and hockey arenas in North America
(with architects and dates of construction/activity)

Skating Rinks, 1862–1908

Building Name	City	Architect	Opening date	NHL use
Quebec City Skating Rink I	Quebec City		1852	
Montreal Skating Club Rink	Montreal		1860	
Victoria Skating Rink	Montreal	Lawford and Nelson	1862–	
Halifax Skating Rink	Halifax		1863	
Skating Arena and Curling Rink	Ottawa	Henry Augustus Sims	1864	
Quebec City Skating Rink II	Quebec City		1864	
Victoria Skating Rink	Saint-John, NB	Charles Walker	1864–65	
Royal Skating Rink	Ottawa		1868	
Boston Skating Rink	Boston		1868	
Quincy Skating Rink	Quincy, IL	Hervey, Johnson and Co.	1868/69	
Velocipede Rink	Toronto		c. 1869–	
Curling and Skating Rink	Toronto	Clarence W. Moberly	1874	
Kingston Skating Rink	Kingston	Robert Gage	1874	
Caledonia Curling and Skating Club (later Mutual Street Rink)	Toronto	William F. McCaw	1875	

Skating Rinks, 1862–1908 (continued)

Toronto Curling and Skating Club	Toronto	William F. McCaw	1876	
Stellarton Rink	Stellarton, NS		1876	
Quebec Skating Club Rink III	Quebec City	William T. Thomas	1877	
Crystal Rink (I)	Montreal		c. 1878	
Public Exhibition Hall and Rink	Yarmouth, NS	Palliser, Palliser and Co.	1878	
Granite Curling and Skating Rink	Toronto	Norman B. Dick	1880	
Manitoba Curling and Skating Rink	Winnipeg	Mancel Wilmot	1880	
Singer Rink	Saint John		c. 1880	
Victoria Rink	Montreal	John W. Hopkins	1881	
Speed Skating Rink	Guelph	John Day	1882	
Skating Rink	London, ON	George F. Durand	1882	
Exhibition Hall and Ice Rink	Dartmouth	Henry Elliot	1883–84	
Dey's Skating Rink (I)	Ottawa		1884	
Skating Rink	St John's, NL	George Henry Jost	1884–85	
Mutual Street Skating Rink	Toronto	Charles Albert Walton	1885	
Prospect Park Skating and Curling Rink	Toronto	Norman B. Dick	1888	
Rideau Skating and Curling Rink	Ottawa	James R. Bowes	1888	1890–96
Quebec Skating Rink IV	Quebec City	Harry Staveley	1889	1910–20
St Alban's Skating and Curling Club	Toronto	Dennison and King	1890	
Duquesne Garden	Pittsburgh		1890*	1925–29
Sarnia Skating and Curling Club	Sarnia	Henry G. Phillips	1892	
Crystal Rink (II)	Montreal		c. 1893	
Victoria Skating and Curling Club	Guelph	George Rawer Bruce	1892	
Ice Palace Rink	New York		1894	
North Avenue Ice Palace	Baltimore		1894	
Schenley Park Casino	Pittsburgh		1895	
Convention Hall	Washington, DC		1896	
Clermont Avenue Rink	Brooklyn		1896	
Dey's Skating Rink (II)	Ottawa		1896	1897–1907
St Nicholas Rink	New York	Flagg and Chambers	1896	
Montagnard Skating Rink	Montreal	Gamelin and Huot	1898	
Sherman Rink	Calgary		1904	

*After 1895 for skating and hockey

First Spectator Arenas, 1898–1954

Building Name	City	Architect	Opening date	NHL use
Montreal (Westmount) Arena	Montreal		1898	1912–18
Chicago Coliseum	Chicago		1900	1926–29
Coliseum	Montreal		1907	
Jubilee Ice Rink	Montreal		1908	1918–19
Forum Roller Rink	Montreal		1908	
Elysium Rink	Cleveland		1908	
Dey's Arena	Ottawa		1907	1908–23
Boston (Matthews) Arena	Boston	Funk and Wilcox	1910	1924–28
Barton Street Arena (The Forum)	Hamilton		1910	1922–25
Victoria Arena	Victoria		1911	
Denman Street Arena	Vancouver	Thomas Hooper	1912	
Mutual Street Arena (Arena Gardens)	Toronto	Ross and McFarlane	1912	1917–31
Public Arena	Quebec	Ross and McFarlane	1912	
Mount Royal Arena	Montreal		1920	1920-26
Ottawa Auditorium	Ottawa		1923	1923–31
Windsor (Border Cities) Arena	Windsor		1924	1926–27
Madison Square Garden III	New York	Thomas W. Lamb	1925	1925–68
Varsity Arena	Toronto	Prof. T.R. Loudon, with Darling and Pearson	1926	
Montreal Forum	Montreal	John S. Archibald	1924	1924–96
Detroit Olympia (Olympia Stadium)	Detroit	C. Howard Crane	1927	1927–79
Boston Garden	Boston	Funk & Wilcox	1928	1928–95
Chicago Stadium	Chicago	Hall, Lawrence and Ratcliffe	1929	1929–94
St Louis Arena	St Louis	Gustel R. Kiewitt	1929	1967–94
Vancouver Forum	Vancouver		1930	
Maple Leaf Gardens	Toronto	Ross and MacDonald	1931	1931–99
Memorial Auditorium	Buffalo	Green and James	1940	1970–96
Cow Palace (California State Livestock Pavilion)	San Francisco		1941	1991–93
Le Colisée	Quebec City	Robert Blatter	1949	1979–95
Calgary Corral	Calgary	John Stevenson	1950	1980–83

NHL Expansion Arenas, 1961–1983

Building Name	City	Architect	Opening date	NHL use
Winnipeg Arena	Winnipeg	Moody and Moore	1955	1979–96
Memorial Sports Arena	Los Angeles	Welton Beckett	1959	1967
Memorial Coliseum	Portland, OR	SOM	1960	
Civic Arena	Pittsburgh	Mitchell and Ritchey	1961	1967–2010
Oakland-Alameda County Coliseum	Oakland	SOM (Myron Goldsmith, Chuck Basset)	1966	1967–76
Pacific Coloseum	Vancouver	W.K. Noppe	1966	1970–95
Metropolitan Sports Center	Bloomington, MN		1967	1967–93
Civic Centre Arena	Ottawa	Craig and Kohler	1967	1992–95
Los Angeles Forum	Inglewood, CA	Charles Luckman Associates	1967	1967–99
Montreal Forum (renovation)	Montreal	Ken Sedleigh	1968	1968–96
The Spectrum	Philadelphia	SOM (Myron Goldsmith)	1967	1967–96
MSG Center	New York	Charles Luckman Associates	1968	1968–
The Omni	Atlanta	Thompson, Ventulett and Stainback, Architects	1972	1972–80
Nassau Veterans Memorial (County) Coliseum	Long Island, NY	Welton Beckett	1972	1972–2015
US Air Arena	Washington	Shaver Partnership	1973	1973–97
Northlands Coliseum	Edmonton	Phillips, Barrett, Hillier, Jones Partners Wynn, Forbes, Lord, Feldberg and Schmidt	1974	1974–78* 1979–
Kemper Arena	Kansas City, MO	Helmut Jahn	1974	1974–76
Richfield Coliseum	Richfield, OH	George E. Ross Architects, Inc.	1974	1976–78
McNichols Sports Arena	Denver	Sink/Combs Architects	1975	1975–82, 1995–98
Hartford Civic Center	Hartford	Kling and Associates	1975	1980–97
Joe Louis Arena	Detroit	Sith, Hinchmen and Gylls Architects	1979	1979–
Reunion Arena	Dallas	Harwood K. Smith and Partners	1980	1993–2001
Brendan Byrne Arena	New Jersey	Grad Partnership, Dilullo, Clauss, Ostroki and Partners	1981	1982–2007
Scotiabank Saddledome	Calgary	Graham McCourt	1983	1983–

*World Hockey Association

Corporate-Entertainment Complex, 1990–2010

Building Name	City	Architect	Opening date	NHL use
Miami Arena	Miami	Lloyd Jones Fillpot Associates	1988	1993–98
Thunderdome	Tampa	HOK Sport, Lescher and Mahoney Sports, Criswell, Blizzard and Blouin Architects	1990	1993–96
American West Arena	Phoenix	Ellerbe Becket	1992	1996–2003
Arrowhead Pond of Annaheim	Anaheim	HOK Sport	1993	1993–
San Jose Arena	San Jose	Sink Combs Dethlefs	1993	1993–
United Center	Chicago	HOK	1994	1994–
Kiel Center	St Louis	Ellerbe Becket	1994	1994–
Fleet Center	Boston	Ellerbe Becket	1995	1995–
MCI Center	Washington, DC	Ellerbe Becket	1995	1997–
General Motors Place	Vancouver	Brisbin Brook Beynon Architects	1995	1995–
Marine Midland Center	Buffalo	Ellerbe Becket	1996	1996–
Bell Centre (Molson Centre)	Montreal	Consortium of Quebec Architects	1996	1996–
Corel Centre	Ottawa	Rossetti Architects, Murray & Murray Architects	1996	1996–
Corestates Centre	Philadelphia	Ellerbe Becket	1996	1996–
Ice Palace	Tampa	Ellerbe Becket	1996	1996–
Gaylord Entertainment Center	Nashville	HOK	1996	1998–
Broward County Civic Arena	Miami	Ellerbe Becket	1998	
Pepsi Center	Denver	HOK	1998	1998–
Staples Center	Los Angeles	NBBJ	1999	1999–
Air Canada Centre	Toronto	HOK, Brisbin Brook Beynon Architects	1999	1999–
Philips Arena	Atlanta	HOK, Arquitectonica	1999	1999–2011
PNC Arena	Raleigh, NC	Odell and Associates	1999	1997–
Nationwide Arena	Columbus	Heinlein + Schrock, Inc., NBBJ	2000	2000–
Xcel Energy Center	Saint Paul, MN	HOK	2000	2000–
American Airlines Center	Dallas	Schwarz/Architectural Services, Inc.	2001	2001–
Glendale Arena	Glendale, AZ	HOK	2003	2003–

Corporate-Entertainment Complex, 1990–2010 (continued)

MTS Centre	Winnipeg	Sink Combs Dethlefs	2004	2011–
Prudential Center	Newark, NJ	HOK, Morris Adjmi Architects	2007	2007–
Consol Energy Center	Pittsburgh	HOK	2010	2010–
Barclays Center	Brooklyn	Ellerbe Becket, SHoP	2012	2015–

Table 2
NHL average seating capacity, 1917–1931

Year	Games Played	Average Seating Capacity Per Game*	Average Seating Capacity Per Season*
1917–18	22	7,166	157,652
1918–20	24	5,916	142,000
1920–23	24	8,167	196,008
1923–24	24	9,167	220,008
1924–25	30	9,050	271,500
1925–26	36	9,049	325,764
1926–27	44	9,165	403,260
1927–28	44	9,736	428,384
1928–29	44	11,057	486,508
1929–30	44	12,485	549,340
1930–31	44	12,485	549,340
1931–32	48	13,195	633,360

*Average capacity for teams that played in cities for more than five seasons: Montreal, Ottawa, Toronto, Boston, Chicago, Detroit, New York.

Table 3

NBA, NFL, MLB expansion-era arenas and stadiums, 1960–1985

NBA

Name	City	Opened	Cost (in millions)
Cobo Arena	Detroit	1960	$56*
Veterans Memorial Coliseum	Portland	1960	$8
KeyArena	Seattle	1962	$7
Baltimore Arena	Baltimore	1962	$14
Arizona Veterans Memorial Coliseum	Phoenix	1965	$7
San Diego Sports Arena	San Diego	1965	$6.4
HemisFair Arena	San Diego	1968	
Hofheinz Pavilion	Houston	1969	$4.2
Salt Palace	Salt Lake City	1969	$17
Market Square Arena	Indianapolis	1974	$23
Compaq Center	Houston	1975	$27
Pontia Silverdome	Pontiac, MI	1975	$55.7
Louisiana Superdome	New Orleans	1975	$134
Kingdome	Seattle	1976	$67
Izod Center	East Rutherford, NJ	1981	$85
Hubert H. Humphrey Metrodome	Minneapolis	1982	$68
Tacomadome	Tacoma	1983	$44
Arco Arena I	Sacramento	1985	

*Includes attached convention center

NFL

Name	City	Opened	Cost (in millions)
Candlestick Park	San Francisco	1960	$24.6
RFK Stadium	Washington, DC	1961	$20
Shea Stadium	New York	1964	$28.5
Astrodome	Houston	1965	$35
Liberty Bowl Memorial Stadium	Memphis	1965	$3.7
Annaheim Stadium	Anaheim	1966	$24
Busch Memorial Stadium	St Louis	1966	$25
Fulton County Stadium	Atlanta	1966	$18
Houlihan's Stadium	Tampa	1967	$4.1
San Diego Stadium	San Diego	1968	$27
Riverfront Stadium	Cincinnati	1970	$45
Three Rivers Stadium	Pittsburgh	1970	$55
Veterans Stadium	Philadelphia	1971	$63
Texas Stadium	Irving, TX	1971	$35
Foxboro Stadium	Foxboro, MA	1971	$7.1
Arrowhead Stadium	Kansas City, MO	1972	$150
Ralph Wilson Stadium	Buffalo	1973	$22
Aloha Stadium	Honolulu	1975	$37
Giants Stadium	East Rutherford, NJ	1976	$78
RCA Dome	Indianapolis	1983	$77.5

MLB

Name	City	Opened	Cost (in millions)
Dodger Stadium	Los Angeles	1962	$23
Arlington Stadium	Arlington, TX	1965	$1.9
Jack Murphy Stadium	San Diego	1967	$27
Kauffman Stadium	Kansas City	1973	$70
	1960–69	22	
	1970–79	15	
	1980–85	5	
	TOTAL	42	

Table 4
Cost of NHL facilities

Expansion Era, 1961–83

Building	City	Opening Date	Cost (in millions)
Winnipeg Arena	Winnipeg	1955	$2.5
Memorial Sports Arena	Los Angeles	1959	$8.5
Memorial Coliseum	Portland, OR	1960	$8
Civic Arena	Pittsburgh	1961	$22
Oakland-Alameda County Coliseum and Arena	Oakland	1966	$25.5 (for arena and stadium)
Pacific Coloseum	Vancouver	1966	$6
Metropolitan Sports Center	Bloomington	1967	$6
Civic Centre Arena	Ottawa	1967	$9.5
The Great Western Forum	Inglewood, CA	1967	$16
Montreal Forum – renovation	Montreal	1968	$10
The Spectrum	Philadelphia	1967	$12
MSG Center	New York	1968	$43
The Omni	Atlanta	1972	$17
Nassau Veterans Memorial (County) Coliseum	Long Island, NY	1972	$31.3
Capital Centre (US Air Arena)	Washington	1973	$18
Rexall Place (Northlands Coliseum)	Edmonton	1974	$68
Kemper Arena	Kansas City, MO	1974	$23
Richfield Coliseum	Richfield, OH	1974	$36
McNichols Sports Arena	Denver	1975	$16
Hartford Civic Center	Hartford	1975	$30
Joe Louis Arena	Detroit	1979	$57
Reunion Arena	Dallas	1980	$27
Brendan Byrne (Continental Airlines) Arena	New Jersey	1981	$85
Scotiabank Saddledome	Calgary	1983	$176

Corporate-Entertainment Complex, 1990–2010

Building	City	Opening Date	Cost (in millions)
Miami Arena	Miami	1988	$52.5
Thunderdome	Tampa	1990	$139
Scottrade Center (American West Arena)	Phoenix	1992	$90
Honda Centre (Arrowhead Pond of Anaheim)	Anaheim	1993	$120
HP Pavilion (San Jose Arena)	San Jose	1993	$170
United Center	Chicago	1994	$150
Savvis Center (Kiel Center)	St Louis	1994	$160
TD Garden (Fleet Center)	Boston	1995	$160
Verizon Center (MCI Center)	Washington, DC	1995	$260
Rogers Arena (General Motors Place)	Vancouver	1995	$160
First Niagara Center (Marine Midland Center)	Buffalo	1996	$122.5
Bell Centre (Molson Centre)	Montreal	1996	$230
Scotiabank Place (Corel Centre)	Ottawa	1996	$200
Wells Fargo Center (Corestates Centre)	Philadelphia	1996	$206
St Pete Times Forum (Ice Palace)	Tampa	1996	$139
Bridgestone Arena (Gaylord Entertainment Center)	Nashville	1996	$144
BankAtlantic Center (Broward County Civic Arena)	Miami	1998	$212
Pepsi Center	Denver	1998	$164.5
Staples Center	Los Angeles	1999	$375
Air Canada Centre	Toronto	1999	$265
Philips Arena	Atlanta	1999	$213.5
PNC Arena	Raleigh, NC	1999	$154
Nationwide Arena	Columbus	2000	$150
Xcel Energy Center	Saint Paul, MN	2000	$170
American Airlines Center	Dallas	2001	$350
Jobing.com Arena (Glendale Arena)	Glendale, Arizona	2003	$170
MTS Centre	Winnipeg	2004	$133
Prudential Center	Newark, NJ	2007	$375
Consol Energy Center	Pittsburgh	2010	$290

Table 5
Dimensions (in square feet) of NHL facilities, 1990–2010

Building	City	Opening Date	Size (sq ft)
Scottrade Center (American West Arena)	Phoenix	1992	665,000
Honda Centre (Arrowhead Pond of Annaheim)	Anaheim	1993	650,000
HP Pavilion (San Jose Arena)	San Jose	1993	450,000
United Center	Chicago	1994	1,000,000
Savvis Center (Kiel Center)	St. Louis	1994	665,000
TD Garden (Fleet Center)	Boston	1995	755,000
Verizon Center (MCI Center)	Washington, DC	1995	1,020,000
Rogers Arena (General Motors Place)	Vancouver	1995	475,000
First Niagara Center (Marine Midland Center)	Buffalo	1996	700,000
Bell Centre (Molson Centre)	Montreal	1996	780,000
Scotiabank Place (Corel Centre)	Ottawa	1996	600,000
Wells Fargo Center (Corestates Centre)	Philadelphia	1996	750,000
St Pete Times Forum (Ice Palace)	Tampa	1996	600,000
Bridgestone Arena (Gaylord Entertainment Center)	Nashville	1996	750,000
BankAtlantic Center (Broward County Civic Arena)	Miami	1998	872,000
Pepsi Center	Denver	1998	675,000
Staples Center	Los Angeles	1999	950,000
Air Canada Centre	Toronto	1999	665,000
Philips Arena	Atlanta	1999	680,000
PNC Arena	Raleigh, NC	1999	700,000
Nationwide Arena	Columbus	2000	700,000
Xcel Energy Center	Saint Paul, MN	2000	650,000
American Airlines Center	Dallas	2001	840,000
Jobing.com Arena (Glendale Arena)	Glendale, AZ	2003	600,000
MTS Centre	Winnipeg	2004	440,000
Prudential Center	Newark, NJ	2007	700,000
Consol Energy Center	Pittsburgh	2010	720,000

Illustrations Credits

0.1 Chamonix, 1924 Winter Olympics hockey match, Canada vs. United States of America.
© 1924 / Comité International Olympique (CIO) / COUTTET, Auguste, PHO10007878. | 7

0.2 Bob Frid/Icon SMI, photographer, fans in stands, Sharks at Canucks, 10 October 2013.
© Bob Frid/Icon SMI/Corbis. | 10

0.3 "Grand Skating Carnival at Halifax, N.S. – from a Sketch by J.J. Henderson." Reproduced
from *Canadian Illustrated News,* Montreal: Burland Lithographic Co. [11 February 1882], 84.
Collection Centre Canadien d'Architecture / Canadian Centre for Architecture, Montreal. | 12

1.1 Skating Rink, Quebec City. Library and Archives Canada, PA23517. | 16

1.2 Victoria Skating Rink, Montreal. Reproduced from *Montreal Herald,* 4 February 1884.
Bibliothèque et Archives nationales du Québec (Massicotte Album). | 18

1.3 Belle Isle Skating Pavilion, Detroit. Library of Congress, LC-D4-33769. | 20

1.4 Currier and Ives, lithographers, "Central Park, Winter, the Skating Pond," 1862, New York
Public Library. | 23

1.5 Caledonian Rink, Toronto. Reproduced from John Kerr, *Curling in Canada and the United
States.* Toronto: Toronto News Co. 1904. | 25

1.6 Thistle Curling Club, Montreal, 1871. Reproduced from *Canadian Illustrated News* (vol. 3, 21).
Library and Archives Canada, C-054213. | 27

1.7 Norman B. Dick, architect, Granite Curling and Skating Rink, Toronto, 1880. Reproduced from
John Kerr, *Curling in Canada and the United States.* Toronto: Toronto News Co. 1904. | 27

1.8 Stratford Ontario Curling Club. Postcard in the collection of the Hockey Hall of Fame. | 28

1.9 Victoria Skating Rink, Montreal. Bibliothèque et Archives nationales du Québec (Massicotte
Album). | 30

1.10 Drill Shed, Hamilton. Reproduced from *Canadian Illustrated News,* 12 September 1863, 211.
Fisher Rare Book Library, University of Toronto. | 30

1.11 Palliser, Palliser and Co., architect, Yarmouth Skating Rink (Public Exhibition Hall and Skating Rink), Yarmouth, NS. Reproduced from *Canadian Illustrated News* 18, no. 13 (28 September 1878): 201 (detail). | 31

1.12 "The Provincial Exhibition of Upper Canada – Opened by HRR the Prince of Wales, September 1860." Reproduced from *Illustrated London News*, London: Illustrated London News and Sketch Ltd, 17 November 1860, 462–3. Collection Centre Canadien d'Architecture / Canadian Centre for Architecture, Montreal. | 32

1.13 "The Arena, St Louis, Mo" (originally the National Dairy Association Building), 1929. Postcard, © W.C. Persons. Author's collection. | 33

1.14 John Saunders Climo, photographer, Victoria Skating Rink, City Road, Saint John, NB, c. 1880. New Brunswick Museum, X11432. | 34

1.15 Matthew Stead, architect, engine house for the European and North American Railway, front elevation, 1858. New Brunswick Museum, Acc. no. 20284/P253-18-18. | 34

1.16 Victoria Skating Rink, Saint John, NB. Reproduced from *Canadian Illustrated News* 1, no. 15 (12 February 1870): 236. | 35

1.17 "A General Prospect of Vauxhall Gardens," 1880. Image courtesy the British Museum, 1113.5465AN806468. | 36

1.18 "An Inside View of the Rotundo in Ranelagh Gardens." Image courtesy the British Museum, J,11.62AN888693. | 37

1.19 "Quebec – Carnival in the New Rink," Quebec City Skating Rink. Reproduced from *Canadian Illustrated News*, 17, no. 4 (26 January 1878): 53. | 38

1.20 "The Great Skating 'Rink' at Chicago." Reproduced from *Harper's Weekly*, 10 February 1866, 93. | 40–1

1.21 "Skaters Festival," 1869. Image courtesy Johns Hopkins University, Lester S. Levy Collection of Sheet Music (box 28, item 135, plate no. 850). | 42

1.22 "Matilda Toots," n.d. Image courtesy Johns Hopkins University, Lester S. Levy Collection of Sheet Music (box 28, item 92, plate no. 19.1–5). | 44

1.23 William Notman, photographer, Captain Huyshe, posed for a composite, Montreal, QC, 1870. © McCord Museum, Montreal, I-43857.1. | 45

1.24 William Notman, photographer, Skating Carnival, Victoria Skating Rink, Montreal, QC, painted composite, 1870. © McCord Museum, Gift of Charles Frederick Notman, N-0000. 116.21.1. | 46

1.25 Victoria Skating Rink, Toronto, 1863. © Toronto Reference Library, JRR 536. | 49

1.26 Alexander Henderson, photographer, hockey game, McGill University, 1884. Library and Archives Canada, Alexander Henderson collection, C-081683. | 50

1.27 William Notman and Son, photographer, hockey match, Victoria Rink, Montreal, QC, composite, 1893. © McCord Museum, Purchase from Associated Screen News Ltd, II-101415. | 52

1.28 "Skating Rink of Real Ice at Chelsea." Reproduced from *Illustrated London News*, London: Illustrated London News and Sketch Ltd, 13 May 1876, 468. Collection Centre Canadien d'Architecture / Canadian Centre for Architecture, Montreal. | 53

1.29 Prince's Skating Rink, Knightsbridge, London. Image courtesy World Figure Skating Museum and Hall of Fame, Colorado Springs. | 54

1.30 Spanish Riding School, Vienna. Wikimedia Commons, dedicated to public domain. Photo by Jebulon. | 55

1.31 "A Race on the Ice – Bicycles v. Skates." Reproduced from *Canadian Illustrated News*, 1881. © McCord Museum, Gift of Mr Charles deVolpi, m975.62.72. | 57

1.32 The Lava Skating Rink, Grove Lane, Camberwell, c. 1910. Postcard, author's collection. | 58

1.33 "Polo on Roller Skates at Newport." Reproduced from *Harper's Weekly*, 8 September 1883. Image courtesy of Royal Ontario Museum, Toronto. | 59

2.1 "Grand Opening of the 'Arena.'" Reproduced from *Montreal Gazette*, 31 December 1898. | 60

2.2 "The Arena, Montreal" (Westmount), c. 1907. Montreal and Toronto: Valentine and Sons Publishing Co., Bibliothèque et Archives nationales du Québec, 0002629366. | 64

2.3 "Le Nouveau 'Hockey Rink.'" Westmount Arena, Montreal, elevation, plan, and section. Reproduced from *La Patrie*, 10 September 1898, 11. Bibliothèque et Archives nationales du Québec. | 65

2.4 "Winter Garden Glide," 1916. Image courtesy Johns Hopkins University, Levy Sheet Music Collection, box 28, item 176. | 67

2.5 Amphidrome, Houghton, mi. Michigan Technological University Archives and Copper County Historical Collection, Image mtu Neg 02680. | 70

2.6 W.J. Oliver, photographer, the Sherman Roller Rink fire, Calgary, Alberta, 25 February 1915. Glenbow Museum, Calgary (nb-16-446). | 72

2.7 Dey's Rink, Ottawa, 1908. Library and Archives Canada, pa203558. | 73

2.8 Duquesne Garden, Pittsburgh. Pennsylvania Department, Carnegie Library of Pittsburgh, Neg# p-4889. | 74

2.9 R.W. Johnston, "Pittsburgh, Pa., Ice Rink, Duquesne Garden." Author's collection. | 75

2.10 Hockey and Skating Rink (Arena), Victoria. Image courtesy of the Royal bc Museum, bc Archives, hp071524. | 76

2.11 Denman Street Arena, Vancouver, 1913. Vancouver Public Library, #6549. | 77

2.12 The Alpine Room, Coloseum, London, 1844. Image courtesy Alexander Turnbull Library, Wellington, New Zealand. | 79

2.13 "Skating Rink. View Showing Pipes before Flooding." St Nicholas Rink, New York. Reproduced from Louis Milton Schmidt, *Principles and Practice of Artificial Ice-Making and Refrigeration* (Philadelphia: Philadelphia Book Co. 1908), 36. New York Public Library. | 80

2.14 "De La Vergne Machine Co, 220-ton Refrigeration Machine." Reproduced from Louis Milton Schmidt, *Principles and Practice of Artificial Ice-Making and Refrigeration* (Philadelphia: Philadelphia Book, Co. 1908), 204. New York Public Library. | 81

3.1 Olympia Arena, Detroit, southwest facade, looking northeast, 5920 Grand River Avenue, Detroit, Wayne County, mi. Library of Congress, habs mich, 82-detro, 25–3. | 84

3.2 Madison Square Garden III, New York, during construction, 25 August 1925. Thomas W. Lamb Archive, Avery Library, Columbia University, New York, box 19, no. 52. | 86

3.3 The Forum, Montreal, under construction, 1924. © McCord Museum, mp-1977.140.18.2. | 87

3.4 Chicago Stadium. Author's collection. | 89

3.5 Maple Leaf Gardens, political rally, 1941. City of Toronto Archives, Fonds 1257, series 1057, item 7098. | 90

3.6 Mount Royal Arena, Montreal. Image courtesy Duggan Family Collection. | 90

3.7 Fairchild Aerial Surveys, Inc., North Station and Boston Garden: Boston and Maine RR, 1930. Boston Public Library, Accession: 08_02_002229. | 91

4.1 "Darling, it's just a building." Advertisement for Decarie Motors, Montreal. Reproduced from *Montreal Gazette*, 11 March 1996, E10. | 94

4.2 Foster Hewitt in his gondola broadcast booth at Maple Leaf Gardens, Toronto. Image courtesy Hockey Hall of Fame, Toronto. Imperial Oil – Turofsky. | 96

4.3 R-100 Airship approaching Toronto, 1930. City of Toronto Archives, Fonds 1244, f1244-it10045. | 97

4.4 Maple Leaf Gardens, aerial view. City of Toronto Archives, Fonds 1244, item 3185. | 98

4.5 Mutual Street Arena, Toronto. City of Toronto Archives, SC 646-37N. | 98

4.6 Ross and Macdonald, architects, Eaton's Department Store, College Street, Toronto. Archives of Ontario, F 229-308-0-517-3. | 100

4.7 Ross and Macdonald, architects, "Maple Leaf Gardens, Toronto," 13 July 1931, negative photostat print. Ross and Macdonald fonds, Collection Centre Canadien d'Architecture / Canadian Centre for Architecture, Montreal, ARCH33050. | 101

4.8 Ross and Macdonald, architects, "New Arena, Toronto, Main Floor Plan." Maple Leaf Gardens, Toronto, 14 February 1931. Graphite on translucent paper, 65.5 × 87.1 cm. Ross and Macdonald fonds, Collection Centre Canadien d'Architecture / Canadian Centre for Architecture, Montreal, ARCH33054. | 103

4.9 "Maple Leaf Gardens, Toronto's New Sports Centre," 1931. Conn Smythe Papers, Archives of Ontario, F 223-3-1-53. | 104

4.10 "Proposed New Arena Toronto." Maple Leaf Gardens, 1931. Conn Smythe Papers, Archives of Ontario, F 223-3-1-53. | 104

4.11 SporTimer Time clock, Maple Leaf Gardens, Toronto. Ross and Macdonald fonds, Collection Centre Canadien d'Architecture / Canadian Centre for Architecture, Montreal, 13 ARCH 120d. | 105

4.12 Paul Chiasson, "A Real Floater," Montreal Canadiens parade to Molson Centre. Photo published in *Vancouver Sun*, 16 March 1996, C3. The Canadian Press / Paul Chiasson. | 106

4.13 Paul Chiasson, Opening ceremony at the Molson Centre, Pierre Turgeon at centre ice. Photo published in *Montreal Gazette*, 17 March 1996, D1. The Canadian Press / Paul Chiasson. | 106

4.14 Corpus Christi parade, Notre Dame Street, Montreal, 1914. © McCord Museum (MP-1984. 25.1.71). | 107

4.15 "The Forum, the Finest and Most Unique Open Air Skating Rink and Amusement Place in the World." Reproduced from *La Presse*, 9 November 1908. Illustration: Archives La Presse. | 109

4.16 Associated Screen News, Ltd. Funeral of Howie Morenz at the Forum, Montreal, 1937. Hockey Hall of Fame, Toronto. | 110

4.17 "Richard appeals to fans." Photo published in *Montreal Gazette*, 19 March 1955, 1. Gazette Photo Service fonds / Montreal Gazette photo archives. | 111

4.18 "Toutes mes excuses." Cartoon of Maurice Richard apologizing to Clarence Campbell, c. 1954. Reproduced from Jean Marie Pellerin, *L'Idole d'un Peuple: Maurice Richard* (Montreal: Les éditions de l'homme 1976), 261. | 112

4.19 An open-air streetcar passes down Sainte Catherine Street in front of the Montreal Forum on a sightseeing tour, July 1947. Library and Archives Canada, PA-129603. | 114

4.20 Montreal Forum, 1968, Image courtesy Hockey Hall of Fame, Toronto Graphic Artists / Hockey Hall of Fame. | 115

4.21 John Giamundo, photographer, Montreal Forum, 1995–96, Getty Images. | 115

4.22 Molson Centre, Montreal, 1999. Photo by the author. | 117

5.1 Madison Square Garden III, New York, on opening night. Thomas Lamb Archive, Avery Library, Columbia University, New York. | 118

5.2 The Arena, St Botolph's Street, Boston. Boston Public Library, Accession number: 08_02_002717. Image courtesy Boston Public Library. | 122

5.3 Boston Arena, interior view. Image courtesy Duggan Family Collection. | 123

5.4 "Novel Winter Sport: Skating on Artificial Ice at the New St. Nicholas Rink, New York," reproduced from *Frank Leslie's Newspaper*, 12 March 1896. Library of Congress, Prints and Photos, LC-USZ62-83505. | 126

5.5 Brown Brothers, photographer, Madison Square Garden I, New York, 1925. Millstein Division of United States History, Local History and Genealogy, New York Public Library, Astor, Lenox and Tilden Foundations, 1691043. | 127

5.6 Brown Brothers, photographer, "P.T. Barnum's Grand Roman Hippodrome – Interior View." Madison Square Garden I, New York, 1925. Millstein Division of United States History, Local History and Genealogy, New York Public Library, Astor, Lenox and Tilden Foundations, 1691041. | 127

5.7 Wurts Brothers, photographer, Madison Square Garden II, New York. McKim, Mead and White, architects. Picture Collection, New York Public Library, Astor, Lenox and Tilden Foundations, 805885. | 129

5.8 Thomas Lamb, architect, "The New Garden." Unexecuted proposal for Madison Square Garden III, New York, photographic print. Thomas Lamb Archive, Avery Library, Columbia University, New York. | 130

5.9 Thomas Lamb, architect, "Plan of Orchestra and Store Floor." Unexecuted proposal for Madison Square Garden III, New York, 15 February 1923. Thomas Lamb Archive, Avery Library, Columbia University, New York. | 130

5.10 Thomas Lamb, architect, "The Home of the New York Hockey Club at New Madison Square Garden." Unexecuted proposal for Madison Square Garden III, New York, published in *The New York Hockey Club*, a brochure soliciting membership. Image courtesy Duggan Family Collection. | 132

5.11 Madison Square Garden III, New York, 8th Avenue entrance before construction of shops. Photographic print. Thomas Lamb Archive, Avery Library, Columbia University, New York, no. 73. | 133

5.12 Madison Square Garden III, New York, view along 50th Street. Photographic print. Thomas Lamb Archive, Avery Library, Columbia University, New York. | 134

5.13 Manhattan Post Card Publishing Co., "New Madison Square Garden, New York City." Author's collection. | 135

Part III.1 King Publishing Company, "The Forum," Los Angeles, Charles Luckman Associates, architect, 1967. Author's collection. | 138

Part III.2 J.M. Stevenson, Arena at Owen Sound, ON. Part of the report "Arena Tour of North America," 9 September 1948. Stevenson Raines fonds, Canadian Architectural Archives, University of Calgary Library, Accession # 114A/81.18 – STE f573(a). | 140

Part III.3 Julius Shulman, photographer, Skidmore, Owings and Merrill, architect, Portland Memorial Coliseum, 1960. © J. Paul Getty Trust. Used with permission. Julius Shulman Photography Archive, Research Library at the Getty Research Institute (2004.R.10). | 142

6.1 Julius Shulman, photographer, Skidmore, Owings and Merrill, architect, Portland Memorial Coliseum, 1960. © J. Paul Getty Trust. Used with permission. Julius Shulman Photography Archive, Research Library at the Getty Research Institute (2004.R.10). | 144

6.2 Aerial view of Veteran's Stadium, the Spectrum, and John F. Kennedy Stadium, Philadelphia, 1971. PhillyHistory.org, a project of the Philadelphia Department of Records. | 146

6.3 Doug Murray/Icon SMI, photographer, Tailgate party – NCAA football, Florida at Miami, 7 September 2013. © Doug Murray/Icon SMI/Corbis. | 147

6.4 Ron Riesterer, photographer, Skidmore, Owings and Merrill, architects, Oakland-Alameda County Coliseum, aerial view of entire complex. © Ron Riesterer. | 150

6.5 Ezra Stoller, photographer, Skidmore, Owings and Merrill, architects, Oakland-Alameda County Coliseum, arena. © Ezra Stoller / Esto, D:12DD.008. | 151

6.6 Pier Luigi Nervi, architect, Palazetto dello Sport, Rome, 1960. Author's collection. | 152

6.7 Matthew Nowicki, architect, J.S. Dorton Arena, State Fairgrounds, Raleigh, NC, c. 1952. Courtesy of the State Archives of North Carolina, N_72_8_8, copied from PC.1487.7. | 153

6.8 Julius Shulman, photographer, Eero Saarinen, architect, David S. Ingalls Rink, Yale University, Hew Haven, CT, 1961. © J. Paul Getty Trust. Used with permission. Julius Shulman Photography Archive, Research Library at the Getty Research Institute (2004.R.10). | 153

6.9 Ezra Stoller, photographer, Skidmore, Owings and Merrill, architects, Oakland-Alameda County Coliseum arena. © Ezra Stoller / Esto, D:12DD.017. | 154

6.10 Julius Shulman, photographer, Skidmore, Owings and Merrill, architect, Portland Memorial Coliseum, 1960. © J. Paul Getty Trust. Used with permission. Julius Shulman Photography Archive, Research Library at the Getty Research Institute (2004.R.10). | 156

6.11 Julius Shulman, photographer, Skidmore, Owings and Merrill, architect, Portland Memorial Coliseum, 1960. © J. Paul Getty Trust. Used with permission. Julius Shulman Photography Archive, Research Library at the Getty Research Institute (2004.R.10). | 157

6.12 Julius Shulman, photographer, Skidmore, Owings and Merrill, architect, Portland Memorial Coliseum, 1960. © J. Paul Getty Trust. Used with permission. Julius Shulman Photography Archive, Research Library at the Getty Research Institute (2004.R.10). | 158

6.13 "The New Uline Ice Arena," Washington, DC, opened 1941. Courtesy DC Public Library, Washingtoniana Division. | 160

6.14 The Beatles performing at the Washington Coliseum, 11 February 1964. © AP Images 640212061. | 161

6.15 The Beatles rehearsing for the *Ed Sullivan Television Show*, New York, 9 February 1964, © Bettmann/CORBIS. | 162

6.16 The Beatles and Cassius Clay meet in Miami, 18 February 1964. © Bettmann/CORBIS. | 164

6.17 Steve Proehl, photographer, Skidmore, Owings and Merrill, architects, Oakland-Alameda County Coliseum arena, after renovation by HNTB, 9 November 2006, © Steve Proehl/Proehl Studios/Corbis. | 167

7.1 Ray Pioch, illustrator, "Arena Rises atop Buried Rail Terminal." Madison Square Garden IV, cutaway perspective. Reproduced from *Popular Science* 188 (May 1966): 80–1. Toronto Reference Library. Used with permission of Popular Science © 2015. All rights reserved. | 168

7.2 Madison Square Garden, arena and convention centre proposal for Columbus Circle between 58th and 60th Streets, plan, aerial perspective, longitudinal section and perspective, 1948. Reproduced from *Architectural Forum* 88 (April 1948): 13. Toronto Reference Library. | 171

7.3 Progressive Publications, Inc., Coliseum, New York, 1950s. Author's collection. | 171

7.4 Charles Luckman Architects, Madison Square Garden IV, unexecuted proposal, perspective, 1960. Reproduced from *Progressive Architecture*, December 1960, 56. | 174

7.5 Charles Luckman Architects, Madison Square Garden IV, 1960, unexecuted proposal, plan. Reproduced from *Progressive Architecture*, December 1960, 56. | 174

7.6 "Madison Square Garden Center, to be Built over Penn Station." Charles Luckman Architects, Madison Square Garden IV, unexecuted proposal, perspective, 1961. Reproduced from *Architectural Record*, September 1961, 14. Collection Centre Canadien d'Architecture / Canadian Centre for Architecture, Montreal. | 175

7.7 Charles Luckman Architects, Madison Square Garden IV, unexecuted proposal, perspective and plan, 1962. Reproduced from the *New York Times*, 23 September 1962, 78. | 176

7.8 Cameron Davidson, photographer, aerial view of Madison Square Garden and Penn Station, Manhattan, New York City. © Cameron Davidson/Corbis, 42-52825248. | 177

7.9 Detroit Publishing Co., bird's-eye view of Pennsylvania Station, New York, between 1910 and 1920. Library of Congress, Prints and Photographs Division, LC-DIG-det-4a24329 (digital file from original) LC-D4-72676 [P&P]. | 178

7.10 John McCann, photographer, Birmingham City Architects Department, architect, Bull Ring shopping centre (rotunda under construction in the right background), 1964. © John McCann / RIBA Collections. | 180

7.11 Vincent G. Kling and Associates, architect, Fort Point Channel stadium/arena project, Boston, photograph of model, 1965. Laurence S. Williams collection, Athenaeum of Philadelphia. | 181

7.12 Houston Astrodome, aerial view. J. Milton Lawless Collection, Houston Public Library, MSS0334. | 182

7.13 Houston Astrodome, interior view. Houston Photograph Collection, Houston Public Library, MSS0157. | 183

7.14 Astrodomain, including Houston Astrodome and Astroworld, aerial view of site. William D. Wurdy Collection, Houston Public Library, MSS0243. | 184

7.15 The Houston Sports Association, Houston Astrodome, luxury suite, 1968. Author's collection. | 186

7.16 Spacettes (ushers) and Earthmen (groundskeepers) in costume at the Houston Astrodome, 7 April 1965. © Bettmann/CORBIS. | 186

Part IV.1 "State-of-the-Art Stadiums." Individual TV screens and concession keypad system proposed for Pacific Bell Park, San Francisco, 1996. Reproduced from *U.S. News & World Report*, 3 June 1996. Wright's Media. | 188

Part IV.2 Warren Wimmer/Icon SMI, photographer, Red Wings at Blackhawks, 25 May 2013. © Warren Wimmer/Icon SMI/Corbis. | 190

Part IV.3 Emmerson, photographer, Iggy Azelea and LA Laker Nick Young caught on the "Kiss Cam" at the Galen Center, USC, Los Angeles, 14 January 2015. © Emmerson/Splash News/ Corbis. | 191

8.1 Aerial view of the United Center, with Chicago Stadium (below), Chicago. AP Images, AP – 9310070132. | 194

8.2 Ellerbe Beckett, architect, Marine Midland Center, Buffalo, view of concourse, 1997. Courtesy Ellerbe Beckett. | 198

8.3 Ellerbe Beckett, architect, Marine Midland Center, Buffalo, view of private suites, 1997. Courtesy Ellerbe Beckett. | 199

8.4 HOK Sport, United Center, Chicago, view from private suite to ice surface. Courtesy HOK Sport. | 200

8.5 HOK Sport, Arrowhead Pond, Anaheim. Courtesy HOK Sport. | 202

8.6 HOK Sport, Arrowhead Pond, Anaheim, interior view of entrance lobby showing "Video Arch" sculpture by Nam June Paik. Courtesy HOK Sport. | 203

8.7 "Superpuck." FoxTrax electronic puck. AP Images, AP – 96011802681. | 205

8.8 Nashville Predators hockey player entering ice surface through jaws of inflated sabre-toothed tiger, Sommett Center, Nashville, TN. AP Images, AP – 9810100504. | 206

8.9 Bruins Ice Girl with smoking T-shirt cannon, 2003. AP Images, AP – 97800726114. | 207

8.10 Buffalo Sabres hockey players on bench watching replay on Jumbotron screen. AP Images, AP – 101105124651. | 208

8.11 Los Angeles Kings vs New York Rangers at Caesar's Palace, Las Vegas, 27 September 1991. Image courtesy Los Angeles Kings. | 212

8.12 HOK Sport, architect, Oriole Park at Camden Yards, Baltimore, c. 2002. © Lance Nelson/ CORBIS. | 214

8.13 Serge Chapleau, "Du Forum au Centre Molson," 13 March 1996. © McCord Museum M997.52.41. | 215

8.14 "Boston Garden Original Unrestored Double Seat," lot 151. Reproduced from Sotheby's, *Important Sports Memorabilia and Cards*, New York, 10 June 2005, 99. Courtesy Sotheby's. | 216

9.1 "$500 Million Blockbuster: Maple Leafs Buy Raptors." Reproduced from *Toronto Star*, 13 February 1998, 1. Torstar Syndication Services. | 218

9.2 Populous, architect, Xcel Energy Center, Saint Paul, Minnesota, 2000. Photo courtesy Xcel Energy Center. | 222

9.3 Eliot Schechter, photographer. Ellerbe Beckett, architect, BB&T Center, Sunrise (Miami), Florida. Image courtesy Florida Panthers. | 223

9.4 Bob Krist, photographer, Watching Ballgame from Hotel Room at the SkyDome, Toronto, 1 August 1990. © Bob Krist/Corbis. | 224

9.5 HOK Sport, "The Proposed Ice Palace," unexecuted proposal for new Maple Leaf Gardens project at Union Station, Toronto. Reproduced from *Toronto Star*, 17 June 1997, B7. Torstar Syndication Services. | 225

9.6 David Cooper, photographer, Fans watching a game on the giant screen in Maple Leaf Square, Air Canada Centre, Toronto. Getty Images. | 227

9.7 Paul Mounce, photographer, L.A. Live at the Staples Center, Los Angeles, 30 June 2014. © Paul Mounce/Corbis. | 228

9.8 360 Architecture, architect, WAM Development, site developers, aerial view of proposed Rogers Place and surrounding "Ice District," Edmonton, 2014. Courtesy WAM Development. | 229

9.9 Lemay, architect, Tour des Canadiens, Montreal, 2012. Courtesy Lemay. | 231

9.10 heneghan peng architects, Bigfoot, a stadium for Los Angeles, aerial view, 1997. Courtesy and © heneghan peng architects. | 233

10.1 HOK Sport, Nashville (now Bridgestone) Arena. Courtesy HOK Sport. | 239

10.2 HOK Sport, Nashville (now Bridgestone) Arena. Courtesy HOK Sport. | 240

Notes

Introduction

1 http://www.arenamaps.com/ (accessed 16 October 2015).

2 For example, Robson Fletcher discussed the possibility of a new hockey facility in Calgary, to be designed by Populous (formerly HOK), in "Calgary Flames Logo in Arena Concept Video Fuels Speculation over New Barn," *Metro*, 29 January 2014, http://metronews.ca/news/calgary/925860/calgary-flames-logo-in-arena-concept-video-fuels-speculation-over-new-barn/ (accessed 25 April 2014).

3 Paula Lupkin, "On Her Book *Manhood Factories: YMCA Architecture and the Making of Modern Urban Culture*," *Rorotoko*, 22 November 2010, http://rorotoko.com/interview/20101122_lupkin_paula_on_manhood_factories_ymca_architecture_modern_urban/?page=3 (accessed 31 March 2014).

4 Adams, *Medicine by Design*, xix, xxii.

5 Longstreth, *City Center to Regional Mall*, xiv–xv.

6 Pevsner, *A History of Building Types*. My work here, on skating rinks and hockey arenas, was preceded by typological studies of Canadian bank architecture and early airport architecture. See Shubert, "Cumberland & Storm and Mies van der Rohe"; "Lloyd Wright and the Lehigh Airport Competition"; and *Airport Origins*.

7 Meeks, "The Life of a Form," 163. Similarly, Dane Lanken writes that "the golden age of movie palace construction lasted just a quarter of a century. It began in the 1900s … and died about 1930." Lanken, *Montreal Movie Palaces*, 166.

8 Carter and Cromley, *Invitation to Vernacular Architecture*, ix, 9, 16.

9 Van Slyck, *A Manufactured Wilderness*; Yanni, *The Architecture of Madness*; Lupkin, *Manhood Factories*.

10 Yanni, *The Architecture of Madness*, 12.

11 The 1924 Winter Olympics were held at Chamonix, France, and the 1928 games at St Moritz, Switzerland. At the 1932 games at Lake Placid, US hockey was played indoors at the Jack Shea Arena. The Garmisch-Partenkirchen rink was finally covered in 1962.

12 Barry Broadfoot, *The Pioneer Years 1895–1914: Memories of Settlers Who Opened the West* (Toronto: Doubleday Canada 1976), as quoted in Morrow, *A Concise History of Sport in Canada*, 123.

13 Nelson, "Baseball," in Raitz, *The Theater of Sport*, 34.

14 Rowan, *The Emigrant and Sportsman in Canada*.

15 James H. Gray, *A Brand of Its Own: The 100 Year History of the Calgary Exhibition and Stampede* (Saskatoon: Prairies Books 1985), 56.

16 Dryden and MacGregor, *Home Game*, 15. On the impact of local hockey arenas on social life and commu-

nity building, see also Gruneau and Whitson, *Hockey Night in Canada*, especially 205–11.

17   On hockey poetry, see Kennedy, *Going Top Shelf*. On hockey literature, see Blake, *Canadian Hockey Literature*, and Buma, *Refereeing Identity*. With the exception of the iconic *Slap Shot* (1977), starring Paul Newman, Hollywood did not take notice of hockey until the 1990s, beginning with the *Mighty Ducks* franchise (both films and team). There have been about a dozen hockey movies, including a musical, *Score* (2010), and one about a Sikh hockey team, *Breakaway* (2011). Film and television producers from French Quebec have shown considerably more interest in hockey: the *Les Boys* franchise of movies (1997–2012); *Lance et Comptes* (1986–2010). See Ransom, *Hockey, PQ*. In 2008 the Art Gallery of Nova Scotia mounted a major exhibition of hockey-themed contemporary art, including work from artists in eight countries. See *Arena: The Art of Hockey*. Twenty years earlier the Pitt Gallery in Vancouver presented *Hockey Night at the Pitt*, from 21 November to 10 December 1988, curated by Donna Hagerman, http://helen pittgallery.org/wp-content/uploads/2010/09/hockey. jpg (accessed 30 March 2016).

18   Examples include: Boyd, *History of Hockey in BC*; Jackson, *The St. Louis Arena*; Podnieks, *The Blue and White Book*; Greenberg, *Full Spectrum*; Goyens, Turowitz, and Duguay, *Le livre officiel Le Forum de Montréal*; and Durso, *Madison Square Garden*.

19   Simon Kuper, "Crowd Pleasers," *Financial Times*, 27 May 2005, http://www.ft.com/cms/s/0/e7099e5a-cf16-11d9-8cb5-00000e2511c8.html#axzz3wCp9RB00 (accessed 3 January 2016). Architecture critic Christopher Hawthorne seemed to concur with Kuper when he noted that "as cities around the world jockey for attention and status, more will surely look to dramatic stadiums as an effective form of global marketing. It even appears possible that stadiums will be to the next 20 years what museums have been to the last 20: architecture's most dynamic specialty." "That Home-Field Advantage," *Los Angeles Times*, 5 June 2005.

20   Windover, "Digging in the Gardens," uses Maple Leaf Gardens as a filter through which to examine aspects of modernity, while Russell Field also looks at Maple Leaf Gardens to study aspects of spectacle, spectator-

ship, and commerce in his dissertation, "A Night at the Garden(s)," and in a pair of articles, "Passive Participation" and "The Ties That Bind." William Keller's 2007 dissertation, "Architecture for Community and Spectacle," takes an art-historical and formalist approach in tracing the development of covered arenas, from ancient Greece to twentieth-century North America.

21   Shubert, "The Montreal Forum"; "The Changing Experience of Hockey Spectatorship"; "The Evolution of the Hockey Arena"; and "Sports Facilities in Canada."

22   Guay, *L'histoire du hockey au Québec*; Mason, "The International Hockey League"; Wong, *Lords of the Rinks*; Kidd, *The Struggle for Canadian Sport*; Ross, *Joining the Clubs*.

23   Bélanger, "Sport Venues and the Spectacularization of urban spaces"; Cha, "*La ville est hockey*."

24   Bell, "Theatrical Design for the Air Canada Centre," 22.

Chapter One

1   The earliest literary description of skating comes from William FitzStephen, clerk to Thomas à Becket, who described the following scene in 1190: "When the Great Fenne or Moore (which washeth the walles of the citie on the north side) is frozen, many young men play upon the yce … Some tye bones to their feete, and under their heeles, and shoving themselves by a little picked staffe, doe slide as swiftlie as a birdie flyeth in the aire, or an arrow out of a crosse-bow. Sometimes two runne together with poles, and hitting one the other, either one or both doe fall, not without some hurt; some break their armes, some their legs, but youth desirous of glorie, in this sort exerciseth it selfe against the time of warre." Quoted in Whedon, *The Fine Art of Figure Skating*, 19. There are still earlier references to skating. In the possibly tenth-century Norse *Poetic Edda*, Thialfe explains to the king that he can run upon skates, and in northern mythology one of the lesser gods, Ullir, was so expert in the use of skates as to outstrip lightning. See Crichton and Wheaton, *Scandinavia, Ancient and Modern*.

2   The word rink has its origins in the Old French word *ranc*, meaning "line, row or rank." The fourteenth-century Middle English word *renc* referred to a joust-

ing ground or other place of contest, to the contest it-self, or to one round of such a contest. Both "rink" and "rank" likely go back to the Germanic root that produced the English word "ring," meaning "circle." By the eighteenth century, the term "rink" began being used for the space of a curling match. See http://dictionary.reference.com/browse/rink and http://www.word-detective.com/021804.html (accessed 1 January 2016).

3 Russell, *Canada; Its Defences*, 84.

4 Stillner, *The Philadelphia Girls' Rowing Club*, 18–20.

5 This period also gave rise to the now long-forgotten skating practice of podography – inscribing letters and words in the ice surface with your skated foot (not to be confused with the twenty-first-century slang definition – porn on your iPod). A reporter for the *New York Times* described the scene at Central Park on 24 December 1865, which included "many graceful professors of podography, whose movements were the 'poetry of motion'; and there were hundreds of novitiates in the art of feet-writing, whose awkward attempts to make, as it were, the initial pot-hooks and hangers, resulted in ludicrous and mirth-provoking scenes." Podography was another means of flirting, as when a young man engraved the initials of his beloved in the ice for her to see.

6 Wolley, *A Two Years Journal in New York*, 96.

7 Edwin Wilson Bullinger claims that attendance during the winter of 1861–62 reached a total of between 500,000 and 600,000, with as many as 28,000–30,000 on a single day. See Bullinger, *Guide to Skating*, 51.

8 *Miller's New York as It Is*, 31.

9 Riess, *City Games*, 45–6, and City of New York, "The History of Ice Skating in New York City Parks."

10 There were sixty-one patents granted for the 1870s, sixty-six for the 1880s, and seventy-one for the 1890s. Lambert, *The American Skating Mania*, n.p.

11 Heathcote, *The Admiral's Niece*, 83–5.

12 Redmond, "Curling."

13 "Women engaged in 'strolls' with small groups of snowshoers but they never tramped or raced." Morrow, "The Knights of the Snowshoe," 29, 31. On page 12, Morrow reproduces the "Song of the Montreal Snow Shoe Club," which reads in part: "All pretty girls take my advice, / On some vain fop don't waste your

'lub,' / But if you wish to hug something nice, / Why marry a boy of the Snow Show Club." Originally published in Beckett, *The Montreal Snow Shoe Club*, 25.

14 Wolley, *A Two Years Journal in New York*, 96.

15 Bullinger, *Guide to Skating*, 55.

16 Chadwick, *Beadle's Dime Guide to Skating and Curling*, 5.

17 Whedon, *The Fine Art of Figure Skating*, 62.

18 "Talk of Paris Fashions: Skating, Christman [sic] Trees and Fine Gowns," *New York Times*, 12 January 1891, 3.

19 Warner, *When the Girls Came out to Play*, 28. In Anthony Trollope's *Phineas Finn*, published serially 1867–68, Madame Max Goesler explains that she does not play croquet any longer because she has "come to think it is only fit for boys and girls. The great thing is to give them opportunities for flirting, and it does that." Anthony Trollope, *Phineas Finn* (Oxford: Oxford University Press 2011), 354.

20 Unknown poet, "With Good Steel Ringing," from William Weaver Tomlinson, *Ballads of Sport* (London: Walter Scott, n.d.), as cited in Hawley, *The Development of Indoor Ice Skating Rinks in London*.

21 Russell, *Canada; Its Defences*, 83–4.

22 *Rules and Regulations of the Brooklyn Skating Rink Association* (Brooklyn: R.M. Whiting, Jr, 1868–69), 7, as quoted in Lambert, *The American Skating Mania*.

23 Edward L. Gill, *The Skater's Manual: A Complete Guide to the Art of Skating* (New York: Andrew Peck and Company 1867), 10, as quoted in Lambert, *The American Skating Mania*.

24 Chadwick, *Handbook of Winter Sports*, 12.

25 Oldenburg, *The Great Good Place*, 21

26 Ibid., 33, 36, 37.

27 Ibid., 24.

28 During a particularly treacherous two-week period between 29 December 1894 and 16 January 1895, *The Times* reported on the deaths by drowning of no fewer than nineteen skaters who had fallen through thin ice.

29 Howell and Howell, *Sports and Games in Canadian Life*, 22.

30 Ibid., 37.

31 This long narrow building with a curved roof was fitted with a natural-ice surface during the winter

months, when it was too cold for boat building. It was a rink measuring 150 × 60 feet, open to all – 15 cents for gentlemen, 10 cents for ladies. Kitchen, *Dey Brothers' Rinks*, 1–2. In 1888 a skating rink was set up in Longueil, Quebec, using freight sheds donated for the purpose by the Canadian Pacific Railway. "Skating, Longueil Skating Rink," *Montreal Gazette*, 22 December 1888, 8.

32 *One Hundred and Fifty Years of Curling*, 18.

33 Hedley, "Curling in Canada," 182.

34 The Mutual Street Rink opened in 1875 as the Caledonian Curling and Skating Club. The article was reprinted as "Curling in the Queen City" in the *Montreal Gazette*, 6 January 1888, 8.

35 Kerr, *Curling in Canada and the United States*.

36 Ibid., 341.

37 "A New Curling Rink," *Ottawa Times*, 14 December 1867, 2. Roller skates were also known as "parlor skates" in the nineteenth century.

38 Metcalfe, *Canada Learns to Play*, 135–6.

39 On the history of baseball parks, see Bennett, *They Play, You* Pay, chapter 3, Gershman, *Diamonds*, and Humber, *Diamonds of the North*.

40 Rowan, *The Emigrant and Sportsman*, as quoted in Roxborough, *The Stanley Cup Story*, 6.

41 Russell, *Canada; Its Defences*, 83.

42 According to an article on curling history in Canada, visitors from the United States upon their first view of curling rinks asked: "Are these big brick buildings drill-sheds or roller skating rinks, or what are they?" Hedley, "History of Curling," 181–2.

43 On the design of nineteenth-century drill sheds, see Adell, "The Structural Design of the Early Drill Sheds in Canada"; Adell, *Architecture of the Drill Hall in Canada*; Fogelson, *America's Armories*; Koch, "The Medieval Castle Revival."

44 London's Paddington Station of 1854 featured a triple-span iron roof spanning 238 feet. See Meeks, "The Life of a Form," 163–4.

45 Adell, "The Structural Design of the Early Drill Sheds in Canada," 45.

46 At Building 4, the drill hall and skating arena at CFB Cornwallis, Nova Scotia, of 1942–43, and Gunner Arena at CFB Shilo, Manitoba, of 1948, each function occupied one-half of the interior space. See "Drill Hall and Skating Arena," Federal Heritage Building Review Office, Building Report 93–01 (Record no. 11713, Access F00–93–001); and Shannon Ricketts, "Gunner Arena, CFB Shilo, Shilo, Manitoba," Federal Heritage Building Review Office, Building Report 87–99 (Record no. 8775, Access F32–87–099).

47 Winnie Hu, "Plan for Ice Center in Bronx Armory Moves Forward," *New York Times*, 23 April 2013, http://www.nytimes.com/2013/04/24/nyregion/bloom berg-announces-ice-sport-center-proposal-for-bronx-armory.html?_r=0 (accessed 25 April 2013).

48 "Grand Opening of the Yarmouth Skating Rink," *Yarmouth Herald*, 7 March 1878, n.p.

49 *The 1999 Canadian Encyclopedia: World Edition* (Toronto: McClelland and Stewart 1998). The population of Yarmouth was 18,550 in 1871, a 70 per cent increase over twenty years earlier. Tonnage handled by ships at the port had increased by over 500 per cent during this same period. J.R. Campbell, *A History of the County of Yarmouth, Nova Scotia* (Saint John, NB: J. and A. McMillan 1876), 195.

50 Palliser, Palliser and Co. is perhaps best known for its publication of nearly a dozen model books between 1876 and 1896. Plans for the Public Exhibition Hall and Skating Rink at Yarmouth, Nova Scotia, were published in 1889 as Plate 71 in *Palliser's Court Houses, Village, Town and City Halls, Jails and Plans of Other Public Buildings* (New York: J.S. Ogilvie 1889). The notes to the plate indicate that it could be constructed for $10,000.

51 "Grand Concert in the Rink!" *Yarmouth Herald*, 4 July 1878, n.p.

52 One exception to this rule is the Crystal Palace in Picton, Ontario, that opened in 1887.

53 The St Louis Arena was designed by Gustel R. Kiewitt. The building was destroyed by implosion on 27 February 1999. See Jackson *The St. Louis Arena*.

54 On the Cow Palace, see Diran, *Cow Palace Great*.

55 *Morning News* (Saint John, NB), Friday, 6 January 1865, 2.

56 I am indebted to Gary Hughes, who first pointed out this connection and who kindly furnished me with copies of drawings and specifications for the Victoria Skating Rink. See Hughes, *Music of the Eye*, 34.

57 Another circular skating rink, based on the model of

that at Saint John, was erected in Fredericton, New Brunswick, in 1868. It was destroyed by fire in 1881. See http://www.heritagefredericton.org/ystour/gallery-j.php (accessed 30 June 2013).

58 On Vauxhall and Ranelagh, see Chancellor, *The XVIIIth Century in London*; Sands, *Invitation to Ranelagh*; Scott, *Green Retreats*; Porter, *London A Social History*.

59 Quoted in Chancellor, *The XVIIIth Century in London*, 102.

60 On her diary, see Monck, *My Canadian Leaves*. On the participation of women at skating and roller rinks in small-town Ontario during the late nineteenth century, see Marks, *Revivals and Roller Rinks*, 127–30. The cost of participating at one of the indoor rinks would have limited those involved to the middle and upper classes, however. An annual subscription to the Montreal Skating Club in 1860 was $10 for an individual and $15 for a family at a time when a labourer might earn one dollar a day.

61 Monck, *My Canadian Leaves*, 115.

62 "Skating: The First Masquerade," *Montreal Gazette*, 30 December 1898, 2.

63 A redowa is a Bohemian folk dance similar to the waltz.

64 Patrick H. Richmond, *History of Quincy and Its Men of Mark; or Facts and Figures Exhibiting Its Advantages and Resources, Manufactures and Commerce* (Quincy, IL: Heirs and Russell 1869), 90.

65 Ibid.

66 Monck, *My Canadian Leaves*, 256–7.

67 Russell, *Canada; Its Defences*, 84.

68 Bullinger, *Guide to Skating*, 24.

69 Gopnik, *Winter Five Windows on the Season*, 144–5, 147.

70 Ibid., 149.

71 Cooke, *Social Etiquette*, 425.

72 Warner, *When the Girls Came out to Play*, 29.

73 "A Skating Party on the Schuylkill," *Harper's Weekly* 24 (28 February 1880): 136–7.

74 Warner, *When the Girls Came out to Play*, 38 and 253n11.

75 Unknown author, *Matilda Toots or You Should Have Seen Her Boots* (New York: Frederick Blume 1855).

76 In January 1867 Notman advertised "a new arrangement for Portraits in Winter Costume … affording to friends at a distance an excellent idea of our Canadian winters." Those interested could choose from the following backdrops: snowshoeing, tobogganing, sleighing, shooting, walking, and skating." *Montreal Gazette*, 19 January 1867, 3. The following month, Notman announced "An artificial rink at his studio, enabling him to photograph persons in the act of skating!" The advertisement suggests that this will afford "an excellent opportunity for those about to appear in fancy costume at the skating carnival to be photographed in character!" *Montreal Gazette*, 5 February 1867, 3.

77 Elaborate fancy-dress balls ranked among nineteenth-century Canada's most splendid of entertainments and were reported on in newspapers across the country. See *Dressing up Canada*.

78 Holt, *Fancy Dresses Described*, viii.

79 The image measures 37 ½ × 53 ½ inches. It was displayed in Notman's studio for fifty-five years before being donated to the McCord Museum in Montreal, which also houses the William Notman photographic archive. See http://www.mccord-museum.qc.ca/en/collection/artifacts/N- 0000.116.21.1.

80 "Victoria Skating Rink," *Montreal Gazette*, 1 March 1865, 2.

81 "Carnival on the Ice," *Canadian Illustrated News* 11, no. 15 (10 April 1875): 227.

82 Morrow, "The Knights of the Snowshoe," 26.

83 On the origins of hockey, see Fitsell, *How Hockey Happened*. I particularly like Fitsell's response to those who ask him where hockey was born. "What do you mean by 'hockey?'" Therein lies a tale.

84 Snowshoeing, for instance, was so popular that in 1881 there were as many as twenty separate clubs for the sport in Montreal alone. Morrow, "The Knights of the Snowshoe," 5n5. French Canadians did not take up hockey seriously until the 1890s. And, writing in 1895, J. Macdonald Oxley comments on the rising popularity of "rink hockey" in Canada, suggesting that "it actually threatens to displace tobogganing and snow-shoeing in the affections of the young men." See Oxley, *My Strange Rescue*, 341–2.

85 "On the Ice," *London Society: An Illustrated Magazine of Light and Amusing Literature for the Hours of Relaxation* 3, no. 1 (1863): 14.

86 Roxborough, *One Hundred – Not Out*, 78.

87 "Victoria Rink," *Montreal Gazette*, 3 March 1875, 3. The game went off without event and merited only a small notice in the next day's *Evening Star*. "An interesting game of Hockey was played at the Rink." The reporter noted that the spectators were "well satisfied with the evening's entertainment." *Evening Star*, 4 March 1875, 2.

88 "Hockey Champions: Defeat Shamrocks in the First Scheduled Senior Match," *Montreal Gazette*, 5 January 1898, 5.

89 "New Rules for the Regulation of the Game," *Montreal Gazette*, 28 January 1886, 8, as quoted in Guay, *L'histoire du Hockey au Québec*, 53. In 1839 Charles Goodyear invented the process of vulcanization, whereby rubber was rendered tough and elastic. According to J.W. Fitsell, the word "puck" derives from the game of Irish hurling, where it refers to a "free poke" or shot. The term was first reported in the Montreal press in 1876. See Fitsell, *How Hockey Happened*, 112.

90 Guay, *L'histoire du Hockey au Québec*, 54.

91 Fitsell, *How Hockey Happened*, 114.

92 In 1890 Montreal's Dominion Rink introduced "a solid wooden fence four feet high, which not only prevents the players breaking their shins … but keeps the spectators from crowding on the ice during the game." "Hockey, M.A.A.A. vs. Victorias," *Montreal Gazette*, 4 January 1890, n.p.

93 According to Ken Dryden, body-checking emerged gradually as a natural consequence of the move indoors to smaller, prescribed ice surfaces. "Cluttered with eighteen players, then fourteen, many of them out-of-season rugby players used to body contact, their hockey skills new and primitive, their equipment clumsy; the unavoidable result would be frequent if inadvertent collisions." Dryden, *The Game*, 171–2.

94 Canada's governor general, Lord Stanley of Preston, donated the silver cup in 1892 as an award for Canada's top-ranking amateur ice-hockey club. It was first awarded in 1893.

95 See Meeks, *The Railroad Station*.

96 Metcalfe, *Canada Learns to Play*, 133.

97 "Skating," *Montreal Gazette*, 19 January 1886, 8.

98 The first purpose-built skating rink intended for public use was not constructed in London until 1929. See Hawley, *The Development of Indoor Ice Skating Rinks in London*, 23–4.

99 The short-lived Boston Skating Rink, which opened on 23 September 1868 at Tremont and Lenox streets, may be the first rink with artificial ice. See Kilham, *Boston after Bulfinch*, 70.

100 Gamgee was responsible for at least two further ice rinks: an even smaller (24×16 feet) experimental rink with a canvas cover that opened in January 1876 (see "A Real Ice Skating Rink," 467); and a floating glacierium that opened in December 1876, another short-lived experiment. Gamgee installed the rink within the floating bath moored in the Thames just above Charing-cross Railway Bridge that had been launched the previous summer ("The Floating Glacierium," *The Times*, 20 December 1876, and "The Floating Bath," *Illustrated London News*, 17 July 1875).

101 Brader, *Leisure and Entertainment in America*, 241.

102 Hawley, *The Development of Indoor Ice Skating Rinks in London*, 47.

103 As illustrated in Lester, *Seattle Arena Souvenir*, 21.

104 T.D. Richardson, *Modern Figure Skating* (London: Methuen 1938), 180, as quoted in Hawley, *The Development of Indoor Ice Skating Rinks in London*, 48.

105 Adams, "Freezing Social Relations," 67.

106 Ibid., 67–8.

107 Ibid., 68.

108 Chadwick, *Handbook of Winter Sports*, 30–3. The *Montreal Gazette* reported that cricket on ice, though rarely attempted, would be played in Boston, on Jamaica Pond, by students from Harvard. "Cricket on Ice," *Montreal Gazette*, 17 January 1888, 8. The invention of the bicycle skate is described in "Fast Time on a Bicycle Skate," *Montreal Gazette*, 28 December 1892, 8.

109 Fitsell, "The Rise and Fall of Ice Polo," 13, see also Hardy, ""Polo at the Rinks,"" 166–71.

110 The rink continued in operation until at least about 1910. See Pout, *The Early Years of English Roller Hockey*, 7.

111 Ibid., 66–7.

112 Turner with Zaidman, *The History of Roller Skating*, 25.

113 *St. Paul Daily Globe*, 2 January 1886, 3, as quoted in Hardy, "'Polo at the Rinks,'" 165.

114 Tuthill, *Ice Hockey and Ice Polo Guide*, 76. On the shift from ice polo to ice hockey, see also Fitsell, *Hockey's Captains, Colonels & Kings*, especially chapter 10, and Hardy, "'Polo at the Rinks,'" 166–71.

115 According to notes compiled by hockey historian Donald M. Clark. See "History of Indoor Ice Rinks in Minnesota," *Vintage Minnesota Hockey,* http://www.vintageminnesotahockey.com/DonClarkMNIndoor IceRinks.html (accessed 18 January 2013).

Chapter Two

1 McKenzie, "Hockey in Eastern Canada," 56–64.

2 By 1887, most important American and Continental theatres were lit by electricity. Penzel, *Theatre Lighting before Electricity*, 74.

3 Whitehead, *The Patricks*, 31.

4 Kerr, "Hockey in Ontario," 107–8.

5 Young, *Beyond Heroes*, 20.

6 Ibid., 18.

7 "Hockey. Montreal vs. Dominion," *Montreal Gazette*, 26 February 1890, 8. Mild weather in February 1892 played havoc with the ice at the Crystal Rink. It was "soft and treacherous and where the roof leaked there were holes in the ice inches deep." "Hockey. The Intermediate Championship," *Montreal Gazette*, 25 February 1892, n.p.

8 Hewitt, *Hockey Night in Canada*, 30.

9 "Victoria Rink," *Montreal Gazette*, 5 February 1884, 5. The scenario was repeated three years later when the obstacle was "a lighthouse about thirty feet high and composed entirely of blocks of ice," in consequence of which "really first class play was prevented." "The Skating Rinks," *Montreal Gazette*, 8 February 1887, 8.

10 The Amateur Hockey Association of Canada, which comprised from four to five teams between 1887 and 1898, competed from 1 January until 15 March. The Montreal Winter Carnival Tournament (1883–89) presented five or six games each year. In the NHL's first season (1917), teams played a twenty-two-game schedule.

11 Kidd, "Brand-Name Hockey," in *The Struggle for Canadian Sport*.

12 Morrow, "The Little Men of Iron," 55, 58. Contracts between the Montreal Hockey Club and the Westmount Arena for the 1904–05 and 1905–06 seasons are held at Library and Archives Canada (MG 28, I 351, vol. 6, file 5). Other Montreal teams also used the Westmount Arena. The contracts are typed, except for a blank space where the team's name has been inked in.

13 See Guay, *L'histoire du Hockey au Québec*, 92; Pinard, "Le Forum," in *Montréal Son histoire*, 69–70.

14 "Depuis quelques années, la vogue du jeu du hockey, le sport par excellence de la saison d'hiver, au Canada, va grandissante, si bien que les patinoirs sont trop petits pour contenir les foules qui assistent aux parties" (author's translation): "Le Nouveau 'Hockey Rink,'" *La Patrie*, 10 September 1898. The article was illustrated with a plan, section, and elevation for the proposed building. The new rink was to accommodate as many as 10,000 people: 4,784 seated within the amphitheatre, 216 in boxes, 1,700 standees, and 3,300 on the ice for non-hockey events.

15 "En tous points semblables à l'Arena, il pourra contient cinq milles personnes confortablement assises et pouvant suivre sans qu'elles soient empêchées par des obstacles quelconques toutes les parties de hockey qui seront jouées la cette année" (author's translation): "Transformation du Montagnard desormais on l'appellera le Stadium," *La Patrie*, 9 December 1903, 2.

16 The names Garden or Gardens (after Madison Square Garden, New York) and Coliseum also begin to appear after this date.

17 "City Items," *Montreal Daily Witness*, 4 March 1875, 2.

18 Kitchen, *Dey Brothers' Rinks Were Home to the Senators*, 3.

19 *Fire Insurance Plan of Ottawa 1901 (1888)*, vol. 2, 61, Library and Archives Canada (NMC 0013793).

20 Henry J. Volz, *Winter Garden Glide* (Pittsburgh: E.J. Murray Music Co. 1916).

21 Nelson, "Baseball," in Raitz, *The Theater of Sport*, 34.

22 Ibid., 39.

23 Ibid., 40. On efforts to encourage women to attend hockey games, see Field, "A Night at the Garden(s)."

24 On the rise of commercial sport and hockey professionalism, see Metcalfe, *Canada Learns to Play*, especially 168–72.

25 Kidd, "Brand-Name Hockey," in *The Struggle for Canadian Sport*. "Shamateurism" was so widespread by 1906 that the Stratford, Ontario, *Daily Herald* reported: "Hockey has been played for ten years or more in Canada by men paid good salaries to play the game. Yet, they are called amateurs … Better to come out boldly as professionals, because this is what most of the big teams in Canada [are] today." As quoted in Mason, "The International Hockey League," 9.

26 Kitchen, *Dey Brothers' Rinks Were Home to the Senators*, 4.

27 The discussion that follows relies heavily on two articles: Mason and Schrodt, "Hockey's First Professional Team"; and Mason, "The International Hockey League."

28 Tuthill, *Ice Hockey and Ice Polo Guide*, 5.

29 See Fitsell, *Hockey's Captains, Colonels & Kings*, especially chapter 11.

30 Mason and Schrodt, "Hockey's First Professional Team," 53, 55.

31 Nelson, "Baseball," in Raitz, *The Theater of Sport*, 33. According to Steven A. Riess, a full third of major-league baseball parks caught fire at some point in 1894. *Touching Base: Professional Baseball and American Culture in the Progressive Era* (Westport, CT: Greenwood 1980), 95. Fifteen new baseball stadiums burned between 1909 and 1923. Bennett. *They Play, You Pay*, 38.

32 Vigneault, "La diffusion du hockey à Montréal."

33 Mason and Schrodt, "Hockey's First Professional Team," 57n73.

34 On the rise of professionalism in hockey, see Wong, *Lords of the Rinks*, and Ross, *Joining the Clubs*, 32–4.

35 Kidd, *The Struggle for Canadian Sport*, 197.

36 Ibid., 197.

37 "Ottawa Wins the First," *Ottawa Journal*, 11 January 1897, 5, as discussed in Kitchen, *Dey Brothers' Rinks Were Home to the Senators*, 3.

38 Bruce Kidd has shown that league seating capacity increased from 27,000 to 112,000 between 1917 and 1929, while the number of games played grew from 20 in 1912 to 48 in 1931 (exclusive of playoffs), representing a tenfold growth in potential revenues. See Kidd, *The Struggle for Canadian Sport*, 199.

39 Van Trump, "The Duquesne Gardens," 55.

40 Fitsell, *Hockey's Captains, Colonels & Kings*, 110.

41 Van Trump, "The Duquesne Gardens," 56.

42 Whitehead, *The Patricks*, 93. Much of the discussion that follows of the Vancouver and Victoria arenas is based on Eric Whitehead's entertaining and informative biography.

43 Ibid., 97–8.

44 "Vancouver's New Sports Arena," *Contract Record* 25, no. 42 (18 October 1911): 43.

45 Whitehead, *The Patricks*, 109.

46 Ibid., 85.

47 "Vancouver's New Sports Arena," *Contract Record*, 43.

48 Whitehead, *The Patricks*, 109.

49 "Vancouver's New Sports Arena," *Contract Record*, 43.

50 "Views of Vancouver's Magnificent New Artificial Ice Rink," *B.C. Saturday Sunset* 6, no. 32 (27 January 1912): 1.

51 Hawley, *The Development of Indoor Ice Skating Rinks in*, 1–2.

52 *The Times*, 21 December 1841, as quoted in Hawley. *The Development of Indoor Ice Skating Rinks in London*, 2.

53 Hawley, *The Development of Indoor Ice Skating Rinks in London*, 3.

54 On the history of artificial ice, see Martin, "Evolution of Ice Rinks"; Briley, "A History of Refrigeration." According to notes compiled by hockey historian Donald M. Clark, William Newton constructed an artificial ice rink in New York in 1870. See "Development of Refrigeration," *Vintage Minnesota Hockey*, http://www.vintageminnesotahockey.com/DonClark Refrigerationinicerinks.html (accessed 18 January 2013). A demonstration ice rink was apparently set up at the Fair of the American Institute in New York in 1870, installed by M.J. Bujac and measuring just 24 × 10 feet. See *Scientific American* 23, 15 October 1870, 248. Thanks to James Laverance for pointing this out.

55 "Southport Glaciarium," *Building News and Engineering Journal*, 36 (24 January 1879): 90; and Adams, "Freezing Social Relations," 69.

56 "A Real Ice Skating Rink," *Illustrated London News*, 13 May 1876, 467.

Chapter Three

1 Between 1902 and 1923, fourteen of sixteen major-league baseball clubs built large, modern stadiums. These ambitious, privately financed buildings, built of durable and expensive materials, represented a long-term investment. None of these new ballparks was ever seriously damaged by fire. Nelson, "Baseball," in Raitz, *The Theater of Sport*, 41.

2 To capitalize on the boxing craze that began in the 1920s, entrepreneurs in about a dozen cities built large new arenas seating thousands of spectators. Rader, *American Sports*, 276.

3 Riess, *City Games*, 144.

4 Rader, *American Sports*, 276.

5 For details of new arena construction, see Table 1.

6 Kidd, *The Struggle for Canadian Sport*, 199. With the opening of Detroit's Olympia, gate receipts increased 250 per cent and attendance almost tripled to 142,000, while at Boston the new Gardens witnessed increases of 97 per cent in attendance and 92 per cent in gate receipts. See Ross, *Joining the Clubs*, 172, 177, and "1,350,000, A Record, Saw League Hockey," *New York Times*, 31 March 1928, 16.

7 "Rapid Construction Features Erection of Large Toronto Arena," *Contract Record and Engineering Review* 45, no. 41 (14 October 1931): 1236.

8 Construction periods for NHL arenas: Madison Square Garden, New York – 192 days (16 February 1924–28 September 1925); Montreal Forum – 159 days (24 June 1924–29 November 1924); Detroit Olympia – 229 days (8 March 1927–22 October 1927); Boston Garden – 223 days (9 January–20 August 1928); Chicago Stadium – 270 days (2 July 1928–28 March 1929); Maple Leaf Gardens, Toronto – 179 days (16 May 1931–12 November 1931).

9 "World's Greatest Sports Palace," *Madison Square Garden Official Program and Guide* (New York, 1927), n.p.

10 Riess, *City Games*, 217.

11 As quoted in Kidd, *The Struggle for Canadian Sport*, 221–2.

12 "Asks Court to Cool Garden for Hockey," *New York Times*, 24 December 1926, 2. I am grateful to Andrew Ross for bringing this episode to my attention and for sharing his research.

13 Walter McMullin, "The Sport Trail," *Hamilton Spectator*, 18 September 1925, as quoted in Kidd, *The Struggle for Canadian Sport*, 204–5.

14 See Quirk and Fort, *Hard Ball*. Table 4–9 (p. 204) measures NHL teams' won-lost records against average player costs over the period 1990–96. Among the top ten teams, in terms of winning percentage, are Boston (#2), with the tenth-ranked payroll, and Calgary (#6), with the twenty-first-ranked payroll.

15 As quoted in Kidd, *The Struggle for Canadian Sport*, 220–1.

16 Mount Royal Arena, Montreal, Montreal Forum, Madison Square Garden, Maple Leaf Gardens, and Chicago Stadium all were designed to include ground-floor shops.

17 Karl Raitz differentiates between "vernacular" and "commercial" buildings. See Raitz, *The Theater of Sport*. For a case study in the move from community, or vernacular, rinks to commercial arenas, see Field, "Passive Participation."

18 Charles Wilkins, "Maple Leaf Gardens (and How It Got That Way)," in *Maple Leaf Gardens Memories & Dreams*, 53–4.

19 Francis Morrone, *The Architectural Guidebook to New York City* (Salt Lake City, UT: Gibbs Smith 1994), 138.

Chapter Four

1 Workers agreed to accept Maple Leaf Gardens shares in partial payment of their salaries.

2 On the Toronto Maple Leafs and Maple Leaf Gardens, see *Maple Leaf Gardens Memories & Dreams*; Podnieks, *The Blue and White Book*; Young, *The Boys of Saturday Night*; Hewitt, *Hockey Night in Canada*.

3 Young, *The Boys of Saturday Night*, 61.

4 Young, *Hello Canada!* 48.

5 Young, *The Boys of Saturday Night*, 60.

6 On Ravina Gardens, see Diana Fancher, "Brilliant Hockey at West End Rink," *Leader and Recorder: West Toronto Junction Historical Society Newsletter* (summer 1996); illustrated in Podnieks, *The Blue and White Book*, 2; blueprints are held at the Architectural Drawing Collection, City of Toronto Archives (CTA) (PT 00627w–1 to 10); notes on file at The Market Gallery, Toronto, from the exhibition *Home Field Advantage*.

7 *Home Field Advantage.*

8 A similar instance occurred in New Jersey where the construction of Newark's Prudential Center in 2007 called into question the financial viability of the Izod Center in neighbouring Meadowlands, eight miles away. The New Jersey Devils moved from Izod to Prudential in 2007 and in 2012 the New Jersey Nets moved to the Barclays Center in Brooklyn. Ted Sherman, "Truce Talks Underway in Dispute between Prudential, Izod Centers," *Star Ledger* (Newark), 15 April 2009, http://www.nj.com/news/index.ssf/2009/04/truce_talks_underway_in_war_be.html (accessed 6 December 2012).

9 "Maple Leafs Gardens, Toronto," *Construction* 24, no. 12 (1931): 369.

10 I am indebted to Russell Field, who first discussed the relationship of Maple Leaf Gardens to the College Street Eaton's store in his doctoral dissertation, "A Night at the Garden(s)."

11 See Wright, *The Most Prominent Rendezvous of the Feminine Toronto.*

12 Field, "A Night at the Garden(s)," 122.

13 Ross and Macdonald to J.A. Gibson, 26 January 1931, Maple Leaf Gardens, General Matters, File M-103, General Files of James Elliot, F229–282, T. Eaton Co. fonds, Archives of Ontario, Toronto, as quoted in Field, "A Night at the Garden(s)," 124.

14 Drawings by Ross and Macdonald for Maple Leaf Gardens are in the collection of the Canadian Centre for Architecture, Montreal (AP013.S1.D164).

15 R.C. Manning, "The Year's Progress in Use of Structural Steel," *Contract Record and Engineering Review* 45, no. 52 (30 December 1931): 1545.

16 A copy of this document is part of the Conn Smythe papers at the Archives of Ontario (Conn Smythe fonds, F223–3–1–53).

17 This unexecuted design is related to two other versions, drawings for which are held at the Canadian Centre for Architecture (CCA), Montreal, and in the Conn Smythe papers at the Archives of Ontario. All three versions can be dated to about 17 March 1931 since they correspond with a plan and sections of that date in the Ross and Macdonald Archive at the CCA.

18 A 1963 plan to extend the building with a projecting element over Carleton Street was refused by Toronto City Council in 1964. *Maple Leaf Gardens Memories & Dreams*, 69.

19 "An Outstanding Construction Accomplishment – Erection of Large Sports Arena in Five Months," *Contract Record and Engineering Review* 45, no. 11 (11 November 1931), 1353, 1357.

20 A version of the following was published in Shubert, "The Montreal Forum."

21 John McCrae, *In Flanders Fields and Other Poems* (Toronto: Briggs 1919). The complete poem reads:

In Flanders fields the poppies blow
Between the crosses row on row,
That mark our place; and in the sky
The larks, still bravely singing, fly
Scarce heard amid the guns below.

We are the Dead. Short days ago
We lived, felt dawn, saw sunset glow,
Loved and were loved, and now we lie
In Flanders fields.

Take up our quarrel with the foe:
To you from failing hands we throw
The torch; be yours to hold it high.
If ye break faith with us who die
We shall not sleep, though poppies grow
In Flanders fields.

Some 600,000 Canadian soldiers saw action in the First World War, out of a population of 6 million. Nearly 60,000 lost their lives, 87 per cent as a result of enemy action in France and Flanders, and more than 150,000 were wounded. Dick Irvin Sr served in the Fort Gary Horse Regiment as a motorcycle dispatcher from late 1917 until war's end. He saw action in France, Belgium, and Holland. (I am grateful to Dick Irvin Jr for generously sharing details of his father's service in the war; telephone conversation with the author, 13 December 2005.)

22 "Au Revoir Forum, Bienvenue Molson Centre," *Associated Press*, 12 March 1996, http://hockey.ballparks.com/NHL/MontrealCanadiens/articles.html (accessed 15 September 2006).

23 For the closing of the Forum and the cultural significance of hockey arenas in Canada, see Shubert, "Hockey Arenas: Canada's Secular Shrines."

24 The banners and other Forum memorabilia were sold at an auction on 12 March 1996 that raised over $700,000 for charity. A hot-dog grill sold for $900, a turnstile for $1,800, and former NHL president Clarence Campbell's seat for $12,000. Peggy Curran, "Fans Bid for Forum Treasures," *Montreal Gazette*, 13 March 1996, A1.

25 Thanks to Nicholas Adams for pointing out this connection.

26 Religious processions date back to the seventeenth century in Quebec and continued into the 1930s, only disappearing completely with the Quiet Revolution of the 1960s. All such processions in Quebec followed a similar pattern: meeting at the church, the faithful would attend Mass, assemble behind the banner for their group, and then parade through the streets while reciting prayers and singing hymns. The ritualistic patterns of religion also find a parallel in the deep strain of superstition that runs through professional sport. Lucky socks, specific bus-seating plans, playoff beards, and game-day rituals are legion. Famously, goaltender Patrick Roy used to step, rather than skate, over the centre-ice line when entering or leaving the ice surface. On parallels between religion and hockey in Montreal, see Bauer and Barreau, *La Religion du Canadien de Montréal*, and Bauer, *Une Théologie de Canadien de Montréal*.

27 Ingrid Peretz, "Wafers Sold as Snacks Showing Mass Appeal," *Globe and Mail*, 27 December 2005, A1.

28 Adam Gopnik discusses the ethnicity of late-nineteenth-century Montreal hockey teams, arguing that "the" great Canadian movie could be made around the story of two French Canadian players who "cross over" and play for the English-speaking Irish Shamrocks team. See Gopnik, *Winter Five Windows on the Season*, 156–61.

29 Johnny Bruno, the promoter for Madison Square Garden, changed the names of Lorne Chabot to "Chabotsky" and Oliver Reinikka to "Ollie Rocco." Kreiser and Friedman, *The New York Rangers*, 1.

30 "Le Canadien est pret a inaugurer sa saison par une victoire ce soir," *La Patrie*, 29 November 1924, 18.

31 Chris Goyens, *Montreal Canadians*, in Diamond, *Total Hockey*, 201.

32 "Habitants" was a French term used to describe the rugged farmer-settlers of seventeenth-century New France (what is now Quebec), while "Canadien" had a similar meaning, referring specifically to the hard-working citizens of Montreal. Goyens, "Montreal Canadiens," in Diamond, *Total Hockey*, 201.

33 On the rise of francophone hockey in Montreal and the role of skating rinks in this development, see Vigneault, "La Diffusion du Hockey à Montréal."

34 "Comme les quatre clubs de programme étaient anglais, le nombre des amateurs de sport canadiens français n'était pas très élevé, mais il le sera d'avantage lorsque le National se mesurera avec les autres clubs de la ligue" (author's translation): "L'Inauguration de la Nouvelle Arena," *La Presse*, 7 January 1920, 6.

35 "Ironically, the first owner [of the Canadiens], J. Ambrose O'Brien, was neither a Montrealer nor a French Canadian [but] the scion of a wealthy mine-owning family… [from] Renfrew, Ontario." Goyens, "Montreal Canadiens," in Diamond, *Total Hockey*, 201.

36 Chris Tredree, "The NHL Entry Draft," in Diamond, *Total Hockey*, 285.

37 Brown, *The Montreal Maroons*, 11.

38 In 1921 Duggan was one of the unsuccessful bidders for the Canadiens when the team was put up for sale. One way to guarantee bookings in your arena was to own your primary tenant.

39 "L'Arena Mont-Royal sera reconstruite de façon à loger douze mille personnes," *La Presse*, 14 July 1925. As would happen later in Toronto, when the arrival of Maple Leaf Gardens forced Arena Gardens out of the hockey business, the Mount Royal Arena struggled financially after the flight of its primary tenant and in 1937 the building was sold and converted into stores and small factories. It was destroyed by fire on 29 February 2000.

40 Montrealers were already accustomed to viewing the Stanley Cup as their property. Montreal teams had won the trophy fourteen times in twenty-five years, from 1893, when the prize was first awarded, to 1917, the year the NHL was formed.

41 Robinson, *Howie Morenz*, chapter 9. See also Perrone, "The King Has Two Bodies," where the author argues that Morenz's funeral and subsequent canonization were promotional tools aimed at shoring up a struggling team and league.

42 Montrealers were familiar with the idea that buildings could symbolize cultural oppositions. Since the mid-nineteenth century they had lived with a particularly apt one at Place d'Armes in the heart of the old city, where the Gothic Revival Nôtre-Dame Church, emblem of French Catholic society, stands across from the Neo-classical Bank of Montreal headquarters, symbol of Anglo-Scottish capital.

43 The reference is to Hugh MacLennan's novel *Two Solitudes* (Toronto: Collins, c. 1945), which treated the alienation and confrontation of Canada's two European founding nations/cultures (English/French) through an individual's struggle for linguistic and cultural identity in the inter-war years.

44 The headline of the *Montreal Star* on 18 March 1955 was "Arrest 41 after Forum Riot Crowd Loots or Damages 50 Stores." The *La Presse* lead was "Défi et Provocation de Campbell."

45 Carrier, *Our Life with the Rocket*, 222.

46 In spite of a stately and dignified manner that personified wisdom and leadership, Clarence Campbell functioned as a servant to the owners, according to David Cruise and Alison Griffiths. Responding to the suggestion that Campbell be replaced, Stafford Smythe, son of Maple Leafs owner Conn Smythe, reportedly replied, "Where would we find another Rhodes scholar, graduate lawyer, decorated war hero, and former prosecutor at the Nuremberg trials, *who will do what he's told*?" Cruise and Griffiths, *Net Worth*, 41. See also Goyens and Turowetz, *Lions in Winter*, 94.

47 O'Brien, *Firewagon Hockey*, 57–8; and Carrier, *Our Life with the Rocket*, 210–12.

48 "Monsieur Campbell, du haut de sa grandeur, écrassait de sa botte anglaise Maurice Richard, et, en celui-ci chaque canadien français se sentait écrasé" (author's translation): Pellerin, *L'Idole d'un Peuple*, 92, as quoted in Dupperault, "L'Affaire Richard," 80.

49 "It was very clear before Thursday night's hockey game that Mr. Campbell's ruling was extremely unpopular, and one could have easily predicted a response on the part of those who attended the game. I am reasonably certain that people would have behaved in an orderly fashion, because it was Mr.

Campbell's provocative presence that caused their protest to take a different turn. Mr. Campbell would be wise to stay away from the Forum, above all to avoid announcing his presence in advance. His attendance could effectively be interpreted as a challenge" (author's translation). "Il est bien évident avant la partie de hockey de Jeudi soir que la décision de M. Campbell était d'une extrême impopularité, et l'on pouvait facilement prévoir une démonstration de la part de ceux qui allaient y assister. J'avais raison d'avoir confiance que la population manifesterait dans l'ordre, puisque ce n'est que sur la provocation causée par la présence de M. Campbell que les protestations ont pris une autre tournure. Il eût été sage de la part de M. Campbell de s'abstenir de se rendre au Forum, surtout d'annoncer publiquement à l'avance sa visite. Sa présence en effet, pouvait être interprétée comme un véritable défi." Jean Drapeau, "La venue de Campbell au Forum constituait un véritable défi," *La Patrie*, 19 March 1955, 1.

50 Goyens and Turowetz, *Lions in Winter*, 87–92; Ulmer, *Canadiens Captains*, 65–72.

51 As quoted in Blake, *Canadian Hockey Literature*, 214.

52 A reference to Yankee Stadium in New York, "The House That Ruth Built." Marc Thibeault, "L'amphithéâtre No 1 du Canada," *Le Petit Journal*, 15 March 1953.

53 "Le fait est que cet organiste, si ça continue, jouera avant longtemps bien plus pour le Bon Dieu que pour les habitués du Forum!" (author's translation). Marc Thibeault, "L'amphithéâtre No 1 du Canada," *Le Petit Journal*, 15 March 1953.

54 The televisual qualities of sports stadiums and their potential as marketing tools are now an accepted fact among designers of sports facilities. Brian Trubey, architect of the Baltimore Colts football stadium, noted that "NFL venues are the most-seen type of architecture on television. As much time as we spend making [the stadium] incredible for the people actually physically there, we believe the balance of the audience – which is probably 99 percent of it – hadn't been leveraged as a participant in terms of enhancing brand through the stadium." Alex Frangos, "New Football Arenas Push Bounds of Stadium Engineering," *Wall*

Street Journal, 29 August 2005, as published in *Pittsburgh Post-Gazette*, http://www.post-gazette.com/pg/pp/05241/561996.stm (accessed 15 September 2006).

55 *Liste des lieux de culte fermés* documents more than 300 Quebec religious buildings that have closed since 1920, according to records of the Fondation du patrimoine religieux du Québec. On this organization, see http://www.patrimoine-religieux.qc.ca/ (accessed 15 September 2006).

56 On the Valleyfield Presbyterian Church, see the *Inventaire des lieux de culte du Québec*, http://www.lieuxdeculte.qc.ca/index.htm (accessed 15 September 2006). On the Centre d'Escalade Vertige, see "Une église qu'il faudra escalader," *Le Soleil de Valleyfield*, 20–21 May 2005, 1, 4; and http://www.vertige-escalade.com/ (accessed 15 September 2006).

57 Vine and Challen, *Gardens of Shame*; and "Maple Leaf Gardens Sex Scandal," *Canadian Encyclopedia*, http://www.thecanadianencyclopedia.ca/en/article/maple-leaf-gardens-sex-scandal/ (accessed 28 October 2015). Stadiums in particular have been the sites of horrific scenes never imagined by their architects. They have been employed as both massive detention centres and as sites for executions. In 2005 Hurrican Katrina flood victims were sheltered at the Louisiana Superdome, which "quickly became a sweltering and surreal vault, a place of overflowing toilets and no showers," where one refugee claimed, "'They're housing us like animals.'" Joseph B. Treaster, "Superdome: Haven Quickly Becomes an Ordeal," *New York Times*, 1 September 2005, http://www.nytimes.com/2005/09/01/us/nationalspecial/superdome-haven-quickly-becomes-an-ordeal.html?_r=0 (accessed 28 October 2015). The following is a partial list of stadiums used for mass executions: Santiago, Chile, 1973; Gagra Stadium, Abkhazia, 1992; Kibuye Stadium, Rwanda, 1994; Gatwara Stadium, Rwanda, 1994; Kigali Stadium Rwanda, 1994; Bratstvo Stadium, Bratunac, Bosnia, 1995; Ghazi Stadium, Kabul, Afghanistan, 1999; Changdou, Sichuan, China, 2001; Haditha Stadium, Iraq, 2005; Conakry Stadium, Guinea, 2009; Baniyas Stadium, Syria, 2011; Sabzevar Stadium, Khorasan Province, Iran, 2013.

58 A similarly discriminatory environment prevailed

during construction of Pittsburgh's Civic Arena. See Robert Trumpbour. "Civil Rights and Sports Landmarks: Discrimination, Jobs and Activism in the Construction of Pittsburgh's Three Rivers Stadium," in Dryeson and Trumpbour, *Cathedrals of Sport*, 1571 and 1569n28.

59 I present Giullianotti's theoretical approach in greater detail in chapter 8. Giulianotti, *Supporters, Followers, Fans, and Flâneurs*, 41.

Chapter Five

1 The Stanley Cup did not become the sole property of the NHL until 1927. The PCHL folded in 1926.

2 "The problem to resolve was that of New York's rink, which was too small to admit large crowds. The owners of the Saint Nicholas rink have agreed to enlarge their rink and everything will surely go smoothly" (author's translation): "Le problème à résoudre était celui du patinoir à New York, qui était un peu restraint pour admettre de grandes foules. Les propriétaires du patinoire Saint-Nicholas ont accepté d'aggrandir ce patinoir et il est certain que tout marchera sur des roulettes." "Ligue de Hockey Internationale," *Le Devoir*, 24 July 1914, 6.

3 Wong, *Lords of the Rinks*, 86.

4 See Kidd, "Brand-Name Hockey," 202, and Fitsell, *Hockey's Captains, Colonels, and Kings*, chapters 10–12.

5 The path to American expansion was, in fact, far more complex than it has been possible to represent here. Fears of rival American leagues and the financial might of teams there even led Canadian teams to sign agreements promising to stay in the NHL for a period of years. See Kidd, "Brand-Name Hockey," 202–7; Wong, *Lords of the Rinks*; Holzman and Nieforth, *Deceptions and Doublecross*; and Ross, *Joining the Clubs*.

6 The Thomas J. Duggan Collection is held privately. It contains documents and correspondence dating from 1923–28 primarily by and between Thomas Duggan, Charles F. Adams, Frank Calder, George C. Funk, and Tex Rickard.

7 Funk and Wilcox installed the artificial-ice plant at Madison Square Garden III. According to a letter in the Thomas Duggan Collection, they also designed arenas, or possibly just the ice plants, at Chicago,

Detroit, Providence, and Springfield. Thomas Duggan to A.B. Smythe, 2 March 1928.

8 George C. Funk to Thomas J. Duggan, 28 February 1924 (Thomas J. Duggan Collection).

9 Ibid.

10 George L. Rickard to Thomas J. Duggan, 20 December 1923 (Thomas J. Duggan Collection).

11 Charles F. Adams to Thomas J. Duggan, 13 February 1924 (Thomas J. Duggan Collection).

12 Charles F. Adams to Frank Calder, 10 April 1924 (Thomas J. Duggan Collection).

13 Charles F. Adams to Thomas J. Duggan, 10 April 1924 (Thomas J. Duggan Collection).

14 Charles F. Adams to Thomas J. Duggan, 15 May 1924 (Thomas J. Duggan Collection).

15 Charles F. Adams to Thomas J. Duggan, 29 May 1924 (Thomas J. Duggan Collection).

16 "Duggan Tells of Talks with Adams: Suing Owner of Bruins to Force Stock Turnover," *Boston Globe*, 6 March 1929, 31.

17 Rickard died in 1929. See Jack Cavanaugh, "Backtalk: The Last Days of a Garden Where Memories Grew," *New York Times*, 16 April 1995, http://www.nytimes.com/1995/04/16/sports/backtalk-the-last-days-of-a-garden-where-memories-grew.html?src=pm (accessed 11 December 2012).

18 Hal Bock, "Hockey," in Hollander, *Madison Square Garden*, 111. Even when quoted in a brochure soliciting membership in the New York Hockey Club, the best Rickard could find to say about the sport was that "it gives me a bigger kick than International Polo." *The New York Hockey Club* (New York, 1925).

19 George C. Funk to Thomas J. Duggan, 28 October 1924 (Thomas J. Duggan Collection).

20 *New Issue New Madison Square Garden Corporation Class A Cumulative Participating Preference Stock* (New York: Allan, Weed and Co., n.d.). The New Madison Square Garden Corporation had been incorporated on 31 May 1923. See "Plan Uptown Arena Twice Garden's Size," *New York Times*, 28 June 1923.

21 *New York Hockey Franchises Holding Company Incorporated* Printed stock offering (Thomas J. Duggan Collection).

22 Bruce Kidd made this point in *The Struggle for Canadian Sport*, 203.

23 *New Issue New Madison Square Garden Corporation Class A Cumulative Participating Preference Stock.*

24 "Profit of $784,639 In Madison Square," *New York Times*, 19 May 1927, n.p.

25 John S. Archibald, *Proposed Arena Building: Schedule #7* (21 February 1924), Molson Papers, Library and Archives Canada. The same was true for Maple Leaf Gardens in Toronto. A preferred stock offering dated 15 May 1931 indicates that professional and amateur hockey revenues are estimated at $350,000, or 70 per cent of the total $500,000 expected earnings for the building. Additional income was anticipated from other attractions, concessions, and store rentals.

26 John S. Archibald, *Report on Proposed New Arena Building, Montreal: Report #2* (13 December 1922), Molson Papers, Library and Archives Canada.

27 On the history and architecture of Madison Square Garden, see "New Garden Dims All Indoor Arenas," *New York Times*, 22 November 1925; Bolling, "Madison Square Garden Is Razed!"; Hollander, *Madison Square Garden*; Durso, *Madison Square Garden*; Stern, Mellins, and Fishman, *New York 1880*.

28 As quoted in Pepe, *Madison Square Garden Hall of Fame*, 7.

29 "Skating at Gilmore's Garden," *New York Times*, 20 January 1879, 8.

30 Stern, Mellins, and Fishman, *New York 1880*, 695.

31 Ibid., 695.

32 *American Architect and Building News* 8 (7 August 1880): 61–2, as quoted in Stern, Mellins, and Fishman, *New York 1880*, 696–7.

33 *New York Times*, 28 February 1900, as quoted in Steven A. Reiss, ed. *Major Problems in American Sport History* (Boston, New York: Houghton Mifflin Company 1997), 148.

34 "Building to Eclipse Madison Sq. Garden," *New York Times*, 22 September 1911.

35 "Garden as Ice Palace," *New York Times*, 5 December 1915, 3, and "Ice Skating at Madison Sq. Garden," *New York Times*, 13 December 1915, 14.

36 On 20 May 1920 New York State passed the Walker law, which legalized boxing.

37 Aycock and Scott, *Tex Rickard*, 136.

38 Ibid., 137.

39 The drawings are part of the Thomas Lamb Archive at Avery Architectural Library, Columbia University.

40 "Plan Uptown Arena Twice Garden's Size: 'Greatest Amusement Centre' to Seat 26,515 to Be at 50th and 7th Av," *New York Times*, 28 June 1923.

41 Ibid.

42 "Rickard to Stage Big Hockey Games," *New York Times*, 19 June 1924.

43 George C. Funk to Thomas J. Duggan, 27 May 1924 (Thomas J. Duggan Collection). The blueprints by Funk and Wilcox for the installation of artificial ice at Madison Square Garden II are also in the Thomas J. Duggan Collection.

44 George C. Funk to Thomas J. Duggan, 27 May 1924 (Thomas J. Duggan Collection).

45 In June 1924 the New York Life Insurance Company asked Rickard to vacate Madison Square Garden II by 1 August 1925.

46 "Rickard to Build Garden on 8th Av.: Boxing Promoter and Associates Buy Car Barn Site between 49th and 50th Streets," *New York Times*, 18 June 1924.

47 The drawing was also published in a brochure soliciting membership in the New York Hockey Club.

48 See Lanken, *Montreal Movie Palaces*, 169n6.

49 "The New Madison Square Garden," in "Madison Square Garden is Razed!" 19.

50 Harold Sterner, "Madison Square Garden, Old and New," *The Arts* 14 (1928): 349–50, as quoted in Field, "A Night at the Garden(s)," 49–50.

51 Hart, *The New York Theatres of Thomas Lamb*, 4–5.

52 According to the agreement between Rickard and Duggan.

53 George C. Funk to Thomas J. Duggan, 25 July and 25 August 1924 (Thomas J. Duggan Collection).

54 Funk and Wilcox to Geo. L. Rickard, 29 October 1925 (Thomas J. Duggan Collection).

55 Thomas Duggan to A.B. Smythe, 2 March 1928 (Thomas J. Duggan Collection).

Part Three

1 The NHL's stability also reflected the limited regional appeal of the sport in the United States and the expenses entailed in building and maintaining adequate sized arenas. Riess, *City Games*, 234–5.

2 J.M. Stevenson, "Arena Tour of North America" (9 September 1948). The document is part of the Stevenson Raines fonds at the Canadian Architectural Archives, University of Calgary Library (Accession # 114A/81.18 – STE f573(a)).

3 Ibid. The Calgary Corral opened in 1950 at a cost of $1.5 million.

4 In fact, there was expansion and contraction, including teams that were added, folded, and relocated. For the details of NHL expansion, see http://www.rauzulusstreet.com/hockey/nhlhistory/nhlhistory.html (accessed 11 June 2012). For details of the new hockey facilities, see Table 1.

5 The twenty-two new franchises were as follows: the NBA added ten teams from 1966 to 1981 – Chicago Bulls (1966), San Diego Rockets (1967), Seattle Sonics (1967), Milwaukee Bucks (1968), Phoenix Suns (1968), Buffalo Braves (1970), Cleveland Cavaliers (1970), Portland Trailblazers (1970), New Orleans Jazz (1974), Dallas Mavericks (1980); MLB added teams six teams from 1969 to 1977 – San Diego Padres, Montreal Expos, Kansas City Royal, Seattle Pilots (all 1969), and Seattle Mariners and Toronto Blue Jays (1977); the NFL added six teams from 1960 to 1976 – Dallas Texans (became the Cowboys) (1960), Minnesota Vikings (1961), Atlanta Falcons (1966), New Orleans Saints (1967), Tampa Buccaneers (1976), Seattle Seahawks (1976). The forty-two new buildings are listed in Table 3. The list does not include those arenas where hockey was also played: United Center, Chicago; Reunion Arena, Dallas; Coliseum at Richfield, OH.

6 See: Ronald A. Smith, "Far More Than Commercialism: Stadium Building from Harvard's Innovations to Stanford's 'Dirt Bowl,'" in Dyreson and Trumpbour, *Cathedrals of Sport*, 1453–74.

7 Riess, *City Games*, 237–8.

8 With the exception of Madison Square Garden, which cost $43 million, expansion-era arenas were erected through 1968 at costs ranging from about $6–16 million. See Table 4.

9 Noll and Zimbalist, *Sports, Jobs, and Taxes*, 2.

10 Riess, *City Games*, 239.

Chapter Six

1 Nelson, "Baseball," in Raitz, *The Theatre of Sport*, 54.

2 Ibid., 55–6.

3 "Oakland-Alameda County Coliseum Complex 'Nation's Most Complete Indoor-Outdoor Sports and Entertainment Center'" (undated typescript document held within the Myron Goldsmith fonds, Canadian Centre for Architecture, Montreal).

4 Bradford and Sherry, "Domesticating Public through Ritual," 146.

5 Ibid., 134.

6 Ibid., 147. See also Shannon Chapla, "Not Simply a Party: Tailgaters Contribute to Team Victory and Even University Brand, New Study Shows," *Notre Dame News*, 6 September 2012, http://news.nd.edu/news/33119-not-simply-a-party-tailgaters-contribute-to-team-victory-and-even-university-brand-new-study-shows/ (accessed 28 June 2013).

7 Discussing spectatorship at international sporting events, Alan Guttman observed that, as a consequence of advances in the quality of equipment and facilities produced by our modern international culture, "when we watch an international sporting event we are participating in a thoroughly modern cultural form and celebrating a thoroughly modern form of human excellence." Alan Guttman, *From Ritual to Record*, as quoted in Hall, Slack, Smith, and Whitson, *Sport in Canadian Society*, 42. These authors believe that, in attending such sporting events, "we are also participating in cultural institutions that have lost any national character they may once have had. Rather, they have become arenas in which our modernism is demonstrated" (ibid.).

8 Nelson, "Baseball," in Raitz, *The Theatre of Sport*, 61.

9 Ibid., 61–2.

10 Allen Guttman, "Mediated Spectatorship," in Pope, *The New American Sport History*, 378, reprinted from Guttman, *Sports Spectators*.

11 Zimbalist, *The Bottom Line*, 64.

12 Ibid., 65.

13 John Pastier, "The Laurel That Oakland Lost," *Los Angeles Times*, 21 October 1975, 1. If baseball stadiums received 1 per cent of architectural criticism, it is fair to assume that hockey arenas, by extension, have been virtually unnoticed. Pastier himself discusses only the stadium, ignoring the pendant arena.

14 "An Elegant Sports and Recreation Center," *Architectural Record* 143, no. 6 (1968): 121–7. The arena was home to the NHL's California Seals (1967); Oakland Seals (1967–70); and California Golden Seals (1970–76).

15 Pastier, "The Laurel That Oakland Lost," 7.

16 Eero Saarinen had employed this approach in his design of the David S. Ingalls Hockey Rink at Yale University in New Haven (1956–59).

17 AIA California Council, "Three San Francisco Architectural Firms Selected for Statewide Firm, 25-Year and Maybeck Awards" (20 March 1993). (Typescript news release held within the Myron Goldsmith fonds, Canadian Centre for Architecture, Montreal.)

18 I am indebted to Cammie McAtee for bringing Matthew Nowicki's J.S. Dorton Arena to my attention. The building was constructed as part of the North Carolina Sate Fairgrounds and used for agricultural displays and a wide range of other activities, including ice hockey. Major-league arenas employing a saddle-dome design include: Arizona Veterans Memorial Coliseum (Phoenix, AZ, 1965), Capital Center (Landover, MD, 1973), and the Olympic Saddledome (Calgary, 1983). On the Dorton Arena, see Henry Petroski, *Pushing the Limits*, 131–40, "Nowicki, Matthew (1910–50)," in *North Carolina Builders and Architects: A Biographical Dictionary*, http://ncarchitects.lib.ncsu.edu/people/P000044 (accessed 27 September 2012); and "Dorton Arena," a ten-minute film, http://video.unctv.org/video/2365276737/ (accessed 17 March 2016).

19 See Shapiro Comte, *Myron Goldsmith*.

20 Goldsmith had explored a similar project in 1954, while in Rome. This unexecuted project featured a roof that was 800 feet in diameter. See Shapiro Comte, *Myron Goldsmith*, 17–18. On the work of SOM and for a discussion of the Oakland-Alameda County Coliseum, see Adams, *Skidmore, Owings & Merrill*.

21 Temko, "Portland's Great Hall of Glass," 108.

22 Libby, "Memorial Coliseum," and "Talking with Bill Rouzie."

23 The project also called for an exhibition hall with

over 50,000 square feet of space. The hall was located below grade, its roof serving as parking space for 1,700 cars.

24 In addition to the article by Allan Temko, cited above, on the Portland Coliseum, see also "Portland Coliseum"; Goodrich, "Portland Memorial Coliseum; "Freezing Ice and Cooling People," *Weather Magic* 25, no. 4 (1961): 10–12.

25 "Portland Coliseum," 30.

26 William Rouzie's comments were originally reported in Sarah Mirk, "Designers Rant about Rose Quarter Process," *Portland Mercury*, 21 April 2009, http://blogtown.portlandmercury.com/BlogtownPDX/archives/2009/04/21/designers-rant-about-rose-quarter-process (accessed 20 June 2012); and Libby "Talking with Bill Rouzie."

27 April Baer, "Looking for a Way to Save Portland's Coliseum," OPB News, 13 May 2009, http://news.opb.org/article/looking-way-save-portlands-coliseum/ (accessed 20 June 2012).

28 Allen Ginsberg, "Portland Coliseum (27 August 1965)," *Planet News, 1961–1967* (San Francisco: City Lights Books 1968), 102–3.

29 Sercombe, "'Ladies and Gentlemen …' The Beatles," 1–15.

30 According to figures compiled by Larry Kane, the journalist who accompanied the Beatles throughout their tour, total attendance for the tour was 824,969. This total was boosted by a number of shows at outdoor stadiums, notably that at Shea Stadium in New York, which attracted 55,600. See Kane, *Ticket to Ride*, 271–2. By comparison, the clubs and halls the band had played previously, in Hamburg (Indra, Kaiserkeller, Star Club), Liverpool (Casbah, Cavern Club, Grafton), and London (Astoria), had a capacity of a few hundred to no more than two thousand.

31 In addition to the fifty-two concerts, the Beatles also appeared four times on the *Ed Sullivan Show*, in New York City and in Miami.

32 On Washington Coliseum, see Christianson, "The Uline Arena/Washington Coliseum," and "Uline Arena."

33 You can see them doing this in a number of YouTube clips, including this one: http://www.youtube.com/watch?v=t-pBqLGhMUo (accessed 21 September 2012).

34 Samuel Shaffer, "Hubert Humphrey Comes on Strong," *New York Times*, 25 August 1963, 62, as quoted in Ethan, *A Spatial History of Arena Rock*.

35 John S. Wilson, "Amplifying System Drowns out Music at Capital Festival," *New York Times*, 2 June 1962, 8. See also Ethan, *A Spatial History of Arena Rock*, 66–7.

36 The twenty-two venues and the dates they opened are: Moby Arena, Fort Collins, CO (1966); Los Angeles Forum (1967); Oakland-Alameda County Coliseum (1966); San Diego Sports Arena (1966); Arizona Veterans Memorial Coliseum (1965); Moody Coliseum, Dallas (1956); University Coliseum, Auburn, TX (1969); Assembly Hall, Champaigne, IL (1963); International Amphitheater, Chicago (1934); Olympia Stadium, Detroit (1927); The Spectrum, Philadelphia (1967); Civic Center, Baltimore (1962); Madison Square Garden, New York (1968); Boston Garden (1928); Palm Beach International Raceway, FL (1965). I have not included the show at the Altamont Speedway on 6 December, which was not officially a part of the tour.

37 Ethan, *A Spatial History of Arena Rock*, 17. See Kathy Orloff, "Bogdanovich Runs a Sound Business," *Los Angeles Times*, 11 October 1970, Q16.

38 As discussed in Ethan, *A Spatial History of Arena Rock*, 11–12. See Jack Boettner, "Top-Name Concerts Planned to Fight Anaheim Stadium Deficit," *Los Angeles Times*, 11 May 1970; Bill Hazlett, "Policing Rock Concerts: A Question of Priorities," *Los Angeles Times*, 12 May 1975; Jack Boettner, "87 Arrested at Stadium Rock Concert," *Los Angeles Times*, 30 August 1977

39 Badman, *The Beatles Off the Record*, 85.

40 Sercombe, "'Ladies and Gentlemen …' The Beatles," 4–5.

41 *New Yorker*, 22 February 1964, 22, as quoted in Sercombe, "'Ladies and Gentlemen …' The Beatles," 5.

42 *New Yorker*, 22 February 1964, 22.

43 Sercombe, "'Ladies and Gentlemen …' The Beatles," 8.

44 Oddey and White, *Modes of Spectating*, 8.

45 On the transformation of the traditional "sender-receiver" or "simple" model of spectatorship to the

postmodern "mass" or "diffused" model, see Kennedy, *The Spectator and the Spectacle*.

46 David Remnick, "American Hunger," *New Yorker*, 12 October 1998, 65. On Gorgeous George, see John Capouya, *Gorgeous George: The Outrageous Bad-Boy Wrestler Who Created American Pop Culture* (New York: HarperCollins 2008).

47 Remnick, *American Hunger*, 65.

48 Sammons, *Beyond the Ring*, 200.

49 James C. McKinley Jr, "Barclays Arena Rivals the Garden's Glow," *New York Times*, 27 September 2012, http://www.nytimes.com/2012/09/28/arts/music/barclays-arena-rivals-the-gardens-glow.html?ref=music (accessed 27 September 2012).

50 Ken Belson, "With New Move, Jay-Z Enters a Sports Agent State of Mind," *New York Times*, 2 April 2013, http://www.nytimes.com/2013/04/03/sports/new-jay-z-lyrics-for-athletes-please-let-me-represent-you.html (accessed 3 April 2013).

51 Photocopied plans dated 29 April 1993 and signed by Ellerbe Becket Architects for a renovated Oakland-Alameda County Coliseum are held within the Myron Goldsmith fonds, Canadian Centre for Architecture, Montreal.

52 Rob Gloster, "Dazzling! Spectatcular! Top-Quality! (The Arena, Not the Team)," *Associated Press*, 1997, http://wwwmediacity.com/~csuppes/NBA/Golden StateWarriors/Articles/110898.htm (accessed 27 June 2000). The average cost of a new NHL arena through 1990s was $176 million.

53 On the renovations, see Rick DelVecchio, "Arena Polished, Ready for Fans: Warriors Betting That $102 Million Upgrade Brings Crowds Back," *San Francisco Chronicle*, 7 November 1997, A21, http://wwwmediacity.com/~csuppes/NBA/GoldenStateWarriors/Articles/110797.htm (accessed 27 June 2000).

54 The California Golden Seals were first known as the California Seals (1967) and then as the Oakland Seals (1967–70) before being renamed the California Golden Seals in 1970. In 1976 the team was relocated to Cleveland and in 1978 merged with the Minnesota North Stars.

55 In 2014 Rick Welts, Golden State Warriors president, announced a change of location to Mission Bay and that Snøhetta would no longer design the building. Eric Young, "Warriors President Explains New Game Plan for San Francisco Arena," *San Francisco Business Times*, 22 April 2014, http://www.bizjournals.com/sanfrancisco/news/2014/04/22/warriors-salesforce.html (accessed 23 April 2014).

Chapter Seven

1 "The New Madison Square Garden Center: She's Changed Her Style and She May Change *Yours*," *Architectural Forum* 129 (December 1968): 6–7.

2 Mickey Herskowitz, "Dome Hits 30: Historic Construction Covers All the Bases," *Houston Post*, 9 April 1995, as reproduced in "Housing the Spectacle," http://www.columbia.edu/cu/gsapp/BT/DOMES/domelst.html (accessed 26 October 2015).

3 "Three Times Bigger," *Architectural Forum* 88 (April 1948): 13.

4 Lionel and Leon Levy's New York Coliseum was a four-storey, 323,000-square-foot convention hall. It opened on 28 April 1956.

5 "Three Times Bigger," *Architectural Forum*, 13.

6 Quirk and Fort, *Hard Ball*, 37.

7 Cruise and Griffiths, *Net Worth*, 26–30.

8 Ownership of more than one team violated NHL league rules. In 1952 Norris and Wirtz sold their stake in the Chicago building and franchise to Norris family members. See Quirk and Fort, *Hard Ball*, 37.

9 Cruise and Griffiths, *Net Worth*, 33.

10 Sammons, *Beyond the Ring*, 164–5.

11 Stern, Mellins, and Fishman, *New York 1960*, 680.

12 Luckman, *Twice in a Lifetime*, 207–14.

13 Ibid., 391–8.

14 The announcement was subsequently reported in the architectural press: "New $38 Million Sports Arena Planned for Manhattan," *Architectural Forum* 113, no. 12 (1960): 9, and "New York Sporting Set Plans to Move Headquarters," *Progressive Architecture* 41, no. 12 (1960): 56.

15 Foster Hailey, "Huge New Madison Sq. Garden is Planned," *New York Times*, 4 November 1960, 1, 39.

16 Ibid., 39.

17 Stern, Mellins, and Fishman, *New York 1960*, 1114.

18 Ibid.

19 Robert E. Bedingfield, "Symes of Pennsy Tells Meeting Central Tries to Block Mergers," *New York Times*, 10 May 1961, 72.

20 "New Madison Sq. Garden to Rise atop Penn Station," *New York Times*, 25 July 1961, 1, 55.

21 Foster Hailey, "'62 Start Is Set for New Garden," *New York Times*, 27 July 1961, 15.

22 Foster Hailey, "Battle over Future of Penn Station Continues," *New York Times*, 23 September 1962, 78.

23 *An Invitation to See … Our Town 1970: New York City: An Exhibit by the Municipal Art Society: at the Union Carbide Building, 270 Park Ave., April 6 to May 11, 1964* (New York: Municipal Art Society 1964).

24 Murray Seeger, "Construction Begins on New Madison Sq. Garden," *New York Times*, 30 October 1964, 25.

25 J.A. Sterner, "Madison Square Garden: Fabrication and Erection of Cable-Supported Roof," *Civil Engineering* 37 (October 1967): 43.

26 Ibid., 46.

27 Sarah Williams Goldhagen, "Architecture Is More Than Just Buildings: In Remembrance of Ada Louise Huxtable," *New Republic*, 12 January 2013, http://www.tnr.com/article/art/111828/architecture-more-just-buildings-in-remembrance-public-minded-critic (accessed 4 February 2013). The authors of *New York 1960* record a litany of outrage from a wide variety of sources: "a giant mambo palace"; "the dump that replaced the masterpiece"; "For this there is no excuse." See Stern, Mellins, and Fishman, *New York 1960*, 1120. An article discussing a competition sponsored by the Municipal Art Society to rethink the Penn Station plan prompted this wish from its author. "New York's grimy Madison Square Garden (MSG) has been an eyesore for all of its 50 years and hope has never died that one day the wrecking ball will swing." James S. Russell, "Fix Penn Station Now; Raze $1 Billion Knicks Garden Later," *Bloomberg*, 15 May 2013, http://www.bloomberg.com/news/2013-05-15/fix-penn-station-now-raze-1-billion-knicks-garden-later.html (accessed 20 May 2013).

28 "A New Old Plan for Penn Station," *New York Times*, 8 January 2016, http://www.nytimes.com/2016/01/09/opinion/a-new-old-plan-for-penn-station.html (accessed 8 January 2016).

29 Christopher Gray, "Is Old Penn Station's Killer Significant? Or Unforgivable?" *New York Times*, 16 October 2005, http://www.nytimes.com/2005/10/16/re...te/16scap.html (accessed 1 February 2013).

30 Ada Louise Huxtable, "A Vision of Rome Dies," *New York Times*, 14 July 1966, 37, 71.

31 *Madison Square Garden Center: A New International Landmark.*

32 Joe Durso, "The Four Gardens and How They Grew," in Hollander, *Madison Square Garden*, 66.

33 "Pennsy Project Luring Builders," *New York Times*, 7 August 1966, 1, 10. On the proposed I Penn Plaza by Kahn and Jacobs, see "Big Deal on 34th Street," *Progressive Architecture* 47 (August 1966): 74.

34 "Fun Palace," *Architectural Review* 141 (January 1967): 2.

35 On Cedric Price's Fun Palace, see Matthews, *From Agit-Prop to Free Space*; Shubert and Wigley, "Il Fun Palace di Cedric Price"; and Shubert, "Cedric Price: Fun Palace."

36 "Fun Palace," *Architectural Review*, 2.

37 The Bull Ring Shopping Centre opened in 1964. Sidney Greenwood designed it in association with James T. Hirst. See Gold, *The Practice of Modernism*, and Holyoak "Street, Subway and Mall."

38 Gold, *The Practice of Modernism*, 122.

39 Ibid.

40 "Stadium Roof Will Come and Go," *Engineering News-Record*, 15 July 1965, 16. The project is illustrated in "1965 Boston Dome," http://www.stadiumpage.com/ (accessed 18 February 2013). See also Don Lawson, "The Year Fenway Was Almost 'Domed,'" *examiner.com*, 9 March 2010, http://www.examiner.com/article/the-year-fenway-was-almost-domed (accessed 18 February 2013).

41 Mark Mulvoy, "Slow Death by Committee in Boston: Politicians Talk and Talk about New Stadium, but Nobody Does Anything," *Sports Illustrated*, 12 June 1967.

42 Mickey Herskowitz, "Historic Construction Covers All the Bases," *Houston Post*, 9 April 1995, http://www.columbia.edu/cu/gsapp/BT/DOMES/HOUSTON/h-dome30.html (accessed 21 March 2013).

43 The Houston baseball team was originally called the Colt 45s. See ibid.

44 See "The Houston Astrodome: Overview," in Columbia University, *Housing the Spectacle*.

45 United States Congress, Department of the Interior, "Houston Astrodome HAER No. TX-108" (Washington, DC: Historic American Engineering Record 1968).

46 Gary Cartwright, "A Barnum Named Hofheinz," *New York Times*, 21 July 1968, 10.

47 Angell, "The Cool Bubble," 131.

48 Robert Lipsyte, "Astrodome Opulent Even for Texas," *New York Times*, 8 April 1965, 50.

49 Louis O. Bass, "Unusual Dome Awaits Baseball Season in Houston," *Civil Engineering – ASCE*, January 1965. The architects were Lloyd and Morgan; Wilson, Morris, Crain, and Anderson.

50 Frank X. Tolbert, "Incredible Houston Dome," *Look*, 20 April 1965, 97, as quoted in Kammer, *Take Me out to the Ballgame*, 328.

51 Gary Cartwright, "There's More Texas Than Technology in the Houston Astrodome," *New York Times*, 7 April 1974, 20.

52 Kammer, *Take Me out to the Ballgame*, 367.

53 The architects are Hellmuth, Obata and Kassabaum and Neuhas and Taylor. In 1990 the Galleria had grown to 3.9 million square feet.

54 Ada Louise Huxtable, "Deep in the Heart of Nowhere," *New York Times*, 16 February 1976, 1, 36. Stephen Fox, *Houston Architectural Guide* (Houston: Herring Press 1990), 234–5.

55 Liz Smith, "Giltfinger's Golden Dome," *Sports Illustrated*, 12 April 1965, http://sportsillustrated.cnn.com/vault/article/magazine/MAG1077072/3/index.htm (accessed 20 March 2013).

56 Angell, "The Cool Bubble," 128.

57 Ibid., 135.

58 Douglas Pegues Harvey, "Il Duomo," *Texas Architect*, May/June 1990, http://www.columbia.edu/cu/gsapp/BT/DOMES/HOUSTON/h-duomo.html (accessed 21 March 2013).

59 Angell, "The Cool Bubble," 130.

60 Al Reinert, "Greetings from the Eighth Wonder of the World," *Texas Monthly*, April 1975, 84.

61 Kammer, *Take Me out to the Ballgame*, 361.

Part Four

1 The construction of NHL facilities was part of a still larger building boom across all major-league sports in North America that saw some $18 billion of new construction in the 1990s alone. Chapin, "Sports Facilities as Urban Redevelopment Catalysts." For a detailed list of arenas and construction costs, see Table 4.

2 Carter, *Money Games*, 173.

3 Saul, *Reflections of a Siamese Twin*, 479.

4 Giulianotti, "Supporters, Followers, Fans, and Flâneurs."

5 Coakley, *Sport in Society*, 345.

6 ANC Sports Enterprises supplies signage, scoreboard, fascia, and dashboard rotational monitors to some thirteen NHL teams and provides marketing services to all thirty (http://www.ancsports.com/). Daktronics supplies thirteen NHL facilities with "super systems" and twenty-two with scoring and/or display equipment (http://www.daktronics.com/Pages/default.aspx).

7 http://www.smgworld.com/company_history.aspx.

8 http://aegworldwide.com/facilities/facilities.

9 Bruck, "The Man Who Owns L.A.," 48.

10 Gerrard, "Media Ownership of Teams," 248–9.

11 Major League Baseball granted its players free agency in 1976, the National Basketball Association in 1983. Gerrard, *Media Ownership of Teams*, 253–4.

12 The term was coined by Alan Suger, former chairman of the English soccer club Tottenham Hotspur. Gerrard, *Media Ownership of Teams*, 256.

13 Ibid., 254.

14 Ibid., 256.

15 Field, "The Ties That Bind," 41, 29–58.

16 S. Miller, "Taking Sports to the Next Level: Start with Teams, Add Arenas, Media and You've Got a Sports Empire," *Street and Smith's Sports Business Journal*, 23–29 August 1999, 23, as quoted in Andrews, "Sport in the Late Capitalist Moment," 15.

17 Gerrard, *Media Ownership of Teams*, 255.

18 Jeff Z. Klein and Karl-Eric Reif point out that the NHL has been complicit in its own homogenization. In 1993 the league decided to rename its current conferences and divisions with generic compass point names (Northeast, Southwest), replacing names that

honoured the league's history (Prince of Wales, Campbell, Adams, Patrick, Norris, Smythe). See Klein and Reif, *The Death of Hockey*, 89.

19 I am paraphrasing the work of David Harvey in *Conditions of Modernity* (London: Wiley-Blackwell 1989) and his earlier article "Down Towns," published in *Marxism Today* (1989) and as discussed in Bramham and Wagg, *Sport, Leisure and Culture in the Postmodern City*, 1.

20 Hannigan, *Fantasy City*, 3–4.

21 Carter, *Money Games*, 203. For more on the application of immersive techniques in the worlds of entertainment and marketing, see Rose, *The Art of Immersion*.

22 On the latest (2016) attempts to wire stadiums, see Kapustka, "Betting the Under."

Chapter Eight

1 Giulianotti, "Supporters, Followers, Fans, and Flâneurs," 25.

2 Ibid., 41. A supporter's relationship with the club resembles those with close family and friends. "In South America, supporters talk of their respective clubs as 'mothers,' whereas they are its 'sons' or 'children.'" Ibid., 33.

3 Giulianotti, "Supporters, Followers, Fans, and Flâneurs," 41.

4 Ibid., 29.

5 Whitson and Gruneau, *Artificial Ice*, 2.

6 Supporting this view were the results of an informal online survey of hockey fans. The website *Slam! Sports: Hockey* asked users to describe their mood in the lead-up to the 2004 player strike. A surprising 57 per cent responded that they were indifferent. See Richard Harrison, "Between a Puck and a Showpiece: Spectator Sport and the Differing Responses to Hockey (and Its Absence) in Canada and the United States – A Canadian Poet Looks at the Fate of the Game," 160n1, in Holman, *Canada's Game*. This state of relative apathy could be discovered again, in 2012, when the NRG Research Group polled 1,001 people in seven Canadian cities about their attitudes to the 2012 lockout by hockey owners. It found that 52 per cent of respondents believed it was either "not too" or "not at all important" for the two sides to reach an agree-

ment. NRG Research Group, "Survey Shows over Half of Canadians Not Interested in NHL Dispute," http://www.marketwire.com/press-release/survey-shows-over-half-of-canadians-not-interested-in-nhl-dispute-1702504.htm (accessed 1 October 2012.)

7 Whitson and Gruneau, *Artificial Ice*, 16. On this phenomenon, see also Rein, Kotler, and Shields, *The Elusive Fan*. In chapter 10, "The Future of Fan Connection," the authors describe the new sport of street ball that is being promoted by the clothing and shoe company *And1* as part of a package that includes clothing, mix tapes, video games, and a strong Internet presence. They call this approach a "textbook case in fan interaction, interrelated media platforms, and a multiple connection fan experience" (294).

8 It has been suggested that Jay Z's presence as investor tipped the balance in smoothing approval for this controversial real estate project in the face of stiff local opposition. As a "home-town boy made good" (he grew up, and dealt drugs, near the site of the facility), his return to the neighbourhood and support for the team and building helped sway public sentiment. Opponents of the project spearheaded by developer Bruce Ratner "complained that residents who might have been wary of Mr. Ratner's promises to create jobs, nonetheless trusted Jay-Z, who invoked his roots and insisted he could never support "anything that's against the people."" David M. Halbfinger, "With Arena, Rapper Rewrites Celebrity Investors' Playbook," *New York Times*, 15 August 2012, http://www.nytimes.com/2012/08/16/nyregion/with-the-nets-jay-z-rewrites-the-celebrity-investors-playbook.html?hp (accessed 15 August 2012).

9 Ticket revenues account for 41 per cent of total NHL income. The figures for the other three major leagues are: MLB = 36 per cent; NBA – 31 per cent; NFL = 23 per cent. See Mason and Howard, "New Revenue Streams in Professional Sports," 126.

10 Tony Keller with Neville McGuire, "The New Economics of the NHL: Why Canada Can Support 12 Teams," Mowat Centre for Policy Innovation, University of Toronto (April 2011), 8.

11 Taub, "Hypocrisy on Ice," 43–4.

12 Keating, "Sports Pork," 17.

13 Ibid.

14 Euchner, *Playing the Field*, 27.

15 Jason Starr, "Marketing Sharks," *Financial World*, 14 February 1995, 43.

16 Bill Saporito, "The Owners' New Game Is Managing," *Fortune*, 1 July 1991, 86, as quoted in, Danielson, *Home Team*, 232.

17 Coakley, *Sport in Society*, 346.

18 Bruck, "The Man Who Owns L.A.," 48.

19 Taub, "Hypocrisy on Ice," 42.

20 San Jose earned $4 million from their sixty-four luxury boxes, $25.4 million from gate receipts, $6 million from concessions, $2.4 million from advertising, and $3 million from parking. Taub, "Hypocrisy on Ice," 44.

21 "It's a Mall … It's an Airport," *New York Times*, 10 June 1998, as quoted in Gordon, *Naked Airport*, 283. Denver's airport has over 100 shops in its 1.5-million-square-foot terminal while Hong Kong's Chek Lap Kok Airport has more than 140. At Ronald Reagan National Airport in Washington, DC, shop sales averaged $950 per square foot compared with $250 to $350 at regular malls. See Gordon, *Naked Airport*, 251.

22 Bale, *Landscapes of Modern Sport*, 8.

23 Interview with the author, 13 March 2000.

24 Interview with the author, 14 March 2000.

25 Donald Eyeberg, "Aesthetics of Arenas," *Facility Manager* 7, no. 3 (Facility Manager, Irvine, TX: IAAM 1996).

26 The tipping point between earnings from admissions versus concessions sales was reached in the 1950s. Cinema owners became aware that drive-in theatres were earning 40 cents for every admission dollar. By 1956, cinema attendance was half that in 1948 but concession sales had increased forty times. Valentine, *The Show Starts on the Sidewalk*, 171.

27 Edward Jay Epstein, "Multiplexities," *New Yorker*, 13 July 1998, 34–5.

28 Christopher Hume, "The Selling of Popcorn Architecture," *Toronto Star*, 19 December 1998.

29 Ibid.

30 Ibid.

31 In 2007 the average price for suites in NHL arenas ranged from $111,501 to $216,333. The 160 suites at the Staples Center sell for $188,278 to $307,000 while the 2,476 club seats sell for an average of $14,000 each, or $34,664,000 per year. See Mason and Howard, "New Revenue Streams in Professional Sports," 128–9.

32 Tim Cronin, "Building's Key: How Suite It Is," *Daily Southtown*, 18 August 1994, 8. Joe Robbie (now Sun Life) Stadium in Miami, home of the NFL Dolphins, opened in 1987 with 216 suites. See Mason and Howard, "New Revenue Streams in Professional Sports," 127–8.

33 Stadium Consultants International, "Calgary Olympic Saddledome Improvement Study" (16 December 1993), as quoted in Graham Edmunds Architecture, "Canadian Airlines Saddledome Improvement."

34 Graham Edmunds Architecture, "Canadian Airlines Saddledome Improvement."

35 Interview with the author, 13 March 2000.

36 Ibid.

37 See Mason and Howard, "New Revenue Streams in Professional Sports," 134.

38 Geert De Lombaerde, "Nissan Name to Grace Bridgestone Arena Atrium, Entrance," *Nashville Post*, 13 October 2011, http://nashvillepost.com/news/2011/10/13/nissan_name_to_grace_bridgestone_arena_atrium_entrance (accessed 26 October 2015).

39 As quoted in Klein and Reif, *The Death of Hockey*, 86.

40 Jon Azpiri, "Hockey Video Games: Better Than Real Thing?" *Vancouver Free Press*, 25 March 2004, http://www.straight.com/article/hockey-video-games-better-than-real-thing (accessed 27 March 2012)

41 Hans Eisenbis, "Take the Body," *Wired*, March 1999, 148.

42 As quoted in Carter, *Money Games*, 64.

43 *The Mighty Ducks*, starring Emilio Estevez, was released in 1992. Two sequels followed: *D2: The Mighty Ducks* (1994), and *D3: The Mighty Ducks* (1996).

44 Michael Lischer, "Like Ducks to Water," *Panstadia International*, September 1994, 112.

45 http://www.southcoastplaza.com/ (accessed 20 February 2012.)

46 Roger Yee, "Just Ducky," *Contract Design* 5 (May 1994), n.p.

47 "Anaheim Arena: 'A Tough Act for Anyone to Follow,'" *Los Angeles Times*, 13 June 1993, http://articles.latimes.com/1993-06-13/news/ss-3216_1_sports-arena (accessed 27 September 2015).

48 The acoustical consultants for GM Place (now Rogers Centre) were BKL Consultants in Acoustics. See

http://www.bkl.ca/bkl-projects/gm-place-arena-acoustical-experience/ (accessed 16 April 2013).

49 Allen, *Audio in Media*, 263.

50 Ibid.

51 Stan Honey, "First-Hand: My Recollections of the Development of the Glowing Hockey Puck," *IEEE Global History Network*, http://www.ieeeghn.org/wiki/index.php/First-Hand: My_Recollections_of_the_Development_of_the_Glowing_Hockey_Puck (accessed 16 February 2012). Honey's development of the glowing hockey puck was an offshoot of his research into digitally inserting billboards into televised sporting events.

52 Andrews, "Sport and the transnationalizing media corporation," 239.

53 Michael Lischer, *Like Ducks to Water*, 112.

54 Nicholas Brown, "Stadiums & Arenas – High-Tech Upgrades Help Aging Spectator Facilities Stay in the Game," *Athletic Business*, October 2008, http://www.athleticbusiness.com/stadium-arena/high-tech-upgrades-help-aging-spectator-facilities-stay-in-the-game.html (accessed 1 April 2016).

55 Jean Baudrillard, "Simulacra and Simulations," in Poster, *Jean Baudrillard*.

56 Rail, *Sport and Postmodern Times*, 150–1.

57 Giullianotti, "Jean Baudrillard and the Sociology of Sport," 234.

58 Marche, "The Meaning of Hockey."

59 Farber, "Why Good Teams Fight," 110.

60 Ibid., 111–12.

61 Bobbi Murray, "Shall We Gather at the Staples?" *Los Angeles*, October 2000, 80. Jacques Herzog, whose firm Herzog and de Meuron designed the Allianz Arena in Munich, which opened in 2005, accepts the corporatization of sports stadiums as inevitable. "Older versions of soccer stadiums were working-class cathedrals. Here there is no more working class: it's a totally different public." Simon Kuper, "Crowd Pleasers," *Financial Times*, 27 May 2005, http://www.ft.com/cms/s/0/e7099e5a-cf16-11d9-8cb5-00000e2511c8.html#axzz3wCp9RB00 (accessed 3 January 2016).

62 Bale, *Landscapes of Modern Sport*, 141.

63 Carter, *Money Games*, 107.

64 Swangard, "Sport in the Digital Domain," in Humphreys and Howard, *The Business of Sports*, 269.

65 Rein, Kotler, and Shields, *The Elusive Fan*, 296.

66 Swangard, "Sport in the Digital Domain," 262.

67 "State-of-the-Art Stadiums," *U.S. News and World Report*, 3 June 1996, n.p., and David Sweet, "With Wired Seats, Fans Get Replays, Rules, Snacks: Little Video Screens Pop up at More Sports Venues, Despite Lingering Resistance," *Wall Street Journal*, 31 May 2000, B1.

68 "Kangaroo TV Expands Partnership with Miami Dolphins," *Canada NewsWire*, 12 March 2010, http://www.newswire.ca/en/story/657399/kangaroo-tv-expands-partnership-with-miami-dolphins (accessed 21 March 2012).

69 Carter, *Money Games*, 139.

70 For an interesting take on this subject, see Craig Hyatt and Julie Stevens, "Are Americans Really Hockey's Villains? A New Perspective on the American Influence on Canada's National Game," in Holman, *Canada's Game*, 27–43.

71 Blake, *Canadian Hockey Literature*. In addition to Blake's study of Canadian hockey literature, see Buma, *Refereeing Identity*, and Hughes-Fuller, *The Good Old Game*.

72 Blake, *Canadian Hockey Literature*, 35.

73 Ibid., 42.

74 Ibid., 14.

75 Ibid., 19.

76 The ads began airing in 2000. Aimed at an eighteen- to twenty-four-year-old white, male demographic, the ads were hugely successful. See Erin Manning, "I AM CANADIAN: Identity, Territory and the Canadian National Landscape," *Theory and Event* 4 (2000): 1–29; Robert M. Seiler, "Selling Patriotism/Selling Beer: The Case of the 'I AM CANADIAN' Commercial," *American Review of Canadian Studies* 32, no. 1 (2002): 45–66; Ira Wagman, "Wheat, Barley, Hops, Citizenship: Molson's 'I Am [Canadian]' Campaign and the Defense of Canadian National Identity through Advertising," *Velvet Light Trap* 50 (2002): 77–89; Robert M. MacGregor, "I Am Canadian: National Identity in Beer Commercials," *Journal of Popular Culture* 37, no. 2 (2003): 276–86.

77 The 2016 Winter Classic, played at a football stadium in Foxboro, Massachusetts, outside of Boston, featured fake snow distributed around the perimeter of the rink, for the benefit of television audiences.

78 Gatehouse, *The Instigator*, 187–8.

79 Justin Piercy, "Winter Classic: Top 5 Outdoor Game Moments," *CBC Sports*, 6 December 2011, http://www.cbc.ca/sports/hockey/opinion/2011/12/winter-classic-top-5-outdoor-game-moments.html (accessed 27 February 2012); Ron Kantowski, "NHL's First Outdoor Game Was Icy Blast at Caesars," *Las Vegas Review-Journal*, 3 January 2012, http://www.lvrj.com/sports/nhl-s-first-outdoor-game-was-icy-blast-at-caesars-136579858.html (accessed 27 February 2012).

80 Ramshaw, "Nostalgia, Heritage, and Imaginative Sports Geographies."

81 Vineberg, *No Surprises, Please*, 26.

82 Ken Belson, "Mets and Yankees Follow Well-Worn Path with New Old Parks," *New York Times*, 1 April 2009, B12, http://www.nytimes.com/2009/04/02/sports/baseball/02design.html?adxnnl=1&pagewanted=1&adxnnlx=1330095670-jJ1qF1c83dGgLdSntrFkJA (accessed 24 February 2012).

83 Joanna Cagan and Neil deMause point out that, as part of the design for Camden Park, the B&O Warehouse was truncated, losing its northern end, in order to afford better views of the downtown skyline from the seats behind home plate. See Cagan and deMause, *Field of Schemes*, 24. Referring to this fact, Tommy Craggs, editor of the blog *Deadspin*, astutely notes: "Those old quirks and odd angles now imitated by modern ballparks were a function of wedging baseball into an urban environment. The game, in other words, had to accommodate the city. Now, large pieces of the urban environment are lopped off to accommodate the game." Tommy Craggs, "Why Your Stadium Sucks: Oriole Park at Camden Yards," *Deadspin*, 10 July 2009, http://deadspin.com/5311876/why-your-stadium-sucks-oriole-park-at-camden-yards (accessed 26 October 2015).

84 Bale, *Landscapes of Modern Sport*, 170.

85 Phil Patton, "Hall Marks," *Metropolis*, August/September 2000, 109.

86 Ibid., 76.

87 Bélanger, "Sport Venues and the Spectacularization of Urban Spaces in North America," 391.

88 Public Communications, "Winning (over the Fans) in New Comiskey Park," http://www.pcipr.com/whowe workwith/culture/casehistory/WinningOverFans.htm (accessed 20 June 2013).

89 William W. Wirtz, "Dear Blackhawk and Stadium Fans," *Remember the Roar: Chicago Stadium 1929–1994* (Chicago: Traversco Productions [1994]), R2.

90 Rein, Kotler, and Shields, *The Elusive Fan*, 295.

91 Ibid., 296.

92 Nauright and White, "Mediated Nostalgia, Community and Nation."

93 John Hannigan, "From Maple Leaf Gardens to the Air Canada Centre: The Downtown Entertainment Economy in 'World Class' Toronto," in Whitson and Gruneau, *Artificial Ice*, 205.

94 Cha, "'*La ville est hockey*,'" 6–8.

95 Ibid., 3–18.

96 "Light a Candle for Sainte-Flanelle," *Montreal Gazette*, 18 April 2014, http://www.montrealgazette.com/sports/hockey/montreal-canadiens/Light+candle+Sainte+Flanelle/9750186/story.html (accessed 23 April 2014). This is not that the first time that a religious organization has sought to co-opt hockey fans. A newspaper advertisement for Billy Graham's 1998 visit to Ottawa's Corel Centre, home of the Ottawa Senators, featured a pair of clasped and praying hockey gloves.

Chapter Nine

1 The significant contradiction to this trend was the NHL, where 66.7 per cent of hockey teams played in privately owned facilities. See Riess, *City Games*, 239. Riess suggests that the reason the NHL bucks the trend is that, historically, hockey had been played in large multi-purpose buildings like Madison Square Gardens.

2 Even privately built arenas have benefited from government support in the form of land acquisition, infrastructure, subsidized loans, and tax concessions. Danielson, *Home Team*, 225. The percentage of publicly financed NHL arenas would be still higher if only US arenas were considered. Federal and provincial governments in Canada have not funded major league sports until very recently.

3 Danielson, *Home Team*, 226.

4 Ibid., 227.

5 "Online News-Hour: The Economics of Pro Football

– January 29, 1999," PBS, http://www.pbs.org/new…orts/jan-june99/economics_1-29.html.

6 Danielson, *Home Team*, 227.

7 See Roger G. Noll and Andrew Zimbalist, "Build the Stadium – Create the Jobs!" in Noll and Zimbalist, *Sports, Jobs, and Taxes*, 2, and Mark S. Rosentraub, "Stadiums and Urban Space," in ibid., 180–2.

8 Among the most frequently cited sources, see Cagan and deMause, *Field of Schemes*; Euchner, *Playing the Field*; Keating, "Sports Pork"; Long, "Full Count"; Noll and Zimbalist, *Sports, Jobs, and Taxes*; Quirk and Fort, *Hard Ball*; Rosentraub, *Major League Losers*; Silver, *Thin Ice*. The argument continues to be made. In 2016 James T. Bennett wrote that "if there is one economic truth upon which almost every practitioner of the art or science of economics agrees, it is that publicly financed ballparks, stadiums, and arenas built by taxpayers for professional baseball, football, basketball, and hockey teams are not good investments." Bennett, *They Play Yoy Pay*, 1.

9 See Zimbalist, "Report on Rexall Place."

10 Chapin, "The Political Economy of Sports Facility Location," 379.

11 Interview with the author, 14 March 2000.

12 "In Tune with Music City," *Panstadia International* 4, no. 2 (1997): 7.

13 See, for instance, Bélanger, "The Urban Sport Spectacle," 52–7.

14 Bale, *Landscapes of Modern Sport*, 168.

15 *Building Culture Downtown: New Ways of Revitalizing the American City* (2 May 1998–3 January 1999), National Building Museum, Washington, DC, brochure, n.d., n.p.

16 On "sports-anchored development," see Carter, *Money Games*, 187–95.

17 Ibid., 173, 186.

18 Danielson, *Home Team*, 242.

19 Walter Shapiro, "Remaking the Field of Dreams," *Time*, 29 April 1991, 80.

20 Bale, *Landscapes of Modern Sport*, 174, 176.

21 Ibid.

22 Bill Knapp, "Hello, Skydome, Brought to You by …" *Canadian Building* 39 (May 1989): 23. The Stadium Corporation of Ontario was the provincially man-dated body created to oversee the government's involvement in building the SkyDome.

23 Silver, *Thin Ice*, 63.

24 Ibid., 63–6. Without a new arena and with ownership problems, the Jets were sold in 1996 and relocated to Phoenix. In 2011 hockey returned to Winnipeg when the Atlanta Thrashers were sold to the Winnipeg group True North Sports and Entertainment. The team plays in the MTS Centre, which opened in 2004.

25 David Israelson, "Stavro Sets Terms for Sharing Arena," *Toronto Star*, 1 November 1996, E1.

26 Damien Cox, "Leafs, Raptors Strike Deal: NBA, NHL Clubs to Share Arena at Union Station," *Toronto Star*, 15 May 1997, A1; James Christie, "Raptors' Arena Bites the Dust: Finding New Use for Big Hole in the Ground Is One Issue Being Worked out in Deal with Leafs," *Globe and Mail*, 16 May 1997, A16.

27 Bruce DeMara and Paul Moloney, "Arena Deal Is Dead," *Toronto Star*, 25 June 1997, A1. The Leafs continued to fight for the Union Station site. On 14 July 1997 they published a full-page newspaper advertisement to make their case directly to the people. "An Open Letter to the Citizens of Toronto," *Toronto Star*, 14 July 1997, A9.

28 Paul Moloney, "Stadium Past Point of No Return: Official," *Toronto Star*, 21 June 1997), A4.

29 Paul Moloney, Bruce DeMara, and Doug Smith, "Last-Ditch Bid to Revive Arena Deal," *Toronto Star*, 26 June 1997, A1.

30 Jack Lakey, "Leafs Eye the Ex: Team Makes Play for 19,000-Seat Arena, and a Retail Complex," *Toronto Star*, 22 November 1997, A1.

31 As quoted in David Shoalts and Michael Grange, "Common Ground Seen in Arena Rift: Two Too Many – Insiders Feel the Leafs Will Share a New Home with the Raptors and End up Controlling It," *Globe and Mail*, 29 November 1997, A26.

32 David Shoalts, "Leafs Buy Raptors, Solve Arena Problem," *Globe and Mail*, 13 February 1998, A14; Bruce DeMara, Paul Moloney, and Dale Brazao, "$500 million Blockbuster: Maple Leafs Buy Raptors," *Toronto Star*, 13 February 1997, A1.

33 Bruck, "The Man Who Owns L.A.," 48.

34 Carter, *Money Games*, 179, 182.

35 Ibid., 184.

36 Dubai Sports City is part of the still larger Dubailand, also announced in 2003, which is projected to stretch over 3 billion square feet and 107 square miles and include 45 mega-projects, including Warner Brothers Movie World, Six Flags Dubai, Universal Studios Dubai, Fantasia, Legoland Dubai, Falcon City of Wonders, and Dreamworks. See Carter, *Money Games*, 184.

37 Matt Chaban, "Gehry'd Away: Gehry Partners Dumped for Ellerbe Becket at Nets Arena, Still Master Planning Atlantic Yards," *Architect's Newspaper*, 4 June 2009, http://archpaper.com/news/articles.asp?id=3561 (accessed 5 April 2013).

38 Charles V. Bagli, "Developer Drops Gehry's Design for Brooklyn Arena," *New York Times*, 4 June 2009, http://www.nytimes.com/2009/06/05/nyregion/05gehry.html?hp (accessed 5 April 2013).

39 Andrea Sands and Gordon Kent, "Katz Group Hires WAM to Develop Land around Arena," *edmontonjournal.com*, 3 February 2012, http://www.edmontonjournal.com/sports/arena/Katz+Group+hires+develop+land+around+arena/6098082/story.html (accessed 27 March 2012).

40 Mike Hager, "Vancouver City Council Approves Aquilini's Three New Highrise Towers beside Rogers Arena," *Vancouver Sun*, 19 July 2012, http://www.vancouversun.com/Vancouver+city+council+approves+Aquilini+three+highrise+towers+beside+Rogers+Arena/6961948/story.html#ixzz2EImYk3DQ (accessed 3 April 2013).

41 Allison Lampert, "Habs-Mania Hits the Condo Market," *Montreal Gazette*, 16 July 2012, http://blogs.montrealgazette.com/2012/07/16/habs-mania-hits-the-condo-market/ (accessed 3 April 2013).

42 Danielson, *Home Team*, 169.

43 Euchner, *Playing the Field*, 50.

44 Danielson, *Home Team*, 218.

45 D. Purdy, "For Whom Sport Tolls: Players, Owners, and Fans," *The World & I* (3, 10, 1988), 573–87, as quoted in Coakley, *Sport in Society*, 346. In *Madden NFL 25*, the American football video game released in 2013, players can select "Connected Franchise" mode, allowing them to own and manage an NFL team.

Game players can then set prices, upgrade their stadium, or move the team to another city.

46 Gruneau and Whitson, *Hockey Night in Canada*, 224

47 Danielson, *Home Team*, 235.

48 Gatehouse, *The Instigator*, 3.

49 I am indebted to Róisín Heneghan for supplying me with information and images of her firm's project. See "A Fantasy Stadium for a Dream Team," *Architectural Record*, 186, no. 39 (1998), and "League at Sea," *Wallpaper*, 14, no. 44 (1998).

50 One such example was Cedric Price's unexecuted Thames Fort project. Price envisioned transforming the seven, interconnected Red Sands Forts, originally constructed in 1942 in the Thames Estuary to provide anti-aircraft fire during the Second World War, into entertainment centres. Documents relating to Price's Thames Fort project are in the collection of the Canadian Centre for Architecture, Montreal (AP144.S2.D75). On the Red Sands Forts, see "Undergroundkent," http://www.undergroundkent.co.uk/maunsell_towers.htm (accessed 22 January 2013).

51 Joe Nocero, "In Losing the Rams, St. Louis Wins," *New York Times*, 15 January 2016, http://www.nytimes.com/2016/01/16/sports/football/st-louis-should-be-glad-it-lost-the-rams.html?ref=sports&_r=0 (accessed 16 January 2016).

52 One team, the Cleveland Barons, merged with the Minnesota North Stars in 1978. The eight relocations and their dates were: California Golden Seals to Cleveland Barons (1976); Kansas City Scouts to Colorado Rockies (1976); Atlanta Flames to Calgary Flames (1980); Colorado Rockies to New Jersey Devils (1982); Minnesota North Stars to Dallas Stars (1993); Quebec Nordiques to Colorado Avalanche (1995); Winnipeg Jets to Phoenix Coyotes (1996); Hartford Whalers to Carolina Hurricanes (1997).

53 In 1997 Atlanta was awarded an expansion franchise, the Thrashers, after its initial team, the Flames, moved to Calgary. The Thrashers began play in 1999. Denver lost the Rockies in 1982 but regained the Avalanche in 1995. The Minnesota North Stars moved to Dallas in 1993 and in 1997 the state was awarded a new franchise. The Wild began play in 2000. The Winnipeg Jets moved to Phoenix in 1996. In 2011 the Jets

were reborn when the Atlanta Thrashers team was relocated to Winnipeg.

54 Malcolm Kelley, "Oilers' Daryl Katz Apologizes to Edmonton Fans: Edmonton Owner Locked in Battle with City over New Arena," *CBC Sports*, 29 September 2012, http://www.cbc.ca/sports/hockey/nhl/story/2012/09/29/sp-oilers-katz-apology.html (accessed 9 April 2013).

55 Sarah O'Donnell, "After Katz Apology, Edmonton Mayor Says Next Step Is Public Discussion with Council," *Edmonton Journal*, 5 November 2012, http://www.edmontonjournal.com/After+Katz+apology+Edmonton+mayor+says+next+step+public+discussion+with+council/7320204/story.html (accessed 10 April 2013); Terry Jones, "Daryl Katz Apology to Edmonton, Oilers Fans a Momentous Move," *Edmonton Sun*, 29 September 2012, http://www.edmontonsun.com/2012/09/29/jones-momentous-move-by-katz (accessed 10 April 2013)

56 *Edmonton Journal*, 29 September 2012, http://www.scribd.com/fullscreen/108046008?access_key=key-217qcz60tgwpxm7glq1q (accessed 10 April 2013).

Conclusion

1 Shel Silverstein, "Zebra Question," in *A Light in the Attic* (New York: Harper and Row 1974).

2 In 2012 there were thirty NHL teams. The buildings they played in were designated: Arena – 6; Center/Centre – 16; Coliseum – 1; Forum – 1; Garden – 2; Pavilion – 1; Place – 2; Saddledome – 1.

3 Hannigan, *Fantasy City*, 3–4.

4 Pevsner, *A History of Building Types*.

5 Ground breaking for the Arrowhead Pond at Anaheim, California, took place in November 1990. Anaheim was awarded an expansion franchise in 1992 and the team played its first game in 1993. HOK Sports also designed the Arrowhead Pond.

6 "Nashville Ready with Second Pro Franchise in Two Years," *Associated Press*, 8 August 1997. In 1997 the Houston Oilers of the NFL relocated to Nashville. HOK designed their new, $290-million stadium, which opened in 1999 on a site just six blocks from the Nashville Arena.

7 Mark Alden Branch, "Nashville Arena Competition," *Progressive Architecture* 74, no. 12 (1993): 18.

8 Ibid.

9 Since 2010 the building has been called the Bridgestone Arena. Formerly it was called: Nashville Arena (1996–99), Gaylord Entertainment Center (1999–2007), and Sommet Center (2007–10).

10 "In Tune with Music City," *Panstadia International* 4, no. 2 (1997): 7.

11 Ibid., 8.

12 J.R. Lind, "Arena Ranks Sixth in Concert Attendance in U.S.," *City Paper*, 6 January 2012, http://nashvillecitypaper.com/content/city-business/bridgestone-arena-ranks-sixth-concert-attendance-us (accessed 8 February 2012).

13 Christopher Hume, "Centre Takes off on the Inside," *Toronto Star*, 19 February 1999, s2.

14 Melissa Bell, "Theatrical Design for the Air Canada Centre, Toronto," *Stadia* 1 (October 1999): 22.

Select Bibliography

Adams, Annmarie. *Medicine by Design: The Architect and the Modern Hospital, 1893–1943*. Minneapolis, MN, and London: University of Minnesota Press 2008.

Adams, Mary Louise. "Freezing Social Relations: Ice Rinks and the Development of Figure Skating." In Patricia Anne Vertinsky and John Bale, eds., *Sites of Sport: Space, Place, Experience*. London and New York: Routledge 2004.

Adams, Nicholas. *Skidmore, Owings & Merrill: The Experiment since 1936*. Milan: Electa 2006.

Adell, Jacqueline. *Architecture of the Drill Hall in Canada 1863–1939*. Ottawa: Historic Sites and Monuments Board of Canada 1989.

– "The Structural Design of the Early Drill Sheds in Canada." *Bulletin of the Society for the Study of Architecture in Canada* 16, no. 2 (1991): 40–51.

Allen, Stanley R. *Audio in Media*. Boston: Wadsworth 2011.

Andrews, David L. "Sport in the Late Capitalist Moment." In Trevor Slack, ed., *The Commercialization of Sport*. London: Routledge 2004.

– "Sport and the Transnationalizing Media Corporation." *Journal of Media Economics* 16, no. 4 (2003): 235–51.

Angell, Roger. "The Cool Bubble." *New Yorker*, 14 May 1966, 125–42.

Arena: The Art of Hockey. Halifax: Art Gallery of Nova Scotia 2008.

Aycock, Colleen, and Mark Scott. *Tex Rickard: Boxing's Greatest Promoter*. Jefferson, NC: McFarland 2012.

Badman, Keith. *The Beatles off the Record*. London: Omnibus Press 2000.

Bale, John. *Landscapes of Modern Sport*. London: Leicester University Press 1994.

– *Sport, Space, and the City*. London: Routledge 1992.

Bale, John, and Olof Moen, eds. *The Stadium and the City*. Keele, UK: Keele University Press 1995.

"Ballparks by Munsey and Suppes." http://www.ballparks.com/ (accessed 15 August 2015).

Baudrillard, Jean. "Simulacra and Simulations." In Mark Poster, ed., *Jean Baudrillard: Selected Writings*. Stanford, CA: Stanford University Press 1988.

Bauer, Olivier. *Une Théologie de Canadien de Montréal*. Montreal: Bayard Canada Livres 2011.

Bauer, Olivier, and Jean-Marc Barreau, eds. *La Religion du Canadien de Montréal*. Montreal: Éditions Fides 2009.

Beamish, R. "The Political Economy of Professional Sport." In J. Harvey and H. Cantelon, eds., *Not Just a Game*. Ottawa: University of Ottawa Press 1988.

Beardsley, Doug. *Country on Ice*. Markham, ON: Paperjacks 1987.

Beckett, H.W. *The Montreal Snow Shoe Club, Its History and Record …* Montreal: Beckett Brothers 1882.

Bélanger, Anouk. "Sport Venues and the Spectacularization

of Urban Spaces in North America: The Case of the Molson Centre in Montreal." *International Review for the Sociology of Sport* 35, no. 3 (2000): 378–97.

– "The Urban Sport Spectacle: Towards a Critical Political Economy of Sports." In Ben Carrington and Ian McDonald, eds., *Marxism, Cultural Studies and Sport*. London: Routledge 2009.

Bell, Melissa "Theatrical Design for the Air Canada Centre, Toronto," *Stadia* 1 (October 1999): 22–6.

Bennett, James T. *They Play, You Pay: Why Taxpayers Build Ballparks, Stadiums, and Arenas for Billionaire Owners and Millionaire Players*. New York: Copernicus Books, 2012.

Betke, Carl. "Sports Promotion in the Western Canadian City: The Example of Early Edmonton." *Urban History Review* 12, no. 2 (1983): 47–56.

– "Winter Sports in the Early Urban Environment of Prairie Canada." In Elise A. Corbet and Anthony W. Rasporich, eds., *Winter Sports in the West*. Calgary: Historical Society of Alberta 1990.

Bidini, Dave. *Tropic of Hockey: My Search for the Game in Unlikely Places*. Toronto: McClelland and Stewart 2000.

Blake, Jason. *Canadian Hockey Literature: A Thematic Study*. Toronto: University of Toronto Press 2010.

Bolling, Esten, ed. "Madison Square Garden Is Razed! Madison Square Garden Is Raised!" *Weather Vein* 6, no. 2 (1926).

Boyd, Denny. *History of Hockey in B.C.: From the Denman Arena to the Pacific Coliseum*. Vancouver: Privately published, 1972.

– *The Vancouver Canucks Story*. Toronto: McGraw-Hill Ryerson 1973.

Brader, Donna R. *Leisure and Entertainment in America*. Dearborn, MI: Henry Ford Museum and Greenfield Village 1998.

Bradford, Tonya Williams, and John F. Sherry Jr. "Domesticating Public Space through Ritual: Tailgating as Vestaval." *Journal of Consumer Research* 42 (2015): 130–51.

Bramham, Peter, and Stephen Wagg, eds. *Sport, Leisure and Culture in the Postmodern City*. Farnham, UK: Ashgate 2009.

Briley, George C. "A History of Refrigeration." In "100 Years of Refrigeration: A Supplement to ASHRAE Journal," *ASHRAE Journal*, November 2004, s31–s34.

Brown, Nigel. *Ice-Skating A History*. London: Nicholas Kaye 1959.

Brown, William. *The Montreal Maroons: The Forgotten Stanley Cup Champions*. Montreal: Véhicule Press 1999.

Bruck, Connie. "The Man Who Owns L.A." *New Yorker*, 16 January 2012.

Bull, William Perkins. *From Rattlesnake Hunt to Hockey: The History of Sports in Canada and of Sportsmen of Peel, 1798–1934*. Toronto: Perkins Bull Foundation 1934.

Bullinger, Edwin Wilson. *Guide to Skating: A Complete Manual of the Art*. New York: Dick and Fitzgerald 1862.

Buma, Michael. *Refereeing Identity: The Cultural Work of Canadian Hockey Novels*. Montreal and Kingston: McGill-Queen's University Press 2012.

Butler, Richard J. *Dock Walloper: The Story of "Big Dick" Butler*. New York: G.P. Putnam's Sons 1933.

Cagan, Joanna, and Neil deMause. *Field of Schemes: How the Great Stadium Swindle Turns Public Money into Private Profit*. Monroe, ME: Common Courage Press 1998.

Cantelon, H., and R.S. Gruneau. "The Production of Sport for Television." In J. Harvey and H. Cantelon, eds., *Not Just a Game*. Ottawa: University of Ottawa Press 1988.

Carrier, Roch. *Our Life with the Rocket: The Maurice Richard Story*. Toronto: Viking / Penguin 2001.

Carter, David M. *Money Games: Profiting from the Convergence of Sports and Entertainment*. Stanford, CA: Stanford Business Press 2011.

Carter, Thomas, and Elizabeth Collins Cromley. *Invitation to Vernacular Architecture: A Guide to the Study of Ordinary Buildings and Landscapes*. Knoxville: University of Tennessee Press 2005.

Cha, Jonathan. "*La ville est hockey*: De la hockeyisation de la ville à la représentation architecturale: une quête urbaine." *SSAC Journal* 34, no. 1 (2009): 3–18.

Chadwick, Henry. *Beadle's Dime Guide to Skating and Curling: Illustrated for Learners and Amateurs*. New York: Beadle Company 1867.

– *Handbook of Winter Sports: Fancy Skating, Plain Skating, Roller Skating, Ice Boating &c. &c. &c.* New York: Beadle and Adams 1879.

Chancellor, E. Beresford. *The XVIIIth Century in London: An Account of Its Social Life and Arts*. London: B.T. Batsford 1920.

Chapin, Tim. "The Political Economy of Sports Facility

Location: An End-of-the-Century Review and Assessment." *Marquette Sports Law Journal* 10, no. 361 (2000): 361–82.

– "Sports Facilities as Urban Redevelopment Catalysts: Baltimore's Camden Yards and Cleveland's Gateway." *Journal of the American Planning Association* 70, no. 2 (2004): 193–209.

Christianson, Justine. "The Uline Arena/Washington Coliseum: The Rise and Fall of a Washington Institution." *Washington History* 16, no. 1 (2004): 16–35.

– "Uline Arena: Written Historical and Descriptive Data." *Historic American Engineering Record* (HAER no. DC–63) 2003, updated 2010

City of New York Parks and Recreation. "The History of Ice Skating in New York City Parks." http://www.nycgov-parks.org/about/history/ice-skating (accessed 2 February 2012).

Coakley, Jay. *Sport in Society: Issues and Controversies*, 6th ed. Boston: McGraw-Hill 1998.

Coates Dennis, and Brad R. Humphreys. "Do Economists Reach a Conclusion on Subsidies for Sports Franchises, Stadiums, and Mega-Events?" *Econ Journal Watch* 5, no. 3 (2008): 294–315.

Cohen, Leonard. *Beautiful Losers*. Toronto: McClelland and Stewart 1966.

Coleman, Charles L. *The Trail of the Stanley* Cup. [Montreal]: National Hockey League 1966–69.

Columbia University. *Housing the Spectacle: The Emergence of America's Domed Superstadiums 1965–1992*.http://www.columbia.edu/cu/gsapp/BT/DOMES/HOUSTON/houston.html (accessed 21 February 2013).

Cooke, Maud C. *Social Etiquette, or Manners and Customs of Polite Society*. London: McDermid and Logan 1896.

Copley-Graves, Lynn. *Figure Skating History: The Evolution of Dance on Ice*. Columbus, OH: Platoro Press 1992.

Craig, Bruce Alan, and Kenneth Ross Craig. *Blades on the Bay: One Hundred Years of Hockey in North Bay and Area*. North Bay, ON: Kenneth Ross Craig 1997.

Crichton, Andrew, and Henry Wheaton. *Scandinavia, Ancient and Modern: Being a History of Denmark, Sweden, and Norway: Comprehending a Description of These Countries*. New York: Harper Brothers 1878.

Cross, Harry. "Garden Is Opened in Blaze of Color." *New York Times*, 16 December 1925.

Cruise, David, and Alison Griffiths. *Net Worth: Exploding the Myths of Pro Hockey*. Toronto: Penguin Books 1991.

Cuthbert, Chris, and Scott Russell. *The Rink: Stories from Hockey's Home Towns*. Toronto: Viking 1997.

Danielson, Michael N. *Home Team: Professional Sports and the American Metropolis*. Princeton, NJ: Princeton University Press 1997.

"David S. Ingalls Hockey Rink, Yale University, New Haven, Connecticut." *Architecture and Urbanism* 4 (April 1984, extra edition): 76–85.

Diamond, Dan. *Total Hockey: The Official Encyclopedia of the National Hockey League*. New York: Total Sports 1998, 2000.

Diran, Edward. *Cow Palace Great Moments: Cow Palace Tales*. San Mateo, CA: Western / Journal Press 1991.

Dressing up Canada, an exhibition held at the Canadian Museum of Civilization (24 October 1997–3 January 1999). http://www.civilization.ca/cmc/exhibitions/hist/balls/i-2eng.shtml (accessed 15 August 2015).

Dryden, Ken. *The Game*. Toronto: Macmillan of Canada 1983.

Dryden, Ken, and Roy MacGregor. *Home Game: Hockey and Life in Canada*. Toronto: McClelland and Stewart 1989.

Dryeson, Mark, and Robert Trumpbour, eds. "Cathedrals of Sport: The Rise of Stadiums in the Modern United States" (special issue). *International Journal of the History of Sport* 25, 11 (2008): 1419–1590.

Dunbar, Nancy J. *Images of Sport in Early Canada*. Montreal: McCord Museum / McGill-Queen's University Press 1976.

Dupperault, Jean R. "L'Affaire Richard: A Situational Analysis of the Montreal Hockey Riots of 1955." *Canadian Journal of the History of Sport* 12 (May 1981): 66–83.

Durso, Joseph. *Madison Square Garden: 100 Years of History*. New York: Simon and Schuster 1979.

Ethan, Michael. "A Spatial History of Arena Rock 1964–79." PhD diss., McGill University 2011.

Euchner, Charles C. *Playing the Field: Why Sports Teams Move and Why Cities Fight to Keep Them*. Baltimore, MD: Johns Hopkins University Press 1993.

Falla, Jack. *Home Ice: Reflections on Backyard Rinks and Frozen Ponds*. Tampa, FL: McGregor Publishing 2000.

Farber, Michael. "Why Good Teams Fight." *Sports*

Illustrated Hockey Talk. Toronto: Fenn / McClelland and Stewart 2011.

Farrington, S. Kip. *Skates, Sticks, and Men: The Story of Amateur Hockey in the United States.* New York: David McKay Company 1972.

Field, Russel. "A Night at the Garden(s): A History of Professional Hockey Spectatorship in the 1920s and 1930s." PHD diss., University of Toronto, 2008.

– "Passive Participation: The Selling of Spectacle and the Construction of Maple Leaf Gardens 1931." *Sports History Review* 33, no. 1 (2002): 35–50.

– "The Ties That Bind: A 2003 Case Study of Toronto's Sport Elite and the Operation of Commercial Sport." *International Review for the Sociology of Sport* 41 (2006): 29–58.

Fischler, Stan. *Cracked Ice: An Insider's Look at the NHL in Turmoil.* Whitby, ON: McGraw-Hill Ryerson 1995.

Fitsell, Bill. "The Rise and Fall of Ice Polo." *Hockey Research Journal*, 4, no. 1 (1999): 11–17.

Fitsell, J.W. *Hockey's Captains, Colonels & Kings.* Erin, ON: Boston Mills Press 1987.

– *How Hockey Happened: A Pictorial History of the Origins of Canada's National Winter Game.* Kingston, ON: Quarry Press 2006.

Flood, Brian. *Saint John: A Sporting Tradition 1785–1985.* [Saint John, NB]: Neptune Publishing Company 1985.

Fogelson, Robert M. *America's Armories: Architecture, Society, and Public Order.* Cambridge, MA: Harvard University Press 1989.

"The Forum Building, Montreal." *Construction* 18 (March 1925): 81–6.

Frayne, Trent. *The Mad Men of Hockey.* Toronto: McClelland and Stewart 1974.

Gatehouse, Jonathon. *The Instigator: How Gary Bettman Remade the League and Changed Hockey Forever.* Toronto: Viking 2012.

Geraint, John, and Rod Sheard. *Stadia: A Design and Development Guide.* Oxford: Architectural Press 1997.

Gerrard, Bill. "Media Ownership of Teams: The Latest Stage in the Commercialisation of Team Sports." In Trevor Slack, ed., *The Commercialisation of Sport.* Oxon, UK: Routledge 2004.

Gershman, Michael. *Diamonds: The Evolution of the Ballpark: From Elysian Fields to Camden Yards.* Boston and New York: Houghton Mifflin Company 1993.

Giullianotti, Richard. "Jean Baudrillard and the Sociology of Sport." In *Sports and Modern Social Theorists.* Houndmills, UK, and New York: Pallgrave Macmillan 2004.

– "Supporters, Followers, Fans, and Flâneurs: A Taxonomy of Spectator Identities in Football." *Journal of Sport and Social Issues* 26 (2002): 25–46.

Giulianotti, Richard, and Roland Robertson. "Forms of Globalization: Globalization and the Migration Strategies of Scottish Football Fans in North America." *Sociology* 41 (2007): 133–52.

Gold, John R. *The Practice of Modernism: Modern Architects and Urban Transformation, 1945–1972.* Oxon, UK: Routledge 2007.

Goodrich, Hollis. "Portland Memorial Coliseum: In Pursuit of Entertainment, 12 Million Pass thru Doors." *Greater Portland Commerce*, April 1961, 18–21.

Gopnik, Adam. *Winter Five Windows on the Season.* Toronto: House of Anansi Press 2011.

Gordon, Alastair. *Naked Airport: A Cultural History of the World's Most Revolutionary Structure.* New York: Metropolitan Books 2004.

Gowdey, David, ed. *Riding on the Roar of the Crowd: A Hockey Anthology.* Toronto: Macmillan of Canada 1989.

Goyens, Chrystian, and Allan Turowetz. *Lions in Winter.* Markham, ON: Penguin Books Canada 1981.

Goyens, Chrystian, Allan Turowitz, and Jean-Luc Duguay. *Le livre officiel Le Forum de Montréal: La fierté pour toujours.* Westmount, QC: Éditions Effix 1996.

Graham Edmunds Architecture. "Canadian Airlines Saddledome Improvement." http://www.architecture.ca/firms/gearch/casaddledome/ (accessed 15 April 2013).

Greenberg, Jay. *Full Spectrum: The Complete History of the Philadelphia Flyers.* Toronto: Dan Diamond and Associates 1996, 1997.

Gruneau, Richard, and David Whitson. *Hockey Night in Canada: Sport, Identities and Cultural Politics.* Toronto: Garamond Press 1993.

Guay, Donald. *L'histoire du hockey au Québec.* Montreal: Les éditions JCL 1990.

Guttman, Allen. *From Ritual to Record: The Nature of Modern Sports.* New York: Columbia University Press 1978.

– *Sports Spectators.* New York: Columbia University Press 1986.

Hall, Ann, Trevor Slack, Garry Smith, and David Whitson. *Sport in Canadian Society.* Toronto: McClelland and Stewart 1991.

Hannigan, John. *Fantasy City: Pleasure and Profit in the Postmodern Metropolis*. London and New York: Routledge 1998.

Hardy, Stephen. "'Polo at the Rinks': Shaping Markets for Ice Hockey in America, 1880–1900." *Journal of Sport History* vol. 33, no. 2 (2006): 157–74.

Hart, Claudia C. "The New York Theatres of Thomas Lamb." MS thesis, Columbia University 1983.

Harvey, Jean, and Hart Cantelon, eds. *Not Just a Game: Essays in Canadian Sport Sociology*. Ottawa: University of Ottawa Press 1988.

Hawley, Joanne. "The Development of Indoor Ice Skating Rinks in London before World War II." MA thesis, City University, London, 1984.

Heathcote, Edmund, Mrs. *The Admiral's Niece, or, a Tale of Nova Scotia*. London: T. Cautley Newby 1858.

Hedley, James. "Curling in Canada." *Dominion Illustrated* 1, no. 3 (1892): 173–82.

Hewitt, Foster. *Hockey Night in Canada*. Toronto: Ryerson Press 1953; rev. ed., 1970.

Hollander, Zander, ed. *Madison Square Garden: A Spectacle on the World's Most Versatile Stage*. New York: Hawthorne Books 1973.

Holman, Andrew C., ed. *Canada's Game: Hockey and Identity*. Montreal and Kingston: McGill-Queen's University Press 2009.

Holt, Arden. *Fancy Dresses Described, or, What to Wear at Fancy Balls*. London, 1896.

Holyoak, Joe. "Street, Subway and Mall: Spatial Politics in the Bull Ring," In Liam Kennedy, ed., *Remaking Birmingham: The Visual Culture of Urban Regeneration*. Oxon, UK: Routledge 2004.

Holzman, Morey, and Joseph Nieforth. *Deceptions and Doublecross: How the NHL Conquered Hockey*. Toronto and Oxford: Dundurn Group 2002.

Home Field Advantage: Toronto Sporting Sites Past and Present. An exhibition presented at the Market Gallery, Toronto, 24 June–22 October 1989.

Horne, John. "Architects, Stadia and Sport Spectacles: Notes on the Role of Architects in the Building of Sport Stadia and Making of World-Class Cities." *International Review for the Sociology of Sport* 46 (2011): 205–27.

Horowitz, Ira. "Sports Broadcasting." In Roger G. Noll, ed., *Government and the Sports Business*. Washington, DC: Brookings Institution [1974].

Howell, Nancy, and Maxwell L. Howell. *Sports and Games in Canadian Life: 1700 to the Present*. Toronto: Macmillan of Canada 1969.

Hughes, Gary K. *Music of the Eye: Architectural Drawings of Canada's First City 1822–1914*. Saint John: New Brunswick Museum and the Royal Architectural Institute of Canada 1992.

Hughes-Fuller, Patricia. "The Good Old Game: Hockey, Nostalgia, Identity," PhD diss., University of Calgary 2002.

Humber, William. *Diamonds of the North: A Concise History of Baseball in Canada*. Toronto: Oxford University Press 1995.

Humphreys, Brad R., and Dennis R. Howard, eds. *The Business of Sports, Vol. 1: Perspectives on the Sports Industry*. Westport, CT: Praeger Perspectives 2008.

Hyde, Ralph. *The Regent's Park Colosseum, or, "Without hyperbole, the Wonder of the World": Being an Account of a Forgotten Pleasure Dome and Its Creators*. London: Ackerman 1982.

Isaacs, Neil D. *Checking Back: A History of the National Hockey League*. New York: W.W. Norton and Company 1977.

Jackson, Patti Smith. *The St. Louis Arena: Memories*. St. Charles, MO: GHB Publishers, 2000.

Jakle, John A., and Keith A. Sculle. *The Gas Station in America*. Baltimore, MD and London: Johns Hopkins University Press 1994.

Jencks, Charles. *The Post-Modern Reader*. London: Academy Editions 1992.

Johnson, Dana. "Montreal Forum / Le Forum de Montréal." Ottawa: Historic Sites and Monuments Board of Canada Agenda Paper (1997–20), 1997.

Kammer, David John. "Take Me out to the Ballgame: American Cultural Values as Reflected in the Architectural Evolution and Criticism of the Modern Baseball Stadium." PHD diss., University of New Mexico, 1982.

Kane, Larry. *Ticket to Ride: Inside the Beatles' 1964 Tour That Changed the World*. Philadelphia: Running Press Book Publishers 2003.

Kapustka, Paul. "Betting the Under: Putting Wi-Fi Antennas under Seats is the Hot New Trend in Stadium Wireless Networks." *mobile sports report*, 28 March 2016, http://www.mobilesportsreport.com/2016/03/betting-the-under-putting-wi-fi-antennas-under-seats-is-the-hot-new-trend-in-stadium-wireless-networks/ (accessed 1 April 2016).

Keating, Raymond J. "Sports Pork: The Costly Relationship between Major League Sports and Government." *Policy Analysis* 339 (5 April 1999).

Keller, William. "Architecture for Community and Spectacle: The Roofed Arena in North America, 1853–1968." PhD diss., University of Pennsylvania, 2007.

Kennedy, Dennis. *The Spectator and the Spectacle: Audiences in Modernity and Postmodernity.* New York: Cambridge University Press 2009.

Kennedy, Michael P.J., ed. *Going Top Shelf: An Anthology of Canadian Hockey Poetry.* Surrey, BC: Heritage House 2005.

Kerr, John. *Curling in Canada and the United States.* Toronto: Toronto News Company 1904.

Kerr, W.H.A. "Hockey in Ontario." *Dominion Illustrated* 2, no. 2 (1893): 99–108.

Kestenbaum, Ellyn. *Culture on Ice: Figure Skating & Cultural Meaning.* Middletown, CT: Wesleyan University Press 2003.

Kidd, Bruce. *The Struggle for Canadian Sport.* Toronto: University of Toronto Press 1996.

Kidd, Bruce, and John Macfarlane. *The Death of Hockey.* Toronto: New Press 1972.

Kilham, Walter H. *Boston after Bulfinch: An Account of Its Architecture 1800–1900.* Cambridge, MA: Harvard University Press 1946.

Kinkema, Kathleen M., and Janet C. Harris. "MediaSport Studies: Key Research and Emerging Issues." In Lawrence A. Wenner, ed., *MediaSport.* London: Routledge 1998.

Kitchen, Paul. "Dey Brothers' Rinks Were Home to the Senators." Unpublished paper. Ottawa: Ottawa City Archives 1993.

– *Win, Tie or Wrangle: The Inside Story of the Old Ottawa Senators, 1883–1935.* Manotick, ON: Penumbra Press 2008.

Klein, Jeff Z., and Karl-Eric Reif. *The Death of Hockey or: How a Bunch of Guys with Too Much Money and Too Little Sense Are Killing the Greatest Game on Earth.* Toronto: Macmillan Canada 1998.

Klingmann, Anna. *Brandscapes: Architecture in the Experience Economy.* Cambridge, MA: MIT Press 2007.

Koch, Robert. "The Medieval Castle Revival: New York Armories." *Journal of the Society of Architectural Historians* 14, no. 3 (1955): 23–9.

Kreiser, John, and Lou Friedman. *The New York Rangers: Broadway's Longest Running Hit.* Champaign, IL: Sagamore Publishing 1996.

Lambert, Luna. *The American Skating Mania: Ice Skating in the Nineteenth Century.* Washington, DC: Smithsonian Institution 1978.

Lanken, Dane. *Montreal Movie Palaces: Great Theatres of the Golden Era 1884–1938.* Waterloo, ON: Penumbra Press 1993.

Lester, C.W., ed. *Seattle Arena Souvenir.* [Seattle]: H.C. Pigott Printing Concern 1915.

Libby, Brian. "Memorial Coliseum – Portland, Oregon." *Architecture Week: Design and Building in Depth* (2009). http://www.architectureweek.com/2009/0708/index.html (accessed 20 June 2012).

– "Talking with Bill Rouzie, One of Memorial Coliseum's Original Architects." *Portland Architecture*, blog (18 April 2009). http://chatterbox.typepad.com/portlandarchitecture/2009/04/talking-with-bill-rouzie-one-of-memorial-coliseums-original-architects.html (accessed 20 June 2012).

Long, Judith Grant. "Full Count: The Real Cost of Public Funding for Major League Sports Facilities." *Journal of Sports Economics* 6 (2005): 119–43.

Longstreth, Richard. *The American Department Store Transformed 1920–1960.* New Haven, CT, and London: Yale University Press 2010.

– *City Center to Regional Mall: Architecture, the Automobile, and Retailing in Los Angeles 1920–1950.* Cambridge, MA: MIT Press 1997.

– *The Drive-in, the Supermarket, and the Transformation of Commercial Space in Los Angeles, 1914–1941.* Cambridge, MA: MIT Press, c. 1999.

Luckman, Charles. *Twice in a Lifetime: From Soap to Skyscrapers.* New York: W.W. Norton and Company 1988.

Lupkin, Paula. *Manhood Factories: YMCA Architecture and the Making of Modern Urban Culture.* Minneapolis: University of Minnesota Press 2010.

McCormack, Pete. *Understanding Ken.* Vancouver: Douglas and McIntyre 1998.

McFarlane, Brian. *One Hundred Years of Hockey.* Toronto: Summerhill Press 1990.

McKenzie, R. Tait. "Hockey in Eastern Canada." *Dominion Illustrated* 2, no. 1 (1893): 56–64.

McKinley, Michael. *Putting a Roof on Winter: Hockey's*

Rise from Sport to Spectacle. Vancouver and New York: Greystone Books, c. 2000.

"Madison Square Garden." *American Architect* 128, no. 2487 (1925).

Madison Square Garden. *Historical Book Issued in Connection with the Opening Events of the Madison Square Garden, 8th Avenue and 50th Street, New York City.* New York: [Madison Square Garden] 1925.

Madison Square Garden Center: A New International Landmark at Pennsylvania Plaza, New York. [New York: Madison Square Garden Center, n.d.]

Madison Square Garden Hall of Fame. New York: Madison Square Garden Center [1968?].

Maple Leaf Gardens Memories & Dreams 1931–1999. Toronto: Maple Leafs Sports and Entertainment 1999.

Marche, Stephen. "The Meaning of Hockey: Our Game Is Like No Other. Nor Is Its History." *The Walrus*, November 2011, http://thewalrus.ca/the-meaning-of-hockey/ (accessed 18 March 2016).

Marks, Lynne. *Revivals and Roller Rinks: Religion, Leisure, and Identity in Late-Nineteenth-Century Small-Town Ontario.* Toronto: University of Toronto Press 1996.

Martin, Ted. "Evolution of Ice Rinks." In "100 Years of Refrigeration: A Supplement to ASHRAE Journal." *ASHRAE Journal*, November 2004, s24–s30.

Mason, Daniel S. "The International Hockey League and the Professionalization of Ice Hockey, 1904–1907." *Journal of Sport History* 25, no. 1 (1998): 1–17.

– "Sports Facilities and Urban Development: An Introduction." *City, Culture and Society* 3 (2012): 165–7, http://www.thecyberhood.net/documents/papers/sports2 013.pdf (accessed 15 January 2016).

Mason, Daniel S., and Barbara Schrodt. "Hockey's First Professional Team: The Portage Lakes Hockey Club of Houghton, Michigan." *Sports History Review*, 27 (1996): 49–71.

Mason, Daniel S., and Dennis R. Howard. "New Revenue Streams in Professional Sports." In Brad R. Humphreys and Dennis R. Howard, eds., *The Business of Sports, Vol. 1: Perspectives on the Sports Industry.* Westport, CT: Praeger Perspectives 2008.

Matthews, Stanley. *From Agit-Prop to Free Space: The Architecture of Cedric Price.* London: Black Dog, c. 2007.

Meeks, Carol L.V. "The Life of a Form: A History of the Train Shed." *Architectural Review* 110, no. 657 (1951): 162–73.

– *The Railroad Station: An Architectural History.* New Haven, CT: Yale University Press 1956.

Melançon, Benoit. *The Rocket: A Cultural History.* Vancouver: Greystone Books 2009.

Metcalfe, Alan. *Canada Learns to Play: The Emergence of Organized Sport, 1807–1914.* Toronto: McClelland and Stewart 1987.

– "The Evolution of Organized Physical Recreation in Montreal, 1840–1895," *Social History* 11, no. 21 (1978): 144–66.

– "The Urban Response to the Demand for Sporting Facilities: A Study of Ten Ontario Towns/Cities, 1919–1939." *Urban History Review* 12, no. 2 (1983): 31–45.

Miller's New York as It Is, or the Stranger's Guide-Book to the Cities of New York, Brooklyn and Adjacent Places: Comprising Notices of Every Object of Interest to Strangers ... New York: J. Miller 1866.

Mills, David. "The Battle of Alberta: Entrepreneurs and the Business of Hockey in Edmonton and Calgary." *Alberta: Studies in the Arts and Sciences* 2, 2 (1990): 1–26.

– "The Blue Line and the Bottom Line: Entrepreneurs and the Business of Hockey in Canada, 1927–1988." In James A. Mangan and Paul Staudohar, eds., *American Professional Sports: Social, Historical, Economic and Legal Perspectives.* Urbana: University of Illinois Press 1991.

Monck, Frances. *My Canadian Leaves.* Dorchester, NB, 1873; facsimile edition, Toronto: Canadian Library Service 1963.

Morrow, Don. "Frozen Festivals: Ceremony and the Carnaval in the Montreal Winter Carnivals, 1883–1889." *Sport History Review* 27 (1996): 173–90.

– "The Knights of the Snowshoe: A Study of the Evolution of Sport in Nineteenth Century Montreal." *Journal of Sport History* 15, no. 1 (1998): 5–40.

– "The Little Men of Iron: The 1902 Montreal Hockey Club." *Canadian Journal of History of Sport* 12, no. 1 (1981): 51–65.

– *A Sporting Evolution: The Montreal Amateur Athletic Association 1881–1991.* Montreal: MAAA and Don Morrow 1981.

Morrow, Don, et al. *A Concise History of Sport in Canada.* Toronto: Oxford University Press 1989.

Mott, M. "One Solution to the Urban Crisis: Manly Sports and Winnipeggers, 1900–1914." *Urban History Review* 12, no. 2 (1983): 57–70.

Nagler, Barney. *James Norris and the Decline of Boxing.* Indianapolis, NY: Bobbs-Merrill Company 1964.

Nauright, John, and Phil White. "Mediated Nostalgia, Community and Nation: The Canadian Football League in Crisis and the Demise of the Ottawa Rough Riders, 1986–1996." *Sport History Review* 33 (2002): 121–37.

Naylor, David. *American Picture Palaces: The Architecture of Fantasy.* New York: Van Nostrand Reinhold Company 1981.

Noll, Roger G., and Andrew Zimbalist, eds. *Sports, Jobs, and Taxes: The Economic Impact of Sports Teams and Stadiums.* Washington, DC: Brookings Institution Press 1997.

O'Brien, Andy. *Fire-Wagon Hockey: The Story of the Montreal Canadiens.* Toronto: Ryerson Press 1967.

Ockman, Joan, and Nicholas Adams. "Forms of Spectacle." *Casabella* 673/674 (December 1999–January 2000): 162–3.

O'Coughlin, Seamus. *Squaw Valley Gold: American Hockey's Olympic Odyssey.* New York and Bloomington, IN: iUniverse 2001, 2009.

Oddey, Alison, and Christine White. *Modes of Spectating.* Bristol, UK: Intellect 2009.

Oldenburg, Ray. *The Great Good Place.* New York: Marlowe and Company 1997 (originally published 1989).

One Hundred and Fifty Years of Curling 1807–1957: The Royal Montreal Curling Club. Montreal, 1957.

"On the Ice." *London Society: An Illustrated Magazine of Light and Amusing Literature for the Hours of Relaxation* 3, no. 1 (1863): 11–18.

Oxley, J. Macdonald. *My Strange Rescue and Other Stories of Sport and Adventures in Canada.* London, Edinburgh: T. Nelson 1895.

Pellerin, Jean Marie. *L'Idole d'un Peuple: Maurice Richard.* Montreal: Les éditions de l'homme 1976.

Penzel, Frederik. *Theatre Lighting before Electricity.* Middletown, CT: Wesleyan University Press 1978.

Pepe, Phil. *Madison Square Garden Hall of Fame.* New York: Madison Square Garden Center, n.d.

Perrone, Julie. "The King Has Two Bodies: Howie Morenz and the Fabrication of Memory." *Sport History Review* 41, no. 2 (2010): 95–110.

Petroski, Henry. *Pushing the Limits: New Adventures in Engineering.* New York: Alfred A. Knopf 2004.

Pevsner, Nikolaus. *A History of Building Types.* London: Thames and Hudson 1976.

Pinard, Guy. "Le Forum." *Montréal Son histoire son architecture* (Vol. 3). Montreal: Les Éditions La Presse 1987–.

Podnieks, Andrew. *The Blue and White Book: From Mutual Street to Maple Leaf Gardens.* Toronto: ECW Press 1995.

Pope, S.W., ed. *The New American Sport History: Recent Approaches and Perspectives.* Urbana and Chicago: University of Illinois Press 1997.

Porter, Roy *London: A Social History.* Cambridge, MA: Harvard University Press 1995.

"Portland Coliseum: The Evolution of Structure." *Western Architect and Engineer*, April 1961, 30–4.

Poster, Mark, ed. *Jean Baudrillard: Selected Writings.* Stanford, CA: Stanford University Press 1988.

Poulter, Gillian. "Becoming Native in a Foreign Land: Visual Culture, Sport, and Spectacle in the Construction of National Identity in Montreal, 1840–1885." PhD diss., York University 1999.

Pout, Roger. *The Early Years of English Roller Hockey, 1885–1914.* Herne Bay, UK: R. Pout, c. 1993.

Quirk, James, and Rodney Fort. *Hard Ball: The Abuse of Power in Pro Team Sports.* Princeton, NJ: Princeton University Press 1999.

Rader, Benjamin G. *American Sports: From the Age of Folk Games to the Age of Spectators.* Englewood Cliffs, NJ: Prentice-Hall 1983.

– *In Its Own Image: How Television Has Transformed Sports.* New York: Free Press 1984.

Rail, Geneviève, ed. *Sport and Postmodern Times.* Albany: State University of New York 1998.

Raitz, Karl B., ed. *The Theater of Sport.* Baltimore, MD, and London: Johns Hopkins University Press 1995.

Ramshaw, Gregory. "Nostalgia, Heritage, and Imaginative Sports Geographies: Sport and Cultural Landscapes." Paper presented at the forum UNESCO University and Heritage, Newcastle-upon-Tyne, April 2005, revised July 2006. http://www.google.ca/url?sa=t&rct=j&q= &esrc=s&source=web&cd=1&ved=0CCgQFjAA&url= http%3A%2F%2Fconferences.ncl.ac.uk%2Funescoland scapes%2Ffiles%2FRAMSHAWGregory.pdf&ei=cYh4UJz CMfTU0gH7uID4BQ&usg=AFQjCNFwhfpwowrbcH-cHQ87b2hZzSSvPg&sig2=A7Xk8x-D_PsPi_FV-WSZrg (accessed 12 October 2012).

Ransom, Amy J. *Hockey, PQ: Canada's Game in Quebec's Popular Culture.* Toronto: University of Toronto Press 2014.

Ray, Edgar W. *The Grand Huckster: Houston's Judge Roy Hofheinz: Genius of the Astrodome*. Memphis, TN: Memphis State University Press, c. 1980.

"A Real Ice Skating Rink." *Illustrated London News*, 13 May 1876, 467–8.

Real, Michael R. "MediaSport: Technology and the Commodification of Postmodern Sport." In Lawrence A. Wenner, ed., *MediaSport*. London: Routledge 1998.

Reddick, Don. *Dawson City Seven*. Fredericton: Goose Lane Editions 1993.

Redmond, Gerald (revised by Patricia G. Bailey). "Curling." *The Canadian Encyclopedia*. http://www.thecanadianencyclopedia.com/articles/curling (accessed 2 February 2012).

Rein, Irving, Philip Kotler, and Ben Shields. *The Elusive Fan: Reinventing Sports in a Crowded Marketplace*. New York: McGraw-Hill 2006.

Richards, David Adams. *Hockey Dreams: Memories of a Man Who Couldn't Play*. Toronto: Doubleday Canada 1996.

Rickard, Mrs. "Tex." *Everything Happened to Him: The Story of Tex Rickard*. New York: Frederick A. Stokes Company 1936.

Riess, Steven A. *City Games: The Evolution of American Urban Society and the Rise of Sports*. Urbana and Chicago: University of Illinois Press 1989.

– "In the Ring and Out: Professional Boxing in New York, 1896–1920." In Donald Spivey, ed., *Sport in America: New Historical Perspectives*. Westport, CT: Greenwood Press 1985.

Robinson, Dean. *Howie Morenz: Hockey's First Superstar*. Erin, ON: Boston Mills Press 1982.

Rose, Frank. *The Art of Immersion: How the Digital Generation Is Remaking Hollywood, Madison Avenue, and the Way We Tell Stories*. New York: W.W. Norton and Company 2011.

Rosentraub, Mark S. *Major League Losers: The Real Cost of Sports and Who's Paying for It*. New York: Basic Books 1999.

– "Stadiums and Urban Space." In Roger G. Noll and Andrew Zimbalist, eds., *Sports, Jobs, and Taxes: The Economic Impact of Sports Teams and Stadiums*. Washington, DC: Brookings Institution Press 1997.

Ross, J. Andrew. *Joning the Clubs: The Business of the National Hockey League to 1945*. Syracuse, NY: Syracuse University Press 2015.

Rowan, John J. *The Emigrant and Sportsman in Canada: Some Experiences of an Old Country Settler: With Sketches of Canadian Life, Sporting Adventures and Observations on the Forests and Fauna*. London: E. Stanford 1876; republished Montreal: Dawson Bros. 1881.

Roxborough, Henry. "The Beginnings of Organized Sport in Canada." *Canada: An Historical Magazine* 2, no. 3 (1975): 30–43.

– *One Hundred – Not Out: The Story of Nineteenth-Century Canadian Sport*. Toronto: Ryerson Press 1966.

– *The Stanley Cup Story*. Toronto: Ryerson Press 1964.

Russell, William Howard. *Canada; Its Defences, Condition, and Resources*. London: Bradbury and Evans 1865.

Sammons, Jeffrey T. *Beyond the Ring – The Role of Boxing in American Society*. Chicago: University of Illinois Press 1988.

Sands, Mollie. *Invitation to Ranelagh 1742–1803*. London: John Westhouse 1946.

Saul, John Ralston. *Reflections of a Siamese Twin: Canada at the End of the Twentieth Century*. Toronto: Viking 1997.

Schmidt, Louis Milton. *Principles and Practice of Artificial Ice-Making and Refrigeration*. Philadelphia: Philadelphia Book Company 1908.

Schrodt, Barbara. *Sport Canadiana*. Edmonton: Executive Sport Publications, c. 1980.

Scott, W.S. *Green Retreats: The Story of Vauxhall Gardens 1661–1859*. London: Odhams Press 1955.

Seifried, Chad, and Donna Pastore. "This Stadium Looks and Tastes Just Like the Others: Cookie-Cutter-Era Sports Facilities from 1953–1991." *Sport History Review* 40 (2009): 30–56.

Sercombe, Laurel "'Ladies and Gentlemen …' The Beatles, *The Ed Sullivan Show*, CBS TV, February 9, 1964." In Ian Inglis, ed., *Performance and Popular Music: History, Place and Time*. Burlington, VT: Ashgate 2006.

Shapiro Comte, Barbara. *Myron Goldsmith: Poet of Structure*. Montreal: Centre Canadien d'Architecture / Canadian Centre for Architecture 1991.

Sheilds, Andrew, and Michael Wright, eds. *Arenas: A Planning, Design and Management Guide*. London: Sports Council 1989.

Shergold, Peter R. "The Growth of American Spectator Sport: A Technological Perspective." In Richard Cashman and Michael McKernan, eds., *Sport in History*. St Lucia and Queensland, Australia: University of Queensland Press 1979.

Shubert, Howard. *Airport Origins: Three Projects by Lloyd Wright.* Montreal: Canadian Centre for Architecture 1990.

– "Cedric Price: Fun Palace." http://www.cca.qc.ca/en/collection/283-cedric-price-fun-palace (accessed 15 August 2015).

– "The Changing Experience of Hockey Spectatorship: Architecture, Design Technology, and Economics." In Colin D. Howell, ed., *Putting It on Ice.* Halifax: Gorsebrook Research Institute, St Mary's University, 2002.

– "Cumberland & Storm and Mies van der Rohe: The Problem of the Banking Hall in Canadian Architecture." *Journal of Canadian Art History* 12, no. 1 (1989): 7–21.

– "The Evolution of the Hockey Arena." In Dan Diamond, ed., *Total Hockey.* New York: Total Sports 2000.

– "Lloyd Wright and the Lehigh Airport Competition." *RACAR* 16, no. (1989): 65–70, 288–97.

– "The Montreal Forum: The Hockey Arena at the Nexus of Sport, Religion, and Cultural Politics." *Journal of the Society for the Study of Architecture in Canada* 36, no. 1 (2011): 107–19.

– "Sports Facilities in Canada." *The 1999 Canadian Encyclopedia World Edition* on CD-ROM. Edmonton: McClelland and Stewart 1988, http://www.thecanadianencyclopedia.com/articles/sports-facilities (accessed 15 August 2015).

Shubert, Howard, and Mark Wigley. "Il Fun Palace di Cedric Price." *Domus* 866 (January 2004): 14–23.

Shubert, Irwin. "Hockey Arenas: Canada's Secular Shrines." *Journal of the Society for the Study of Architecture in Canada* 23, 2 (1998): 49–54.

Silver, Jim. *Thin Ice: Money, Politics, and the Demise of an NHL Franchise.* Halifax: Fernwood Publishing 1996.

Simpson, R.W. "Hockey." In D. Morrow et al. eds., *A Concise History of Sport in Canada.* Toronto: Oxford University Press 1989.

Slack, Trevor, ed. *The Commercialization of Sport.* Oxon, UK: Routledge 2004.

Stein, Gil. *Power Plays.* Toronto: Carol Pubishling Group 1997.

Stephenson, Lois, and Richard Stephenson. *A History and Annotated Bibliography of Skating Costume.* Meriden, CT: Bayberry Hill Press 1970.

Stern, Robert A.M., Thomas Mellins, and David Fishman. *New York 1880: Architecture and Urbanism in the Gilded Age.* New York: Monacelli Press 1999.

– *New York 1960: Architecture and Urbanism between the Second World War and the Bicentennial.* New York: Monacelli Press 1995.

Sterner, Harold. *Madison Square Garden, Old and New.* New York: Arts Publishing Corporation 1928.

Stillner, Anna "The Philadelphia Girls' Rowing Club: An Incremental Historic Structure Report," MSC thesis, University of Pennsylvania, 2005.

Taub, Stephen. "Hypocrisy on Ice: Hockey's Player-Cost Inflation Is Slowing While Revenues Are about to Explode. So What's the Problem?" *Financial World,* 14 February 1995, 39–46.

Temko, Allan "Portland's Great Hall of Glass." *Architectural Forum* 114 (April 1961): 106–11.

Trumpbour, Robert C. *The New Cathedrals: Politics and Media in the History of Stadium Construction.* Syracuse, NY: Syracuse University Press 2007.

Turner, Michael, with Michael Zaidman. *The History of Roller Skating.* Lincoln, NE: National Roller Skating Museum 1997.

Tuthill, J.A. *Ice Hockey and Ice Polo Guide 1898.* New York: American Sports Publishing Company 1897.

Ulmer, Michael. *Canadiens Captains.* Toronto: Macmillan Canada 1996.

Valentine, Maggie. *The Show Starts on the Sidewalk: An Architectural History of the Movie Theatre, Starring S. Charles Lee.* New Haven, CT, and London: Yale University Press 1994.

Van Slyck, Abigail. *A Manufactured Wilderness: Summer Camps and the Shaping of American Youth, 1890–1960.* Minneapolis: University of Minnesota Press 2006.

Van Trump, James D. "The Duquesne Gardens." *Pittsburgher Magazine* 2, no. 8 (January 1979): 55–6.

Vass, George. *The Chicago Black Hawks Story.* Chicago: Follett Publishing Company 1970.

Vieyra, Daniel I. *Fill'er Up: An Architectural History of America's Gas Stations.* New York: Macmillan 1979.

Vigneault, Michel. "La diffusion du hockey à Montréal, 1895–1910." *Canadian Journal of History of Sport* 17, no. 1 (May 1986): 60–74.

– "Montreal Ice-Hockey Rinks 1875–1917." *Society for International Hockey Research Journal* 3, (1997): 8–14.

Vine, Cathy, and Paul Challen. *Gardens of Shame: The Tragedy of Martin Kruze and the Sexual Abuse at Maple Leaf Gardens.* Vancouver: Greystone Books 2002.

Vineberg, Steve. *No Surprises, Please: Movies in the Reagan Decade.* New York: Schirmer Books 1993.

Warner, Patricia Campbell. *When the Girls Came out to Play: The Birth of American Sportswear.* Amherst and Boston: University of Massachusetts Press 2006.

Whedon, Julia. *Ice Skating: An Illustrated History and Portfolio of Stars.* New York: Harry N. Abrams 1988.

Whitehead, Eric. *Cyclone Taylor: A Hockey Legend.* Toronto: Doubleday Canada 1977.

– *The Patricks: Hockey's Royal Family.* Halifax: Goodread Biographies 1980.

Whitson, David. "Circuits of Promotion: Media, Marketing and the Globalization of Sport." In Lawrence A. Wenner, ed., *MediaSport.* London: Routledge 1998.

Whitson, David, Jean Harvey, and Marc Lavoie. "Government Subsidisation of Canadian Professional Sport Franchises: A Risky Business." In Trevor Slack, ed., *The Commercialization of Sport.* Oxon, UK: Routledge, 2004.

Whitson, David, and Richard Gruneau, eds., *Artificial Ice: Hockey, Culture and Commerce.* Peterborough, ON: Broadview 2006.

Windover, Michael. "Digging in the Gardens: Unearthing the Experience of Modernity in Interwar Toronto." In Rhodri Windsor Liscombe, *ed., Architecture and the Canadian Fabric.* Vancouver: UBC Press 2011.

Wolley, Charles. *A Two Years Journal in New York, and Part of Its Territories in America.* New York: W. Gowans 1860.

Wong, John. "The Development of Professional Hockey and the Making of the National Hockey League." PhD diss., University of Maryland, 2000.

Wong, John Chi-Kit. *Lords of the Rinks: The Emergence of the National Hockey League, 1875–1936.* Toronto: University of Toronto Press 2005.

Wright, Cynthia. "The Most Prominent Rendezvous of the Feminine Toronto: Eaton's College Street and the Organization of Shopping in Toronto 1920–50." PhD diss., University of Toronto, 1992.

Yanni, Carla. *The Architecture of Madness.* Minneapolis: University of Minnesota Press 2007.

Young, A.J. "Sandy." *Beyond Heroes: A Sporting History of Nova Scotia.* Hantsport, NS: Lancelot Press 1988.

Young, Scott. *The Boys of Saturday Night: Inside Hockey Night in Canada.* Toronto: McClelland and Stewart 1990.

– *Hello Canada! The Life and Times of Foster Hewitt.* Toronto: Seal Books 1985.

Zeman, Brenda. *88 Years of Puck-Chasing in Saskatchewan.* Regina: WDS Associates and Saskatchewan Sports Hall of Fame 1983.

Zepp, Ira G., Jr. *The New Religious Image of Urban America: The Shopping Mall as Ceremonial Center,* 2nd ed. Niwot: University of Colorado Press 1997.

Zimbalist, Andrew. *The Bottom Line: Observations and Arguments on the Sports Business.* Philadelphia, PA: Temple University Press 2006.

– "Report on Rexall Place, the Edmonton Oilers and Plans for a New Arena," 27 September 2010, http://www.edmonton.ca/city_government/projects_redevelopment/arena-reports-and-presentations.aspx (accessed 16 March 2012).

Index